Regulating Refugee Protection Through Social Welfare

Law, Policy and Praxis

Edited by Peter Billings

Routledge
Taylor & Francis Group
a GlassHouse Book

First published 2023
by Routledge
4 Park Square, Milton Park, Abingdon, Oxon OX14 4RN

and by Routledge
605 Third Avenue, New York, NY 10158

This is a GlassHouse book

Routledge is an imprint of the Taylor & Francis Group, an informa business

British Library Cataloguing-in-Publication Data
A catalogue record for this book is available from the British Library

Library of Congress Cataloging-in-Publication Data
A catalog record has been requested for this book

ISBN: 978-0-367-48041-7 (hbk)
ISBN: 978-1-032-28806-2 (pbk)
ISBN: 978-1-003-29859-5 (ebk)

DOI: 10.4324/9781003298595

Typeset in Bembo
by Apex CoVantage, LLC

Regulating Refugee Protection Through Social Welfare

This book analyses the use and abuse of social welfare as a means of border control for asylum seekers and refugees in Australia.

Offering an unparalleled critique of the regulation and deterrence of protection seekers via the denial or depletion of social welfare supports, the book includes contributions from legal scholars, social scientists, behavioral scientists, and philosophers, in tandem with the critical insights and knowledge supplied by refugees. It is organised in three parts, each framed by a commentary that serves as an introduction, as well as offering pertinent comparative perspectives from Europe. Part 1 comprises three chapters: a rights-based analysis of Australia's "hostile environment" for protection seekers, a searing critique of welfare policing of asylum seekers as "necropolitics," and a unique philosophical perspective that grounds scrutiny of Australia's policing of asylum seekers. Part 2 contains five chapters that uncover and explore the lived experiences and adverse impacts of different social welfare restrictions for refugee protection seekers. Finally, the chapters in Part 3 offer distinct views on human rights advocacy movements and methods, and the scope for resistance and change to the status quo.

This book will appeal to an international as well as an Australian readership with interests in the areas of human rights, immigration and refugee law, social welfare law/policy, social work, and public health.

Peter Billings is Professor in the TC Beirne School of Law at The University of Queensland, Australia. He teaches administrative law and immigration and refugee law and has published widely on public law, refugee law, human rights, and "crimmigration." He is the editor of *Crimmigration in Australia: Law, Politics and Society* (2019).

Contents

Preface

For over twenty years Australia has, for much of that time, pursued a suite of deterrence policies and practices that, effectively, outlaw asylum seeking by unauthorised maritime means. These deterrence measures include offshore regional processing in third countries, prolonged and indefinite detention, and interdiction at sea. In addition to these forms of "crimmigration" control limitations have also been placed upon access to justice for the "Legacy Caseload"—a group of approximately 30,000 asylum seekers who arrived between 13 August 2012 and 1 January 2014—including accelerated "fast track" administrative procedures and the withdrawal of legal aid for immigration advice/assistance. These measures are designed to control and deter maritime migration and, arguably, serve to punish those arriving by irregular/clandestine means.

Less visible than the "crimmigration" controls previously outlined, migration management is also carried out by restricting access to social security and welfare support services for asylum seekers and refugees. The social welfare system (and sector) has become an important site of post-arrival post-entry border control, migration management, and policing. Accordingly, this book breaks new ground by carefully examining, from assorted perspectives, the regulation of social security and welfare provision for groups of non-citizens living in Australia, and those who have lived under Australia's effective control in "regional processing countries" hosting asylum seekers and refugees at Australia's invitation.

The genesis of this volume was the commissioning of papers by the editor in 2019, several months prior to a workshop held at the University of Queensland, School of Law, on 29 November 2019. The workshop, entitled "Migration Management through Social Welfare" aimed to provide a holistic examination of the intersection, effects, and impacts of immigration law, policy, and practice on the provision of social welfare, and the human rights of asylum seekers and refugees in Australia. Invited participants, drawn from diverse disciplinary backgrounds, community legal and charitable sectors, presented their ideas and research data, inviting feedback and commentary from other workshop participants. Papers were duly refined and submitted to the editor in mid-2020 and, subsequently, subjected to a double-blind peer review process prior to their revision and completion later in the year. The three comparative commentaries were then authored and added to the collection between March and June 2021.

The manuscript's production and completion were unavoidably delayed by around six months due to the assorted and acute impacts of COVID-19 on various contributors to the project during 2020–21. Though the book's completion was prolonged, the authors' commitment to the project was steadfast and collegiality unwavering throughout the difficulties encountered over the past eighteen months. I extend my deepest gratitude to them all for their patience and staying the course.

This is the first book to be dedicated to the multidisciplinary study of social welfare as a governance tool to regulate asylum seekers and refugees in Australia and two neighbouring states (Nauru and Papua New Guinea) in the Pacific—states which have received funding from Australia to host "regional processing centres" (most recently, since August 2012). This edited collection provides a unique and wide-ranging examination and socio-legal critique of the complex nature, fluidity, and diverse effects and impacts (including lived experiences) of the immigration control–social welfare nexus as it affects protection seekers in Australia.

Although the focus of this edited collection is on Australian law, policy, and practice, the three commentaries authored by European-based scholars offer valuable comparative insights and critical perspectives. As such, this book is purposely situated within a broader context of socio-legal scholarship that has critically examined the creation of "hostile" environments (including through stringent social welfare regulation) for asylum seekers and refugees in Europe since the 1990s.

This book comprises ten chapters, three commentaries, and a short introduction. For thematic coherence the book utilises three parts, although the themes and critical perspectives contained within each part, and in individual chapters, intersect and complement each other. The chapters can be read and comprehended in isolation but are best understood and appreciated when the collection is read entirely.

I'm very thankful to all the contributors—the outstanding academics, researchers, community lawyers, social welfare sector employees, and refugee advocates—who participated at the workshop in November 2019, and to all those who expended their time and intellectual energy (during such a challenging period) to prepare and finalise their respective contributions to the book. Additionally, I extend my appreciation to the many anonymous peer reviewers who provided timely and constructive observations on each chapter in the latter part of 2020. Their comments greatly assisted both the editor and other authors and added significant value to the overall collection.

I also extend thanks to the publisher, to Dr Colin Perrin (commissioning editor at Routledge) for his support and kindness, and to Manjusha Mishra (editorial assistant at Routledge) for her guidance and assistance in preparing the manuscript for publication. Finally, I express my gratitude to the TC

Beirne School of Law for the financial grant that facilitated the gathering of scholars, legal/welfare sector professionals, and refugee advocates in Brisbane in November 2019.

Peter Billings
Brisbane, QLD, Australia
September 2021

Contributors

Atefeh Andaveh is a student in the Master of Science (Geophysics) program at Curtin University, Perth, Australia, and works as an office administrator. She has advocated for the rights of her family and all other people who have sought asylum in Australia over the past eight years.

Salem Askari is from Afghanistan and came to Australia to seek asylum. He has been living in Perth, Western Australia, for eight years. He is currently working as a stonemason and is actively involved in raising awareness about the experiences of people seeking asylum within government and the community.

Vanessa Barker is Professor of Sociology at Stockholm University, Sweden. She writes on democracy and punishment, welfare states and immigration, and border criminologies. She is the author of *The Politics of Imprisonment* (2009) and *Nordic National and Penal Order* (2018) and the current editor-in-chief of *Punishment & Society*.

Behrouz Boochani is an adjunct associate professor of social sciences at University of New South Wales, Australia, and affiliated to Birkbeck Law, University of London, and University of Melbourne. He is an author and journalist based in New Zealand and was incarcerated by the Australian Government on Manus Island, Papua New Guinea (2013–2019). His book *No Friend but the Mountains* (2018) won numerous awards including the 2019 Victorian Prize for Literature.

Linda Briskman holds the Margaret Whitlam Chair of Social Work at Western Sydney University, Australia. She conducts research, writes, and advocates across a range of human rights issues including Indigenous rights, asylum seeker rights, and anti-racism. Her most recent book is the co-edited *Indigenous Health Ethics* (2021).

Clemence Due is a senior lecturer in the School of Psychology at the University of Adelaide, Australia. She is the author of over 90 publications, with particular interest and expertise in mental health in culturally and linguistically diverse populations, especially people with refugee and migrant backgrounds.

Emma Fell holds a Bachelor of Laws (Hons) and a Bachelor of Arts from the University of Queensland, Australia. She works at the Refugee and Immigration Legal Service (RAILS) in Brisbane assisting refugees and asylum seekers with their immigration processes.

Caroline Fleay is an associate professor at the Centre for Human Rights Education, Curtin University, Australia, where she engages in research and advocacy with people seeking asylum. She has written extensively about the impacts on people seeking asylum of indefinite detention and being released into the community with minimal supports.

Margaret Greenfields is a professor of social policy at Anglia Ruskin University, England. Her participatory action research is focused on developing policy interventions to enhance inclusion and cohesion. She works predominantly with vulnerable migrants including refugees and asylum seekers as well as Gypsy, Traveller, and Roma communities at risk of social exclusion.

Rohullah Hassani is a member of the Hazara community who lives in Australia on a safe haven enterprise visa. He works in construction and participates in meetings to advocate for a pathway to permanency for all temporary protection visa holders.

Asher Hirsch is a senior policy officer with the Refugee Council of Australia, the peak body for refugees and the organisations and individuals who support them. His work involves research, policy development, and advocacy on issues impacting refugee communities. He is a PhD candidate and lecturer in public law, human rights, and refugee law at Monash University, Australia.

Mary Anne Kenny is an associate professor in the School of Law, Murdoch University, Australia. She researches and teaches in migration and refugee law. She has a special interest in the intersection of refugee law and mental health. She is a registered migration agent and legal practitioner.

John van Kooy is a senior researcher with experience in community-based research and program development across Australia, South Asia, and East Africa. His doctoral research in the School of Social Sciences, Monash University, Australia, focuses on the neighbourhood conditions for successful settlement and integration of refugees in Australia.

Kate Leaney is an advocate, campaigner, and communications professional who has worked alongside refugees and people seeking asylum, in Australia, for the past ten years. She is the campaigns and communications manager for Welcoming Australia and has developed and implemented initiatives including the Welcoming Centre, Adelaide.

Teresa Lee is a social worker at Riverview Community Services in Perth, Western Australia. She specialises in providing advocacy and assistance for people seeking asylum navigating the legal and migration system.

Greg Marston is professor of social policy in the School of Social Science and deputy executive dean of the Faculty of Humanities and Social Sciences at the University of Queensland, Australia. His research interests include unemployment and poverty, social security, and comparative social policy.

Lucy Mayblin is senior lecturer in sociology at the University of Sheffield, England. Her research focuses on asylum, human rights, policy making, and the legacies of colonialism. She is the author of *Asylum After Empire* (2017), *Impoverishment and Asylum* (2019), and *Migration Studies and Colonialism* (2021).

David Neil is a lecturer in the philosophy program at the University of Wollongong, Australia. His teaching is primarily in the area of ethics. His research interests are in ethical theory and applied ethics, particularly at the intersection of bioethics and political philosophy.

Michelle Peterie is a research fellow in sociology at the Sydney Centre for Healthy Societies, University of Sydney, Australia. She has published widely on immigration detention and social welfare and is the author of *Visiting Immigration Detention* (2022).

Claudia Tazreiter is a professor in the Institute for Research on Migration, Ethnicity and Society (REMESO), University Linköping, Sweden. She researches the social and affective impacts of forced and irregular migration, human rights culture, the role of civil society in social change, and visual cultures of dissent. She is author of *Asylum Seekers and the State* (2017) and co-edited the *Handbook of Migration and Global Justice* (2021) with Leanne Weber.

Omid Tofighian is a lecturer, researcher, and community advocate, combining philosophy with interests in citizen media, popular culture, displacement, and discrimination. He is affiliated with Birkbeck Law, University of London, University of New South Wales, and the University of Sydney, Australia. His publications include *Myth and Philosophy in Platonic Dialogues* (2016) and translation of *No Friend but the Mountains* (2018).

Moira Walsh is an early career researcher at the Flinders Health and Medical Research Institute, Flinders University, Australia. Her work focuses on the social determinants of health, health equity, and integration of people from migrant and refugee backgrounds.

Leanne Weber is professor of criminology in the Canberra Law School at the University of Canberra, Australia, and a research associate at the Centre for Criminology, Oxford University. She researches policing and border control using criminological and human rights frameworks.

Hanne Worsoe completed a PhD in anthropology at the University of Queensland, Australia, on "fast track" refugee processing in Australia. Working with people of asylum seeker and refugee backgrounds for the past nine years, she is interested in policy as a cultural artefact and its effects on identity and citizenship.

Anna Ziersch is associate professor (research) at the Flinders Health and Medical Research Institute, Flinders University, Australia. Her research focuses on the social determinants of health and health equity, with a particular focus on migrant and refugee health. She is a co-convenor of the Migration and Refugee Research Network (MARRNet).

Introduction

Regulating Refugee Protection Through Social Welfare: Law, Policy and Praxis is a multidisciplinary collaboration that supplies a holistic analysis via legal-doctrinal, theoretical, and empirical critiques of the immigration control–social welfare nexus as it affects "irregular" migrants: primarily "unauthorised" maritime arrivals seeing refugee protection in Australia. It serves as an Antipodean companion to the flourishing body of literature that examines provision of welfare services for irregular (or unwanted) migrants in general, and asylum seekers in particular (e.g. Ataç and Rosenberger 2019).

Contributors to the book (offering, *inter alia* legal, anthropological, criminological, sociological, philosophical, and psychological perspectives, along with insights drawn from lived experience) scrutinise the nature and diverse effects of a system of stratified work and social welfare rights/services applicable to certain asylum seekers, and "declared" refugees. This enterprise entails a careful study of how social welfare provision, access to justice and legal aid, and pathways to permanent protection/residency are delimited for certain cohorts of asylum seekers and refugees who are branded with inferior socio-legal status by reason of their *mode* and *date* of arrival in Australia. Namely:

(i) Asylum seekers arriving by boat *before* 13 August 2012 (when "offshore regional processing" was resuscitated pursuant to the "No Advantage" policy) who were initially detained then released subject to bridging visa conditions.

(ii) Asylum seekers arriving by boat *after* 13 August 2012 and before 1 January 2014 who were not removed from Australia and processed under offshore arrangements—the so-called Legacy Caseload—numbering around 30,000 people.

(iii) Asylum seekers arriving (or attempting to arrive) by boat *after* 19 July 2013 who were forcibly sent offshore to regional processing countries, with prospective resettlement in third countries (this cohort includes transitory medical transferees to Australia).

(iv) Refugees in Australia granted either a temporary protection visa (TPV) or safe haven enterprise visa (SHEV) following the withdrawal, in 2014, of permanent protection visas for "unauthorised" arrivals.

DOI: 10.4324/9781003298595-1

The authors contributing to this collection each supply original insights (including subjective knowledge and understanding) about the intersection of immigration law, policy, and administration with aspects of social welfare law, policy, and administration: specifically, access to income security, housing assistance and healthcare, education and employment rights, provision for family unity, and legal assistance.

The aim is to reveal the nature, effects, and outcomes of policies, legal frameworks, and practices that produce precarity—socio-economic vulnerabilities—for many people seeking asylum and manufacture insecurity for "declared" refugees, both in Australia and regional processing countries. Indeed, revealing the lived experiences of asylum seekers and refugees in Australia (and offshore) over the recent past is a key objective and builds on the published research of various contributors to this collection (e.g. Hartley and Fleay 2014).

Additionally, the book uncovers and explores some of the multilevel governance structures/relationships pertinent in social welfare provision for asylum seekers and refugees. This correlates, in certain ways, to Weber's (2013) excellent analysis of different federal and state authorities and service providers conscripted to surveil, report on, and so "police" irregular migrants. Therefore, the book investigates the roles, associations, conflicts, and co-operation between a mélange of federal/state actors and non-state agents (including legal and healthcare professionals, not-for-profit organisations, and market actors contracting with government) as they manage access to and administer social welfare provision, take decisions, and negotiate socio-legal issues, contradictions, and moral tensions between welfare provision and immigration regulation/enforcement away from the geographical border (see further Gerard and Weber 2019).

From "crimmigration" controls to the regulation of irregular migration and asylum through social welfare

Australia's "crimmigration" control system is characterised by use of coercive state power directed at (what is perceived as) undesirable forms of mobility, and the total exclusion or at least segregation of unwanted migrants (asylum seekers) from the community. Notably, "irregular" maritime arrivals have been the subjects of coercive and punitive immigration controls (including maritime interdiction and prolonged detention offshore). The merger or interweaving of criminal law/procedure with administrative immigration law/procedure is a hallmark of crimmigration globally, and one important element of crimmigration is the management of migration through the use and enforcement of criminal law. For example, via accessorial liability—harsh criminal sanctions relating to the facilitation of irregular migration ("people smuggling"). The criminalisation *(de jure* or *de facto)* of irregular migration and normalisation of punitive immigration law enforcement (including administrative detention) is intended to deter irregular migration and encourage voluntary returns to countries of origin.

Relatedly, immigration law and its administration/enforcement coalesce with social welfare law, policy, and practice in many states in the Global North as explained by several contributors to this edited collection. Migration is managed internally, through increasingly strident and parsimonious approaches to social welfare for irregular migrants (including, but not limited to, asylum seekers and those denied asylum). This has manifested in the purposeful creation of hostile socio-politico and regulatory environments that push border controls into different areas of everyday life, generating discomfort and facilitating destitution, homelessness, labour exploitation, and ill health for irregular migrants in general, including asylum seekers.

Arguably most palpable, was (then Home Secretary) Theresa May's announcement of a "really hostile environment" for *all* irregular migrants, living in the United Kingdom, in 2012 (Lewis et al. 2017). A harsh policy later cemented via civil exclusions in the 2014 and 2016 Immigration Acts (Bowling and Westenra 2020). Within this ecosystem, all irregular migrants have been subject to bordering practices routinely by a range of public and private actors. Banks, healthcare workers, and landlords have been required to check on service users' immigration status. As people's entitlement to welfare is determined by their immigration status, those unable to prove their regular visa status have been confronted by the denial of access to essential public services, including access to healthcare.

The rationale for the hostile environment policy is to force the departure of all people without valid legal status, and to discourage others from making clandestine and dangerous journeys to the United Kingdom. As Lewis et al. (2017: 190) explain, "The idea that discomfort and hostility can dissuade potential new arrivals from travelling to the UK or encourage those already in the country to leave is particularly prevalent in deterrence policies aimed at people seeking asylum."

But of course, this objective isn't new: the legacy of inhospitality towards asylum seekers in the United Kingdom pre-dates 2012. For instance, erosion of social supports for asylum seekers was a striking and contentious feature of immigration law and policy in the 1990s and early 2000s (e.g. see Billings and Edwards 2006; Billings 2007; Morris 2009).

In Australia, the depletion of social welfare supports for certain "irregular" migrants has not been attended by explicit statements of intent like Theresa May's (2013) public declaration about driving down illegal immigration to the United Kingdom. However, in combination with its strict crimmigration controls operationalised within and beyond state borders, the Australian Federal Government has employed social welfare as an instrument of internal migration control and enforcement: to influence asylum seekers' behaviour or hasten their departure, and to signal deterrence to others contemplating "irregular" migration to Australia.

Several contemporary shifts in law and policy reinforce the view that social welfare provision is an important site for immigration control/policing in Australia. For example, in 2017 changes to Status Resolution Support Services (SRSS)—which provides people with 89% of the Newstart allowance, casework support, and counselling—included a controversial "welfare crackdown" on asylum seekers brought to Australia for emergency medical treatment, to coerce their return to regional processing centres on Nauru and Papua New Guinea (Baines 2017; Hamilton-Smith 2017). Additionally, in 2018 restrictions were placed on asylum seekers' eligibility for SRSS, making it a highly conditional support system, pending resolution of protection visa claims (Chalmers 2018). It is noteworthy that these sorts of strategies for border policing have been achieved via executive policy (not legislation) with little transparency and parliamentary scrutiny and accountability.

As several chapters in this book keenly demonstrate, punitive approaches to social welfare provision for protection seekers undermine key international law principles and obligations that stipulate non-discriminatory access to a range of economic and social rights. Several contributions evidence how the production of hostile socio-legal environments for asylum seekers and refugees causes ill health, destitution, and housing insecurity, and facilitate labour insecurity and exploitation. Later chapters show that by excluding asylum seekers and "declared" refugees from access to income security and assorted welfare supports, ethical dilemmas and practical challenges arise for legal and healthcare professionals who bear witness to the impacts of Australia's own "hostile environment," as it conflicts with their core values: social justice and human rights.

The structure of the book

The book is organised in three parts. Opening Part 1 ("Context and Critique"), Vanessa Barker begins with a commentary on the first three chapters entitled "A crescendo of violence that might better be called a war." Offering a comparative (Nordic) viewpoint on what she, aptly, describes as "the violent case of Australia," Barker invites readers to consider important, bigger picture questions arising from her reading of the first three chapters. Questions such as "How are we to understand developments in Australia in relation to similarly situated countries? Are these the same across democratic societies? Is Australia simply more violent than Europe or the United States?" And she poses a potent question about whether it is "possible to find sources and sites of opposition to this holistic regime" (that employs totalising force against refugees)?

In tandem with the other, avowedly comparative contributions (written by Lucy Mayblin and Margaret Greenfields, respectively) and later chapters in the book, Barker's perspective goes some way to addressing these critical questions, offering points of convergence among affluent democracies. She opines:

> Australia, Denmark, Sweden, and the United States, among many others, all engage in what I would call *racialised nationalism*. Racialised nationalism is

> organised around the goal of statecraft to protect the territory, people, and resources of the nation for those considered to belong.

Indeed, Barker helpfully illuminates that "Part 1 of this edited collection details the excessive use of force against racialised others deemed outside Australian white heritage, displaced people perceived to be mortal threats to the society."

In Chapter 1, "Regulating refugee protection through welfare," Peter Billings sets out social welfare law, policy, and regulatory techniques deployed against different cohorts of migrants, notably: (i) asylum seekers within Australia on bridging visas pending resolution of their visa claims, (ii) refugee visa holders subject to temporary protection, and (iii) transitory persons brought to Australia from offshore sites, ostensibly, for emergency medical care. The chapter identifies, explains, and analyses the impacts of important judicial decisions that have reviewed the legality of the management of "irregular" migrants seeking protection from harm. Additionally, Billings points to key human rights law issues raised by social welfare and work restrictions that are imposed by the state due to a person's mode/date of arrival. He argues that the Australian Federal Government has weaponised social welfare to discipline asylum seekers for their irregular mode of arrival and presence in Australia, and to coerce asylum seekers into departure.

Leanne Weber also argues that social welfare policy works as a form of border control in her rich and empirically grounded contribution in Chapter 2, "The welfare policing of asylum seekers as necropolitics." Weber claims that Australia's meagre financial support ("SRSS") for asylum seekers operates as a system of "necropolitics" (a term popularised by Achille Mbembe). Supposedly established to provide support to asylum seekers in the community, the system provides minimal financial assistance while subjecting people to intensive surveillance. She concludes that the SRSS serves the instrumental goal of engineering "voluntary departures" by blocking access to the essential requirements for a dignified life, thereby creating conditions of suffering and fear that align with Mbembe's account of necropolitical governance in colonised societies. Weber clearly shows how ostensibly protective (welfare) provisions are, instead, used to coerce and punish non-citizens for their assumed transgression of travelling to Australia irregularly.

Finally, the third chapter in Part 1, "Spectres of subjugation/inter-subjugation/resubjugation of people seeking asylum," authored by Claudia Tazreiter and Omid Tofighian with Behrouz Boochani, presents a powerful and complex examination of the violence of Australia's bordering practices. Drawing on a unique philosophical framework called "Manus Prison Theory," which Iranian journalist and author Boochani first developed and articulated with Tofighian, the chapter uses first-hand accounts, poetry, and knowledge production of asylum seekers and refugees impacted by Australia's border policing practices to demonstrate how Australia's carceral-border archipelago uses isolation, denial of welfare support, and physical violence to render life abject for people.

Part 2 ("The depletion of social welfare for refugees") houses five chapters that uncover the lived experiences and impacts of social welfare denial and diminution for people seeking asylum, and refugees with temporary protected status, in Australia. This part starts with Lucy Mayblin's commentary ("Slow violence in Australia and the United Kingdom") that aims to draw out the similarities between Australia and the United Kingdom and to conceptualise what is happening in both countries within the critical context of connected histories of colonial racial exclusion. Without recognising the racist histories of both countries, she argues, we cannot make sense of the exclusionary politics of asylum (and welfare). Mayblin (informed by Canning and Nixon) observes that the harms done to those in search of refugee protection in both the United Kingdom and Australia are the outcomes of slow structural violence. Those harms, including destitution, homelessness, and health problems, occasioned by and through immigration welfare regimes, are carefully detailed throughout the following five chapters in Part 2.

In Chapter 4, "Destitution by design," John van Kooy and Asher Hirsch draw upon an analysis of nearly fifty public consultations facilitated by the Refugee Council of Australia from 2017 to 2018. These qualitative data provide compelling insights into the deteriorating mental health, poverty, and widespread insecurity of asylum seekers with limited means to participate in mainstream social and economic life. Participant accounts were characterised by lengthy waiting periods for visa status resolution, leading to material dependence on limited forms of state welfare, and more so on community and charitable sources of support. Van Kooy and Hirsch argue that asylum seekers' relative material destitution, with associated negative physical and mental health effects, signifies the outcomes of the state's intentional abdication of its duty of care to people who arrive seeking refugee protection.

Matters raised by van Kooy and Hirsch in Chapter 4 are developed in Chapter 5 by Emma Fell's thorough exploration of the housing issues and growing homelessness experienced by members of the "Legacy Caseload." In her socio-legal contribution entitled "The growing challenge of precarious housing and homelessness for refugees and asylum seekers in Australia," Fell maintains that the denial of suitable housing is one important feature of Australia's hostile environment that serves to punish asylum seekers for their irregular mode of travel to Australia and to coerce their return. She captures and conveys how the absence of federal government sympathy and support for the welfare of the Legacy Caseload has resulted in civil society (or, the third sector) and several state governments (such as Queensland and Victoria) filling the welfare gaps.

Following Fell's analysis of housing issues in Chapter 5, Clemence Due, Moira Walsh, and Anna Ziersch explore the health impacts of visa insecurity in Australia in Chapter 6 called "Financial precarity and health for temporary refugee and asylum-seeking visa holders in Australia." They draw upon in-depth interviews with both temporary visa holders enduring financial hardship and several charitable service providers offering emergency relief to them. The data harvested through these interviews enable the authors to explore the ways in which financial and visa precarity intersects to produce adverse physical and mental health impacts for refugees and asylum seekers.

In Chapter 7 entitled "Navigating the threat of *refoulement* arising from the trifecta of welfare conditionality, behavioural codes, and short-term visas," Hanne Worsoe and Greg Marston argue that the threat of *refoulement* is a necropolitical strategy that diminishes the lives of asylum seekers subject to Australia's "fast track" administrative process for determining refugee status. In support of this claim Worsoe and Marston use a powerful case study (based on participant observation and semi-structured interviews) to examine how an accelerated procedure (with depleted legal protections), in tandem with social welfare conditionality and surveillance and scrutiny of asylum seekers' behaviour, pushes protection seekers towards departure from Australia in breach of the *non-refoulement* principle.

In the final chapter encased in Part 2 entitled "Asylum seekers, healthcare, and the right to have rights," informed by Hannah Arendt's work, David Neil and Michelle Peterie focus on the political controversies surrounding provision of the most fundamental welfare right (healthcare) to asylum seekers and refugees forcibly sent offshore to Nauru and Papua New Guinea. In particular, Neil and Peterie critically address the short-lived "medevac" laws that enabled very sick people to access emergency healthcare more readily in Australia and the surrounding political furore. The authors argue that Australia's denial of access to adequate healthcare to asylum seekers "offshored" is part of an elaborate strategy for refusing people the "right to have rights."

Part 3 ("Protecting and promoting respect for refugees' human rights") is directed at examining human rights welfare advocacy movements and methods and the scope for reconsideration and resistance in order to challenge, subvert, and change asylum-welfare laws and practices. Chapter 9 and Chapter 10 offer different approaches to advocacy and action to realise reform to social welfare law/policy for asylum seekers and refugees on temporary visas.

In her carefully considered comparative commentary on both chapters in Part 3, Margaret Greenfields explains that "activist practitioners, civil society, and academics, who are engaged in humanitarian and legal practices to support asylum seekers and refugees in the UK, are facing broadly similar ethical and practical challenges to those described" in Australia.

Greenfields carefully addresses and engages with the thoughtful and eloquent claims advanced by Linda Briskman, in Chapter 9 entitled "Social welfare paradoxes for asylum seekers," regarding the conflictual relationship and moral responsibilities of health and social welfare professionals attempting to deliver services and support ("second generation" rights) to protection seekers who are denied civil and political ("first generation") rights. While supportive of many of Briskman's persuasive claims, including her argument about the interdependence of human rights, Greenfields queries Briskman's "despairing claim that the provision of welfare services and social work to those labouring under diminished human rights is both 'ineffective and futile.'" For Greenfields the implications of Briskman's principled argument are sombre because, on the one hand, it raises the spectre of withdrawal of trained welfare professionals and all but minimum levels of welfare support for asylum seekers. And on the other hand, the argument has the potential to undermine the values, motivations, and opportunities for supporting health professionals working in detention settings.

The challenges and dilemmas for health and social workers working under repressive asylum welfare regimes, effectively canvassed by Briskman, opens up critical lines of enquiry about forms of resistance and challenge and a gateway to the analysis provided by Caroline Fleay et al. Thus, in Chapter 10, called "I spoke the truth about myself and that's when you connect with people," the authors explore how a network of professionals, advocates, and refugees (with temporary visas) in Western Australia worked together to influence politicians and policy makers to realise practical and positive changes to social welfare (restoring human dignity) for people trapped in temporary refugee protection regimes.

The value of this collaborative and localised approach in bringing about modest but important changes in welfare for people with temporary protection resonates with Greenfields who (in previously published work) argued for empowerment ("voice") for those directly affected by law and policy, high-quality research and data to support arguments for law and policy reform, and engagement with policy professionals, including politicians.

This edited collection offers a valuable and timely critique of the regulation of immigration/refugees via social welfare in Australia, permeated, as it is, with comparative perspectives. Considering the regulation of asylum seekers and refugees through welfare, via a distinctively broad but interconnected range of socio-legal perspectives, this book expands upon existing scholarship in Australia (much of it authored by contributors to this collection), that critically evaluates and challenges Australia's own brand of "hostile environment" for protection seekers. In addition to the telling critiques of refugee welfare law, policy, and administration, and its adverse impacts for non-citizens, several authors offer important ideas about the advancement of social protections and social justice for asylum seekers and refugees in the future.

Bibliography

Ataç, I. and Rosenberger, S. (2019) 'Social policies as a tool of migration control', *Journal of Immigrant and Refugee Studies*, 17(1): 1.

Baines, R. (2017) 'Asylum seekers face welfare crackdown under Government changes', *ABC News*, 27 August.

Billings, P. (2007) 'The treatment of asylum seekers in the UK', *The Journal of Social Welfare and Family Law*, 29(1): 49.

Billings, P. and Edwards, R. (2006) 'R (Adam, Limbuela and Tesema) v Secretary of State for the Home Department—"A case of mountainish inhumanity"', *Journal of Social Security Law*, 13(3): 167.
Bowling, B. and Westenra, S. (2020) '"A really hostile environment": Adiaphorization, global policing and the crimmigration control system', *Theoretical Criminology*, 24(2): 163.
Chalmers, M. (2018) 'Removing asylum seekers from support payments "sends a message"', *ABC News*, 6 September.
Gerard, A. and Weber, L. (2019) '"Humanitarian borderwork": Identifying tensions between humanitarianism and securitization for government contracted NGOs working with adult and unaccompanied minor asylum seekers in Australia', *Theoretical Criminology*, 23(2): 266.
Hamilton-Smith, L. (2017) 'Churches offer sanctuary to asylum seekers affected by welfare crackdown', *ABC News*, 29 August.
Hartley, L. and Fleay, C. (2014) *Policy as Punishment: Asylum Seekers in the Community without the Right to Work*. CHRE, Curtin University.
Lewis, H., Waite, L. and Hodkinson, S. (2017) '"Hostile" UK immigration policy and asylum seekers susceptibility to forced labour', in Vecchio, F. and Gerard, A. (eds) *Entrapping Asylum Seekers: Social, Legal and Economic Precariousness*. Springer.
May, T. (2013) Second reading of the Immigration Bill, House of Commons (U.K. Parliament), *Hansard*, vol. 569, col. 156, 22 October 2013.
Morris, L. (2009) 'Civic stratification and the cosmopolitan ideal: The case of welfare and asylum', *European Societies*, 11(4): 603.
Pickering, S. and Weber, L. (2013) 'Policing transversal borders', in Fanko Aas, K. and Bosworth, M. (eds) *The Borders of Punishment*. Oxford University Press.
Schweitzer, R. (2019) 'Health care versus border care: Justification and hypocrisy in the multilevel negotiation of irregular migrants' access to fundamental rights and services', *Journal of Immigrant and Refugee Studies*, 17(1): 61.
Weber, L., Wilson, A. and Wise, J. (2013) 'Cops and dobers: A nodal cartography of onshore migration policing in New South Wales', *Australian & New Zealand Journal of Criminology*, 46(1): 32.

Part I

Context and critique

Part I commentary

A crescendo of violence that might be better called a war

Vanessa Barker

Regulating Refugee Protection Through Social Welfare: Law, Policy and Praxis is a devastating critique of Australian migration control in all its variation, scale, and insidiousness. Based on a wide range of law and society scholarship and human rights activism, this collection provides in-depth analyses of the legal frameworks, social policy practices, and the lived experiences of migration control in Australia and its offshore camps in Nauru and Papua New Guinea. In Part 1 "Context and critique," Peter Billings, Leanne Weber, and Claudia Tazreiter, Omid Tofighian and Behrouz Boochani, all exceptional contributors to the collection, lay out in empirical detail how Australia has mobilised both internal and external border controls to thwart asylum seekers and refugees at every turn. The empirical details are a major strength of the volume as they make clear that Australia used almost every policy tool available and every legal, political, and geographic opportunity to carry out its assault on asylum seekers and refugees over a sustained period with one innovation followed by the next. To compliment much of the brute force of border restrictions, Australia turned what would seem like legal protections for refugees, or social support mechanisms for the newly arrived, into coercive tools of control and deprivation.

In the first chapter, for example, Billings shows how Australia has inverted its social welfare provisions to deter and deprive asylum seekers and refugees so they will leave the country rather than try to settle. By denying them the right to work as well as by denying them social assistance this puts people on a fast track to deprivation. For a time, Australia imposed a "no work" condition on temporary visa holders, essentially making them dependent on the state, which ushered in a vicious circle of dependence, social stigma, and social blame. By taking away the right to earn a living or support oneself, the state created the conditions to blame asylum seekers and refugees for their own desperation, increasing hostility and making them drains on the state. In this context, we can see how social welfare does not buffer or moderate coercive state practices, but rather is integral to it. Next to the inversion of social welfare support, Billings outlines how legal frameworks for protection were similarly turned against refugees. Analysing the work found in the *Report of the Expert Panel on Asylum Seekers* (Australian Government 2012), he shows how asylum seekers

DOI: 10.4324/9781003298595-3

were transformed from rights-bearing individuals into illegal or unauthorised migrants simply because they arrived by boat. These "unauthorised maritime arrivals" and the related excision laws created a separate and second-class legal protection for those who arrived by sea—they made refugees illegal by virtue of their transportation method. Billings further details how temporary protection visas (TPVs), the denial of family reunification and its prolongation of up to 20 years for some families, and the catch-22 of welfare provisions, all worked to uphold Australia's border regime with its expressed aim of deterrence.

Likewise, in Chapter 2, Weber argues that Australian welfare policy functions as a form of border control. In Weber's provocative conceptualisation, this border control through welfare is really a way for the state to control the lives of refugees, the literal life and death of refugees. Drawing on Achille Mbembe's concept of "necropolitics," Weber describes how Australian welfare agents provide refugees with just enough support to stay alive without killing them. In a series of revelatory interviews with welfare officials, Weber illustrates how and why the state withholds certain entitlements, benefits, and even needed medical care. As one official stated, "I think it's very much about notions of citizenship and who's Australian and who's not Australian and the punishment that people have for wanting to seep through our borders." In other words, the ameliorative benefits of social welfare are restricted to citizens, while the coercive elements of social welfare are reserved for non-citizens—and not only to deprive non-citizens but also to punish them for their assumed transgression for coming to Australia "irregularly."

Finally, in Part 1, Tazreiter, Tofighian and Boochani present an unfiltered look at the absolute violence of Australia's border regimes and offshore sites of detention for asylum seekers and refugees. Specifically, the authors outline the "Manus Prison Theory" which Boochani developed while imprisoned on Manus Island, weaving together his lived experience with poetical reflections and political philosophy. Boochani's remarkable work was transmitted over encrypted social media and later published as an award-winning book. The Manus Prison Theory argues that Australia's carceral archipelago is designed to dehumanise, deter, deprive, and torture those who cross its borders uninvited. Like Kafka's fictionalised penal colony in which the machinery of harm, suffering, and torture literally wrote the death sentence on the body of the condemned, Australia's use of isolation, denial of healthcare and treatment, and recurring physical violence and epistemic violence about the nature of reality is a full-on assault on fellow humans, not for a crime they have committed but simply because a border was crossed. Manus Prison Theory goes on to detail how this system further corrupts those who implement it as our shared systems of knowledge for understanding border violence have been transformed if not obliterated. As a society, we can no longer recognise what is happening at the border, and most do not want to know.

Taken together, the three chapters in Part 1 of this collection build on one another to reach a crescendo of violence—this crescendo of violence might be better called a war. I take up this point in more detail ahead after first considering a few comparative questions, which may, counterintuitively, push this warfare approach forward.

The violent case of Australia raises several pressing questions, particularly in global and comparative perspective. How are we to understand these developments in Australia in relation to similarly situated countries? Are these the same across democratic societies? Is the Global North at war with certain types of migrants? Is Australia simply more violent than Europe or the United States? Why is this happening now? Has Australia always been this way? Is Australia's intricate use of welfare provision to deter, if not starve, asylum seekers and refugees, emulated elsewhere? If Australian society is based on settler colonialism and long histories of racialised coercion, what explains changes in migration policies? The totalising use of force against refugees in Australia sets up questions about resistance and agency. Is it possible to find sources and sites of opposition to this holistic regime?

In what follows, I outline a few key points of convergence in comparative perspective. At first glance, it may be gratuitous to compare Australia with the Nordic countries. The Nordic countries are often thought to be progressive, inclusionary, and egalitarian; they are often noted for their humanitarianism, support for human rights around the globe, and more recently, at least with the case of Sweden, as proponents of a feminist foreign policy based on gender equality and international peace and security. Yet, like Australia and the United States, the Nordic countries have their own set of carceral apparatuses that similarly restricts and deters unwanted mobility (Barker 2018; Franko 2020). The Nordic countries are not exceptions to global border control developments even when they may travel under the radar or are simply dismissed as small scale or not as bad or inhumane as the rest. This is a major misunderstanding of the Nordic countries. It is also a failure to recognise those who are crushed by the welfare state, as if their lives and life chances do not matter.

Let's take the case of Denmark, for example. Denmark made international headlines in 2021 for its proposal to deport Syrian refugees in cases where their homes or neighborhoods have been destroyed by war. In June 2021, the Danish Parliament passed new legislation to process asylum seekers offshore, much like Australia, to prevent refugees from making landfall in Denmark. As my colleague Peter Scharff Smith and I (Barker and Smith 2021) document in a recent article "This is Denmark: Prison Islands and the Detention of Immigrants," Denmark has undertaken a flurry of restrictive migration controls as it relies on the extensive use of prison and prison-like facilities to confine asylum seekers and other unwanted migrants. The government actively seeks to discourage refugees and migrants from coming to Denmark. In the words of former Immigration Minister, Inger Støjberg: "These people are unwanted in Denmark . . . it should be as intolerable as possible to be on a tolerated stay" (Støjberg quoted in Barker and Smith 2021: 1548). In other words, the conditions upon arrival, reception, and confinement should all be so horrible and intolerable than no one would want to stay. This is the 21st-century version of the 19th-century British "less eligibility" principle and approach to crime and punishment—conditions should be so bad inside workhouses and prisons, including hard labour sustained by a diet of gruel, even the poorest and most destitute would do anything to avoid going to prison. In 2021, the Danish government has pursued this less eligibility approach for people fleeing war and persecution in the hopes that refugees would elect not to enter Denmark, let alone want to stay, settle in the country, and make a life for themselves and their families, echoing similar developments in Australia, outlined earlier.

The detention regimes themselves are bleak, regimented, and cold, as they inflict the pains of punishment on those people who have not committed a crime but are rather seeking refuge. These difficult conditions have been well documented and reported by the Red Cross, the Committee for the Prevention of Torture (CPT), border criminologists such as Vicky Canning (2020), and detention researchers such as Julia Suárez-Krabbe et al. (2018). For example, following antiquated less eligibility conditions, detainees are denied mobile phones, spend almost 24 hours confined in the cells, are allowed one hour of exercise outside and one phone call per week (Barker and Smith 2021: 1548). For those confined in these institutions, their mobility inside and outside the facilities is highly regulated and monitored by a well-developed security apparatus. At the Ellebæk Detention Centre and the Nykøbing Falster Holding Centre, for instance, its security system includes walls, fences, and extensive surveillance that are deployed to ensure that no one gets in or out. At another facility in Vridløselilles, isolation chambers and security cells with restraints have been used on immigrant detainees without their understanding what was happening to them or why they were shackled to a bed (Barker and Smith 2021: 1551–1552). Like the less eligibility principle, the shackling of inmates is a remnant of the 19th century, a cruel relic of the past that surely confounds Danish high ground on human rights. Developments that parallel Australia's machineries of harm.

In these cases, we can ask how these societies were able to manage or subsume the apparent contradiction of reliance on repression within liberal democracies. Like mass incarceration in the United States, we need to ask at what point does the scale of coercive confinement undermine the very nature of the democracy itself? As various contributors to this edited collection point out, Australia's growing migration controls were not challenged or opposed on democratic grounds. Instead, they were part of a popular political project that garnered electoral votes for whichever political party pursued them. Why are these repressive approaches so popular in democratic societies such as Australia, the United States, Denmark, and beyond? How is it that these societies can deny the dignity and human rights of so many people, particularly people of colour?

And that factor, the disproportionate impact of people of colour from the Global South, is the key to understanding the proliferation of migration controls across the Global North, long recognised by pioneering figures in the field such as Liz Fekete (2001) and Gurminder Bhambra. As Tazreiter, Tofighian, and Boochani explain in Chapter 3, rather than see these illiberal practices as an aberration to democratic society, the intricacies and range of migration controls can be understood as part of a continuum and colonial legacy of control, coercion, and expulsion of people of colour outside of Australia's white settler heritage. The carceral archipelago has a long history in Australia.

What I would add there is the necessary component of statecraft and nationalism (see Kaufman 2015; Barker 2017; van der Woude 2020; Bosworth 2008). Part 1 of *Regulating Refugee Protection Through Social Welfare* makes this dimension evident and compelling. The Kafkaesque nature of the legal frameworks and welfare provisions in Australia depend on a high level of state capacity and agency to exclude so many asylum seekers and refugees, and to be perceived as legitimate by the public for doing so. As such, I suggest that Australia, Denmark, Sweden, and the United States, among many others, all engage in what I would call *racialised nationalism*. Racialised nationalism is organised around the goal of statecraft to protect the territory, people, and resources of the nation for those considered to belong. In other words, "It is very much about notions of citizenship and who's Australian and who's not." Racialised nationalism includes the two central features of the dynamics of nationalism and the dynamics of racism:

(1) The dynamics of nationalism refer to nation-state's drive to protect its territories; to uphold national interests, national identities, and national resources; and to do so with primary tools of statecraft—warfare and policing power, all documented in this volume.
(2) The dynamics of racism refer to colonial legacies and contemporary xeno-racism, that is the fear of the displaced and dispossessed, particularly racialised others (Fekete 2001; Parmar 2018).

It is the combined force of racism and the perceived legitimacy of nationalism that enables rich states to exclude so many from its private club of democracy (Benhabib 2004). The perceived legitimacy of the state's authority to use force against existential and material threats is difficult to pierce, even as it clearly imposes substantial harms on those people subjected to it at the border. This why I think it is imperative to incorporate the nationalistic elements into our understanding of the dynamics of border control, especially when these efforts are highly racialised. It is by considering these features that we may be able to better connect the extreme violence of border controls with a new kind of warfare, a war against certain migrants carried out inside and outside the territories of the nation-state. Part 1 of this edited collection details the excessive use of force against racialised others deemed outside Australian white heritage, displaced people perceived to be mortal threats to the society. Warfare is usually defined as armed conflict between states or insurgents. But given the details of Manus Island offshore and the forced destitution of asylum seekers and refugees onshore in Australia, it is difficult to go on denying the brutality of the organised violence: violence that is integral to the nation-state, whose rise and fall depends on such practices.

Taken together, these three chapters from *Regulating Refugee Protection Through Social Welfare* present a damning case against Australia as well as affluent democracies more broadly, as we can see significant points of convergence in the response, treatment, and heavy reliance on state violence. For example, Australia and Denmark use the criminological logics of deterrence and less eligibility to stop refugees from coming into the respective countries and to make their lives as miserable as possible if they do arrive. Both logics, moreover, are deeply flawed as they misunderstand the nature of forced displacement. Refugees are, by definition, forced to leave their homes or territories under duress, they do not simply choose to travel anywhere they please. With its clear-sighted critique of state power to control the lives and well-being of those seeking asylum, this volume opens up new avenues of research; it shows how intricate and entrenched these policies and practices are and how difficult it will be to undo this web of pain. It advances a more complex view of the relationship between social welfare, border control, and racialised violence, connecting contemporary practices to the legacies of colonialism, similarly entrenched but often denied. And finally, with the inclusion of the Manus Prison Theory, the collection makes it apparent that state violence against racialised and displaced others has escalated to such an extent that contradictions of democracy are on full display but now without resistance and creativity. The question now is how can we build on this creativity and human spirit to rebuild our societies and bring about a different future?

References

Australian Government. (2012) *Report of the expert panel on asylum seekers*, August 2012.

Barker, V. (2017) 'Penal power at the border: Realigning state and nation', *Theoretical Criminology*, 21: 441.

Barker, V. (2018) *Nordic Nationalism and Penal Order: Walling the Welfare State*. Routledge.

Barker, V. and Smith, P. S. (2021) 'This is Denmark: Prison islands and the detention of immigrants', *British Journal of Criminology*, 61: 1540.

Benhabib, S. (2004) *The Rights of Others: Aliens, Residents, and Citizens*. Cambridge University Press.

Bosworth, M. (2008) 'Border control and the limits of the Sovereign State', *Social Legal Studies*, 17: 199.

Canning, V. (2020) 'Bureaucratised banality: Asylum and immobility in Britain, Denmark and Sweden', in Abdelhady, D., Gren, N. and Joormann, M. (eds) *Refugees and the Violence of Welfare Bureaucracies in Northern Europe*. Manchester University Press, p. 210.

Fekete, L. (2001) 'The emergence of xeno-racism', *Race and Class*, 43: 23.

Franko, K. (2020) *The Crimmigrant Other: Migration and Penal Power*. Routledge.

Kaufman, E. (2015) *Punish and Expel: Border Control, Nationalism, and the New Purpose of the Prison*. Oxford University Press.

Parmar, A. (2018) 'Policing belonging: Race and nation in the UK', in Bosworth, M., Parmar, A. and Vázquez, Y. (eds) *Race, Criminal Justice and Migration Control: Enforcing the Boundaries of Belonging*. Oxford University Press.

Suárez-Krabbe, J., Lindberg, A. and Arce-Bayona, J. (2018) *Stop Killing Us Slowly. A Research Report on the Motivation Enhancement Measures and the Criminalisation of Rejected Asylum Seekers in Denmark*. http://refugees.dk/media/1757/stop-killing-us_uk.pdf

van der Woude, M. A. H. (2020) 'Euroskepticism, nationalism, and the securitization of migration in the Netherlands', in Koulish, R. and van der Woude, M. A. H. (eds) *Crimmigrant Nations: Resurgent Nationalism and the Closing of Borders*. Fordham University Press.

Chapter 1

Regulating refugees through welfare

Australia's hostile response to unauthorised maritime arrivals

Peter Billings

Introduction

Australia's contemporary approach to border policing and enforcement is premised on an understanding of the border as "a complex continuum stretching offshore and onshore, including the overseas, maritime, physical border and domestic dimensions of the border" (Finnane 2015). In the recent past an assemblage of policies has been deployed beyond the physical borders, entailing the *externalisation* and *internalisation* of border controls (Menjívar 2014) directed at preventing and disincentivising "irregular" (or, "unauthorised") maritime migrants seeking asylum and strong-arming asylum seekers already present in the Australian community. Accepting that there are competing ethical concerns around irregular maritime migration these policies appear predicated on a desire to, effectively, punish asylum seekers and to pressurise them to "voluntarily" return home or to resettle in third countries.

This chapter identifies and critically examines the internal, or, "domestic," dimensions of immigration control with an emphasis on stratified social welfare policies and regulatory techniques deployed against some asylum seekers and refugees behind the border. Conceiving of border control as a continuum has enabled the imposition and acceptance of social policies that disregard and neglect asylum seekers and refugees' social welfare needs, and which deliberately inflict hardship—to the point of destitution—on asylum seekers and refugees in Australia. This chapter examines aspects of social welfare provision for three cohorts of people:

(i) Those non-citizens on temporary "bridging" visas while awaiting finalisation of refugee protection claims and status resolution.
(ii) Those "declared" refugees subject to temporary protection regimes.
(iii) Medical transferees: so-called transitory persons brought to Australia from regional processing countries (Nauru and Papua New Guinea) in exceptional circumstances, and temporarily, for emergency treatment.

DOI: 10.4324/9781003298595-4

Law and policy background: an overview

Arrival by boat before 13 August 2012

Asylum seekers (legally dubbed "offshore entry persons" at the time)[1] arriving at an "excised offshore place" (remote islands), were placed in mandatory immigration detention with no legal right to apply for a protection visa: they were statutorily barred from doing so. They would be permitted to seek refugee protection in Australia *if* the Immigration Minister considered it to be in the "public interest." Thus, if government officials (or independent reviewers) assessed a person's claims and determined that, in fact, they engaged Australia's protection *(non-refoulement)* obligations, the Minister would consider exercising their discretionary powers, allowing a visa application to be formally lodged. This cohort of asylum seekers could obtain permanent protection visas with limited family reunion rights.

Asylum seekers arriving by boat rose steadily in number in the period 2009–2012, resulting in increasing numbers of people subject to mandatory detention pending resolution of their protection visa claims. To relieve the growing pressure on the detention estate, from 18 October 2010, several thousand asylum seekers (children and vulnerable families were prioritised) who arrived by boat were released from a prison-like situation in detention and into "community detention" (Australian Human Rights Commission n.d.).[2] Accordingly, those asylum seekers made subject to a "residence determination" were given access to a social welfare support program in the form of simple accommodation, a basic living allowance, and assistance to access to healthcare and education for school-age children, but with no work rights (Buckmaster 2012: 11).

Subsequently, from late November 2011, the Federal Government transferred more adult asylum seekers out of detention into the community detention program and the wider community. Following initial identity and health and security checks, asylum seekers were granted short-term "bridging" visas (BVEs) pending status resolution (Australian Human Rights Commission n.d.). This community-based cohort could get access to transitional welfare support for six weeks upon release from detention, after which time they could apply for financial assistance under (what was then termed) the Asylum Seeker Assistance Scheme (ASAS) if they could not meet their basic living needs or, alternatively, Community Assistance and Support Program (CASP) for those especially vulnerable, including certain asylum seekers and non-citizens who had experienced domestic and family violence (Buckmaster 2012: 8–10).

Welfare support comprised a "special benefit," a hardship payment to cover basic living expenses and healthcare, and rent assistance, along with access to general healthcare, casework support, and referrals to other agencies. Asylum seekers eligible for welfare payments received no more than 89% of the equivalent benefit payable to Australians or permanent residents, leaving individuals well below the poverty line for a single adult in Australia (UNHCR 2013:

6) and reliant on charities (Jesuit Social Services 2015). As Reilly (2016: 5) explained, "By offering a lower level of assistance to asylum seekers than that offered to Australian residents with similar needs, the government draws a bright line between asylum seekers and others in the community."

Asylum seekers reported that they were left demoralised at not being permitted to work, and that refuge without work was poisonous (Mares 2014). Furthermore, they were unable to meet their basic needs and were living in a state of destitution, with little money left for food, medication, and travel after paying rent for poor and overcrowded properties (UNHCR 2013: 6). Moreover, those asylum seekers whose protection claims had been refused, initially and on appeal ("double negatives"), became ineligible for income support and, with no work rights, faced destitution.

From March 2012, most boat arrivals on bridging visas had visa restrictions on the right to work lifted (Parliamentary Joint Committee on Human Rights 2013: 18), but this policy change was short lived. The right to work was, once more, denied to asylum seekers from 13 August 2012, consistent with the Federal Government's "No Advantage" policy to deter irregular maritime migration. Without work rights and with income support levels (under ASAS) below the poverty line, this left thousands of asylum seekers in Australia with bleak prospects, as the next section explains.

Arrival by boat after 13 August 2012: "no advantage"

Australia's policies towards asylum seekers arriving by boat (now legally recast as "unauthorised maritime arrivals") shifted following the *Report of the Expert Panel on Asylum Seekers* (Australian Government 2012). The new approach was premised on a belief that policy settings influence the flow of unauthorised migration to Australia (Australian Government 2012: 31). The Expert Panel was tasked, in June 2012, with providing policy options to the Federal Government to address concerns about the increase in the number of boat arrivals.[3] In particular, to prevent deaths at sea, deter irregular maritime voyages, and tackle the scourge of people smuggling. Indeed, there were 1,437 border-related deaths at sea, mostly asylum seekers, between January 2000 and July 2014 (Weber and Pickering 2014: 186–187), with a striking increase in the number of deaths at sea from 2009 (Parliamentary Joint Committee on Human Rights 2013: 53). In this context, and with a political impasse in respect of how to respond to unauthorised maritime arrivals, the Expert Panel proposed a series of integrated measures that were "driven by a sense of humanity as well as fairness" (Australian Government 2012: 10). The coexistence of humanitarian logic ("saving lives at sea") and assertions about protecting state sovereignty over borders in the face of transnational crime (people smuggling) supplied a powerful moral alibi for politicians' intent on reintroducing stringent deterrence policies. As it transpired, it was mostly the austere aspects of the Expert Panel's suite of recommendations that were progressed into law and policy. Moreover, the Expert

Panel made no suggestions about social welfare policy settings for asylum seekers already present in Australia.

The first element of the new regime of, ostensibly, compassionate borderwork involved reducing Australia's attractiveness as a destination point for irregular migrants by forcibly relocating people outside of Australia. Legislation commenced on 18 August 2012 enabling the transfer of all asylum seekers to detention centres in designated third countries (Nauru and Papua New Guinea/Manus Island)[4] where their asylum claims would be slowly processed.

Asylum seekers sent offshore were to be administered under domestic laws in the host country, and those who were declared refugees were to be allowed to apply for a visa and resettle in Australia. There was no time frame for regional processing and resettlement. Seemingly, the lived experience of waiting for a visa outcome under punishing living conditions was a temporal technique of migration control used to deter others from seeking asylum by maritime means.

When the regional processing centres on Nauru and Manus Island soon reached their capacity, newly arriving asylum seekers were, first, detained and then released on bridging visas into the Australian community but without work rights. Instead, they were made welfare dependent, eligible for just 89% of special benefit and rent assistance. Additionally, they lived with the lingering possibility of transfer offshore at any time (Parliamentary Joint Committee on Human Rights 2013: 14) and a protracted period of administrative processing and uncertainty about resettlement in Australia, with restrictions on family reunion (see ahead). By November 2013, it was estimated that there were around 27,000 asylum seekers living in the community without the right to work (Fleay et al. 2013: 478).

A second element of the deterrence regime advocated by the *Report of the Expert Panel on Asylum Seekers* involved legal reforms that extended so-called excision laws to the whole country (Australian Government 2012: 17, 52). Excision laws function to decouple a person's physical presence in Australia from substantive and procedural legal protections. Consequently, asylum seekers reaching, say, the shores of Western Australia by boat would not have their refugee status governed by the *Migration Act 1958* (Cth). Pursuant to the *Migration Amendment (Unauthorised Maritime Arrivals) Act 2013* (Cth), from 1 June 2013, asylum seekers reaching *any* part of Australia by boat were liable to be transferred offshore.[5] The rationale was fairness (uniform treatment for all asylum seekers travelling by sea) and humanitarianism (saving lives at sea).

A third measure advocated by the Expert Panel was to alter family reunion rules, as a means of dissuading asylum seekers from undertaking maritime voyages with the help of people smugglers, (Australian Government 2012: 40–41). In September 2012, the Labor Government proceeded to change migration rules relating to family reunification in the following ways.[6]

First, by barring asylum seekers, arriving by boat *after* 13 August 2012, from nominating family members for reunion under the auspices of the Special Humanitarian Program (SHP)—the overseas component of Australia's humanitarian program. Instead, those granted refugee protection visas would have to seek family reunion via the family stream of the regular migration program (Bowen 2012). This reform served to disrupt families, separated by conflict or persecution, indefinitely because of an (estimated) twenty-year wait for reunification under the regular migration program (Barchetti and Moradi 2016).

Second, for *adult* asylum seekers travelling to Australia by boat *before* 13 August 2012, family reunion concessions were removed. These concessions had meant that the spouse, dependent children and, in some cases, parents of refugees residing in Australia could be granted a SHP visa *solely* because of that familial relationship and connection to Australia. By removing that allowance family members of boat arrivals were required to meet all four of the standard, "compelling reasons," SHP visa criteria. They were assessed against the level of persecution or discrimination in their home country, their connection to Australia, their protection options elsewhere, and Australia's capacity to help.

Subsequently, in March 2014, the newly elected, conservative, Liberal/National Coalition Government further adjusted and toughened the family reunion policy vis-à-vis "processing priorities" for SHP applications. Family reunion applications from irregular maritime arrivals arriving *prior* to 13 August 2012 were now given the lowest "processing priority" relative to other visa holders.

In the case of *M64/2015 v Minister for Immigration and Border Protection*, an unaccompanied minor with refugee status—who had entered Australia "irregularly" in May 2010—challenged the legality of a decision refusing his immediate family visas under the SHP. An immigration official determined that there were not "compelling reasons" to grant the visas because Australia did not have the capacity to resettle all humanitarian applicants and, furthermore, the family's visa applications were afforded the lowest priority. The plaintiff argued that the priorities policy was unlawful, and in effect a punishment imposed by reason of his mode of arrival in Australia. The High Court of Australia (HCA) disagreed. The processing priorities policy was held to be consistent with the *Migration Act 1958* (Cth) and regulations and could accommodate a consideration of the proposer's irregular mobility:

> The evident rationale of the priorities policy is that no-one should receive a migration advantage as a result of arriving in Australia as an irregular maritime arrival. . . . The policy means only that, in conducting the evaluation of whether there are compelling reasons for giving special consideration to the grant of a visa, an advantage will be conferred on an applicant whose application was proposed by a person who arrived in Australia in a "regular", rather than "irregular", fashion. . . .] it is not irrational, or unreasonable, or punitive to prefer an application from the family of a proposer who came to Australia by regular means over an application from the family of a proposer who came to Australia as an irregular maritime arrival. It

is not irrational that the former application might be regarded as of a kind which should be encouraged in preference to others.[7]

In short, although refugee family reunion for "split families" in Australia was not formally prohibited for those who arrived irregularly by sea prior to 19 July 2013, the limited humanitarian visa allocation quotas annually, the priorities policy, and the prolonged processing delays relating to the regular family migration stream function to keep families separated indefinitely. Arguably, this frustrates the enjoyment of two interrelated human rights principles: the right to protection of family life and right to family unity/reunification found in international law instruments (Darling 2019), as discussed ahead.

Arrival by boat after 19 July 2013: no advantage and no resettlement in Australia

Diverting asylum seekers to third countries under the offshore regional processing regime did not immediately deter boat arrivals, with an estimated 18,000 people seeking asylum in the ten months immediately after the release of the Expert Panel's report (Parliamentary Joint Committee on Human Rights 2013: 55). So, with a growing backlog of asylum seekers in Australia the government reacted by hardening policy settings in July 2013. Maritime arrivals would not, henceforth, be granted bridging visas and released into the community. Rather, they would *all* be transferred offshore and, under new refugee resettlement arrangements—brokered with Papua New Guinea and Nauru—they would *never* be resettled in Australia, even if they were declared refugees.

This punitive, neo-colonial turn in asylum seeker policy was a hurried and costly political response that was exploitative, unsuitable, and unsustainable (Gerard and Kerr 2016; Perera and Pugliese 2014; Dastyari and O'Sullivan 2016; Higgins 2016). Nauru (Australia's former protectorate) is the smallest island nation in the world (21 sq km) with a population of 9,000 people and is reliant on foreign aid. Papua New Guinea (Australia's former colony) is a country with its own economic struggles, scarcity of jobs, public services and housing, and human rights problems. Thus, for social, economic, and cultural reasons permanent resettlement in Nauru or Papua New Guinea never was a viable "durable solution," enabling refugees to live safely and rebuild their lives. Indeed, Australia helped generate toxic, nativist conditions in those two neighbouring countries that have fuelled unrest and human rights violations, with violent and deadly consequences for asylum seekers and refugees (The Senate, Legal and Constitutional Affairs References Committee 2014; The Senate, Legal and Constitutional Affairs References Committee 2017; Gerard and Kerr 2016; Grewcock 2017; Togiba 2020).

Whether the brokerage of resettlement arrangements with Papua New Guinea and Nauru would have reduced irregular maritime migration will remain a source of conjecture because, in September 2013, a change in political leadership marked a decisive shift in the response to asylum seekers extra-territorially and in Australia. The newly elected Coalition Government was publicly committed to a reform agenda that included interdiction at sea with enforced turn-backs, as well as the reintroduction of temporary protection visas for refugees who had arrived irregularly. These two measures formed key elements of a multipronged approach to "stopping the boats" and managing the backlog of 30,000 asylum claims from maritime arrivals (dubbed the asylum legacy caseload, "Legacy Caseload" hereafter)[8] inherited from the former Labor Government (Morrison 2014b).

The balance of this chapter critically examines policy measures and regulatory changes introduced from 2012 to date,[9] with a particular focus on different means of governing, coercing, and punishing asylum seekers, through cuts to Federal Government–funded social welfare provisions. The expansion of internal bordering measures is less conspicuous than interdiction at sea, offshore regional processing, or mandatory immigration detention in Australia, but no less harmful in terms of its impacts on people and the enjoyment of their human rights.

Bridging visa holders, work rights, and social welfare

Policy U-turns about work rights

As outlined earlier, *prior* to 13 August 2012, asylum seekers on a BVE could apply for scant levels of income support and had work rights. Access to the formal labour market is recognised as important for people's dignity and settlement prospects, though in practice it is, generally, very challenging to obtain secure employment given *(inter alia)*: limited government assistance to secure employment, language barriers, the dehumanising experience of long-term immigration detention, and the precarious socio-legal status of those on temporary visas (Fleay et al. 2013: 481–487).

After 13 August 2012 a "no work" condition was added to bridging visas. Those detected breaching this condition faced severe legal and practical consequences: visa cancellation, re-detention for an indeterminate period, and a bar on further bridging visa applications. The "no work" condition served to increase dependency on the welfare state among asylum seekers. Moreover, asylum seekers in the workplace, despite the no work condition, were vulnerable to exploitation by unscrupulous employers and with limited protections under domestic law. As Reilly (2016: 13) explained:

> There is a risk that unscrupulous employers can hold the threat of visa cancellation over asylum seekers with a no work condition in their visa to require them to work without complaint in dangerous conditions or for inadequate pay. . . . The problems of illegal work and exploitation are

> structural. They arise as a result of the conditions of living [below the poverty line] imposed on asylum seekers who are on bridging visas, which create a strong incentive for them to work in breach of their visa conditions.

In February 2014, five months after the formation of the Coalition Government, there were 19,353 asylum seekers living in the community on social welfare support *without* work rights (Mares 2014). They faced many more months of uncertainty with little, if any, administrative progress made on their protection visa status. This was due to the backlog arising under the former (Labour) Government in the period 2009–2013, and a lengthy pause on processing claims initiated by the Coalition Government in late 2013, pending substantial reforms to immigration-asylum law enacted in December 2014.

Overall, the legislative reforms of December 2014 served to weaken refugee protection generally, and especially for the Legacy Caseload who were subject to a procedurally flawed, "fast track" status determination. However, the restriction on work rights for BVE holders was lifted. In mid-2015, when the processing of the protection claims restarted after the administrative hiatus, almost 30,000 asylum seekers were living in the community on BVEs (Reilly 2018: 4).

The reintroduction of work rights was, in theory, a progressive step as a means of subsistence, self-realisation, and social inclusion (Fleay et al. 2013: 475). Moreover, it helped strengthen Australia's compliance with its international human rights law obligations relating to employment and may have strengthened compliance with obligations relating to health because a lack of work rights has been identified as a factor contributing to ill-health (Australian Human Rights Commission 2019: 62). However, asylum seekers in the community have been inadequately supported given the increasingly limited welfare assistance available under the compliance-oriented Status Resolution Support Services (SRSS)—a program that replaced ASAS and CASP in 2014. The government insists SRSS is "not a social welfare program." Officially, it is tiered support temporarily available for people who do not have a substantive visa to address the barriers they face while resolving their immigration status (Golightly 2018: 90).

Status Resolution Support Services: "a compliance program, not welfare"

SRSS includes social worker support and access to counselling and subsidised medication, with payments benchmarked at 89% of equivalent benefits payable to single adults and families. As noted previously, this figure falls significantly below the poverty line; consequently, the Federal Government is not meeting people's basic living needs (Australian Human Rights Commission 2019: 51). In 2017, the UN Committee on Economic, Social and Cultural Rights (CESCR) expressed its alarm at the punitive approach taken by Australia towards asylum seekers arriving by boat (CESCR 2017: 17). The CESCR expressed anxiety about the insufficiency of benefits under the SRSS program for asylum seekers on a bridging visa and advocated for an increase in the levels of benefits so that asylum seekers could enjoy an adequate standard of living consistent with international human rights law.[10]

Policy changes initiated in 2017 saw people studying full-time exited out of the SRSS program, purportedly because they could not work if they were studying full time. Additionally, people transferring money overseas, amounting to $1000 or more over a 12-month period, also lost access to SRSS income supports (RCOA 2018: 6–7). Subsequently, from February 2018, the Federal Government revised SRSS policy guidelines, setting more stringent eligibility criteria for access to welfare supports. Government officials reassessed just over 12,000 SRSS recipients to ascertain what level of support was warranted; with withdrawal of income supports anticipated for those deemed capable of finding employment (Golightly 2018: 90). People with work rights who did not meet a high threshold of vulnerability were exited from SRSS, even if they were unemployed, with just seven to ten days to transition off. The four elements of vulnerability being: (i) ongoing physical health barriers; (ii) mental health barriers; (iii) single parents with preschool-age children, pregnant women, elders (age 70+), and primary carers for someone with significant vulnerability; and (iv) a major crisis for a person (e.g. family violence, house fire). The status and condition of people moved off income supports (and into seeking employment) is supervised by fortnightly reporting requirements.

The rationale for these policy changes was that if people have the capacity to work and can support themselves through employment, the government expects them to do so (van Kooy and Ward 2018: 5). To that end, asylum seekers were, seemingly, to be referred to Australia's employment support service ("Jobactive"). However, that scheme had proven ineffective for refugees (and has since been replaced), with a 2017 study suggesting some refugees were treated with hostility by staff (Tahiri 2017: 12–13). Subsequently, the number of people accessing the SRSS scheme dropped, generating a significant risk of poverty and homelessness for between 75% and 80% of people cut off from SRSS, with only 20% considered to be job ready (van Kooy and Ward 2018).

Cost shifting is another consequence of the restrictions on welfare support for asylum seekers in the community. As a substitute for Federal Government–funded social welfare support, NGOs, community groups, churches, and some provincial (State and Territory) governments[11] have supported the needs of asylum seekers through emergency financial and material relief. These alternative support services are not available as of right or consistent across Australia.

Immiserating asylum seekers, breaching human rights

The Australian Human Rights Commission (AHRC) recently confirmed the findings of earlier studies on social welfare policy for asylum seekers on BVEs. The AHRC survey found that those receiving income supports under

SRSS experienced financial hardship or destitution (Australian Human Rights Commission 2019: 52). And the AHRC, concurring with the CESCR, stated that paying asylum seekers at a lower rate than others on government welfare payments might not be compliant with Australia's human rights obligations to maintain an adequate standard of living for adults and children (Australian Human Rights Commission 2019: 53). Moreover, the changes to SRSS were labelled "ruthless" by Philip Alston, the then UN Special Rapporteur for Extreme Poverty and Human Rights. Alston added that ensuring a minimum level of social protection was needed for human decency, but that "[t]his program [SRSS]—or the proposed changes to it—seem designed precisely to undercut that and to send the message that if you are an asylum seeker in Australia, you will live in absolutely miserable conditions." (Chalmers 2018). Equally, the UN Committee on the Elimination of Discrimination Against Women (CEDAW) expressed particular concern that women and girls seeking asylum in Australia were exposed to further restrictions on access to SRSS from 1 July 2018 (Committee on the Elimination of Discrimination Against Women 2018: 53).

"Failed" asylum seekers: ineligible for welfare and with access to justice impeded

The cohort of people ineligible to receive SRSS support extends to those who have had visa applications refused at both the primary and review stages: "double negatives." As such, bridging visa holders, who may have work rights theoretically, but who face substantial barriers to finding secure employment, are typically in penury while exercising their constitutional right to access the courts to check the legality of administrative decision-making processes. Ordinarily, judicial review processes are lengthy (usually exceeding a year). Accordingly, asylum seekers challenging adverse visa decisions face the grim prospect of surviving without income for a considerable period pending the final resolution of their matter. This leaves a significant number of asylum seekers impaled on the horns of an intolerable dilemma: either abandon judicial review or pursue their basic right to check government decision-making but in a state of utter destitution (see further, Australian Human Rights Commission 2019: 55–57). The right to equality before the law, to safeguard the rule of law, is absent when asylum seekers are pressured into abandoning judicial review because they lack adequate support.

Compounding those problems was the Federal Government's exorbitant hike—from $690 to $1,330—in filing fees for "failed" asylum seekers seeking judicial review before the Federal Circuit Court (Stayner 2020). Even with a partial fee exemption for applicants experiencing financial hardship this fee rise critically affects people seeking to challenge adverse temporary protection/safe haven visa decisions (see ahead in Part 2) made by the Immigration Assessment Authority (IAA) under the fast-track administrative scheme. Judges have expressed their concerns regarding *(inter alia)* the effect of statutory limits on procedural fairness obligations (fast track reviews are conducted "on the papers" without an oral hearing typically) upon the quality of the IAA's decision-making (Peyton 2020: 25). With access to justice impaired by excessive filing fees, legal errors made by the IAA in the appeal process will go uncorrected, meaning substantive injustice for asylum seekers erroneously refused visas.

In summary, by cutting welfare support from asylum seekers on bridging visas awaiting the outcome of their visa applications, or by denying it to those who are "double negatives" and exercising their right to judicial review, the government weaponised welfare to pressure asylum seekers. This is one striking example of how the Federal Government has used this technique to regulate asylum seekers. Other instances are examined ahead, in Part 3 (to enforce an arbitrary visa application deadline) and Part 4 (to coerce medical transferees to leave Australia and return to regional processing countries or elsewhere).

Perpetual uncertainty: unauthorised arrivals and temporary protection

Introduction

Asylum seekers seeking to enter Australia without a valid visa, who engage *non-refoulement* obligations, are *perpetually* ineligible for permanent protection visas (PPV). Because they travelled to Australia "illegally," they are treated as undeserving of the same socio-legal entitlements as holders of PPVs. The deterrence rationale for this measure is dubious and its conformity with human rights law is doubtful.

This section critically explores safe haven enterprise visas (SHEV) and temporary protection visas (TPV), two kinds of temporary visa that offer restricted social welfare support, little or no prospect of permanent residency, no family reunion rights, and no right re-enter Australia if refugees depart. Additionally, upon expiration of the temporary visa (a maximum of three years for a TPV holder and five years for SHEV holder) refugees must re-apply for protected status and undergo re-examination and refugee status adjudication. Accordingly, those refugees relegated to temporary legal status are as much repressed as they are protected. Without the security of permanent protection, the omnipresent spectre of bureaucratic rejection and immigration detention-deportation, is the governing basis of their residency, serving disciplinary and coercive purposes.

Rising numbers of refugees by sea and the resuscitation of temporary protection

One of the Coalition's top policy priorities taken to the 2013 election was to secure borders by "stopping the boats." The reintroduction of TPVs was a key element of that policy (Liberal Party 2013: 47–48). After the election returned a Coalition Government, in September 2013, several attempts to reintroduce TPVs via subordinate legislation (regulations) ensued. Political opponents claimed TPVs were "punishment for punishment's sake" and that there was little evidence they deterred irregular migration (Hanson-Young 2013: 595). The regulations were duly disallowed by the Senate (the upper parliamentary chamber) where the Coalition did not enjoy a majority of Members of Parliament as it did in the House of Representatives (the lower chamber).

The Coalition Government's response to this parliamentary reverse was to regulate the number of PPVs available by capping the number to be granted in the financial year. The illegality of this "freeze" on PPVs was established by the HCA in cognate proceedings: *Plaintiff S150 of 2013 v Minister for Immigration and Border Protection* and *Plaintiff S297/2013 v Minister for Immigration and Border Protection*. In these two cases the plaintiffs' refugee status had been established and both had lodged valid PPV applications that were pending. The visa applications were left undetermined because the Immigration Minister imposed a quota on the number of PPVs that could be granted in the financial year ending 30 June 2014. And, by granting either plaintiff a protection visa the numerical limit would have been exceeded. The evident purpose of the cap was to delay decisions on valid PPV applications.

Plaintiff S297 concerned a refugee applicant who had arrived, irregularly, by boat at Christmas Island, in May 2012, before the resumption of offshore processing. The HCA unanimously agreed that the Minister lacked the power to cap PPVs. For the plurality judgment this was because the Minister was under a statutory duty to make a timely decision (within a period of ninety days) to grant or refuse a protection visa, meaning he couldn't sit on his hands. Enforcing this duty was welfare enhancing, because it provided greater certainty for PPV applicants and had the benefit of placing greater limits on the potential for the prolongation of their immigration detention.[12]

In related legal proceedings, *Plaintiff M150* concerned a child refugee who had, atypically, reached the east coast of Australia as a stowaway on a cargo ship. For the reasons given in *Plaintiff S297*, and because the Minister had offered no reason why he had not made a visa decision *other than* the existence of the purported visa "cap," the HCA ordered the Minister to determine the visa application and delay no further.[13]

Following those two court rulings the Immigration Minister stubbornly refused to grant a PPV to *Plaintiff S297*, instead deciding that the refugee did not meet regulatory requirements. The Minister decided it was not in the "national interest" to grant the PPV because the applicant was an unauthorised maritime arrival. In new proceedings the HCA rejected what was, effectively, the government's attempt to penalise a refugee who had arrived three years prior, and who had properly applied for protection under the (then) prevailing law and policy framework. The HCA held that "the status of unauthorised maritime arrival cannot be treated as a sufficient reason in itself for refusing to grant the visa."[14] Additionally, the HCA rejected the government's argument that sweeping legislative reforms that had reintroduced TPVs conclusively, in December 2014 (see ahead), functioned to *convert* the plaintiff's PPV application into an application for temporary protection. This was because the Minister had, in fact, *already* made an adverse PPV decision on national interest grounds.[15] In short, the HCA decisively quelled the controversy by commanding the Minister to grant the plaintiff a visa to which he was entitled.[16]

TPVs and SHEVs: temporary protection or forms of repression?

When introducing changes to the *Migration Act 1958* (Cth), in September 2014, the Coalition Government lauded TPVs as a key element of border protection. The Immigration Minister explained:

> TPVs will provide refugees with stability and a chance to get on with their lives while at the same time guaranteeing that people smugglers do not have a "permanent protection visa product" to sell to those who are thinking of travelling illegally to Australia.
>
> (Morrison 2014a)

However, temporary protection measures were not just deployed prospectively, in respect of future arrivals, they were used retrospectively. At the time TPVs were reintroduced,[17] maritime arrivals already present in Australia fell into two categories: (i) asylum seekers who arrived *before* 13 August 2012 with PPV applications pending. Strikingly, by legislative command, any PPV applications that were not finalised were "converted" into TPV applications; and (ii) asylum seekers in Australia who arrived *between* 13 August 2012 and December 2013, who were vulnerable to regional processing offshore but who were not transferred from Australia (the "Legacy Caseload").[18]

As TPVs captured more than potential "illegal maritime arrivals" the deterrence rationale for TPVs, advanced by the government, was disingenuous. Essentially, as the government appeared to acknowledge, the reintroduction of TPVs was about disciplining people "by ensuring that those who flagrantly disregard our laws and arrive illegally in Australia are not rewarded with a permanent protection visa" (Morrison 2014a).

An alternative to the TPV, the SHEV, applied solely to members of the Legacy Caseload cohort who were declared refugees. SHEV holders are legally required to live in designated regional parts of Australia and fill regional job vacancies or study full time. Unlike TPV holders, SHEV holders may later apply for other forms of substantive visa (e.g. family visa, skilled worker visa) other than a PPV. But they must satisfy a challenging visa requirement that obliges them to work in regional Australia without requiring access to social (income) support, for three and half years out of the five-year lifespan of the visa. Any paid work undertaken while receiving "special benefit" does not count towards meeting the work requirements of the SHEV. The prospect of securing a skilled or family stream visa, upon expiration of the SHEV, for refugees is unrealistic and remote for many people, due to the strict visa criteria (Reilly 2018). As the government conceded, SHEV's present a very limited opportunity to secure permanent residency in the future (Morrison 2014b).

Additionally, by incentivising employment in the regions, away from established refugee communities and settlement services in cities,[19] via the (faint) prospect of a pathway to a permanent visa in the future, SHEV holders became more reliant on maintaining employment regardless of pay and conditions. Accordingly, their risk of vulnerability in the workplace stemmed from a readiness

> to take on precarious work for low pay out of ignorance of their rights, or will accept poor pay and conditions in exchange for the evidence of employment they require to apply for a non-humanitarian visa at the conclusion of the SHEV.
>
> (Reilly 2018: 883)

There is also the risk of destitution arising from the twin requirements of paid work and avoidance of social welfare assistance. Reilly (2018: 887) has argued, persuasively, that avoiding welfare while undertaking low paid work presented a poverty risk for SHEV holders and would place them in a worse position than those on bridging visas.

Critics of temporary protection argued the new restrictive visas were a "relic of Australia's past abuses of refugees' rights" because the first time around (1999–2008), "TPVs were shown to inflict serious harm on refugees' mental health, with higher levels of stress, anxiety, depression and post-traumatic stress, compared to those with permanent protection" (McGregor 2014). Indeed, a parliamentary committee inquiry concluded that "there is little real evidence of its deterrent value, . . . But there is no doubt that its operation has had a considerable cost in terms of human suffering" (The Senate, Legal and Constitutional References Committee 2006: 252).[20] Moreover, there was a general consensus among health practitioners that the social conditions imposed by TPVs tended to impact negatively on the mental health of refugees, attributable to their state of uncertainty intersecting with other factors including the impact of mandatory detention, time spent in the community without work rights, lack of family reunification, and fear of repatriation (Hafeez-Baig 2016: 129). Children articulated their experience of TPVs in necropolitical terms:

> [L]ike a brain tumour or something—you know that you are going to die after three years. Even if you have a brain tumour, you know that you are going to die in that certain time, and you know you are going to die, so you live happily. With this, you just die every day.
>
> (Human Rights and Equal Opportunity Commission (HREOC) 2004: 815)

As well as the adverse effects on people's health, scholars identified a lack of access to appropriate and affordable housing options and insecure rental housing for TPV holders (Marston 2003). Marston also cited multiple barriers to entering the workforce for TPV holders, concluding that the right to work was "somewhat theoretical" (2003: 58).

Before turning to outline the human rights implications of temporary protection, it is important to reflect on how Federal Government's hostility towards unauthorised maritime arrivals was evidenced in May 2017. The then Immigration Minister branded them as "fake refugees" who were gaming taxpayers.[21] These banal caricatures stemmed from people's failure to apply for a TPV or SHEV "promptly" after the statutory bar on visa applications had been lifted, six months prior. Having denigrated and devalued the moral status of these asylum seekers—who had previously been left in legal limbo for *several years* due to bureaucratic inertia including the deliberate visa processing delays—the Federal Government proceeded to set an arbitrary deadline of 1 October 2017 for all outstanding visa applications to be lodged. This occurred in circumstances where public funding for legal assistance had been cut for maritime arrivals, a cohort who had violated Australia's orderly humanitarian program, according to conservative politicians (Loughland 2014). The prospective cessation of income support and destitution was threatened by the government in order to leverage 7,500 asylum seekers who had failed or refused to lodge visa applications (Norman 2017). Remarkably, all but seventy-one people lodged claims before the deadline amid a climate of distress and fear. However, assisting asylum seekers in lodging their visa applications in time placed considerable strain upon community law centres, pro bono lawyers, and community groups (Koziol 2017). For the seventy-one people failing to meet the deadline, social welfare supports were cut off and detention-deportation became a real possibility.

Temporary protection and human rights

Temporary protection arrangements for asylum seekers arriving by boat breach human rights. The measures are "punitive" (UN CESCR 2017: [17]) and inconsistent with international law. This is because the arrangements use people as a means to an end. They are

> predicated on the idea that it sends a message to the smugglers and the potential candidates for maritime smuggling operations. However, it is a fundamental principle of human rights law that one person cannot be punished only for the reason of deterring another.
>
> (Crépeau 2017: 9)

Additionally, the UN Special Rapporteur on the human rights of migrants (among others) asserted that placing restrictions on *(inter alia)* social welfare services, family reunion, and access to permanent residence and citizenship, due to a refugee's *mode of arrival*, constitutes unjustifiable discrimination: "this two-tier system, with differentiations in the rights enjoyed by those on full protection visas and those on temporary protection visas, is discriminatory" (Crépeau 2017: 18).

Extending this point further, using temporary protection visas to encourage orderly migration is not rationally connected to that objective, nor is it a reasonable and proportionate means of achieving that objective (Australian Human Rights Commission 2019: 68; and Hafeez-Baig 2016: 137–140). As noted earlier, temporary forms of visas cannot discourage asylum seekers (the Legacy Caseload, already present in Australia) from making maritime journeys, and the available evidence shows that TPVs were not an effective deterrent in the past.

Additionally, the UN Committee on the Rights of the Child (CRC) has cautioned Australia that contrary to human rights law the best interests of the child are not a primary consideration in asylum, refugee, and migration processes. The CRC cited the many thousands of children in the Legacy Caseload (along with children transferred to Australia from Nauru on medical grounds [see Part 4]) who will not be permanently settled in Australia, who are left in limbo for an undetermined period (UNCRC 2019).

In view of the substantial body of evidence about the adverse consequences of the first iteration of TPVs for people's health, the government's stance, in 2014, that TPVs would give refugees stability is incongruous. Indeed, informed by numerous studies, a recent report (Australian Human Rights Commission 2019) suggested that the impacts of TPVs/SHEVs "may be particularly pronounced for people in the legacy caseload, who have already experienced a prolonged period of uncertainty due to delays in processing their claims," and that "the mental health impacts of temporary protection arrangements in their current form may be even more significant than under the previous TPV regime" (Australian Human Rights Commission 2019: 72). Accordingly, the negative effects on mental health and well-being of those subject to temporary protection laws and policies may mean that Australia is interfering with the right to the highest attainable standard of health, enshrined in international human rights law.

In theory, TPV/SHEV holders enjoy a work entitlement, but studies show that temporary visa status can compromise access to stable and secure employment and attracts the real risk of exploitation. TPV and SHEV holders do not enjoy the same access to social welfare supports and assistance as refugees on PPVs or humanitarian entrants admitted from overseas. They can access public health services (e.g. Medicare), but strictly limited social security support ("special benefit" payment). They cannot access other income support payments or the National Disability Insurance Scheme.

While children can access free primary and secondary education, high international student fees for tertiary education are prohibitive for refugees. They are effectively barred from higher education in many cases due to an absence of federal government funding (Refugee Council of Australia 2015). For refugees with temporary protection, obtaining commercial loans or raising the money needed to cover fees, in addition to their basic subsistence, is impractical. Even with fee subsidies and scholarships that higher education providers have made directly available to asylum seekers and refugees with temporary status, income support restrictions for special benefit recipients can serve to preclude people's participation in tertiary education programs of twelve months or longer. By a policy of "deterrence and de-education" Australia "may be condemning them to a lifetime of poverty and disadvantage and all the subsequent corollaries of increased welfare burdens and reduced tax revenue" (Hirsch and Maylea 2016: 22).

The Australian Human Rights Commission (2019: 78) has maintained that the restrictions on the human rights of TPV/SHEV holders are not for a legitimate aim, nor a reasonable and proportionate means of achieving that aim (for the reasons stated earlier). As such, Australia may be in breach of obligations arising under international human rights law in respect of *(inter alia)*: rights to work and to just and favourable conditions of work, and the right to an adequate standard of living (including adequate food, clothing, and housing) and in ensuring that the right to education was equally accessible to all.

Moreover, as noted earlier, the protection of family life and family unity are interrelated. The right to protection of the family manifests in the right to family reunion for refugees. However, all TPV and SHEV holders who arrived in Australia by boat on or after 13 August 2012 are ineligible to propose any family members for resettlement under the Refugee and Humanitarian Program. Notably, they are also ineligible to utilise the alternative family stream of the general migration program because they do not hold citizenship or permanent residency. These blanket restrictions mean that majority of refugees in the Legacy Caseload face indefinite family separation, as they have no legal avenues through which to reunite with relatives living overseas. Even those few refugees who eventually secure permanent residency (via the SHEV pathway) are likely to be parted from their families for many years before reunification becomes possible. This is because applications for family stream members lodged by permanent residents who arrived by boat receive the lowest processing priority unless there are special or compassionate reasons.

The Australian Government maintains that its policy on refugee family reunion is complaint with human rights, partly on the basis that refugees were to blame for their own misfortune. They were framed as irresponsible for having *chosen* to leave family members at home and migrating in a disorderly way outside of regular channels.[22] Therefore, the state could not be held morally or legally responsible for causing family separation. This logic wilfully ignores the realities of forced migration and the financial and human costs of being smuggled. Though not the initial cause of family separation, Australia's restrictive refugee policies and practices intentionally prolong family separation on an indefinite and possibly lasting basis. As such, the policy interferes with human rights treaty obligations, including affording "the widest possible protection and assistance to the family" (Australian Human Rights Commission 2019: 82, 86). And it creates a risk of constructive *refoulement*, whereby refugees feel compelled to return to their families at home.

Offshored refugees and medical transferees to Australia

Introduction: outsourcing refugee protection

A critical dimension of the "No Advantage" policy was offshore regional processing. As noted earlier, the policy applied to unauthorised maritime arrivals seeking asylum after 13 August 2012 compelling such persons to lodge asylum claims while in a "regional processing country." The government's subsequent policy shift, in July 2013, forever prohibiting refugee resettlement in Australia for later boat arrivals, left a large cohort of asylum seekers devoid of a durable refugee resettlement solution. In total, 4,100 persons were transferred into regional processing, with 3,127 sent after 19 July 2013 (post "no resettlement in Australia" policy). Just under half of that cohort remain trapped in limbo, either contained offshore (290 people, as at October 2020) or "transitory persons" living temporarily in Australia (more than 1,000) having been evacuated on medical grounds or in order to accompany a sick family member or friend (Ryan 2020).

While contained offshore, welfare provision—income support, accommodation, education, and health services—has been provided for refugees and their families at Australia's expense. However, the structural complexity of offshore processing and reliance on the private sector to administer key aspects of the regime "led to a lack of accountability and transparency in the administration of the policy, and a failure to clearly acknowledge where the duty of care lies in relation to asylum seekers and refugees" (Legal and Constitutional Affairs References Committee 2017–18: v).

Through its regional processing laws (*Regional Processing Act 2012* (Cth)) Australia sought to formally transfer legal responsibility for asylum seekers to designated third countries. Yet behind this legal fiction Australia effectively controlled and managed offshore processing. Grewcock aptly described the Manus Island Centre as a "gulag within which Australian state agencies, through an opaque and complex chain of command, wield control over detainees' basic means of survival, their daily routines and the key decisions affecting their lives" (Grewcock 2017: 76).

Judicial intervention and a "duty of care" to offshored refugees

Australia's ambition to divest itself of legal responsibility for asylum seekers arriving by boat was only ever partially realised. Although regional processing arrangements did survive several legal challenges before the HCA (e.g. *Plaintiff M68/2015 v Minister for Immigration and Border Protection*)[23] importantly, the courts identified that by virtue of the Australian Government's effective control over many facets of people's lives offshore, a "duty of care" exists. Beginning with *Plaintiff S99/2016 v Minister for Immigration and Border Protection*, the courts have considered negligence claims centred on the suitability or adequacy of medical treatment in regional processing countries.

Plaintiff S99 concerned a female refugee living in the Nauruan community with complex medical needs. She was raped outside her accommodation while unconscious during a seizure. Having become pregnant the plaintiff sought an abortion that could not occur in Nauru because the procedure was criminalised. The Australian Government could have procured an abortion in Australia but, remarkably, refused to do so on the basis that exceptional circumstances were not involved. Instead, they opted to facilitate a transfer to Port Moresby (Papua New Guinea) for a termination procedure with provision for her accommodation and care in Papua New Guinea. The plaintiff commenced legal proceedings to resist this course of action because it was uncertain whether an abortion would be lawful in Papua New Guinea and whether she would receive proper medical care.

The Federal Court determined, *inter alia*, that the Immigration Minister owed the plaintiff a duty of care to exercise reasonable care in the discharge of the responsibility he had assumed to procure a safe and lawful abortion.[24] This was because the statutory regime that provided for a scheme of regional processing for unauthorised maritime arrivals erected or facilitated a relationship between the Australian Government and persons transferred to third countries.[25] And the facts disclosed that the Australian Government had provided very substantial assistance to the regional processing functions taken up by Nauru:

> [T]he facts show that the applicant was dependent upon the assistance provided by the Commonwealth to sustain her very existence. In that respect, the Commonwealth provided or was directly responsible for the provision to her of food, water, housing, security and medical services to maintain her health and wellbeing. . . . The facts are clear. The applicant had no means of survival independent of the services provided by the Commonwealth through its Service Providers. She was dependent upon the Commonwealth for her very existence.[26]

A duty to exercise care in the discharge of the responsibility to procure a safe and lawful abortion arose because the plaintiff was reliant on the Minister to obtain an abortion for her, the Minister had assumed responsibility to procure an abortion and controlled whether and where it took place, the applicant was in a generally dependent relationship with Australia, and the Minister had knowledge and foresight of the harmful risks to the plaintiff in Papua New Guinea. The plaintiff had no capacity to protect herself from that potential harm other than by not having the abortion, which would also have been harmful.[27] The Court found that the Minister breached the established duty of care because he had failed to take reasonable care in the discharge of the responsibility he had assumed. Procuring an abortion in Papua New Guinea exposed the plaintiff to legal (a risk of criminal prosecution and conviction) and medical risks (physical and psychological).[28] To restrain the Minister from committing the anticipated tort of negligence, a permanent injunction was issued.

The impact of *Plaintiff S99* was, in principle and practice, considerable: the reasoning in this case was subsequently applied in a raft of other interlocutory cases brought before the courts involving apprehended breaches of the duty of care relating to the provision of an adequate standard of medical services to meet the healthcare needs of refugees offshore (Baxter 2019: 125–127). The impact of injunctive orders made in most of these cases was to effect the evacuation of people to Australia, for the temporary and limited purpose of receiving appropriate medical treatment.[29]

These cases serve to expose how the general medical transfer system put in place by Australia to evacuate refugees wasn't functioning properly; it was seemingly driven by political considerations. Bureaucratic inefficiency resulted in lengthy delays in transferring people for treatment.[30] For example, in the case of *FRX17 v Minister for Immigration and Border Protection*, Justice Murphy did not consider that the Overseas Medical Referral process on Nauru was "likely to be sufficiently swift to adequately protect against the risk of suicide."[31] In *DJA18* the facts disclosed that clinicians had requested transfer to Australia for two young girls but instead they were removed to Papua New Guinea at the behest of Australian bureaucrats. Justice Murphy stated, pointedly, "If the Commonwealth is to be involved in medical decisions, such as where the patient will be treated, it must do so competently."[32] Furthermore, in *DCQ18 v Minister for Home Affairs*,[33] the court ordered the urgent transfer of a refugee (who had undergone infibulation in Somalia) from Nauru to Australia, for termination of her pregnancy, in circumstances when the Australian Government contended she could and should be removed to Taiwan for the required treatment.

The bureaucratic and political imperatives to keep refugees offshore have had deadly consequences. For example, on 23 August 2014 Hamid Khazaei presented to the Manus Island medical clinic with flu-like symptoms and a small lesion on his leg. The clinic lacked the antibiotic to treat his common infection and, despite treatment, Khazaei developed severe sepsis. Doctors urged his immediate transfer to Australia, but this was first ignored and then rejected by officials based in Canberra. Two days after the initial transfer request he was moved to hospital in Port Moresby where there were delays in responding to his critical needs. He grew gravely ill. By the time he was transported to Brisbane's Mater hospital, he was profoundly brain-damaged, and he died on 5 September 2014. The Queensland Coroner found that there were systematic failures with the offshore healthcare system, and that Australia was solely responsible for his care and the failures that led to his death (Ryan 2018).

Medevac laws

For a brief period of time, access to timely medical treatment or assessments for refugees and asylum seekers offshore was facilitated under specific medical transfer provisions (called the "medevac process") inserted into the *Migration Act 1958* (Cth) in March 2019, against the Federal Government's wishes.[34] This statutory scheme, which diminished the importance of political or bureaucratic discretion, and elevated the role of medical officials in transfer decisions, meant people were no longer forced to litigate in court on "duty of care" grounds to secure a medical transfer. However, this reform was short lived. Following an election, in December 2019, the Coalition party secured power and sufficient support within the new Parliament to repeal the medevac laws. The prominence of political discretion over medical transfers was re-established. This has served to delay, if not deny, subsequent transfer requests from the few remaining refugees (or "failed" asylum seekers) living offshore.

Social welfare provisions for medical transferees: a bifurcated governance regime

Over 1,200 people have been brought to Australia from offshore sites for medical assessment and treatment (Pezullo 2020: 74). Less than a handful have been forcibly returned to Nauru or Papua New Guinea, due to court injunctions or ongoing court cases, but they have been increasingly subjected to coercive compliance measures.

Unless they are admitted to a medical facility, "transitory persons" are placed in immigration detention. They may be the subject of a ministerial "residence determination" order (*qua* community detention) if they are not adjudged to be a risk to community safety. Under community detention arrangements people have access to supported housing, schooling, and medical care and, depending on their circumstances, income support under SRSS (Golightly 2018: 88). However, from around August 2017, people who had finished (or were close to finishing) their medical treatment were moved onto "final departure" BVEs. This meant they had to subsist in the community and, notionally, prepare to leave Australia (albeit with no straightforward destination apparent in most cases). This visa signifies another push, another welfare policy ploy, in the (now nine-year-long) war of attrition waged against unauthorised maritime arrivals by the Australian Government.

The six-month BVE has work rights. So, where people are judged to be capable of supporting themselves there is no access to income supports and supported accommodation, only Medicare. The policy of moving "transitory persons" onto "final departure" BVE's was apparently born out of the government's frustration with financially supporting a group of asylum seekers initially brought to Australia temporarily but whose removal was stymied by legal proceedings. This "welfare crackdown" appeared designed to make people destitute and homeless and to coerce them to return offshore, to their home countries, or resettlement elsewhere (Baines 2017). Presently, there is no effort to deport them; indeed, the government is attempting to wind down offshore processing arrangements. In practice, the "final departure" BVE is harsh for a vulnerable cohort and shifts the cost of refugees' welfare and well-being from the Federal Government and onto the State and Territory governments.

Conversely, those transferred to Australia under the medevac laws have been managed differently—even more punitively—by being held in immigration detention facilities ("Alternative Places of Detention," or, hotels typically) and subject to repeated, arbitrary transfers between detention facilities (Middleton 2020). The Australian Government rejects the claim that medevac transferees (nearly 200) are singled out for particularly punitive treatment compared with other transferees. However, at the end of 2020, some medevac detainees had been deprived of their liberty, secured in hotel rooms for nearly two years, with only a handful released into the community on visas (Hermant 2020).

Conclusion

This chapter has argued that by reducing and removing social welfare supports from asylum seekers on bridging visas awaiting the outcome of their protection claims, and by refusing welfare to those who are "double negatives" seeking judicial review before the courts, the Australian Government weaponised social welfare to coerce asylum seekers into departure from Australia. Furthermore, this chapter has shown how the Australian Government used the potential cessation of income support to leverage several thousand asylum seekers who had not lodged TPV/SHEV applications sufficiently promptly, after years of living in limbo when visa processing was halted.

Moreover, it has been argued that temporary visas for refugees are as oppressive as they are protective, effectively disciplining asylum seekers for their mode of arrival in a discriminatory way that violates human rights principles relating to *(inter alia)*: secure employment, an adequate standard of living, access to education, and family reunion. These human rights failings mean dire living conditions, prompting some refugees to contemplate returning home. In such circumstances repatriation would, arguably, constitute constructive *refoulement*.

Finally, this chapter has critically explored how the welfare (especially healthcare) of offshored asylum seekers and refugees has suffered because of mismanagement by Australia politicians, bureaucrats, and private contractors. And it has revealed how, recently, the government pursued a welfare crackdown on asylum seekers and refugees brought to Australia for urgent medical assessments and treatment following litigation (or the threat of litigation) on "duty of care" grounds. The policy of shifting people onto final departure bridging visas (gesturing that they are required to leave Australia) has predictably rendered people destitute and homeless in violation of their human rights. However, the global health pandemic has presently stymied that policy in practice, leaving State and

Territory governments, churches, and charities to manage the welfare of refugees and asylum seekers within their communities.

Notes

1 Continual use of dehumanising language (detainees, unauthorised/illegal maritime arrivals, transferees, transitory persons, etc.), in law and political debates, rather than the label of asylum seeker or refugee, is a feature of how Australia has fostered an environment that distances protection seekers from its citizenry and which can serve to deplete their humanity.
2 The Immigration Minister has the statutory power (s 197AB *Migration Act 1958* (Cth)) to make a "residence determination" in respect of a person in immigration detention; this allows that person to live in a specified residence in the community ("community detention"). People can move about in the community subject to conditions (e.g. curfew and reporting requirements).
3 In 2012, 17,202 asylum seekers arrived in Australia by boat, a significant increase from the 2,726 arrivals in 2009 and the 161 arrivals in 2008 (Spinks and McClusky 2013).
4 *Migration Legislation Amendment (Regional Processing and Other Measures) Act 2012 (Cth).*
5 *Migration Amendment (Unauthorised Maritime Arrivals and Other Measures) Act 2013* (Cth).
6 *Migration Amendment Regulation 2012 (No. 5).*
7 (2015) 258 CLR 173, 192 [49].
8 *Migration and Maritime Powers Legislation Amendment (Resolving the Asylum Legacy Caseload) Act 2014* (Cth).
9 On interdiction at sea, see *(inter alia)*: Klein 2014; Little and Vaughan-Williams 2017; Ghezelbash 2018. On offshore processing, see Gleeson 2016.
10 Ibid at [31]–[32].
11 e.g. Queensland Government, "Asylum Seeker and Refugee Assistance Program," supporting asylum seekers and vulnerable refugees on temporary visas in Queensland ($3.988 million, 2018–2021).
12 *Plaintiff S297/2013* (2014) 255 CLR 179 [23], [64] (Crenan, Bell, Gageler and Keane JJ).
13 *Plaintiff M150 of 2013* (2014) 255 CLR 199 [95].
14 (2015) 255 CLR 231 [21].
15 Ibid., [27]–[41].
16 Ibid., [45], [47].
17 For a short history of TPVs in Australia, see Marston 2003 and Hafeez-Baig 2016: 118–120.
18 Additionally, the asylum legacy caseload was "fast-tracked" to meet government concerns about the backlog of cases and unmeritorious claims for asylum from people who wished to "game the system" (2014a). See McDonald and O'Sullivan 2018.
19 A designated regional area was broadly defined but excluded the main capital cities of Sydney, Melbourne, Brisbane, and Perth.
20 See Hafeez-Baig 2016: 126–130.
21 The claim that undeserving refugees were an economic threat, consuming $250 million in income support per year, must be considered in light of the government's willingness to detain asylum seekers (most of whom have been declared refugees) offshore at exorbitant cost. The Federal Government has spent $12 billion on offshore processing in eight years (Green 2020).
22 House of Representatives, Migration and Maritime Powers Legislation Amendment (Resolving the Asylum Legacy Caseload) Bill 2014 *[Explanatory Memorandum]* Attachment A (Statement of Compatibility with Human Rights) 12.

23 (2016) 257 CLR 42, 84 [93].
24 (2016) 243 FCR 17, 83 [243].
25 Ibid [244]–[248].
26 Ibid [250] and [252]. Also, see *AYX v Minister for Home Affairs* [2018] FCA 283 [26], per Perram J: "As in *S99/2016* the evidence suggests an arguable case that the boy and his mother are dependent on the Commonwealth either directly or indirectly for their survival and sustenance."
27 Ibid [257]–[265], [276].
28 Ibid [284]–[387].
29 *Migration Act 1958* (Cth) s 198AB.
30 *FRX17 as litigation representative for FRM17 v Minister for Immigration and Border Protection* (2018) 262 FCR 116 [32]–[37].
31 Ibid at [70].
32 *DJA18 as litigation representative for DIZ18 v Minister for Home Affairs* [2018] FCA 1050 [13].
33 [2018] FCA 918.
34 *Home Affairs Legislation Amendment (Miscellaneous Measures) Act 2019* (Cth) Sch. 6.

References

Australian Government. (2012) *Report of the Expert Panel on Asylum Seekers*, Commonwealth of Australia, August 2012.

Australian Human Rights Commission. (2019) *Lives on hold: Refugees and asylum seekers in the 'Legacy Caseload'*. AHRC.

Australian Human Rights Commission. (n.d.) *Community Arrangements for Asylum Seekers, Refugees and Stateless Persons*. AHRC.

Baines, R. (2017) 'Asylum seekers face welfare crackdown under Government changes', *ABC News*, 27 August.

Barchetti, V. and Moradi, K. (2016) 'The 20 year queue: Family reunion for 'genuine' refugees unlikely', *Law and Justice: La Trobe Law School Blog*. https://law.blogs.latrobe.edu.au/2016/11/16/the-20-year-queue-family-reunion-for-genuine-refugees-unlikely/

Baxter, T. (2019) 'The slow death of past damage as an essential element of negligence', *Tort Law Review*, 26: 123.

Bowen, C. (2012) 'Minister for immigration and citizenship, "Government Implements Expert Panel's Family Reunion Recommendation"', *Media Release*, 24 September.

Buckmaster, L. (2012) 'Australian government assistance to refugees: Fact v fiction', *Parliamentary Library (Background Notes)*, 28 September.

Chalmers, M. (2018) 'Removing asylum seekers from support payments "sends a message"', *ABC News*, 6 September.

Committee on Economic Social and Cultural Rights. (2017) *Concluding Observations on the Fifth Periodic Report of Australia*, 61st sess. UN Doc E/C.12/AUS/CO/5, 11 July.

Committee on the Elimination of Discrimination against Women. (2018) *Concluding observations on the eight periodic report of Australia*, 70th sess. UN Doc CEDAW/C/AUS/CO/8, 25 July.

Crépeau, F. (2017) *Report of the Special Rapporteur on the Human Rights of Migrants on His Mission to Australia and the Regional Processing Centres in Nauru*. UN Doc A/HRC/35/25/Add.3, 24 April.

Darling, E. (2019) 'The right to refugee family reunion', in Juss, S. (ed.) *Research Handbook on International Refugee Law*. Edward Elgar, p. 353.

Dastyari, A. and O'Sullivan, M. (2016) 'Not for export: The failure of Australia's extraterritorial processing regime in Papua New Guinea and the Decision of the PNG Supreme Court in Namah (2016)', *Monash University Law Review*, 42(2): 308.

Finnane, M. (2015) 'The border is everywhere: The policy overreach behind operation fortitude', *The Conversation*, 31 August.

Fleay, C., Hartley, L. and Kenny, M.A. (2013) 'Refugees and asylum seekers living in the Australian community: The importance of work rights and employment support', *Australian Journal of Social Issues*, 48(4): 473.

Gerard, A. and Kerr, T. (2016) 'Lethal violence and legal ambiguities: Deaths in custody in Australia's offshore detention centres', in Fitz-Gibbon, K. and Walklate, S. (eds) *Homicide, Gender and Responsibility: An International Perspective*. Routledge, p. 130.

Ghezelbash, D., Moreno-Lax, V., Klein, N. and Opeskin, B. (2018) 'Securitization of search and rescue at sea: The response to boat migration in the Mediterranean and Offshore Australia', *International and Comparative Law Quarterly*, 67: 315.

Gleeson, M. (2016) *Offshore: Behind the Wire on Manus and Nauru*. New South Books.

Golightly, M. (2018) The Senate, Legal and Constitutional Affairs Legislation Committee, *Estimates*, 21 May.

Green, M. (2020) 'Budget blowouts: Offshore processing costs $1.2bn for fewer than 300 people', *The Guardian*, 11 December.

Grewcock, M. (2017) '"Our lives is in danger": Manus Island and the end of asylum', *Race & Class*, 59(2): 70.

Hafeez-Baig, M. (2016) 'Putting the "Protection" in temporary protection visa', *Bond Law Review*, 28(2): 115.

Hanson-Young, S. (2013) 'The Senate', *Hansard*, 2 December, p. 595.

Hermant, N. (2020) 'Farhad Bandesh among first asylum seekers brought to Australia under medevac legislation to be granted visa', *ABC News*, 11 December.

Higgins, C. (2016) 'The (un-)sustainability of Australia's offshore processing and settlement policy', in Moreno-Lax, V. and Papastavridis, E. (eds) *Boat Refugees and Migrants at Sea: A Comprehensive Approach*. Brill, p. 303.

Hirsch, A. and Maylea, C. (2016) 'Education denied: People seeking asylum and refugees trapped in limbo', *New Community Journal*, 14(3): 19–35.

Human Rights and Equal Opportunity Commission. (2004) *A Last Resort? National Inquiry into Children in Immigration Detention*. HREOC.

Jesuit Social Services. (2015) 'The Living Conditions of People Seeking Asylum in Australia', *Jesuit Social Services*, December 2015.

Klein, N. (2014) 'Assessing Australia's push back the boats policy under international law: Legality and accountability for maritime interceptions of irregular migrants', *Melbourne Journal of International Law*, 15: 1.

Koziol, M. (2017) 'Peter Dutton's crackdown on 'fake refugees' prompts nearly 7500 asylum claims', *Sydney Morning Herald*, 12 October.

Legal and Constitutional Affairs References Committee. (2017–18) 'Additional estimates, question on notice no. 99', Portfolio question number: AE18/104.

Liberal Party. (2013) *Our Plan—Real Solutions for All Australians: The Direction, Values and Policy Priorities of the Next Coalition Government*, Bambra Press, 1 February.

Little, A. and Vaughan-Williams, N. (2017) 'Stopping boats, saving lives, securing subjects: Humanitarian borders in Europe and Australia', *European Journal of International Relations*, 23(3): 533.

Loughland, O. (2014) 'Legal aid denied to asylum seekers who arrive through unauthorized channels', *The Guardian*, 31 March.

Mares, P. (2014) 'Refuge without work: "This is a poison, a poison for the life of a person"', *Griffith Review*, 45: 103.

Marston, G. (2003) *Temporary Protection Permanent Uncertainty*. Centre for Applied Social Science Research, RMIT University.

McDonald, E. and O'Sullivan, M. (2018) 'Protecting vulnerable refugees: Procedural fairness in the Australian fast track regime', *University of New South Wales Law Journal*, 41(3): 1003.

McGregor, G. (2014) 'TPVs: human rights used as bargaining chips', *The Drum*, 25 September.

Menjívar, C. (2014) 'Immigration law beyond borders: Externalizing and internalizing border controls in an era of securitization', *Annual Review of Law and Social Sciences*, 10: 353.

Middleton, K. (2020) 'Medevac refugees: We face special punishment', *The Saturday Paper*, 5–11 December.

Morrison, S. (2014a) 'House of representatives', *Hansard*, 25 September, p. 10545.

Morrison, S. (2014b). 'Reintroducing TPVs to resolve labor's asylum legacy caseload, Cambodia', *Transcript of Press Conference*, 25 September.

Norman, P. (2017) 'Peter Dutton declares "game is up" for "fake refugees" living in Australia', *ABC News*, 21 May.

Parliamentary Joint Committee on Human Rights. (2013) 'Migration legislation amendment (regional processing and other measures) Act 2012', *Ninth Report of 2013*, June.

Perera, S. and Pugliese, J. (2014) 'Manifesto for a pogrom: Hostility to resettled refugees grows on Nauru', *The Conversation*, 20 November.

Peyton, T. (2020) 'Judicial review of the fast-track asylum seeker assessment process', *Australian Journal of Administrative Law*, 27: 20.

Pezullo, M. (2020) 'The Senate, Legal, and Constitutional Affairs Legislation Committee', *Estimates*, 19 October.

Phillips, J. and Spinks, H. (2013) 'Boat arrivals in Australia since 1976' (Research Paper, Parliamentary Library), *Commonwealth of Australia*, 23 July.

Refugee Council of Australia. (2015) 'Barriers to education: For people seeking asylum and refugees on temporary visas', *Refugee Council of Australia*, December 2015.

Reilly, A. (2016) 'Asylum seekers in the community: the importance of work for a decent life', *Australian Journal of Human Rights*, 22(1): 1.

Reilly, A. (2018) 'The vulnerability of safe haven enterprise visa holders: Balancing work, protection and future prospects', *University of New South Wales Law Journal*, 41(3): 871.

Ryan, H. (2020) 'Revealed: 1500 people in limbo under Australia's "bizarre and cruel" refugee deterrence policy', *The Guardian*, 10 December.

Ryan, T. (2018) 'Inquest into the death of Hamid Khazaei', *Coroners Court of Queensland—Findings of Inquest*, 30 July.

Spinks, H. and McClusky, I. (2013) 'Asylum seekers and the Refugee Convention', Parliamentary Library (Briefing Book—Key Issues for the 44th Parliament), p. 156.

Stayner, T. (2020) 'Fears refugees will be denied justice under "exorbitant" hike of court fees for migration cases', *SBS*, 19 November.

Tahiri, S. (2017) 'Not working: Experiences of refugees and migrants with jobactive', Report No. 03/2017, Fairfeld Multicultural Interagency and Refugee Council of Australia, August.

The Senate, Legal and Constitutional References Committee. (2006) *Administration and operation of the Migration Act 1958*, March, Commonwealth of Australia.

The Senate, Legal and Constitutional Affairs References Committee. (2014) *Incident at the Manus Island Detention Centre from 16 February to 18 February 2014*, December, Commonwealth of Australia.

The Senate, Legal and Constitutional Affairs References Committee. (2017) *Serious Allegations of Abuse, Self-harm and Neglect of Asylum Seekers in Relation to the Nauru Regional Processing Centre, and any Like Allegations in Relation to the Manus Regional Processing Centre*, 21 April, Commonwealth of Australia.

The Senate, Select Committee on the Recent allegations Relating to Conditions and Circumstances at the Regional Processing Centre in Nauru. (2015) *Taking Responsibility: Conditions and Circumstances at Australia's Regional Processing Centre in Nauru*, August, Commonwealth of Australia.

Togiba, L. (2020) 'Manus Island refugees recount violent attacks by armed locals on apartment compound', *The Guardian*, 11 March.

UN, Committee on Economic, Social and Cultural Rights. (2017) *Concluding Observations on the Fifth Periodic Report of Australia*, 61st sess. UN Doc E/C.12/AUS/CO/5, 11 July.

UN, Committee on the Rights of the Child. (2019) *Concluding Observations on the Combined Fifth and Sixth Periodic Report of Australia*. CRC/C/AUS/CO/5–6, 1 November.

UNHCR. (2013) *Asylum Seekers on Bridging Visas in Australia: Protection Gaps*. UNHCR Consultation.

van Kooy, J. and Ward, T. (2018) 'An unnecessary penalty: Economic impacts of changes to Status Resolution Support Services', *Policy Paper*, September.

Weber, L. and Pickering, S. (2014) 'Counting and accounting for deaths of asylum seekers en route to Australia', in IOM (ed.) *Fatal Journeys: Tracking Lives Lost During Migration*. IOM.

Chapter 2

The welfare policing of asylum seekers as necropolitics

Leanne Weber

"We really feel helpless and hopeless when we think that Australian politicians do not care if we live or die." (Manus Island detainee)[1]

Introduction

"Necropolitics" translates literally as the politics of death. We can easily imagine that the spectre of physical death permeates the consciousness of many asylum seekers as they live with memories of the horrors they have fled and might yet be forcibly returned to. But in many cases the conditions they are exposed to once reaching the putative safety of Australia may cultivate new and equally deadly risks. Indeed, deaths have occurred as a direct result of the deprivations deliberately inflicted by Australian border control policies, such as offshore detention and—although information is much harder to find—refoulement to danger. The Australian Border Deaths Database[2] has recorded at least 33 deaths following return to danger and 17 deaths in offshore detention since records began in 2000.[3] As well as violent deaths, such as the killing of Reza Berati during unrest at Manus Island Detention Centre (The Senate, Standing Committee on Legal and Constitutional Affairs 2014), there are deaths that are caused by medical neglect or are self-inflicted as a result of protracted emotional suffering (Powell et al. 2015).

But death, or the spectre of death, may also follow other asylum seekers living in the seemingly more hospitable environment of the Australian community. In these cases, Australian border control measures operate in more nuanced, and less visible, ways by creating conditions of prolonged insecurity and destitution. The Australian Border Deaths Database records 16 border-related deaths since the year 2000 of asylum seekers or other visa holders living within the community.[4] This is roughly the same number as the number of deaths in offshore detention and very likely a significant undercounting. Moreover, the same reasons predominate—despair over lack of legal recognition, social isolation, and lack of medical care. A recently reported death in the community tells an often-repeated story. In October 2019 a 33-year-old Bangladeshi asylum seeker

DOI: 10.4324/9781003298595-5

Mohammad Mohsin took his own life in Lakemba, Sydney. Ian Rintoul, an activist with the Refugee Action Coalition (RAC), said of his death:

> Like so many others on a bridging visa, Mohammad had no income and did not have the right to work. He was destitute and had become homeless, relying on charity and support from others in the Bangladeshi community. After being supported for many months by friends, he had spent the last few months going from couch to couch. Friends said that his precarious situation had weighed heavily on him and that he had spoken of ending his life even several months ago . . . The government's punitive anti-refugee regime is killing people—offshore and onshore.[5]

The regime this refugee advocate is referring to is the Status Resolution Support Services (SRSS), a bespoke welfare system exclusively for asylum seekers living in the Australian community on bridging visas (BVEs). The scheme was introduced in 2015 after release into the community had become more frequent for asylum seekers who had arrived without visas by boat and were therefore subject to Australia's harsh mandatory detention laws. The SRSS scheme is administered by the Department of Home Affairs (DHA) and is separate from the cumbersome social security system the serves the rest of the nation. This facilitates government discretion in constantly shifting and tightening the rules.[6] The scheme is marked by extreme complexity, uncertainty, and discretion. BVE holders may or may not be granted work rights on their visas, may or may not be eligible for financial support through SRSS, and may or may not be covered by the national health system Medicare. As they are issued on a short-term, renewable basis, frequent lapses of bridging visas occur due to administrative backlogs and for a multitude of other reasons, amplifying the precarity that is already built into the system. Both work rights and financial support are withdrawn completely after a "double negative" result involving rejection of an asylum application at both the first instance and merits review stage, even though options for judicial review may still be available.

The SRSS system operates on the basis that services be provided at a level no greater than is applicable for the wider population. However, it is immediately apparent that SRSS provision falls well short of the already low level of income support available to other population groups. Most SRSS recipients receive 89 per cent of the minimum social security payment available to Australian citizens, placing them well below the poverty line (Jesuit Social Services 2015). A review conducted by the Australian Human Rights Commission (AHRC) concluded that most asylum seekers on BVEs were "unable to meet their basic needs" (AHRC 2019: 50).

Since the SRSS clearly fails as a system of even minimalist welfare provision, the question that arises is, what is its purpose? Vanessa Barker has established, in relation to Sweden, that "welfare chauvinism" whereby social security is reserved for citizens at the expense of outsiders, is not driven by economic rationalism, but reflects the role of welfare as a bonding mechanism (Barker 2018). Inclusion in the generous welfare state within that social democracy signals membership but it also exercises control over members who are supported by the exclusion of others. Barker therefore associates the welfare state in Sweden with the exercise of penal power, and rather than seeing the two as negatively correlated, concludes that the Swedish system delivers more of both. While Australia's welfare system and Sweden's cannot be readily equated, Barker's analysis alerts us both to the in/exclusionary nature of welfare provision and the close association between systems of welfare and penal power.

The specialist welfare support system in Australia for asylum seekers who have arrived by boat is organised around a bordering logic, in which the endgame of possible removal is perpetually in play. The stated reason for the introduction of the SRSS is to encourage this group of asylum seekers—all of whom would previously have remained indefinitely in closed detention—to stay in touch with immigration authorities while their applications are finalised. A separate system of provision is considered necessary, both to reflect the non-entitlement to welfare of those who have already flouted the law by arriving at Australia's border without authorisation and reinforce their status as putative outsiders and to establish a system of surveillance and control.

The provision of casework support to SRSS recipients is contracted out by the DHA to non-government agencies. Case workers assigned to certain SRSS recipients are contractually obliged to report even minor breaches of visa conditions to DHA officials and to enforce a code of conduct that facilitates loss of financial support, visa cancellation, and possible re-detention for behaviours ranging from alleged criminal offending to perceived failure to uphold "community values" (Vogl and Methven 2015; Vogl 2019; Weber and Powell 2020). Individuals with serious health problems or other recognised vulnerabilities receive additional casework support within the SRSS system, which is accompanied by more surveillance and control. The highest level of support is provided to unaccompanied minors in "community detention" who reside in designated accommodation under close supervision and may be returned to closed detention for minor breaches such as non-attendance at school.

So the SRSS reflects the merging of welfare and penal mentalities observed by Barker in relation to the Swedish welfare system that is reserved for citizens. But as a system applicable only to non-citizens the SRSS may also serve an additional purpose of border control. In previous research I have articulated the characteristics of the "structurally embedded border" that is regularly encountered by non-citizens living in Australia with a precarious legal status (Weber 2013, 2019). This internal border is composed of networks of public and private agencies, including law enforcement, regulatory and service-providing bodies, most of which do not have an obvious role in border control. The structurally embedded border has two modes of operation. First, it facilitates information exchange within these "migration policing networks" to identify potentially deportable non-citizens. This surveillance function of the SRSS has already been described. But the structurally embedded border also operates through a modality of attrition, whereby essential services are systematically withdrawn with a view to generating "voluntary" departures. This achieves a border control outcome, without the direct application of penal power, while creating the illusion of individual choice (Weber and Pickering 2014).

In this chapter I discuss the SRSS as a system of welfare policing which relies on both these modalities to bring the determination of asylum claims for BVE holders to a preferred conclusion of removal from Australia. Systems that use systematic deprivation and surveillance to achieve a border control objective have previously been described in terms of "minimalist biopolitics" (Johansen 2013). In this chapter I develop this analysis further, employing the ideas of Achille Mbembe (2003, 2019) to critique the SRSS scheme as an example of "necropolitics." This governmentality not only minimises welfare provisions for certain groups—as in "minimalist biopolitics"—but also may be directed towards the production of literal or figurative death. In the discussion that follows I will draw on original material derived from interviews with service providers, government officials, and legal representatives, conducted between 2015 and 2017.[7] The interviews focused on access to services for various categories of non-citizens and information provision between immigration authorities and service-providing agencies. Before proceeding to that discussion, I will set out the main features of necropolitics as a mode of governance applied to a range of subjugated peoples who are systematically denied the protections of citizenship.

Necropolitics as a mode of governance

Colonial politics as "the work of death"

First coined by postcolonial theorist Achille Mbembe (2003), the concept of necropolitics invites immediate comparison with the Foucauldian term biopolitics, the aim of which is to "sustain, confirm and multiply life" through the exercise of "biopower" over populations (Foucault 1976).[8] Michel Foucault conceives of biopower as largely a positive force, contrasting it with more repressive forms of sovereign power in which a more direct power over life and death is expressed. This does not mean that the exercise of biopower leads solely to life-affirming outcomes. Rather, biopower constitutes "a power to foster life *or disallow it to the point of death*" (Adams 2017, emphasis added). In his later writings Foucault emphasised how the objective of war had shifted from the defence of the sovereign to the protection of whole populations against external threats. This mentality might also be applied internally, he argued, in the form of "state racism" directed against those who deviate from the norm (Foucault 2003). The concept of biopolitics therefore did allow for differential expression of biopower in relation to different population sub-groups distinguished primarily on the basis of race. However, these more life-threatening dimensions of biopower were never fully elaborated in Foucault's writings.

Mbembe (2003) has built on this foundation, noting that Foucault failed to develop a coherent theory of how biopolitics is actually put to work in deciding who will live and who will die. Mbembe developed his theory of necropolitics in this lacuna left by Foucault, posing the key question of "Under what practical conditions is the right to kill, to allow to live, or to expose to death exercised?" Mbembe began by defining biopower as "that domain of life over which power has taken control." He criticises liberal theories of democracy that posit individuals as rational and autonomous players in a collective process that supposedly differentiates politics from war. Imagining (bio)politics as a form of war, he places sovereignty at the centre of his formulation. In so doing, he merges the Foucauldian paradigms of biopolitics and sovereignty that are more usually treated as distinct and employs additional concepts such as states of exception, which are distinguishing features of the governance of colonised peoples.

Drawing on this counter-colonial perspective, Mbembe posits a reading of the politics of modernity, which is based on the instrumentalisation of human existence and the ever-present capacity for destruction. In contrast to Foucault, he argues for a more physical reading of human interaction: "[i]nstead of considering reason as the truth of the subject, we can look to other foundational categories that are less abstract and more tactile, such as life and death" (Mbembe 2003: 14). Politics as "the work of death" is realised most clearly in the Nazi totalitarian state. But Mbembe argues that necropolitics can be recognised within any set of power relations in which the Other, by their mere presence, is depicted as a mortal threat:

> The perception of the existence of the Other as an attempt on my life, as a mortal threat or absolute danger whose biophysical elimination would strengthen my potential to life and security—this, I suggest, is one of the many imaginaries of sovereignty characteristic of both early and late modernity itself.
>
> (Mbembe 2003: 18)

Mbembe acknowledges Foucault's reference to racism as an inherent principle of biopower, noting that "in the economy of biopower, the function of racism is to regulate the distribution of death and to make possible the murderous functions of the state" (Mbembe 2003: 17). But he makes explicit what is perhaps left implicit in Foucault's formulation that "race has been the ever present shadow in Western political thought and practice, especially when it comes to imagining the inhumanity of, or rule over, foreign peoples" (Mbembe 2003: 17). Necropolitics therefore makes explicit the colonial constellations of power that are not articulated in Foucault's account of biopolitics, including also forms of "social death" that are exemplified most clearly in slavery.

In relation to colonial rule, the key point for Mbembe is that "the colony represents the site where sovereignty consists fundamentally in the exercise of a power outside the law" (Mbembe 2003: 23). Necropolitics, as practiced in the colony, is the power to decide who should exist in a state of exception and therefore be exposed to death:

> The ultimate expression of sovereignty largely resides in the power and capacity to dictate who is able to live and who must die. To kill or to let live thus constitutes sovereignty's limits, is principle attributes. To be sovereign is to exert one's control over mortality and to define life as the deployment and manifestation of power.
>
> (Mbembe 2019: 66)

Hannah Arendt also explored this terrain at the junction of imperial and authoritarian rule, arguing that Nazism allowed previously unknown levels of violence that were associated with colonial conquest and reserved for "savages" to be unleashed domestically onto "civilized peoples" (Arendt 1968, cited in Mbembe 2003: 23). These distinctions between "savages" and "civilized peoples" have their origins, according to Mbembe (2003: 24), in the bordering and colonial practices of the international order:

> The colonies are the location par excellence where the controls and guarantees of judicial order can be suspended—the zone where the violence of the state of exception is deemed to operate in the service of "civilization" . . . All manifestations of war and hostility that had been marginalized by a European legal imaginary find a place to re-emerge in the colonies.

The outcome is for colonised peoples to live not only in a state of material deprivation but also in a state of terror, viewed by their rulers as, at best, unworthy, and, at worst, as enemies of the state.

From colonial subjects to "enemies of the state"

In his most recent writing, Mbembe builds on the idea of necropolitics being directed towards a variety of internal enemies of the state, observing that global developments have led to a "planetary-scale renewal of the relation of enmity and its multiple configurations" (Mbembe 2019: 1). This allows for the technologies and mentalities of necropolitics that Mbembe claims are always latent within democracies, and that have hitherto been most apparent in the colonies, to be revealed in the heart of the "civilized" state. In societies of enmity, Mbembe observes, the populations of the former colonial powers now experience the existential dread and insecurity previously reserved for colonised, or enslaved, peoples; even citizens are labelled by him as "terrorized humans." "Having an enemy at one's disposal," Mbembe notes, "has become an obligatory stage in the constitution of the subject" and is required in order to fulfil "the compulsion to be afraid" (Mbembe 2019: 48).

Since enemies must be identified in societies of enmity, these societies are inevitably marked by separation and inequality, with race and citizenship becoming the predominant markers of non-belonging:

> Two orders exist within it—a *community of fellow creatures* governed, at least in principle, by the law of equality, and a *category of non-fellows*, or even of those without part, that is also established by law. A priori, those without part have no right to have rights. They are governed by the law of inequality. This inequality and the law establishing it, and that is its base, is founded on the prejudice of race.
>
> (Mbembe 2019: 17)

Noting also the "unequal redistribution of capacities for mobility" in a world in which mobility may indeed be a question of survival (Mbembe 2019: 3), Mbembe observes that "[n]early everywhere the political order is reconstituting itself as a form of organization for death" (Mbembe 2019: 7), with the distinction between citizen and non-citizen becoming the key vehicle of separation.

While this presents an exceptionally bleak and totalising view of the present human condition, other commentators are presenting more limited analyses which identity the construction of "public enemies" as a feature of contemporary governance, accompanied by a retreat from liberal democratic principles. For example, Susan Krasmann (2007) has critiqued the "enemy penology" approach advocated by German legal theorist Günther Jakobs, in which the liberal underpinnings of criminal law are increasingly jettisoned in response to public enemies deemed to be irredeemably at odds with fundamental social values. Jakobs' list of primarily internal enemies includes terrorists, paedophiles, and habitual offenders (see also Weber and McCulloch 2019). The enemy penology thesis has been applied to asylum seekers arriving in Australia without visas, who have been constructed as an extraordinary threat to Australian values by virtue of their mere presence (Weber and Powell 2020). And, in relation to migrant deaths at sea arising from border externalisation policies, Schindel (2019: 1) has noted that "sovereign violence operates not only through an unconditional power of death but also through the abandonment and exposure of migrants to the elements and therefore the production of a zone of mere biological survival."

The logic of borders, both internal and external, can be seen to mobilise the same constellation of power relations that Mbembe posits as the foundation for necropolitics. Tracing the many ways in which "public enemies" are being constructed in our insecure and globalising world highlights conceptual connections between necropolitics and domestic policies in which exercising the power over life and death is increasingly normalised. In fact, Mbembe himself offers us a link between necropolitics and the very modes of governance that are the subject of this chapter, noting that strategies to deal with enemies who "lie beyond the confines of humanity" involve not only death but also the technologies of siege (reflected in the prolonged denial of support) and banishment (reflected in the ultimate objective of removal) (Mbembe 2019: 64). This everyday modality of necropolitics is described by Mbembe (2019: 58) as "nano-racism":

> It consists in placing the greatest number of those that we regard as undesirable in intolerable conditions, to surround them daily, to inflict upon them repeatedly, an incalculable number of racist jabs and injuries, to strip them of all their acquired rights, to smoke them out of their hives and dishonour them until they are left with no choice but to self-deport.

Everyday necropolitics as "slow violence"

While necropolitics is most often associated with the spectre of war and death, I have argued so far that we can see the same dynamic of power relations that underpins necropolitics playing out in seemingly everyday responses to social groups identified as an ontological threat. The "political warfare" at the heart of necropolitics need not involve the use of weapons or the direct imposition of death: the "invisible killing" of the siege is a frequent feature of the colony. As Mbembe (2003: 27) says of townships in colonised Africa: "[t]he native town is a hungry town, starved of bread, of meat, of shoes, of coal, of light." And, in Palestine: "[t]he besieged population is deprived of their means of income. Invisible killing is added to outright executions" (Mbembe 2003: 30). Although bridging visa holders may not be concentrated in townships or visibly besieged, this more "everyday" dimension brings the necropolitics framing into closer proximity to the deliberate deprivations of welfare policing discussed in this chapter. In his later writing, Mbembe used the terminology of *deathworlds* to describe "new and unique forms of social existence in which vast populations are subjected to living conditions that confer upon them the status of the *living dead*" (Mbembe 2019: 92, italics in original). This reinforces the fact that the endgame of necropolitics may not always be death, or even physical expulsion, but instead being "kept alive but in a *state of injury*" (Mbembe 2003: 21, italics in original).

Understood in this light, necropolitics begins to share common ground with the concept of "slow violence," which is widely attributed to sociologist Rob Nixon (2013). In the perpetration of "slow violence," the sovereign right over life and death is disguised within protracted and destructive social processes. Contemporary borders are starting to be understood in these terms. As Estela Schindel argues in relation to externalised borders, this is "a violence that occurs gradually and out of sight" and is "dispersed across time and space"; it is an "attritional violence that is typically not viewed as violence at all" (Schindel 2019: 13, citing Nixon). According to Schindel, this framing avoids the determinism associated with terms such as "structural violence," emphasising instead fluidity and change. Being continual rather than episodic, invisible rather than visible or even spectacular, this is the violence that slowly and relentlessly erodes hope.

This form of potentially lethal violence can be incorporated under the umbrella of necropolitics through the idea that populations, rather than being exterminated, may be subjected to sustained conditions of living death. The system supporting asylum seekers in the United Kingdom has recently been analysed in terms of both necropolitics and slow violence, identifying the everyday harms deliberately inflicted on asylum seekers by the state (Mayblin et al. 2020). Those authors attribute these harms to "a general consensus among politicians and publics that some human lives are worth less than others" and argue that this perspective is embedded historically in colonial worldviews. They note that "[a]sylum seekers offer a good case study for exploring the postcolonial everyday because many are close to economic, social and cultural death at the hands of governments who nevertheless subscribe to human rights law" (Mayblin et al. 2020: 108). According to these authors, the juxtaposition of universalist rhetoric alongside the disregard of human rights in practice typifies colonial rule, while historical hierarchies in the value of human lives are clearly visible in migration control today. Just as Foucault, and Mbembe, see racism as inherent within the liberal state, Mayblin et al. (2020: 110) argue that "this logic is internal to liberal western values, not a denigration of them."

The policies described by these authors in the United Kingdom share many features with the SRSS regime to which bridging visa holders in Australia are subjected. In both cases, asylum seekers often lack work rights and other entitlements, are subject to a separate system of welfare provision with reduced payment rates, and must demonstrate absolute destitution to access services. Mayblin et al. reported many instances of sustained hunger, shame, dehumanisation and physical suffering, trauma, and forced dependency, and noted that most asylum seekers endured far lower living conditions in "civilisation" than they had enjoyed in their home countries, although circumstances prevented their return. Their overall assessment of the "living death" into which this population had been placed was as follows:

> From this we can see that being kept alive through the provision of just enough support to cover essential living needs nonetheless inflicts harms which are difficult to quantify. The woundings of poverty are slow but relentless. Equally, in being viewed as inferior in the design of policy, asylum seekers are then produced as inferior, internalising a sense of being "less than" in their presentation of self.
>
> (Mayblin et al. 2020: 116)

Mayblin et al. obtained their insights into the impact of these policies by conducting interviews with asylum seekers, noting that "[i]t is through these narratives of the everyday lives of asylum seekers that we can see the logics of postcolonial necropolitics at work in the slow violence inflicted upon them" (Mayblin et al. 2020: 109). In the remainder of this chapter I uncover the necropolitical logic of the equivalent system that supports the most disadvantaged group of asylum seekers in Australia, using interviews—not with asylum seekers themselves—but with the legal advocates and service providers who support them.

The deliberate deprivations of welfare policing

Destitution by design

A senior public servant responsible for administering the SRSS system explained to me that "the theory behind the program is that by meeting someone's basic needs we put them in a better position to engage with the process of resolving their immigration status" (Interview Gov1). As noted earlier, any objective assessment of the scheme concludes that the level of support provided to BVE holders falls well short of this minimum standard. Echoing the observations of Mayblin et al. (2020) about asylum seekers in the United Kingdom being "kept alive" by providing "just enough support," one community support worker told me:

> It feels to me that the system works basically to manage risk for the department, to ensure that the people who are under that system do not kill themselves. And beyond that, the actual support, or I guess, welfare provisions, are very minimal.
>
> (Interview NGO9)

Another refugee advocate backed up this assessment, saying, "Essentially, facilitating enough support for you to get through the process without you breaking down seems to be the new approach" (Interview NGO1).

An interviewee from an agency providing material support to destitute asylum seekers explained that

> the cohort that are the most vulnerable pretty much on any kind of metric are people who are denied access to all these essential services and opportunities. So, we generally describe this as no work rights, no Medicare, obviously no employment.
>
> (Interview NGO10)

This group of people who had been left in abject destitution due to the misfortune of the date of their arrival by sea, or because they had received two negative rulings on their asylum applications, had been given their own special category within the organisation as "people denied essential services." As the prognosis was that this cohort would grow, the agency was even working on a "projection tool" to estimate the numbers of people deliberately rendered entirely destitute.

The networks of surveillance and information exchange set up to police the provision of welfare support to BVE holders assist in the relentless pursuit of maintaining levels of support at the absolute minimum. This is exemplified in the experience of a seriously ill asylum seeker as recounted by a community caseworker:

> He's gone into hospital and the hospital has informed the Department of Immigration that he is an in-patient there, and his SRSS payments have ceased for the duration of his stay, and they've given some explanation about him having the food and housing and services and that being the reason for his—the cessation of his payment.
>
> (Interview NGO7)

A legal advocate explained the distress that could be caused to clients who lacked entitlements to essential government services and were often left carrying impossible levels of debt:

> A client a few months ago, who had to be taken in an Ambulance and have an emergency appendectomy and then gets hit with a hospital bill after and the hospital says, "Well you're entitled to Medicare, but you didn't have a current card at that time, so sorry, you need to pay the bill." Or yeah, ditto with Ambulance . . . which of course is hugely distressing for the client, who says "I don't have the money."
>
> (Interview NGO2)

Moreover, the difficulties of maintaining precarious welfare entitlements were compounded by bureaucratic hurdles and seemingly arbitrary rulings about access to essential services:

> People aren't going to keep a three-month Medicare card always current. And so then when an emergency happens, then yeah, it just blows up into this big mess . . . Very frequently the client will go into Medicare to get it renewed and be told they're not entitled to it, even though they've been entitled to it for years.
>
> (Interview NGO2)

To add further to the persistent state of struggle and uncertainty, SRSS payments and other entitlements could be deliberately cut in response to even minor breaches of visa conditions:

> You know, if they've not been coming to school for a certain period of time, does that mean they've broken their code of conduct or whatever? And therefore, they're denied that—they're cut off from all their services? Denied access to school, all those sorts of things?
>
> (Interview Education5)

The picture painted by service providers aligned closely with Mbembe's characterisation of necropolitics in the townships, in which subordinated groups were destined to be "kept alive but in a *state of injury*" (Mbembe 2003: 21, emphasis in original). Persistent denial of access to essential resources operated as a tactic of *siege*, in which asylum seekers released into the community from detention were subjected to regimes of control that operated through sustained deprivation and welfare-based surveillance.

Penal power and the creation of terror

Against this backdrop of being 'kept alive but in a *state of injury*,' direct expressions of penal power are also evident. In line with Barker's notion of "welfare chauvinism" discussed earlier, the deprivations visited on BVE holders tended to be perceived by participants in this study as expressions of punitivism and deliberate exclusion, rather than simply as cost-cutting measures. As one community worker explained:

> I don't think government is thinking, "Oh, it's cheaper to not let them access services." I think government is spending a lot of money already, keeping them in detention. So, I don't think that's the driver . . . I think it's very much about notions of citizenship and who's Australian and who's not Australian and the punishment that people have for wanting to seep through our borders.
>
> (Interview NGO8)

Denial of support was backed up by the involvement of service providing agencies in surveillance networks, with the ever-present spectre of re-detention following breaches of visa conditions that were opaque and changeable. This merger of welfare and penal control could deter asylum seekers from trying to access even the services to which they were entitled: "[it] just made people feel very vulnerable and very afraid of the authorities, which no doubt they already are, but much more reluctant to talk to authorities than they would have been otherwise" (Interview NGO1). The code of behaviour which contained demeaning instructions about adherence to "Australian values" was described as "insulting" and as "just another, almost, indignity" (Interview NGO2) that was said to be having a "chilling effect" (Interview NGO1).

Government-contracted SRSS caseworkers were the most visible embodiment of this penal-welfare machinery, as they were required to deliver services to BVE holders while at the same time monitoring their compliance with immigration rules. Their capture into networks of welfare policing is described here by a senior government official:

> One of the obligations our service providers have is to provide us with incident reports when certain things happen. And that might be that there's a major health event in someone's life that we need to know about. If it's a

non-accompanied minor, write it up at that high end of support. It might be that they've missed school; that would trigger a report. But it can also be if someone is a victim or a perpetrator or a witness to a criminal activity, for example. Those incident reports can trigger a number of different things.

(Interview Gov1)

A senior manager in one of the contracted providers confirmed that "I've certainly seen clients be re-detained over quite minor incidents" (Interview Gov2). This example provided by a secondary school principal illustrates the policing role of SRSS caseworkers:

> We have a family who are in community detention at the present time and the student is 18 early next year and he wasn't attending. And one of the issues was that if he didn't attend school up until he was 18, the family might be returned to detention because he wasn't attending school. So that was—and that was a warning that came through the [SRSS] case worker in a meeting we had with them as well.
>
> (Interview Education5)

Other independent service providers gave numerous examples of the persistent fear of re-detention that prevented their clients from participating fully in community life. A caseworker from a faith-based service provider described the dilemma he had faced while trying to help a client navigate the tertiary education sector. The lack of clarity over working rights, and the danger that even making enquiries might attract adverse attention, rendered the process fraught with danger:

> So, we were told that we needed to get what's called a Unique Student Identifier (USI). So, we put in applications for these people, only to be told that once they were logged on the system, that their information could be passed on to any government agency, including the Department of Immigration and Border Protection (DIBP) . . . They could have got a USI without having study rights and then, technically, be reported to the Department as breaching the conditions of their visa.
>
> (Interview NGO9)

While systems of welfare policing can be traced to specific practices of information exchange between service providers and immigration authorities, the potential for exposure via the media created an even more ubiquitous terror. This high school principal recounted an incident where two unaccompanied minors attending her school had been re-detained after launching a campaign against their deportation via the media:

> It's sending a message to everybody else—You talk to the media, we'll get you. We can take you at any time . . . It doesn't matter that you're about to do the [High School Certificate]. We don't give a fuck about that. We're

going to put you into detention and that will show everyone just how powerful we are.

(Interview Education2)

Although this pair were ultimately successful with their campaign, this had created such a sense of dread that another student at the school who had won a university scholarship created specifically for asylum seekers had asked that his success not be publicised even in the school newsletter for fear of repercussions: "[h]e was fearful that they would say 'Hello, this guy's got into university, we'll stuff him up, we'll remove him. We'll put him back into closed detention'" (Interview Education2).

Refugee advocates confirmed that there was good reason to be cautious about seeking to expose injustices in the media, saying, "We've learnt from bitter experience that individuals will get punished. And because these people have been left with nothing, they're so incredibly vulnerable" (Interview NGO1). The separation of the immigration enforcement function from the administrative department through the formation of a uniformed Australian Border Force was said to have ramped up the intimidation levels still further: "I think it has also come from the top in terms of the politics. The hostile and the military language, all that from the top, and it's clearly percolated all the way down" (Interview NGO1).

For Mbembe, colonial subjugation entailed, not only being held in a *state of injury*, but also experiencing sustained *terror*, by being subjected to the arbitrary violence of necropolitical, sovereign power. While denial of access to essential welfare services operates via the modality of the *siege*, the direct threat of re-detention and removal adds a terror-inducing element that corresponds to the exclusionary tactic described by Mbembe as *banishment*.

Fashioning "voluntary" departures from despair

Underpinning the SRSS system is the highly instrumental objective of maintaining contact with, and control over, asylum applicants until their legal status is finalised. One SRSS provider described the system as "not [being] around the support. The end game or the start game isn't the client. The end game is the status being resolved" (Interview Gov2). Amongst the refugee supporters interviewed in this study, it was widely believed that the preferred resolution was to effect removal, and many suspected that the policy of intimidating asylum seekers and starving them of essential resources was intended to achieve this outcome through the withdrawal of applications. One legal advisor said she couldn't "speak for the motivations of it" but added that "it does feel like there is that aspect to it—that it's making things really difficult to encourage somebody to depart Australia" (Interview NGO2). A community case worker confirmed that at least one of his clients perceived the SRSS system in those terms: "[h]e conceptualises it as a way—as another way the Department's trying to push him out of Australia" (Interview NGO9). This refugee support worker speculated about how this process might work:

> If you're destitute and you don't have access to health services, and you're not allowed to work, that clearly—I mean it's impossible to imagine anything other than you're going to more seriously consider leaving the country. If your life is going okay, though you're in limbo, you might hang in there. If your life is absolutely shit from day to day and you don't know what you're going to be eating tomorrow, and you can't feed your children, the likelihood of departure surely is much higher . . . There are certain policies that you'd think are pretty strongly encouraging people to depart, and deny[ing] all services must be one of them.
>
> (NGO10)

However, there were mixed views about the efficacy of these efforts to generate "voluntary departures." This legal advocate suspected that living in the community, even under these challenging conditions, was still more tolerable than experiencing prolonged detention:

> I definitely think that's a reason—a policy reason, as I think all these punitive measures are, you know—I think it is all about trying to force people to return. I don't know how successful that is, though. I know it's very successful on places like Nauru and Manus, you know, where conditions are just dire.
>
> (Interview NGO4)

Where BVE holders did opt for "voluntary" departure, it was thought to be difficult to disentangle the different factors that may have led to that outcome:

> [The IOM] do report that people leave because of destitution. They collect quite a lot of information from people. And they can't tell us everything because they are funded by the Department, but that's been made very clear, that people say to them, "I'm leaving because I can't survive in Australia." Not because they think it's safe to go home, or because, "Okay, you've got me, my claim was bogus." I mean I suppose no one's going to say that. But they've specifically said that's why they're leaving.
>
> (Interview NGO10)

Most research participants did see other factors as contributing to these decisions beyond the operation of the SRSS system itself:

> I think it's the compound disadvantage, that whole feeling of hopelessness that the world has stacked against you. It does also seem to depend very much on which country people are maybe coming or going from. Certainly,

> communities who have experienced, I suppose, a more stable state. . . . say they're Iranians, for example—yes, the state is oppressive, but at least it's functioning, as opposed to the ones who have never experienced any kind of stable state, have different expectations and they know their rights. Well they don't know their rights because they actually don't have very many rights.
>
> (Interview NGO1)

Delays in processing asylum claims, deliberate or otherwise, added to the accumulating misery:

> It's not [lack of] services per se, but delays in processing plus events back home that wear people down. Anecdotally, that has been something that I guess has worn people down enough to leave. I think if anything, it's delay. That is what—yeah, is the big one . . . it is another deliberate response that immigration has taken, is yeah—just sitting on these applications for years and years and years.
>
> (Interview NGO2)

Ultimately, this refugee advocate thought that prolonged separation from family, itself a product of government policy, was usually the decisive factor.

> The main thing, actually, that people report is family. So, the lack of family reunion at the moment and effect on their family of knowing that they're stuck here. . . . So often it would be things like, well my family are at home; I'd rather die with them than live this long, slow death.
>
> (Interview NGO1)

Surviving in a state of "living death"

Those who resist the pressure to abandon their claims must continue to survive with "the status of the *living dead*" (Mbembe 2019: 92, italics in original). This was generally expressed by participants in this study in terms of the severe impacts on mental health arising from sustained destitution: "[t]hey just live in extreme poverty, and the effects on their mental health and, yeah, it's really bad" (Interview NGO4). Some asylum seekers were worn down beyond their endurance and could slip into a state of detachment from everyday life: "[w]e've certainly heard of people voluntarily returning because it's just too difficult. We've certainly heard of more people, I suppose, just giving up internally, so they might just be here in body but not in spirit anymore" (Interview NGO1). For one legal advisor, "voluntary" departure had not been an option for any of her clients. Rather, they were more likely to endure the protracted misery of their lives at the cost of their mental health:

> You're throwing more horrific circumstances at them and my experience is not that they return home, it's just they go mad. Like, they—the effect

> on people's mental health of getting to a place where they have this dream of safety and protection and then to reach it and not receive that is just devastating on their mental health.
>
> (Interview NGO4)

One medical practitioner saw this outcome as almost inevitable:

> I've seen many people over the years who appear incredibly damaged. They're really genuinely frightened about going home and to have those people in the community without access to work and without access to health care is—it doesn't take a rocket scientist to figure out that the consequences are not going to be good.
>
> (Interview Health4)

Different aspects of policy were said to have compounding effects, including social isolation, protracted anxiety about application outcomes, and other deprivations:

> So, it's about not being able to work, not being able to learn, not being able to do anything and not being able to be part of the community at all, and there were some pretty nasty bits of the policy—for example, that you couldn't get any kind of settlement. Someone was telling me as a provider they couldn't tell them about basic laws about driving, for example, because that might indicate they might one day settle here and that wasn't allowed . . . There's just levels of vindictiveness all through the policy which just compound each other.
>
> (Interview NGO1)

The response from some of these practitioners was to work around the extreme limitations placed on the lives of this group in order to enable social participation:

> We know that's the law and the policies and procedures which are what kind of entitlements they are allowed to have or not. So, it's very clear in that sense. So, it's trying to find them other ways of participating in community. It's one way of alleviating that sense of anxiety is finding them connections.
>
> (Interview NGO8)

Survival as resistance

Mayblin et al. (2020: 120) found in their UK study that "[p]articipants in this research were very busy with survival, so docile in the face of perpetual wounding, that any possibilities for resistance were quietened." However, if the modus operandi of necropolitics is to subject population groups to the "work of deat" (Mbembe 2003), then perhaps the sheer fact of survival—the choice to continue to live—can be viewed as an act of resistance. Indeed, Mayblin et al. (2020: 113) cite examples of everyday solidarity between asylum seekers in the United Kingdom aimed at bolstering their chance of survival, as in this report from an Iranian asylum seeker:

> We are living with minimum of everything. We had a friend here and he was very good at knowing where to buy different things, for example he knew that we can find tuna in Poundland for £1 but in Tesco it's £1.50; so, we were buying tuna from Poundland not Tesco. If a pack of tuna was £1 and there were 5 inside, then we share it between 5 people and everyone had to pay only 20p.

Some practitioners interviewed for this study reported similar levels of resilience:

> Most of my clients . . . didn't have that SRSS payment to start with anyway. So, they're already used to living in this state of relying on charity, friends. It's quite astounding the way their communities support each other, and the way they pool money . . . They just live on a basis where they borrow money and lend money and it just goes around, and whoever is able to work at the time shares amongst the household, you know. It's quite astounding. But that's how they survive.
>
> (Interview NGO4)

But asylum seekers living with the fear of re-detention and expulsion had few opportunities to openly protest their treatment. While organisations that provided material support for BVE holders also frequently engaged in efforts to subvert or reform oppressive policies, some research participants commented on the degree of acceptance in the wider community for the government's approach: "[w]e're not a community that seems to be so outraged about detention as we should be" (Interview NGO4). This effect was believed to be compounded by the invisibility of the slow violence to which this group of asylum seekers were subjected, which was becoming normalised:

> I think we've just become so jaded now and unless someone is setting themselves on fire now—that's the new bar, and even then it doesn't seem to necessarily trigger as much outrage as you would have thought . . . People don't really even seem to care anymore. I think that slow drip feed of gradual emotion to this process has been really toxic.
>
> (Interview NGO1)

As Mbembe (2019: 60) has noted, "the camp" and the associated techniques directed against enemies of the state, have "ceased to scandalize," have arguably become "a form of government of the world." This creates the conditions in which the differential distribution of death, which is the hallmark of necropolitics, can thrive.

Conclusion

Necropolitics had its origins in colonial rule. But, as Mbembe (2019: 27) reminds us, "The colony is not external to democracy and is not necessarily located outside its walls. Democracy bears the colony within it." For a settler society such as Australia, necropolitics has always been the principal mode of internal governance directed towards First Nations peoples. The power of the settler state over life and death was expressed initially through wars of dispossession and later through processes of systemic racism that remain deeply embedded within the national psyche, and manifest, *inter alia*, through persistently high rates of deaths in custody.[9]

Under contemporary conditions, in which even citizens are characterised by Mbembe as "terrorized humans," necropolitics is seeping further into the fabric of neoliberal governance. Nowadays, necropolitics can be recognised within any set of power relations in which the Other, by their mere presence, is depicted as a mortal threat. In Australia, those who have arrived "irregularly" by sea without visas have been singled out for particular vilification as a threat to social order and to an idealised conception of "Australian values." In this chapter, I have demonstrated how welfare has been weaponised to create a system of necropolitical power in which asylum seekers released from mandatory detention are kept alive, but in a state of injury, with a view to expediting their expulsion, or *banishment*, in Mbembe's terminology. This goal has been pursued through denial of access to essential resources (a variant of the necropolitical technology of *siege*) and is reinforced by the ever-present threat of detention (which maintains an ongoing state of *terror*).

The SRSS system therefore demonstrates all the key features of necropolitics. Moreover, parallels with Australia's colonial practices are readily apparent, as recognised in the writings of Behrouz Boochani.[10] He considers the exceptional measures directed towards asylum seekers and, over a much longer period, against First Nations peoples, to be united under a broader "kyriarchal system" that creates a "web of intersecting oppressions." Importantly, this web is not confined to the exceptional spaces created by offshore detention camps but pervades the whole of Australian society (Boochani 2018).[11] While the politics of death can, and must, be resisted, the increasing visibility and reach of necropolitical power within neoliberal governance provides support for Mbembe's reading of the politics of modernity as based on the instrumentalisation of human existence and the ever-present capacity for destruction.

Notes

1 Quoted by Marcella Brassett in "They are happy for Behrouz but his 'brothers' remain in PNG, begging for freedom," *Sydney Morning Herald*, 17 November 2019 www.smh.com.au/national/they-are-happy-for-behrouz-but-his-brothers-remain-in-png-begging-for-freedom-20191115-p53b3a.html
2 "Australian Border Deaths Database," www.monash.edu/arts/border-crossing-observatory/research-agenda/australian-border-deaths-database
3 Australian Border Deaths Database, "Border Crossing Research Brief No. 14" www.monash.edu/__data/assets/pdf_file/0008/1703636/BOb-Annual-Report-2018.pdf
4 Australian Border Deaths Database, "Border Crossing Research Brief No. 14" www.monash.edu/__data/assets/pdf_file/0008/1703636/BOb-Annual-Report-2018.pdf
5 Personal communication distributed by the RAC. See also www.sbs.com.au/news/bangladeshi-asylum-seeker-dies-by-suicide-at-a-lakemba-mosque
6 Refugee Council of Australia, (26 January 2019). "How cuts to support for people seeking asylum will affect people, states and local communities" www.refugeecouncil.org.au/srss-cuts-factsheet/
7 Twenty-eight key informant interviews were conducted between 2015 and 2017 with healthcare providers (8), education providers (7), not-for-profit providers of legal and community support services (8), and related government agencies at the state (primarily Victoria) and federal level (5).
8 Given the interest in these concepts now it is surprising that they were set out only briefly in an early work: Michel Foucault, *The Will to Knowledge: The History of Sexuality Volume 1*, 1976 (trans R. Hurley 1998)
9 "Deaths inside: Indigenous Australian Deaths in Custody 2021," *The Guardian*, www.theguardian.com/australia-news/ng-interactive/2018/aug/28/deaths-inside-indigenous-australian-deaths-in-custody
10 Behrouz Boochani resides in New Zealand as a recognised refugee. He developed his ideas about offshore detention in his extraordinary book, *No Friend but the Mountains* (2018), written during his six-year detention in the Australian offshore detention facility he insists on calling Manus Island Prison.
11 Other examples include the relentless pursuit of social security recipients for alleged welfare support overpayments under the so-called Robodebt scheme www.abc.net.au/triplej/programs/hack/2030-people-have-died-after-receiving-centrelink-robodebt-notice/10821272 and the demoralising ordeals faced by those seeking supports under the National Disability Insurance Scheme www.perthnow.com.au/community-news/western-suburbs-weekly/rather-be-dead-than-deal-with-ndis-user-c-894948; www.theguardian.com/australia-news/2018/jun/01/agency-head-apologises-to-family-of-man-who-died-waiting-for-ndis-equipment

References

Adams, R. (2017) 'Michel Foucault: Biopolitics and biopower', *Critical Legal Thinking*. https://criticallegalthinking.com/2017/05/10/michel-foucault-biopolitics-biopower/#fn-22546-12

Arendt, H. (1968) *The Origins of Totalitarianism*. Harcourt, Brace and Jovanovich.

Australian Human Rights Commission. (2019) *Lives on Hold: Refugees and Asylum Seekers in the 'Legacy Caseload'*. AHRC.

Barker, V. (2018) *Nordic Nationalism and Penal Order: Walling the Welfare State*. Routledge.

Boochani, B. (2018) 'Manus Prison Theory', *The Saturday Paper*, 11–17 August. www.thesaturdaypaper.com.au/opinion/topic/2018/08/11/manus-prison-theory/15339096006690

Foucault, M. (1976) *The Will to Knowledge: The History of Sexuality, Volume 1*. Editions Gallimard.

Foucault, M. (2003) *Society Must Be Defended: Lecture Series at the College de France, 1975–76*. Picador.

Jesuit Social Services. (2015) *The Living Conditions of People Seeking Asylum in Australia*. Jesuit Social Services.

Johansen, N. (2013) 'Governing the funnel of expulsion: Agamben, the dynamics of force, and minimalist biopolitics', in Aas, K. and Bosworth, M. (eds) *The Borders of Punishment: Migration, Citizenship, and Social Exclusion*. Oxford University Press, p. 257.

Krasmann, S. (2007) 'The enemy on the border: critique of a programme in favour of a preventive state', *Punishment and Society*, 9(3): 301.

Mayblin, L., Wake, M. and Kazemi, M. (2020) 'Necropolitics and the slow violence of the everyday: Asylum seeker welfare in the postcolonial present', *Sociology*, 54(1): 107.

Mbembe, A. (2003) 'Necropolitics', *Public Culture*, 15(1): 11.

Mbembe, A. (2019) *Necropolitics*. Durham University Press.

Nixon, R. (2013) *Slow Violence and the Environmentalism of the Poor*. Harvard University Press.

Powell, R., Weber, L. and Pickering, S. (2015) 'Every death counts: An argument for counting deaths in immigration custody in the national deaths in custody collection', *Current Issues in Criminal Justice*, 27: 113.

Schindel, E. (2019) 'Death by "nature": The European border regime and the spatial production of slow violence', *EPC Politics and Space* (published online, 10 November 2019).

The Senate, Legal and Constitutional Affairs References Committee. (2014) 'Incident at the Manus Island Detention Centre from 16 February to 18 February 2014', Report, 11 December.

Vogl, A. (2019) 'Crimmigration and refugees: Bridging visas, criminal cancellations and 'living in the community' as punishment and deterrence', in Billings, P. (ed.) *Crimmigration in Australia: Law, Politics and Society*. Springer, p. 149.

Vogl, A. and Methven, E. (2015) 'We will decide who comes to this country, and how they behave', *Alternative Law Journal*, 40(3): 175.

Weber, L. (2013) *Policing Non-Citizens*. Routledge.

Weber, L. (2019) 'From state-centric to transversal borders: Resisting the 'structurally embedded border in Australia', *Theoretical Criminology*, 23(2): 228.

Weber, L. and McCulloch, J. (2019) 'Penal power and border control: Which thesis? Sovereignty, governmentality, or the preemptive state?', *Punishment & Society*, 21(4): 496.

Weber, L. and Pickering, S. (2014) 'Constructing voluntarism: Technologies of 'intent management', in Australian border controls' in Schwenken, H. and Russ, S. (eds) *New Border and Citizenship Politics*. Palgrave Macmillan, p. 17.

Weber, L. and Powell R. (2020) 'Crime, pre-crime and sub-crime: Deportation of risky non-citizens from Australia as "Enemy Crimmigration"', in Pratt, J. and Anderson, J. (eds) *Criminal Justice, Risk and the Revolt against Uncertainty*. Palgrave Macmillan, p. 245.

Chapter 3

Spectres of subjugation/inter-subjugation/resubjugation of people seeking asylum

The kyriarchal system in Australia's necropoleis

Claudia Tazreiter and Omid Tofighian, with Behrouz Boochani*

Introduction

This chapter offers critical and original insights into the mistreatment of asylum seekers who arrived (or attempted to arrive) by boat after 19 July 2013, people who the Australian authorities forcibly sent offshore to regional processing centres on Nauru and Manus Island. Importantly, this chapter reveals the lived experience of asylum seekers and refugees exposed and subjected to the "carceral-border archipelago" (which encompasses Australia's immigration detention centres on the mainland and on Christmas Island, Papua New Guinea (PNG) [Manus Island detention centre has closed with remaining refugees held in Port Moresby], Nauru, and the Australian-funded facilities in Indonesia). At the time of writing some asylum seekers and refugees remain in Nauru and Papua New Guinea, some people have been transferred to Australia on medical grounds,[1] and others have been resettled in third countries including the United States, Canada, and Europe.

By late August 2020, some eight years after the Australian Government resuscitated regional 'processing' of asylum seekers entering Australia by sea—"unauthorised maritime arrivals" under the *Migration Act 1958* (Cth)—the government moved to what some analysts label the "final phase in a war on refugees" (Morton 2020), with the issuing of letters to hundreds of asylum seekers and refugees who were moved from detention offshore into "community detention" in Australia for medical treatment. The letters outline that individuals and families would be moved to a different visa class: bridging visa E (BVE) and, for the first time, given work rights. However, they are stripped of all other government support, including housing and income assistance, and only school-age children can access education. They are expected to make departure arrangements—during the coronavirus pandemic. While this particular cohort gained access to Australia's public healthcare scheme (Medicare) they lost specific support for the complex health issues that led to their medical evacuation

DOI: 10.4324/9781003298595-6

from Nauru or Manus Island in the first place. While lawyers and advocates working closely with this group indicate that most have been assessed as refugees, the issue is a humanitarian one regardless of the determination outcomes; crucially, many of the health conditions of detainees and ex-detainees were caused by the systemic violence of the indefinite detention/processing program offshore. They suffer from a range of medical conditions including malnutrition, untreated dental infections, cancer, stroke, autoimmune conditions and other infections and chronic health problems (including severe mental health conditions caused or exacerbated by indefinite detention) (Morton 2020).

The move to the "final phase of the war on refugees" in August 2020 is part of a steady stream of new austerity measures imposed on refugees and asylum seekers living temporarily in Australia, without long-term residency rights and a pathway to permanent resettlement. Since 2017, the Australian Federal Government has shifted individuals and families onto (six-month) final departure bridging visas. The group that is now being targeted have previously had exemptions from final removal due to a vulnerability criterion that exempted couples, families with children, and the seriously ill. Having lived for years without work rights, this group now has work rights at a time when unemployment numbers are very high due to the economic impacts of the Federal Government's coronavirus-related restrictions. Additionally, the demonisation of asylum seekers is absorbed by all facets of society and the economy with opportunities for all levels of work limited by the realities of racism and anti-refugee aggression.

In this chapter we assert a link between the treatment and experiences of people seeking asylum in offshore and onshore carceral sites (including those in community detention and on temporary visas). This link is evident in the three decades of mandatory, indefinite detention of asylum seekers and in the cruelty that policies of austerity design to render life utterly abject. Although our focus is squarely on the experiences of people seeking asylum in relation to the actions and policies of the Australian state, our argument is ultimately coextensive to other individuals and groups that also experience cruelty, isolation and silencing, neglect and death. To develop this argument, we explore the core ethos of the neoliberal, racial state and importantly consider "Manus Prison Theory" (MPT) articulated by Boochani (2018a, 2018b), Tofighian (2018b, 2020) and Boochani and Tofighian (2019, 2020). MPT articulates a form of governmentality based on cruelty, domination, and submission that is redirected onto other groups and individuals deemed marginal/outsiders/disrupters. This conceptualisation, together with reflections and voices from asylum seekers and refugees with lived experience of the onshore and offshore austerity regime, is considered in the context of abolitionist philosophy and advocacy.

The context for detention: Australia as an immigrant nation and the development of carceral borders

Australia has a long history of a proactively determined yearly intake of immigrants including refugees (the humanitarian resettlement quota) and a highly formalised immigration bureaucracy, underpinned by the *Migration Act 1958* (Cth). This carefully regulated system is premised on a logic of state-authorised, predetermined arrivals, a system that denotes "irregular migrants" (people seeking asylum) as disturbing and disruptive, often described as security threats in attempts to exploit their bodies for political profit. Over more than three decades, Australia has implemented policies that effectively punish people seeking asylum due to the undocumented and unauthorised mode of their arrival, with the logic of deterring future unauthorised arrivals.

The mandatory and indefinite detention of people seeking asylum began in the early 1990s under the social-democrat Labor Party with the incarceration of people arriving in Australian territory irregularly by boat. In 2001 the conservative Liberal/National Coalition Government began the "Pacific Solution," which involved agreements between Australia and two of its former colonial subjects, Manus Island in Papua New Guinea (PNG) (colony) and the Republic of Nauru (protectorate). The detention centre on Manus Island incarcerated men travelling alone—although women and children were held there temporarily for short periods before transfer to other sites. The detention centre on Nauru incarcerated women, families, and unaccompanied minors. Both offshore carceral sites also held queer and transgender people. Same-sex relations are punishable with up to fourteen years in prison in PNG and Nauru.

In September 2013, the Coalition Government launched Operation Sovereign Borders (OSB), a maritime border protection policy and a coercive, militarised, and highly secretive operation. OSB encompassed the following policies and practices: offshore (regional) processing for irregular maritime arrivals in third countries, in conjunction with a permanent bar on refugee resettlement in Australia; covert maritime interceptions of vessels carrying asylum seekers, with modalities of return to transit countries or direct repatriation; offshore disruption of people smuggling ventures in transit and source countries; enhanced maritime aerial surveillance; strategic communications used for diaspora communities within Australia and offshore in source and transit countries—messaging the personal and financial hazards and risks of travelling on people smugglers' boat; and law enforcement and intelligence co-operation with regional partners. These deterrence practices constitute what the Australian Government claims as having "stopped the boats."

Considerable research and critique indicate the impact over time of demonising political rhetoric in relation to asylum seeker arrivals as undeserving, suspicious, and even fraudulent refugees—due to their spontaneous mode of arrival. As argued elsewhere (Grewcock 2013, 2017; Juss 2017; McAdam and Chong

2019; Martin 2015; Mountz 2011; McAdam 2013; Tazreiter 2015, 2017), the lifeboat narrative and rhetoric of moral panics are thoroughly effective tools used by Australian political leaders from both major political parties to build impressions of scarcity, fear, and an immeasurable change of life for average Australians if boat arrivals are not stopped.

Rather than being separate spheres of administration and legal regulation, we assert that a strong political narrative is created over time between "onshore" and "offshore" refugee and asylum seeker arrivals, that validates administrative and legal "reform" experienced as punishment and austerity. This political narrative is most evidently expressed in border control as visual and textual messaging, though no less effective and potent are the historical links in a colonial settler society such as fear of outsiders, of invasion, of unspecified dangers (Martin 2015; Gleeson 2016; Tazreiter 2004). The international legal obligations to asylum seekers through the core protection principle of *non-refoulement* are sidelined in the dominant Australian public debates in favour of racialised messages. For instance, in the 2013 Federal election, the Liberal candidate for the electorate of Lindsay in Western Sydney, Fiona Scott, claimed that asylum seekers were the cause of traffic jams and overcrowding in hospitals: "[m]y recommendation is go and sit in the emergency department of Nepean hospital and go and sit on the M4, and people see 50,000 people come in by boat" (Elson 2013). The Australian state's approach to asylum seekers and refugees does not emerge in isolation from other social and political processes of marginalisation and exclusion.

Australia's carceral-border archipelago has produced multiple and multiplying sites of subjugation and death of displaced and exiled peoples. In addition to onshore immigration detention centres the state has funded and constructed offshore facilities in PNG and Nauru and financed places of confinement in Indonesia (operated by the International Organization for Migration [IOM]). Australia's relationship with PNG and Nauru exhibits neocolonial dynamics because aid and development have been factored into the equation as the developing nations remain dependent of the wealthier nation for recovery from the fallout of colonialism. Also, employment hierarchies in detention centres, sociocultural disruptions, and environmental hazards caused by the regional detention facilities have created long-term problems for the Indigenous peoples.

A key feature of Australia's border-industrial complex is the multinational companies contracted to build, maintain, and/or manage the carceral sites. Companies such as Transfield Services/Broadspectrum, G4S, Serco, International Health and Medical Services (IHMS), and Paladin have secured lucrative contracts with little oversight and accountability in the way they manage and care for asylum seekers and refugees. Such privatisation of immigration detention in Australia mirrors similar "outsourcing" developments in other Western countries (Ackerman and Furman 2013; Leerkes and Van Houte 2020; Mountz 2020) and is critically challenged by new abolitionist claims and movements (Brown and Schept 2017; Tofighian 2020a).

On 5 December 2014, the Australian Parliament passed the *Migration and Maritime Powers Legislation Amendment (Resolving the Asylum Legacy Caseload) Act 2014*. These changes to the *Migration Act 1958* reintroduced temporary protection visas for "illegal maritime arrivals." Specifically, those asylum seekers arriving by boat without a visa on or after 13 August 2012, who were liable to offshore 'processing' but who were not part of the cohort (arriving by boat after July 2013) forever barred from resettlement in Australia. Significantly, and by contrast with refugees on permanent visas, an individual granted a temporary visa also cannot apply for family reunion, hampering their resettlement.

The legislation also changed administrative decision-making review processes for asylum seekers by replacing an independent merits review process with an inferior "fast track" procedure for boat arrivals on or after 13 August 2012 (Kenny and Proctor 2016). The 2014 reforms signalled the beginning of increasingly stringent measures targeting refugees and asylum seekers who had arrived in Australia without authorisation.

Hartley and Fleay (2017) have argued that dehumanising people is an important aspect of these stringent policies. Moreover, in 2019 the Australian Human Rights Commission documented the circumstances of financial hardship, deteriorating mental health, and poorer settlement outcomes resulting from the austerity measures directed at boat arrivals in Australia. The report detailed the daily circumstances of refugees and asylum seekers that arrived in the period 2012–14 when governments opted for more punitive asylum policies for those existing both offshore and onshore (AHRC 2019).

Knowledge production at the carceral-border

This chapter continues by drawing on the unique theoretical framework developed by Behrouz Boochani and Omid Tofighian as a way of understanding and conceptualising refugee detention. Importantly, MPT emerges from Boochani's lived experience of Australia's carceral-border as a detainee for over six years in Manus Island. We also draw upon the voices and perspectives of those impacted by Australia's carceral borders approach both onshore and offshore: refugees, asylum seekers, and advocates. We assert the importance of voice, knowledge production, and positionality that has those with lived experience at the heart of research design, epistemologically and methodologically (Anthias 2008; Moya 2011). Our approach is in line with migration scholars who highlight the agency of migrants and refugees, by contrast with the prevalent view, among some policy makers and political leaders in many parts of the world, of migrants as victims or as causing an existential and identity crisis to the state (de Haas, Castles and Miller 2019; Mezzadara and Neilson 2013; Tazreiter 2019).

Our novel contribution to this field of study is to show that the treatment of refugees and asylum seekers is not exceptionalism, as is so often asserted by politicians and researchers. The governments that practice border externalisation would like domestic populations to believe that their responses to refugees and asylum seekers *is* exceptional, that tough border policies, interdiction and pushbacks at sea, detention and deportation are necessary for national security, securing borders, and financial resources. By contrast, the linkage we wish to make is between the logic of the neoliberal state in lock-step with global capitalism and the necropolitics that shapes policies targeting populations through dehumanisation, silencing, austerity, and annihilation (Mbembe 2019).[2] The theorising of the racialised state that supports our argument is developed later in the chapter.

The section ahead draws out and selects from the experiences of those who have directly experienced Australia's internal and externalised borders. These connections are personal and they are political. The connections and collaborations developed between Boochani and Tofighian over years of writing, activism, creative work, and friendship. By foregrounding the voices, the ways of knowing and experiences, of those subject to Australia's carceral-border archipelago onshore and offshore, we introduce two different critical discussions and approaches to studies of border violence. These two perspectives aim to situate the border-industrial complex within discourses pertaining to the logic of austerity and kyriarchy.

First, in relation to austerity (Darling 2016; Scarpa and Schierup 2018), we argue that it is necessary to understand the inside/outside dynamic that characterises border politics and the symmetrical relationship between border control and practices of bordering within the nation; that is, the logic of austerity is normalised through border politics and justified through xenophobic rhetoric of hate and competition. Second, in terms of kyriarchy, we refer to the "kyriarchal system" introduced in Boochani's *No Friend but the Mountains: Writing from Manus Prison* (2018a, 2018b) and further theorised by Boochani and Tofighian (2019, 2020) and Tofighian (2018b) within the framework of MPT. By interpreting the nature of the detention industry through the lens of interlocking, multiplicative, and replicating systems of oppression, domination, and subjugation, we open up new spaces for understanding the colonial continuities manifested in these carceral sites and the profound effects that such technologies have on Australia's socio-political landscape and its social imaginary. We support these two different critical discussions and approaches by drawing on Boochani's work in addition to the writing and resistance of other people with lived experience of border violence.

Manus Prison Theory and austerity: border technologies and resistance from inside detention

Manus Prison Theory

In exploring the lived experience of exile in detention (offshore), as well as the legitimation of austerity practiced on refugees and asylum seekers living in the community and in various forms of "community detention" (onshore), racialised hierarchies are a key point of reference. For Boochani and Tofighian, MPT is a form of carceral-border knowing (i.e. knowledge born from the lived experience of exile and indefinite detention) that strikes at the core of the border-industrial complex. A carceral-border system that violently disrupts and controls human life.

Australian settlers with "citizen privilege" are addressed directly through these ideas, not only in documenting the conditions of the Manus Prison, but also, importantly, in highlighting the processes of dehumanisation that are able to target any number of vulnerable populations and groups (Boochani 2018b: 362). In their writing, Boochani and Tofighian address those who choose to turn away from the pain and suffering caused through the offshore detention regime in acts of "knowing unknowing," as the theorist Paul Geissler (2013) explicates acts of willing denial (see also Mills 1997; Dotson 2012; Pohlhaus 2012). Individuals, from whatever political affiliation, who do not make spaces for asylum seekers to genuinely speak and represent their own experiences are also implicated in giving legitimacy to the regimes of power that create "asylum seeker" and "refugee" as categories, labels, to be hated and feared. In Australia's case it is the lie perpetuated by political leaders, in a bipartisan manner, that mode of arrival by boat implicates people seeking asylum as security risks, disruptive and contagious. Importantly, the approach of MPT has synergies with the ethos and critique of the black radical tradition, explored later in the chapter, calling out the normalisation of the legacies of slavery and theft through colony and empire (Mbembe 2017; Robinson 1983). MPT, and its discussion of the kyriarchal system, is deeply influenced by Black feminist, Chicana feminism, Mujeristas, Kurdish women's movements including Jineology, and transnational feminist philosophies. Boochani and Tofighian's collaboration targets the narrative that creates the attitudes and norms that drive systemic violence and empower the authorities who sustain those systems.

While Boochani was incarcerated in Manus Prison he published in international media, presented speeches, posted and engaged on social media, participated in interviews, shot and codirected a feature film, and wrote a book. These forms of intellectual and cultural production were written and created using a mobile phone with the writing being typed, stored, and sent using WhatsApp messaging. The translating, reviewing, researching, planning, ordering, editing, and distributing, in addition to the promotional work, was conducted in conjunction with a small group of supporters (Tofighian 2018a). What has received less popular attention is the theoretical developments and philosophical critique that emerged during Boochani's imprisonment on Manus, which has continued after his escape to Aotearoa New Zealand. Tofighian translated and edited for Boochani, and the two researched—individually and together—various aspects of the border-industrial complex in addition to Australia's colonial past and present (Tofighian 2018b; Boochani 2018b). They laid down the foundations for "Manus Prison Theory" (MPT), a philosophical framework that continues to take shape and which has benefited from different working relationships and networks (Boochani et al. 2020; Boochani and Tazreiter 2019). Boochani uses the concept of the kyriarchal system to explain the working of the Manus Prison camp and how it is also part of Australia.

The kyriarchal system: the soul of the system

In the original Farsi text of *No Friend but the Mountains* Boochani introduces a neologism named *system-e hākem*. In search for a word or phrase that described the complex, expanding, unrelenting, and fluid forms of violence that targeted the body, mind, emotions, and spirit of detainees he constructed his own concept and term. Recognising the limitations of language and theoretical frameworks he endeavoured to create a phrase that identified individual acts of violence, systemic violence, intersecting systems of violence, perpetual replication of violence, and the soul of the violent system. To find the most appropriate term in English for this neologism it was necessary to also create a new phrase: Tofighian drew from radical feminist theology and philosophy, settling on the term 'kyriarchy' as coined and developed by Elisabeth Schüssler Fiorenza (1992). From this foundation, the kyriarchal system emerges as the heart of MPT.

A basic description of the kyriarchal system includes the following: interlocking systems of oppression such as race, misogyny, classicism, heteronormativity, ableism, militarism, colonialism, neoliberal capitalism, and ecological degradation; interlocking systems that are both multiplicative (i.e. they reinforce and invigorate each other) and replicating (i.e. they produce more sites of kyriarchal violence and oppressed groups based on newly created vulnerabilities and anguish); a pyramidal system, as opposed to hierarchies, where people and groups can be both oppressor and oppressed in multifarious ways and positionalities are altered in different circumstances and periods; an insatiable and unrelenting desire to not only oppress and dominate but also to force into submission—the aim is essentially to grind individuals down, prolong the state of subjugation, and pursue new subjects of violence and construct new technologies of harm; that ultimately there are no victors in the kyriarchal system since oppressors have their capacity for compassion reduced and their moral compass distorted, while they reproduce violence by also inflicting it on their own family and social group; and, that the legacy of settler-colonialism is manifest in all instantiations of the kyriarchal system—traditions and a politics based on Indigenous genocide, anti-Blackness and exploitation of bodies, excessive resource extraction and destruction of the ecosystem, the control of human mobility driven by a damaging form of Orientalism, and whiteness as the moral centre of settler-colonial subjectivity.

The myth of the errant traveller: criminalising narratives as justification for incarceration

> When the British Empire invaded and colonized Australia and dispossessed Aboriginal and Torres Strait Islander peoples of their lands in 1788, the British claimed the land based on the myth of *terra nullius* (no one's land). Their lives and cultures destroyed, Aboriginal and Torres Strait Islander peoples were forced from their traditional lands to cattle stations, missions and reserves. The British turned them into indentured servants whose wages, to this day, have not been fully paid. In "I Still Call Australia Home," Aileen Moreton-Robinson explains: "Indigenous people were denied their customary propriety rights under international law and their rights as British subjects of the crown." Britain instructed Captain James Cook to make a treaty with the Aboriginal people, but he refused on the basis of the lie that the land was unoccupied. Therefore, Cook's strategy in colonizing the land was based on the myth of *terra nullius* and involved implementing laws under which native peoples were dispossessed of land and livelihood. In doing so, he directly contravened international laws which regulated the British colonies.
>
> (Tofighian 2018b: 7)

The indispensable power of narrative in political ambition and garnering support for a socio-cultural vision based on violence and suppression is a frightening reality; mythmaking conditions all forms of biopolitics and all interactions with ecosystems, nowhere is it more fundamental than in the necropolis. One of the driving forces behind MPT is to expose, satirise, and dismantle colonial narratives by imposing narratives of resistance and decolonisation, literature that reclaims and replaces: the myth of "illegal" refugees; the myth that allows for the false dichotomy of genuine and fake/political and economic refugee; the myth that evokes the sense of entitlement in settlers with citizen-privilege to demand performances of refugeehood and play off of deservingness; the myth of uniform, fair, and informed asylum claim determination systems; the myth that justification must precede humanity—one must first justify their humanity according to some "refugee imaginary" to then be treated as human; and, the myth of the errant traveller which constitutes border politics and bordering practices—it is intertwined with the colonial violence imposed on First Nations people and is, in fact, one extension of its technologies and ideologies. Crimmigration becomes both the narrative source for producing "illegals" in the intertwining of criminal and immigration law (Weber and McCulloch 2018) and itself is the product of earlier mythmaking.

It is apt that MPT was born from a literary endeavour, a writing and translation process that crossed borders and genres and facilitated an emerging language that then supported storytelling about new horizons, characterised by abolition of immmigration detention and debordering. It is apt to imagine *No Friend but the Mountains* as new language for a new way of knowing, it is an anti-genre about a new kind of subject created by late capitalism and experimented on by new bordering technologies. *No Friend but the Mountains* is also a myth about the future, a narrative with ravaging potential to become a far-reaching reality. MPT is as much a story as it is a theory.

The penal state: expanding and morphing, the original penal colony, bordering practices creating imprisoned thinking

The dispossession of Aboriginal lands for a penal colony used by the British Empire in 1788 has expanded into multifarious prisons and other carceral sites. Australia's current prison estate—which represents a disproportionate number of Aboriginal and Torres Strait Islander men, women, and children—and its carceral-border archipelago of detention facilities, must be critically analysed as part of this legacy, and interpreted as interdependent with the formation and development of significant and numerous bordering practices over time. Significant examples of subjugation/inter-subjugation/resubjugation dynamics include the removal of Indigenous peoples from their countries and confining them to cattle stations, missions, and reserves for forced labour (slavery and stolen wages); islands converted into prisons to incarcerate Indigenous peoples and convicts; the forced exile of citizens to the newly established penal colony; over-imprisonment of Chinese migrant workers; prolonged internment of Italians, Japanese, and Germans (including German Jews) during the First and Second World Wars; the exile and detention of West Papuas or West Irians in the Salasia Camp on Manus Island, Papua New Guinea; and, indefinite onshore and offshore detention of people seeking asylum.

A pivotal argument within MPT involves an examination of the "two island" thought experiment. Influenced by Charles Mills' reading of W.E.B. Du Bois' metaphor of the veil, the story about the two islands is designed to reveal the ways in which settlers are imprisoned; that is, how the island of Australia kills their "vision, creativity and knowledge—it imprisons thought." In contrast, the mind of imprisoned refugees is free because they have intimate, direct knowledge of state violence and understand first-hand border violence and its relationship with other bordering practices. In many respects, they know Australia in ways the settlers do not. Imprisoned refugees are subject to the experiments and developing technologies of oppression, domination, and subjugation and, therefore, are privy to the machinations and responses of state violence in a perversely uninhibited form. And, in many cases, before the methods and ideas are used on citizens. Through an uncanny inversion, we interpret the settlers as prisoners, and the refugees see things that the prisoners cannot, they create things that the prisoners cannot, and they certainly know things that the prisoners cannot. Using this thought experiment to induce an imagination of this inversion we can analyse both offshore and onshore detention and the positionality and knowledge production of people harmed by detention and austerity measures, its residual effects, and different ways it conditions life out of detention and after austerity.

Creative works of resistance

Hani Abdile's way of knowing border violence has been by her detention experience and precarious visa status after her release, but her forms of creative resistance and survival have also been empowered by her Somali heritage, history, and traditions. Her political and cultural understanding and innovation have been a driving force behind her stance against border politics and anti-Blackness in Australian society. Abdile established her literary reputation in Australia by publishing her work and performing spoken word poetry regularly. She developed her craft while in Australian immigration detention (Christmas Island) as an unaccompanied minor after fleeing Somalia and losing contact with her family. She was released from detention in 2015 after eleven months in custody but has yet to be granted residency to stay in Australia. The uncertainty of the situation and the arbitrary features associated with the immigration process are another form of torture. During her time in the community she has had few opportunities to educate herself and work, but she persists and makes the most of her limited options. She states:

> Many people are still on this Bridging visa but it can't stop them doing what they're passionate about. People just want a peaceful world where they can be proactive. They want to contribute and build a life in their new home. But a wall has been put up. A wall of hardship and mental imprisonment holds us back.
>
> (Tofighian 2018b: 10)

The work of Mohamed Adam and Hass Hassaballa (two Sudanese writers who were held on Manus Island) has been integral to unpacking complex aspects of the offshore regional 'processing' system (particularly the way anti-Blackness operates), generating new interpretations and forms of resistance, and creating writing that acts as a foundation for future research and action. As Tofighian explains:

> These three writers [Mohamed, Hass, and Hani] have introduced me to many ideas, thinkers, critiques, research and, of course, their experiences. They were more than collaborators: they helped shape my project into a more nuanced and multidimensional reading of Australia's broader immigration detention regime. Their [writing] includes firsthand accounts of detention on Manus and poems from a woman who endured that same system.
>
> Together we built an intellectual framework for analysing the subjugation of black bodies by Australia's border policies. Mohamed, Hass, and

> Hani also helped me find ways to align their experiences with other examples of confinement, including forced labour, internment camps, human trafficking and slavery. They gave me particular Sudanese and Somali standpoints to inform my analysis of the ongoing humanitarian crisis on Manus and Nauru.
>
> (Tofighian 2018b: 10–11)

Offshore, onshore, Indonesia: carceral-border archipelago and the case for abolition

The carceral-border pertains to physical locations, and it is also symbolic and epistemic. It targets bodies, minds, emotions, and spirits. More accurately, carceral borders refer to evolving processes, institutions, narratives, concepts, and categories—the border is not just a thing, bordering is not an event. Processes of bordering cover a whole range of different features, notions, and factors from the demarcation of spaces and processes of territorialisation to the multiple dimensions of boundaries which extend to different kinds of meaning-making, meaning imposition, and methods of sustaining meaning. Processes of bordering also determine how movement is controlled using ideas, emotions, and wills. The events, ideas, and processes that determine all forms of bordering are contingent; the carceral-border shifts and morphs in line with other socio-political and cultural phenomena in Australia and globally. Social elements and facets such as law, racialisation, economy, religion, trade, and other determining factors interweave, and this makes identification of the roots of marginalisation, stigmatisation and exclusion of asylum seekers difficult. When bordering practices are arranged and directed to embolden and maintain colonial manifestations then territorialisation becomes a horrific phenomenon. As Boochani writes:

> Our greatest adversity is not that as imprisoned asylum seekers we are unequal before the law; the greatest adversity is that there is no formulation of laws that applies to us. . . . Our bodies have been directly exploited by a cruel and violent political strategy; a new form of fascism born at the beginning of the 21st century. During this extended period in detention, government policy has targeted our bodies and minds. We resist so that we do not lose our sense of self and individuality—maintaining our identities has been our primary motivation and goal over the past three years.
>
> (Boochani 2016)

Mardin Arvin was transferred to Australia under the now repealed "medevac" laws[3] and was locked up in a Melbourne hotel without access to the urgent medical treatment he was supposed to receive while in Australia. Prior to this transfer he was confined in Port Moresby and two sites in Manus Island—another example of the fluid, ever-changing, and unpredictable nature of the carceral-border. Bordering practices are transnational in far-reaching ways. His punishment extends to his family back in Iran, in addition to a new family that he was accepted into and forced to leave in Manus Island. Arvin explains:

> Refugees lose their lives to war, political persecution or economic exploitation—they flee their homelands and no one knows whether they end up living a happy life or not. The future is unknown, no one knows what the future holds.
>
> Like me, I have not been able to feel the touch of my mother's hands. I have not been able to hold her for all these years. It has been years since I have had the chance to see her wrinkled face, to see her fading smile, to see her staring back at me. This is what I dream for while incarcerated, locked up without ever having committed a crime.
>
> (Arvin 2020)

Hani Abdile resists the carceral-border regime and the anti-Blackness that makes up its network of oppression, domination, and subjugation. As an unaccompanied minor who was denied the right to education while detained, she used the language of the oppressor, appropriated it through poetry, and disrupted it with her mother tongue to help build her own support networks. Through writing she was able to maintain her culture and identity and also find ways to navigate racism and isolation as someone on a temporary visa living in Australia. Her poetry became one form of defence against the war on refugees living onshore:

> My mother tongue has guided my life
> Teaching me words like
> *Walaltinimo*. Brotherhood.
> In my mother tongue we call people of all kinds *walalo*
> And the word that is strange, that is really hard to find is
> *Xurnimo*. Freedom.
> Freedom has been the key word of my people's speech
> Even though you will be told that they found their freedom
> sixty years ago
> Still mentally they are captives of others.
> *Biladanimo*. Humanity.
> In our poetry humanity is discussed and
> Judged by many great poets, but it is yet to be extinguished
> Because my mother tongue taught me to see humanity, not
> Bureaucracy built by those who hate unity.
> With my tongue I say these words with passion.
> With these three words I communicate with the universe
> And the salve beneath my tongue tastes of love.
> I am not just pretending, but here I really speak a language of love,
> Kindness and generosity
>
> (Abdile 2018)

The violence of bordering practices is interwoven in the fabric of Australian society and impacts people in different ways, including activists working to support people seeking asylum. As convenor of *Writing Through Fences* with Abdile, Janet Galbraith has written about the toll that the carceral-border takes on the physical and mental health of detainees; she is also an example of the extent to which a commitment to justice for people affects citizens:

> I hold so much knowledge of the intimate violences being perpetrated by the state and its allies, including the legal and medical professions. I want to tell you about what it is to watch as someone you love, and have loved for years, is kept alive by a system that aims to destroy, has already succeeded in destroying a life, many lives—and any will to live. I want to tell you of the torture that this person, these people, are forced to undergo in our hospitals, here in our suburbs throughout Australia. Tortures that are seldom even whispered about.
>
> I want to tell you of the way in which two SERCO guards are present 24/7 in the room of a dying person, of someone who cannot walk, hardly talk, cannot eat, drink, function, and when communicating, communicates with absolute visceral fear of the knowledge that they (Australia) are killing her/him. I want to tell you of how these guards say "this is what happens when you come by boat"; of how they sit and record every detail of a conversation between family members; of how bags are checked; of how the toilet door is held open by a guard even though the person who has been placed on the toilet is not able to move. I want to tell you of how it takes so much effort, so many submissions and interventions to enable a doctor to have some private time with their patient; of the arguments and numerous phone calls it takes to ABF before a social worker is allowed inside the room.
>
> (Galbraith 2018)

Erfan Dana (also known as Shams Hussaini) has written about the situation for people seeking asylum in Indonesia. A Hazara from Afghanistan, he was an unaccompanied minor when he arrived and has been critical of the role of the IOM and the UN. He also addresses issues pertaining to subjugation, inter-subjugation, and resubjugation, issues that relate to Australia's "stop the boats" policies that have left asylum seekers in a state of semi-permanent limbo in Indonesia:

> The hardest part of all these difficulties has been spending three years of my life in the corner of a prison. I have been reduced to a prisoner, forced to live in the worst state possible, even though I have not committed any crime—stripped of a life of freedom and dignity due to my status as a displaced person and my weak financial situation. I have ended up wasting time in this repulsive and depressing place. In most cases I have been resisting the injustice and violence of the guards and immigration officers, and I have become a somewhat expert in using whatever strategies humanly

possible. Without fear of damaging my case for protection, I have been defending homeless and vulnerable refugees.

Ultimately, after all these bitter and edifying encounters I have realised that no one is your friend, no one will come to your aid, no one recognises you as a soul who deserves freedom. No one is there for you, just because you are not religiously inclined, because you do not have religious faith. And I have come to understand that humans, and humanity as a whole, have lost their values and principles.

(Dana 2018)

Writing from the Manus Island prison camp during a "23-day siege" (Boochani and Tofighian 2018) at the time it was officially closed down and essential services discontinued, in November 2017, Hass Hassaballa reveals the horrors of the carceral-border regime:

> The days when the leaders of the world came together to form humanitarian agencies dedicated to observing and protecting human rights were extraordinary days. But, sadly, today's leaders are leading us into an abyss. It is frustrating to see a county like Australia, which is perceived to be a great nation, now becoming a country that tortures people. And Australia, as a member of the United Nations, is part of a global community that claims to protect the vulnerable. In recent years Australia has established a ruthless refugee detention regime. Innocent people fleeing danger and persecution have been targeted. They are in breach of the noble humanitarian laws that they claim to uphold. It is clear that we are going backwards when it comes to human rights and compassion. It is tough to say farewell to the days of democracy. In this world the actions of our indifferent leaders will ultimately abolish democracy. What an irony. The Australian politicians are now showing off. They are boasting about how heroic they are. They have suppressed all humanitarian initiatives; they have supported the ongoing tragedy in their immigration detention centres. . . .
>
> Believe me, Australia, you are on the wrong side of history . . . It does not matter how brutal you are. Days of freedom await us.
>
> (Hassaballa 2018: 32)

During the same 23-day siege Mohamed Adam analysed the brutality visited on people, as water, food, power, and medical services were cut off, to coerce people to leave the camp. Both Adam and Hassaballa—in addition to other detainees—have contributed to history by documenting the atrocities inside the Manus Island prison camp (and other carceral sites) and made a considerable difference to the imaginary pertaining to incarcerated refugees by introducing themselves as knowledge producers as well as resisters. Adam states:

> I have been betrayed by the Australian government. I have been swapped and sold like a slave. I have been treated like an animal in this prison. On 31

> October 2017 the Australians tried to close down the prison for good, they tried to remove us and reimprison us in another prison camp in town. We refused to move, we refused to be abused in this way. The Australians cut off the power. They cut off the water. They cut off the food supply.
>
> (Adam 2018: 19–20)

Borders are physical, symbolic, and epistemic instruments that create social imaginaries to support rhetorics and practices of marginalisation, exclusion, and stigmatisation. The bordering practices that characterise and shape the social imaginaries determine us/ours from them/theirs, create enmity, and also keep human beings and the ecosystem on the threshold of death, sickness, and loss. As the coronavirus pandemic amplifies the dangers of immigration detention and puts the lives of refugees and staff at risk—and by extension their families, friends, and communities—the need for abolitionist thinking and acting is paramount. MPT argues that we are relational beings and our physical and mental well-being is interdependent with others and the environment; our moral imagination, capacity for compassion, and ability to care for one another is put at risk by the brutal and punitive bordering practices discussed in this chapter. Therefore, border, detention, and prison abolition is a necessary step to ensure everyone's human rights and help protect society.

The racialised, neoliberal state: austerity as normality

In view of the purpose of this chapter, in linking dehumanising and austerity measures targeting refugees and asylum seekers onshore, to the practices of cruelty in offshore detention, it is critical to bear in mind the role of racialised capitalism as the primary driver of the economic system, neoliberalism, and in turn, the state that utilises the levers of neoliberalism and racialisation in governing. This is a fundamental, yet often overlooked, historical feature of the embeddedness of deep, "structuring structures" (following Pierre Bourdieu) that in the case of the racialised state rest on differential "value" attached to humans (Mbembe 2019; Robinson 1983; Weheliye 2014). This is evident in hierarchies that come to be practiced in the micropolitics of state bureaucracies in identifying particular populations in developing administrative, juridical, and resource "reforms." Here, the lived experience of asylum seekers subject to Australian legislation and policy, both onshore and offshore, as detailed earlier, provide evidence of the stigmatised circumstances experienced through cruelty and austerity, with "normal" life on hold. While neoliberal capital claims to be "disinterested" and value neutral, it carries deeply embedded features from the legacies of colony and empire (Fanon 1963; Gilroy 2005; Berlant 2011; Mbembe 2019; Robinson 1983; Storper 2001; Streeck 2016; Wang 2018).

Violence—symbolic, institutional, and physical—is embedded in the very DNA and micro practices of neoliberal capital (Bourdieu 1991, 1993). Tyner argues that violence and crime are constituted together—or at least intimately related in how lives are valued in society and, therefore, neither neutral nor objective (Tyner 2016: 3). Tyner argues, following Foucault, that neoliberal capitalism orients towards letting die those people who are not valued as full contributors to the "system" (ibid). An important distinction with necropolitics, that writers such as Mbembe (2019) outline, is where administrative systems, policy, and law is organised in such a manner as to "make die": a calibrated design of death for the targeted populations.

Indeed, the neoliberal economic systems, values, and the contemporary manifestations and alignments with neo-nationalism and neoliberal politics and policies, eschew the harmonious coexistence that classical liberalism promised through the project of modernity and enlightenment values. The negative consequences of these processes are most visible and felt by vulnerable populations all over the world, notably displaced persons, refugees, and asylum seekers. One of the key threads we wish to draw together is the impact of neoliberalism as a totalising ideology on all forms of life (Braidotti 2013; Berlant 2011; Fraser and Jaeggi 2018; Mezzadara and Neilson 2013).

Analysts from different perspectives regularly assert and identify the insecurity felt and experienced by the poor and marginalised, by the materially cushioned middle class in the West, and even by elites, as a consequence of neoliberal policies and values that eschew cultures and practices of solidarity, care, and social connectivity (Fraser and Jaeggi 2018; Hardt and Negri 2004; Sassen 2014; Berlant 2011; Wang 2018). Brown's assessment of the end stages of neoliberalism (2015, 2019) take shape through late capitalist desublimation in this way:

> Free, stupid, manipulable, absorbed by if not addicted to trivial stimuli and gratifications, the subject of repressive desublimation in advanced capitalist society is not just libidinally unbound, released to enjoy more pleasure, but released from more general expectations of social conscience and social comprehension.
>
> (Brown 2019: 167)

The rise in a politics of indifference is evident in many parts of the world, but perhaps most perplexing when expressed by those benefitting from the legacies of colony and empire, such as White Australia (Hage 2003; Dauvergne 2015).

Racialised capitalism and continuities of extraction, expulsion, and necropolitics

To contextualise the evidence of cruelty and austerity practiced by Australia (and through her agents and proxies) onshore and offshore towards refugees and asylum seekers, we consider the persistence of the colonial imaginary in the contemporary nation-state. This colonial imaginary extends to the present, often expressed in racism observable as systematised devaluation of some humans. Importantly, the embedded value system that undergirds racialisation extends to many forms of "difference" through highlighting fundamental characteristics of people. Racialisation takes many forms, perhaps most commonly in state-implemented policies, laws, and administrative measures of dividing and categorising populations. The processes of racialisation evident in the creation of hierarchies of humans are manifest and driven by the technologies of the state. This racialisation is evident in the processes of dividing, categorising, and stigmatising humans according to a range of biological and/or acquired qualities and characteristics used in regimes of power to dominate and to marginalise (Mignolo 2011; Weheliye 2014). Racialisation relies on a range of techniques that draw on embodied characteristics of persons (such as gender, disability, sexual orientation) and to target such fundamental aspects of personhood for exclusion. Racialisation occurs where biological or cultural characteristics are equated with values and qualities attached selectively to some persons in creating divisions and hierarchies of deserving or "better" persons. Such divisions and hierarchies are drawn on, whether consciously or unconsciously, in policy decision-making and resource allocation. Such hierarchies, and the categories that result in the bureaucracies of the state, have the effect of allocating differential value to persons.

The empires of the West and their reach to all parts of the world through practices, policies, and mentalities of colonisation still reverberate today. The legacies of empire and colonial conquests remain as lived experience, including the exploitative and extractive logics that are founded on hierarchies of persons (and other living entities) used to justify the violence of conquest and its continuities to the present (Gilroy 1993; Mignolo 2011; Mbembe 2017; Weheliye 2014; Robinson 1983). The racialised histories of colony and empire, and the deep relation between these histories and process with modernity and capitalism are vital histories to excavate rather than relegate to the dustbin. The legacies of these histories manifest in contemporary practices of creating punitive border(s), so evident in the Australian context. Importantly, state-led projects of racialisation, including the institutions of care such as hospitals, schools, and churches, are normalised over time as legitimate aspects of governing populations (Braidotti 2013; Foucault 1997; Haraway 1989; Mbembe 2017). Indeed, racialisation and its broader social effects are invidious in historical legitimation of valuing persons according to biological or cultural factors, rather than the qualities, dispositions, and ethics of what it is to be human, as manifest in human rights values.

Austerity is a method for enforcing conformity, creating more competition and enmity, and forming spaces that determine new rules and regulations in support of power. Austerity in every context is a bordering practice—when it occurs in society it will then be reflected in carceral sites, and when it occurs in carceral sites it will then be reflected in society. Under austerity, many situations in life transform you into a particular subject, one feels confined and made into a prisoner by the institution that has promised to protect you. This is not unlike the situation of refugees in immigration detention, especially in indefinite detention. Refusing to allow these measures and restrictions to hinder your desire to collaborate with others, to stop you from hoping and celebrating in creative ways with others, is a political act in these circumstances and can be leveraged for meaningful change. It is a form of reclaiming power. Austerity is designed to separate people and force them to eliminate each other from paths of social mobility in perverse and complex ways. Joy, celebration, hope, and pride become a way to rebuff austerity when they are combined.

Bureaucratic rules and regulations already control so many aspects of our lives and these technologies of domination are exacerbated under austerity regimes. So many decisions are made and policies created to justify the stripping away of rights and liberties, stripping us of our capacity to be compassionate, limiting our ability to dream and love, quashing hope. But when we look at the histories of collective struggle, we find inspirations that have been built by persistence especially through writing and creativity. Examples such as *No Friend but the Mountains* reveal cracks through which we can escape from and then overturn the system, we can expose it and bring other people in and work together for change. Any form of activism that does not continue to produce unique and creative possibilities runs the risk of becoming routine and ineffective, and possibly counter-productive.

By incorporating the notion of kyriarchy, we argue that the relentless, self-destructive ambitions of border politics—especially detention regimes—create anomalies for descriptions and interpretations of neoliberalism as efficient, rational, and profit driven. Also, kyriarchy allows for a reading of necropolitics beyond the control and destruction of bodies to include disregard for and destruction of ecosystems. Oppression and domination here shift into an obsessive zeal for submission. Kyriarchy is a concept that informs debates regarding border violence by helping to articulate the perverse drive for subjugation. Kyriarchy unpacks the tragic dynamics of inter-subjugation at the carceral border and within the nation. And resubjugation represents how a system determined by kyriarchy oversees the cyclical and frequent technologies for grinding human beings into submission and represents why in most cases death is not always the desired outcome, people are frequently left on a threshold of life-death/human-animal/law-lawlessness.

Conclusions

We have built an argument, through first-hand accounts and knowledge production, of the mistreatment and violence experienced by asylum seekers and refugees seeking Australia's protection. We argue that, rather than constituting a form of exceptionalism, cruelty, dehumanisation, and austerity directed towards refugees and asylum seekers is a continuum of violence perpetrated through the seemingly benign economic prism of neoliberal logic, together with the disciplining practices of a racialised state. When austerity measures are introduced, we witness how immigration/border systems express creativity in brutal and diabolical ways. One of the problems with austerity measures is its ability to drain and blur perspective—it becomes impossible to determine when the system will attack the vulnerable again. Therefore, creativity is central to strategies for resistance and for developing a diversity of tactics. Through art and imagination one can interpret the individual instances of control and domination and recognise the "soul of the system"—the ideological base of the system, the social imaginary, and the foundational narrative.

This area of public policy operates within a wider field of the "politics of care," raising questions of who the state cares for, what are priorities and ultimately the matrix of value attached to human life (Yuval-Davis 2011; Braidotti 2–13, Mbembe 2019). In the Australian Government's response to the global coronavirus pandemic, an assertion of care and assistance is articulated along the lines of formal, legal membership/citizenship as well as socio-cultural belonging, with temporary migrant workers, international students, and many others excluded from "care" and the significant financial security (or, welfare supports) the government has extended to workers and business. While these are important discussions, for the remit of this chapter, the aspect of care that is of particular importance is the matrix of value attached to human life that policy and law references in asylum/refugee policy. And this challenge is at the heart of MPT. That is, the exercise of state power is akin to the necropolitics that Mbembe (2019) outlines where the intention is not merely to let die, but to kill. Through the first-hand accounts, narratives, and poetic interpretations presented in this chapter, and through research, we demonstrate the Australian Government as having instituted a necropoleis in its carceral-archipelago.

Notes

1 See further Chapter 1 by Billings and Chapter 8 by Neil and Peterie.
2 Also, on the necropolitical aspects of the management of asylum seekers and welfare, see Chapter 2 by Weber and Chapter 7 by Worsoe and Marston.
3 Medevac laws were introduced in early 2019 to allow sick refugees and asylum seekers to be promptly transferred from offshore detention to Australian hospitals for treatment not available in offshore sites.

References

Abdile, H. (2018) 'My mother tongue/untitled/home far from home', *Transition*, (126): 25.

Ackerman, A. and Furman, R. (2013) 'The criminalization of immigration and the privatization of the immigration detention: Implications for justice', *Contemporary Justice Review*, 16(2): 251.

Adam, M. (2018) 'Betrayal: A prison under siege', *Transition*, (126): 19.

Anthias, F. (2008) 'Thinking through the lens of translocational positionality: An intersectionality frame for understanding identity and belonging', *Translocations: Migration and Social Change*, 4(11): 5.

Arvin, M. (2020) 'From Manus Island to Melbourne: We do not even know what we are being punished for', *The Guardian*, 8 August.
Australian Human Rights Commission. (2019) *Lives on Hold: Refugees and Asylum Seekers in the 'Legacy Caseload*. AHRC.
Berlant, L. (2011) *Cruel Optimism*. Duke University Press.
Boochani, B. (2016) 'A cruel and violent political strategy'', trans. by Tofighian, O. *The Huffington Post* (published 18 October 2016).
Boochani, B. (2018a) *No Friend but the Mountains: Writing from Manus Prison*, trans. by Tofighian, O. Picador, Pan Macmillan.
Boochani, B. (2018b). 'Manus Prison theory', trans by Tofighian, O. *The Saturday Paper*, 11–17 August.
Boochani, B. and Tazreiter, C. (2019) 'Notes on exile: Behrouz Boochani in conversation with Claudia Tazreiter', *Australian Journal of Human Rights*, 25(3).
Boochani, B. and Tofighian, O. (2018) 'The Last Days in Manus Prison', *Meanjin Quarterly*. https://meanjin.com.au/essays/the-last-days-in-manus-prison/
Boochani, B. and Tofighian, O. (2019) 'Manus prison theory: Borders, incarceration and collective agency'. *Griffith Review*, 65.
Boochani, B. and Tofighian, O. (2020). 'No friend but the mountains and Manus prison theory: In conversation', *Borderlands*, 19(1): 8.
Boochani, B., Tazreiter, C. and Tofighian, O. (2020) 'The multiple faces of the people smuggler', in Balint, R. and Kalman, J. (eds) *SMUGGLED: An Illegal History of Journeys to Australia*. New South Press.
Bourdieu, P. (1991) *Language and Symbolic Violence*. Harvard University Press.
Bourdieu, P. (1993) *The Weight of the World. Social Suffering in Contemporary Society*. Standford University Press.
Braidotti, R. (2013) *The Posthuman*. Polity Press.
Brown, M. and Schept, J. (2017) 'New abolition, criminology and a critical carceral studies', *Punishment & Society*, 19(4): 440.
Brown, W. (2015) *Undoing the demos: Neoliberalism's stealth revolution*. Zone Books.
Brown, W. (2019) *In the Ruins of Neoliberalism. The Rise of Antidemocratic Politics in the West*. Columbia University Press.
Dana. E. (2018) www.writingthroughfences.org/writers/erfan-dana/
Darling, J. (2016) 'Asylum in Austere Times: Instability, privatization and experimentation within the UK asylum dispersal system', *Journal of Refugee Studies*, 29(4): 483.
Dauvergne, C. (2015) *The End of Settler Societies and the New Politics of Immigration*. Cambridge University Press.
de Haas, H., Castles, S. and Miller, M. J. (2019) *The Age of Migration. International Population Movements in the Modern World*. Macmillan).
Dotson, K. (2012) 'A cautionary tale: On limiting epistemic oppression', *Frontiers: A Journal of Women Studies*, 33(1): 24.
Elson, R. (2013) 'Candidate links traffic congestion to asylum seekers', *SBS News Online*, 3 September.
Fanon, F. (1963) *The Wretched of the Earth*. Grove.
Foucault, M. (1997) 'The birth of biopolitics', in Rabinow, P. and Faubion, J. D. (eds) *Ethics, Subjectivity, and Truth*. New Press, p. 73.
Fraser, N. and Jaeggi, R. (2018) *Capitalism: A Conversation in Critical Theory*. Polity Press.
Galbraith, J. (2018) 'How could it all have happened', *Overland*. https://overland.org.au/previous-issues/solidarity-beyond-borders/essay-janet-galbraith/

Geissler, P. (2013) 'Public secrets in public health: Knowing not to know while making scientific knowledge', *American Ethnologist*, 40(1): 13.
Gilroy, P. (1993) *The Black Atlantic: Modernity and Double Consciousness*. Harvard University Press.
Gilroy, P. (2005) *Postcolonial Melancholia*. Columbia University Press.
Gleeson, M. (2016) *Offshore: Behind the Wire on Manus and Nauru*. Newsouth.
Grewcock, M. (2013) 'Australia's ongoing border war', *Race & Class*, 54(3): 10.
Grewcock, M. (2017) '"Our lives is in danger": Manus Island and the end of asylum', *Race & Class*, 2(59): 1.
Hage, G. (2003) *Against Paranoid Nationalism: Searching for Hope in a Shrinking Society*. Pluto Press.
Haraway, D. (1989) 'The biopolitics of postmodern bodies: Constitutions of self in immune system discourse', *Differences: A Journal of Feminist Cultural Studies*, 1(1): 3.
Hardt, M. and Negri, A. (2004) *Multitude: War and Democracy in the Age of Empire*. Harvard University Press.
Hartley, L. and Fleay, C. (2017) '"We are like animals": Negotiating dehumanising experiences of asylum-seeker policies in the Australian community', *Refugee Survey Quarterly*, 34: 45.
Hassaballa, H. (2018) 'Time, torture . . . and tomorrow/artist's statement,' *Transition*, (126): 31–3.
Juss, S. (2017) 'Detention and delusion in Australia's Kafkaesque refugee law', *Refugee Survey Quarterly*, 36(1): 146.
Kenny, M.A. and Proctor, N. (2016) 'The fast track refugee assessment process and the mental health of vulnerable asylum seekers', *Psychiatry, Psychology and Law*, 23(1): 62.
Leerkes, A. and Van Houte, M. (2020) 'Beyond the deportation regime: Differential state interests and capacities in dealing with (non-) deportability in Europe', *Citizenship Studies*, 24(3): 319.
Martin, G. (2015) 'Stop the boats! Moral panic in Australia over asylum seeker', *Continuum: Journal of Media & Cultural Studies*, 29(3): 304.
Mbembe, A. (2017) *Critique of Black Reason*, trans by Dubois, L. Duke University Press.
Mbembe, A. (2019) *Necropolitics*, trans by Corcoran, S. Duke University Press.
McAdam, J. (2013) 'Australia and asylum seekers', *International Journal of Refugee Law*, 25(3): 435.
McAdam, J. and Chong, F. (2019) 'How did our treatment of refugees come to this?', *Sydney Morning Herald*, 5 July.
Mezzadara, S. and Neilson, B. (2013) *Border as Method, or, the Multiplication of Labor*. Duke University Press.
Mignolo, W. D. (2011) *The Darker Side of Western Modernity: Global Futures, Decolonial Options*. Duke University Press.
Mills, C. (1997) *The Racial Contract*. Cornell University Press.
Morton, R. (2020) 'Exclusive: War on refugees moves to the final phase onshore', *The Saturday Paper*, 17–23 October.
Mountz, A. (2011) 'Specters at the port of entry: Understanding state mobilities through an ontology of exclusion', *Mobilities*, 6(3): 317.
Mountz, A. (2020) *The Death of Asylum. Hidden Geographies of the Enforcement Archipelago*. University of Minnesota Press.
Moya, P. (2011) 'Who we are and from where we speak', *Transmodernity: Journal of Peripheral Cultural Production of the Luso-Hispanic World*, 1(2): 79.

Pohlhaus, G. (2012) 'Relational knowing and epistemic injustice: Toward a theory of willful hermeneutical ignorance', *Hypatia: A Journal of Feminist Philosophy*, 27(4): 715.

Robinson, C. J. (1983) *Black Marxism*. University of North Carolina Press.

Sassen, S. (2014) *Expulsions: Brutality and Complexity in the Global Economy*. Harvard University Press.

Scarpa, S. and Schierup, C. (2018) 'Who undermines the welfare state? Austerity-dogmatism and the u-turn in Swedish asylum policy', *Social Inclusion*, 6(1): 199.

Schüssler Fiorenza, E. (1992) *But She Said: Feminist Practices of Biblical Interpretation*. Beacon Press.

Streeck, W. (2016) '"The post-capitalist interregnum" the old system is dying, but a new social order cannot yet be born', *Juncture*, 23(2): 68.

Storper, M. (2001) 'Lived effects of the contemporary economy: Globalization, inequality, and consumer society', in Comaroff, J. and Comaroff J. (eds) *Millennial Capitalism and the Culture of Neoliberalism*. Duke University Press, p. 98.

Tazreiter, C. (2004) *Asylum Seekers and the State: The Politics of Protection in a Security-Conscious World*. Ashgate.

Tazreiter, C. (2015) 'Lifeboat politics in the Pacific: Affect and the ripples and shimmers of a migrant saturated future', *Emotion, Space and Society*, 16: 99.

Tazreiter, C. (2017) 'The unlucky in the "lucky country": Asylum seekers, irregular migrants and refugees and Australia's politics of disappearance', *Australian Journal of Human Rights*, 23(2): 242.

Tazreiter, C. (2019). 'Crisis politics of asylum seekers and migrant arrivals in Australia', in Menjivar, C., Ruiz, M. and Ness, I. (eds) *The Handbook of Migration Crises*. Oxford University Press, p. 619.

Tofighian, O. (2018a) 'Translator's tale: A window to the mountains', *Sydney Review of Books*.

Tofighian, O. (2018b). 'Black bodies for political profit: Sudanese and Somali standpoints on Australia's racialized border regime. *Transition*, 126: 5.

Tofighian, O. (2020) 'Introducing Manus Prison theory: Knowing border violence', *Globalizations*, 17(7): 1138.

Tyner, J. A. (2016) *Violence in Capitalism. Devaluing Life in an Age of Responsibility*. University of Nebraska Press.

Wang, J. (2018) *Carceral Capitalism*. Semiotext(e).

Weber, L. and McCulloch, J. (2018) 'Penal power and border control: Which thesis? Sovereignty, governmentality, or the pre-emptive state?' *Punishment & Society*, 21(4): 496.

Weheliye, A. G. (2014) *Habeas Viscus: Racializing Assemblages, Biopolitcs, and Black Feminist Theories of the Human*. Duke University Press.

Yuval-Davis, N. (2011) *The Politics of Belonging. Intersectional Contestations*. SAGE.

Part 2

The depletion of social welfare for refugees: impacts and experiences

Part 2: commentary

Slow violence in Australia and the United Kingdom: connected histories and contemporary exclusions

Lucy Mayblin

Introduction

The preceding chapters of this volume (Part 1) detail a policy regime for asylum applicants and refugees that is complex, punitive, and dehumanising. In spite of having signed and ratified international legal agreements, which should guarantee people who are fleeing persecution a set of rights and entitlements that will allow them to access sanctuary, Australia is demonstrably failing to live up to these commitments. In this regard, Australia is certainly not unusual. While the vast majority of refugees in the world seek refuge in a "low income," "developing" country in what has come to be known as the "Global South" (a symbolic geography rather than an actual place), wealthier countries in the "Global North" have effectively closed their doors. Through a range of deterrence and control measures, they have gone to significant effort over the past 30 years, at great expense, to prevent refugees from finding sanctuary in their countries (for an overview, see Fitzgerald 2019). Indeed, in her recent book Alison Mountz (2020) argues that what is being observed is not an *erosion* of the right to asylum, but in fact the *death* of asylum.

My aim, in this commentary on Part 2 of this edited volume, is to draw out the similarities between Australia and the United Kingdom, but also to explain how we can make sense of what is happening in both countries, theoretically and historically. I discuss how we can conceptualise the effects of these measures, particularly at the immigration/welfare nexus detailed across the chapters of this volume, as a form of slow violence (Nixon 2011; Mayblin 2019b). I then situate asylum policy in Australia and the United Kingdom in the context of histories of colonial racial exclusion. In doing so, I draw attention to the connected histories (Bhambra 2014) which can help us to understand the similarities between Australia and the United Kingdom in the present.

Asylum in the United Kingdom and Australia

For many years a growing body of work has explored, from a range of perspectives and locations, the erosion (or even death) of the right to asylum. The

DOI: 10.4324/9781003298595-8

chapters that make up this volume attest to this phenomenon in Australia, and there is a large body of work which describes similarly punitive measures being used against people seeking asylum in the United Kingdom (e.g. Darling 2009; Allsopp et al. 2014; Canning 2017; Fitzgerald 2019; Mayblin 2019b). In both countries a shift has taken place in which politicians and policy makers have ceased to construe asylum seeking as primarily a humanitarian phenomenon; they now construe it as primarily an economic phenomenon (Mayblin 2019a). Asylum seekers, in short, are treated as unwanted economic migrants. This shift has a range of implications, including the curtailment of welfare provisions for those awaiting a decision on their asylum application. Such measures constitute slowly unfolding structural violence measured out against sanctuary seekers.

The contributions that make up Chapters 4–8 of this volume describe the lived experience of awaiting a decision on one of the many applications that can be involved in someone's asylum journey in Australia. Because the asylum journey is often so protracted, access to a means of survival in the form of welfare support payments or work becomes essential. Yet the complex bureaucratic process, littered with hierarchies of visas, rights, entitlements, acronyms, and opaque and illogical rules, seems designed to confuse, confound, and exclude. For example, John van Kooy and Asher Hirsch (Chapter 4) explain how socio-legal rights and entitlements are used as a form of deterrence for asylum seekers, in spite of seeming like they would constitute protections. This passage from Chapter 4 on people who find themselves in the "Legacy Caseload" conveys the deterrence-by-complexity of the system facing applicants:

> TPV and SHEV holders do not have access to the SRSS program, nor are they eligible for the suite of settlement services available to permanent refugees. Under certain conditions they may access a modest income support payment, but unlike permanent refugees they are not eligible for government-subsidised education, housing, disability and mental health services, or public transport concessions . . . After their visa expires, TPV and SHEV holders may reapply for another TPV or SHEV, but they may not apply for permanent refugee protection. In addition, SHEV holders, should they meet the stipulated condition of living, working, and/or studying in a designated regional area for at least three-and-a-half out of five years, are technically eligible to apply for a subsequent family or skilled visa. However, the visa fees, English language requirements, and skills tests associated with these visas make the bar "very high to clear" for any refugee group.

Alongside this complexity, systemic inefficiencies appear also to be a strategy in the Australian asylum system to deter people through attrition. The story of Reza, who had been navigating the asylum system in Australia since 2012 at the time of writing, which is detailed by Hanne Worsoe and Greg Marston in Chapter 7, is a powerful testament of this approach. In this way, we can observe the Australian state acting upon those who are in the country in order to influence not only their actions but also the actions of an imagined group of others who have yet to arrive (see Mayblin 2019b, on the same tactic in the UK context). The intention is to deter them, though there is no evidence that this form of deterrence has any impact on numbers of people seeking sanctuary. The only impact on numbers that deterrence measures appear to have is to increase deaths at (or beyond) borders as people seek ever more dangerous modes of entry in the absence of safe and legal routes to safety (Brambilla and Jones 2020; Mountz 2020).

Together, the experience of precarity and extended periods of waiting has both physical and mental health implications for many people (see Clemence Due, Moira Walsh, and Anna Ziersch, Chapter 6). This is in part because, as Emma Fell (Chapter 5) shows, the system reaches out beyond welfare payments into housing precarity, even for those who are entitled to work and rent privately. Poor quality and unsafe housing alongside financial precarity result in people experiencing periods of destitution, and third sector organisations become some people's only means of survival through ad hoc and piecemeal support (see Mayblin and James 2019 in the UK context). For those who arrive by boat in Australia and find themselves deported to detention camps in Nauru and Papua New Guinea this state of liminality is then compounded by literal incarceration. David Neil and Michelle Peterie describe the struggles of the incarcerated to access emergency medical care in Chapter 8 and, more widely, the critical literature on these offshore detention camps has consistently found conditions to be in violation of human rights law (Grewcock 2017; Mountz 2020).

The labyrinthine system faced by asylum applicants within Australia ("onshore") seems designed to curtail access to the right to asylum and has much in common with the UK system. This system has also gone through a process in which rights and entitlements for those seeking asylum have steadily been eroded over at least the past two decades (see Mayblin 2019b). In the United Kingdom people who have made an application for asylum are not generally permitted to work. In the absence of the right to work they are therefore dependent on welfare support payments, which are delivered through a separate welfare system to that which supports unemployed citizens. Those going through the asylum system receive weekly support payments of £37.75 at the time of writing. This figure is determined on the basis of what the poorest ten per cent of British citizens spend on essential living items only (*R (Refugee Action) v Secretary of State for the Home Department,*[1] (see the discussion of this judicial review in Mayblin 2017). It is, then, around one third of the weekly income of the poorest citizens, themselves having undergone a decade of austerity policies which have left one third of British children living in poverty (Department for Work and Pensions 2018). People who are receiving asylum support are rarely able to take buses to travel around the cities in which they live, to buy clothes, or even to eat sufficient food in many cases. As a group they experience higher than average rates of infant and maternal mortality, domestic violence, mental and physical health problems, social isolation, and struggle to access basic services to which they are entitled (Allsopp et al. 2014). As in the Australian case, the role of the voluntary and community sector in supporting those who should be supported by the state is then extended, and the sector becomes highly over-burdened with tackling destitution amongst asylum seekers.

Also in the United Kingdom, there is a complex landscape of different types of benefits with opaque names, just as there is in Australia. Not for those who arrived at different periods of time, as in Australia, but for people at different stages of the process from an initial application ("Section 95" support); to people who have been refused asylum and yet (somewhat contradictorily) cannot be returned to their country of origin as it is unsafe to do so or their country of origin denies that they are a citizen ("Section 4" support); to those who have been refused asylum but are not detained or deported and, therefore, live in the United Kingdom as denizens with the label "no recourse to public funds," no right to housing (even privately rented), or to work. If someone is granted leave to remain this is not refugee status but a time-limited "humanitarian," "indefinite," or "limited" leave to remain. Though the details of these different statuses of course become of great significance for those who are seeking asylum and their legal representatives, the real concern for critical scholars is not in the particulars but in the totality of the regime—what it aims to do overall, to who, and to what end. In his regard we can say that it aims to foreclose access to the right to asylum. In bringing this foreclosure it aims to inflict slow violence upon those who do make an application for asylum in order to both force people to give up and leave, at the same time as "sending a message" to those who have not yet arrived.

The harms done to those going through the asylum system in both the United Kingdom and Australia are, thus, the outcomes of structural violence. Canning (2017: 48) argues that "where there is capacity for people to live free from suffering, but no political will exists to implement change to alleviate such suffering, structural violence is present." Asylum policy constitutes violence because it inflicts serious physical and mental harms upon its victims, and it is structural because it is impossible to identify a single perpetrator (Gupta 2012). One of the utilities of the concept of structural violence is that it focuses attention on mortality—literal or potential. That is, not necessarily immediate deaths such as drowning at sea, but belated harm potentially leading to death, through impoverishment and the stress of being trapped within an asylum system which does not wish for you to succeed. The negative health impacts of poverty, of anxiously waiting for a response from the authorities, of "racism and discrimination, ongoing uncertainty. . . [and] acculturative stress" (as detailed in Chapter 6) evidence the "intertwined nature of the relationships between financial and visa precarity and health."

Both the Australian and British cases have temporal commonalities. In spite of regular promises to speed up the asylum system and "fast track" cases, people applying for asylum in both countries are routinely kept in a lengthy state of waiting (see particularly Chapter 7). Such is the extent of this phenomenon that a burgeoning international literature on waiting in asylum systems around the world has grown in recent years (e.g. Conlon 2011; Hyndman and Giles 2011; Refugee and Asylum Voice 2019). The violence inflicted on asylum seekers going through these systems is both spatially removed from any single perpetrator and temporally removed. The violence, in other words, is slow.

Thinking of these phenomena as "slow violence" draws attention to the ways in which the harms of dispersed violence are wrought gradually by the asylum system. Nixon (2011: 2) writes, in a different context:

> By slow violence I mean a violence that occurs gradually and out of sight, a violence of delayed destruction that is dispersed across time and space, an attritional violence that is typically not viewed as violence at all . . . a violence that is neither spectacular nor instantaneous, but rather incremental and accretive, its calamitous repercussions playing out across a range of temporal scales.

Nixon's work on slow violence focuses on physical or natural environments which have been damaged, in ways that bring delayed harms to humans and other species, but it has many resonances with the situation of people seeking asylum. For example, they are placed in hostile environments in many senses: in the sense of being subject to a hostile asylum system driven by a culture of disbelief; in the sense of being placed in very poor-quality housing, which is often not a healthy environment in which to live; and in the sense of being situated in a hostile social environment in which people who have sought asylum are routinely subject to hostility and racist abuse. Policies both produce and place certain people within hostile environments, therefore, in which suffering will be inevitable under a thin veil of helping them to survive. Indeed, the concept of slow violence allows us to make sense of the extent of the harm done by the state, within the context of that state claiming and, perhaps, just meeting certain human rights commitments.

Slow violence inspires an idea that temporality is important and that impoverishment is connected to more visible acts of border control on a continuum of violence. In a broad sense then, the structural violence of asylum regimes can be slow, but it can also give rise to moments of sudden violence, such as detention centre riots, deportations, or drownings at sea. In the case of those on the receiving end of economic restrictions, it is the slowly unfolding everyday violence of enforced poverty which characterises the phenomenon, though this may of course be punctuated by sudden moments of violence (Weber and Pickering 2011). The slow degradation of the bodies and minds of people who are in the asylum system through impoverishment means that, like other examples of poverty, their suffering is individualised and diffused; it happens quietly behind closed doors, making it largely invisible to the majority of the wider population. We might contrast this with highly visible refugee crises, which can have a dramatic, even violent, immediacy, which is harder to ignore.

We can use the concept of slow and structural violence to aid our understanding of what is happening to people caught up in the asylum regimes in Britain and Australia. But we must also be cognizant of the fact that this is only one element of a broader strategy of foreclosing the right to seek and enjoy asylum. In the Australian context the treatment of in-country applicants is tied to the island detention camps in Nauru and Papua New Guinea (see Chapter 8). These practices of "externalising" asylum are themselves just one part of a host of measures that seek to prevent the arrival in Australia of people who wish to seek asylum, and the prevention of those who do in fact arrive from being successful. Alongside proposals to "offshore" asylum on former colonial islands, disused ferries, and oil rigs (Davies et al. 2021), the United Kingdom also follows the same approach of curtailing access to the right to asylum by any means. Taken together, Mountz (2020) calls these symptoms of the death of asylum.

Connected colonial histories and the exclusionary politics of asylum

Having discussed the measures described and critiqued in Part 2 of this volume, and conceptualised them as a form of slow violence, in this section I dig deeper. My aim is to draw attention to the colonial origins of the 1951 *Convention relating to the Status of Refugees* ("Refugees Convention") as an entry point to understanding how the phenomena detailed in this book came about. The international refuge regime was exclusionary at its inception, and colonial histories of racial exclusion can, therefore, give us a deeper understanding of the contemporary moment. Such an analysis is undertaken to make sense of, not to justify, contemporary instantiations of the exclusionary politics of asylum.

The human rights framework, as we know it today, was devised in the middle of the twentieth century. It was based on the idea that there was a need for some legal constraints on (non-colonised) states' sovereignty, in order to prevent a repeat of the atrocities committed in Nazi Germany. Refugee rights were an integral part of this because many of those who fled the Nazi regime found that once they had crossed an international boarder they had, in the words of Hannah Arendt, 'lost the right to have rights' (Arendt 1973). That is because, until this point, rights, where people had them, were tied to citizenship, making the uprooted and stateless effectively without recourse to rights or justice. The Refugees Convention was meant to rectify this. It enshrined the right to seek asylum in international law for those displaced in Europe prior to 1951.

Both Britain and Australia signed the Refugees Convention and also the 1967 *Protocol relating to the Status of Refugees*, which made it applicable to refugees from outside Europe. The reason that the Refugees Convention did not originally open up the possibility of non-Europeans having the right to asylum in a foreign country if their own government had persecuted them was because colonial powers and settler colonies, including Britain and Australia, argued forcefully for their exclusion (Mayblin 2017). This was not because there were no refugees outside of Europe at this time. On the contrary, there were millions across Pakistan and India alone. In spite of strong opposition from countries that had recently gained independence and had significant refugee challenges to face—such as Pakistan and India—the colonial powers won the insertion of a territorial application clause in the Refugees Convention. This meant that it applied only to European refugees unless a colonising power deemed otherwise. Suffice to say, none did.

It is no coincidence, then, that both Britain and Australia are hostile to non-European people seeking asylum in their countries today. The only reason it took until the 1990s for the particularly hostile and exclusionary policies to begin to be implemented is because before this time non-Europeans seeking asylum were not arriving, spontaneously, in any significant number in either country. Two phenomena—the increase in asylum applications, and the punitive response by many Western states—have garnered a significant amount of academic attention. Often they are seen as causally linked: restrictive measures were introduced because numbers of applications were "at intolerably high levels" (Hansen 2003: 35). This assessment is founded on what Chimni (1998) dubs the "myth of difference." Chimni argues that during the first four decades of the refugee regime, Cold War priorities dominated. Those seeking asylum in the West were assumed to be white, male, European, and fleeing the Soviet Union. Whether they were fleeing because of individual persecution or mixed motives related to poverty and "seeking a better life" was not a matter of interest to Western states. When, in the late 1980s, and accelerating into the 1990s and 2000s, different cohorts of asylum seekers began to arrive, they were construed as "new asylum seekers." At this point "the nature and character of refugee flows in the Third World were represented as being radically different from refugee flows in Europe since the end of the First World War" (Chimni 1998: 351). Third-world refugees clashed sharply with the image of the "normal" refugee described earlier, and this difference was seen by Western states as diminishing their claims for asylum.

The arrival of these new refugees, the start of which roughly coincided with the end of the Cold War, thus led to a policy shift. This shift can be summed up as the dawn of the *non-entrée* regime. The refugee "no longer possessed ideological or geopolitical value" (Chimni 1998: 351) and as such powerful states individually, and through the UN, shifted the policy agenda away from refuge (or the "exilic bias") towards a focus on repatriation as the ideal solution to the refugee challenge. So, while the shift occurred in the policy preferences of powerful Western states, this had global implications. There was, concurrently, a change in emphasis amongst those seeking to make sense of population displacements away from the international contexts that precipitated them towards an emphasis on the immediate contexts that existed in sending countries.

In this way, we cannot make sense of the exclusionary politics of asylum in either Britain or Australia without recognising the racial, and racist, histories of these countries. Of course the literature on these topics is vast and there is not space to cover such histories at length here. However, it is well documented that British immigration history is one which has sought racial exclusion of those not racialised as white. The British government began to turn black and brown citizens of the British Empire and Commonwealth into migrants in order to exclude them from entering UK territory in the 1970s and 1980s (Hampshire 2005; Bhambra 2017). Australia famously operated a "white Australia" immigration regime until the 1970s and was deeply indebted to ideas of white racial superiority developed in and through the British Empire. As a settler colony, then, Australia has a long history of explicit state racism against non-white people seeking to enter the country, as well as towards those Indigenous peoples already there when Europeans first arrived (Carey and McLisky 2009; Moreton-Robinson 2015).

Writing on the question of "race equality" in 1921, a British Foreign Office Official observed:

> The white and the coloured races cannot and will not amalgamated. One or the other must be the ruling caste; and countries where the white population is in power have determined from a sure instinct for self-preservation that they will never open their doors to the influx of the coloured race, which might eventually become dominant. In this policy the United States of America, taught by the Negro trouble (and especially California, where the Asiatics are most numerous) have taken the lead, and have been closely followed by the British Dominions of Canada, Australia New Zealand, and South Africa. In varying forms and degrees all the countries have excluded and will exclude Oriental immigration.
>
> (Foreign Office 1921)

Writing about the "white Australia" policy in 1929, Prime Minister Billy Hughes argued something similar:

> The idea of a "white Australia", and one peopled in the main by men and women of British stock, reflects the traditions and achievements of our race. Racial purity pays in the long run . . . we cannot assimilate these coloured peoples; their ways are not ours . . . we cannot marry their women nor they ours without producing a race of half-castes at which both races would spit contempt.
>
> (Hughes 1929: 366)

The history of both countries then, as (settler) colonial states, and nations imagined as white, is deeply entangled with the contemporary dehumanisation of people who are seeking asylum. It should be no surprise that twenty years after the previous quotes, both Britain and Australia refused to sign the Refugees Convention unless a "territorial application clause" were inserted that would give them control over who the right to asylum applied to. Britain then used this right to exclude people in the majority of its territories. Only in 1967, with movements for decolonisation developing apace, and threats that the African Union would develop its own, competing, legal instrument, did the world powers consent to extend the *non-refoulement* principle, and related rights, to anyone in the world.

These connected histories (Bhambra 2014) of race, blood, and lineage, as well as of racial otherness and inferiority, can help us to understand the accounts of slow violence related in this volume. In the absence of recognising these connected racist histories, the actions of the British and Australian states appear bafflingly cruel and indefensibly inhumane. What is it that makes some people more easily impoverished, excluded, detained, denied life-saving medical treatment that is readily available nearby; drowned, deported to war zones, impaled on razor wire, and denied the human rights which their host states have signed up to? When we recognise that these states view some human lives as worth less than others, and that there is a long lineage to which such dehumanisation is indebted, and draws upon, we can then better understand what is happening. In exploring connected histories, and the longevity of ideas, which aim to categorise and exclude, we can grasp the global historical context to contemporary slow violence.

Conclusion

This critical commentary has discussed the similarities between asylum policy Australia and the United Kingdom. The focus has particularly been in relation to welfare policies that seek, explicitly, to impoverish people as a means of deterrence. I have discussed how we can conceptualise the effects of these measures as a form of slow violence (Nixon 2011; Mayblin 2019b) and how thinking about violence as a continuum can aid us in understanding what is happening in a range of different locations and amongst people of different statuses. While policy and legal detail is important, then, in contesting the exclusionary politics of asylum, we also need to be able to stand back and conceptualise these phenomena as linked to much broader structures and logics. The similarity of logics of exclusion in both Australia and Britain is striking, making such connections urgent in challenging such policies.

In the second half of this commentary, I briefly discussed how histories of colonial racial exclusion, particularly in relation to the international refugee regime, must be part of this broader understanding. This touched upon my own work on the colonial origins of the refugee regime (Mayblin 2017). I drew attention to the connected histories (Bhambra 2014) which can help us to understand the similarities between Australia and the United Kingdom in the present, especially colonial logics of racial exclusion. Such historical work can aid in developing an understanding of state actions in the present, which seem needlessly cruel and violative of people's human rights. Because the category "refugee" is a legal one and is, in principle, open to all people irrespective of background or social status, researchers in refugee studies have tended to avoid analyses that connect the mistreatment of people who are seeking asylum with racism. It has been the case only recently that a growing number of scholars have drawn on colonial histories of racial differentiation and exclusion to make sense of the exclusionary politics of asylum today (see Mayblin and Turner 2021). In doing so, they have been able to show how colonial ideas of racial difference—whether biological or cultural—are so often drawn upon in discursive moves to make dehumanising practices seem logical, sensible, and appropriate. As scholars, it is important that we denaturalise these discourses and practices, as the scholars of this volume have done so clearly.

Note

1 [2014] EWHC 1033 (Admin).

References

Allsopp, J., Sigona, N. and Phillimore, J. (2014) 'Poverty among refugees and asylum seekers in the UK: An evidence and policy review', Iris Working Paper Series No. 1/2014.

Arendt, H. (1973) *The Origins of Totalitarianism*. Harcourt Brace Jovanovich.

Bhambra, G. K. (2014) *Connected Sociologies*. Bloomsbury.

Bhambra, G. K. (2017) 'Brexit, Trump, and 'methodological whiteness': On the misrecognition of race and class', *British Journal of Sociology*, 68(S1): 214.

Brambilla, C. and Jones, R. (2020) 'Rethinking borders, violence, and conflict: From sovereign power to borderscapes as sites of struggles', *Environment and Planning D: Society and Space*, 38(2): 287.

Canning, V. (2017) *Gendered Harm and Structural Violence in the British Asylum System*. Routledge.

Carey, J. and McLisky, C. (2009) *Creating White Australia*. Sydney University Press.

Chimni, B. S. (1998) 'The geopolitics of refugee studies: A view from the South', *Journal of Refugee Studies*, 11(4): 350.

Conlon, D. (2011) 'Waiting: Feminist perspectives on the spacings/timings of migrant (im) mobility', *Gender, Place and Culture*, 18(3): 353.

Darling, J. (2009) 'Becoming bare life: Asylum, hospitality, and the politics of encampment', *Environment and Planning D: Society and Space*, 27(4): 649.

Davies, T., Isakjee, A., Mayblin, L. and Turner, J. (2021) 'Channel crossings: Offshoring asylum and the afterlife of Empire in the Dover Strait', *Ethnic and Racial Studies*, 44(13) (published online 17 May 2021).

Department for Work and Pensions. (2018) 'Households below average income: An analysis of the UK income distribution: 1994/95–2016/17', National Statistics Reporting. Office for National Statistics.

Fitzgerald, D. S. (2019) *Refuge Beyond Reach: How Rich Democracies Repel Asylum Seekers*. Oxford University Press.

Foreign Office. (1921) *General Correspondence: Far-Eastern: Japan* (FO 371/6684). National Archives.

Grewcock, M. (2017) '"Our lives is in danger": Manus Island and the end of asylum', *Race & Class*, 59(2): 70.
Gupta, A. (2012) *Red Tape: Bureaucracy, Structural Violence and Poverty in India*. Duke University Press.
Hampshire, J. (2005) *Citizenship and Belonging: Immigration and the Politics of Demographic Governance in Postwar Britain*. Palgrave Macmillan.
Hansen, R. (2003) 'Migration to Europe since 1945: Its history and lessons' *Political Quarterly* 74(1): 25.
Hughes, W. M. (1929) *A Splendid Adventure: A Review of Empire Relations Within and Without the Commonwealth of Britannic Nations*. London: Ernest Benn Ltd.
Hyndman, J. and Giles, J. (2011) 'Waiting for what? The feminization of asylum in protracted situations', *Gender, Place & Culture*, 18(3): 361.
Mayblin, L. (2017) *Asylum After Empire: Colonial Legacies in the Politics of Asylum Seeking*. Rowman and Littlefield International.
Mayblin, L. (2019a) 'Imagining asylum, governing asylum seekers: Complexity reduction and policy making in the UK Home Office', *Migration Studies*, 7(1): 1.
Mayblin, L. (2019b). *Impoverishment and Asylum: Social Policy as Slow Violence*. Routledge.
Mayblin, L. and James, P. (2019) 'Asylum and refugee support in the UK: Civil society filling the gaps?', *Journal of Ethnic and Migration Studies*, 45(3): 375.
Mayblin, L. and Turner, J. (2021) *Migration Studies and Colonialism*. Polity.
Moreton-Robinson, A. (2015) *White Possessive: Property, Power, and Indigenous Sovereignty*. University of Minnesota Press.
Mountz, A. (2020) *The Death of Asylum: Hidden Geographies of the Enforcement Archipelago*. University of Minnesota Press.
Nixon, R. (2011) *Slow Violence and the Environmentalism of the Poor*. Harvard University Press.
Refugee and Asylum Voice. (2019) *The Waiting Game: The Impact of Delayed Asylum Decisions*. RAS.
Weber, L. and Pickering, S. (2011) *Globalisation and Borders: Death at the Global Frontier*. Palgrave Macmillan.

Chapter 4

Destitution by design

The impacts of Australia's in-country deterrence regime on people seeking asylum

John van Kooy and Asher Hirsch*

Introduction

Extending the state's hospitality towards a foreign visitor, writes Derrida (2002), implies a prior invitation from the host to share their resources. State invitations of this nature are normally only offered to "integratable immigrants," the "assimilable visitors" with whom cohabitation is deemed "liveable" (Derrida 2002: 363). Conversely, for visitors without an invitation—the "absolutely unforeseeable strangers"—there can be no such state hospitality.

The notion of "visitation without invitation" is at the heart of sharp policy distinctions made in Australia between people seeking asylum—especially those who have arrived by boat without a valid visa—and people with predetermined refugee status. The latter arrive on the official invitation of the Australian Government, many as part of a resettlement arrangement with the UN High Commissioner for Refugees (UNHCR). Though successful long-term resettlement is an elusive goal, refugee entrants are welcomed at the border and supported by a variety of Australian Government institutions and welfare programs. People seeking asylum, by contrast, are treated very differently. In attempts to stop unauthorised immigration, successive Australian governments have created both physical obstacles (such as naval operations to intercept boats and immigration detention centres run by private security firms) and extensive socio-legal barriers for those who do manage to gain entry (Hirsch 2017). People who arrive without travel documentation are classified as illegal maritime arrivals (IMAs), and experience prolonged obfuscation and delays on the processing of asylum claims, combined with restrictions on accessing the state's welfare system.[1] This policy strategy aims not only to warn off any future "uninvited" arrivals, but also by creating situations of destitution for asylum seekers, to deter those who are already in Australia from seeking to remain.

This chapter examines the impacts of recent immigration and welfare policy directions concerning people seeking asylum in Australia. We do so through an analysis of nearly 50 consultations facilitated by the Refugee Council of Australia from 2017 to 2018; a series of workshops, roundtables, and public conversations involving people who have sought or need humanitarian protection

DOI: 10.4324/9781003298595-9

and the organisations who support them. The consultations reveal accounts of deteriorating mental health, poverty, and widespread insecurity among asylum seekers who have, at best, limited means to participate in mainstream social and economic life. Two interrelated themes of *waiting* and *dependence* characterise our analysis of these lived experiences, which we argue represent the intentional outcomes of the Australian Government's in-country deterrence strategy.

Distinctions of deservingness

While in social democratic states the guiding principle of welfare policy design may be equality of access for all, in selective welfare regimes like Australia there is greater attention on "deservingness" (Larsen 2008; van Oorschot 2000). Scrutiny on "who should get what, and why" is also heightened when economic resources and government budgets are stretched, or perceived as such. Sandelind (2019: 338) argues that defining deservingness is about demarcating the limit where the welfare system becomes "destabilised"—an imagined threshold that, when crossed, renders the welfare state unsustainable and, in the case of immigrant claimants, is thought to cede an unacceptable degree of sovereign control. Paraphrasing Derrida (2002: 360–361), to extend state hospitality to uninvited outsiders, to "host and shelter" them with public resources, is to risk the welfare state being "overtaken . . . violated." Welfare policy design, thus, institutionalises group boundaries and perpetuates the power structures that give voice to the "majority citizen" (Sandelind 2019), while "othering" the unwanted.

Larsen (2008) outlines five criteria commonly used to assess or assign deservingness to welfare claimants in selective regimes: (1) the individual's degree of control over their own need for support; (2) actual, objective need; (3) perceived identity and group belonging to the national community; (4) a demonstrated attitude of docility, compliance, gratefulness, or "pleasantness" on the part of the recipient; and (5) the potential for reciprocity (e.g. through taxation). Selective welfare regimes, argues Larsen, use these deservingness criteria to distinguish welfare recipients from the "well-adjusted majority" between those who can give and those who receive (Larsen 2008).

People seeking asylum who arrive by boat, "irregularly," without valid visas represent the "hard line" of welfare deservingness in Australia—and fail on virtually all of Larsen's five criteria. In Australian political discourse, the association of asylum seekers with transnational crime, their supposed willingness to be "smuggled" into the country and speculated links to terrorist networks (see Cameron 2013; Goot and Watson 2011; Pickering 2001) implies individual agency—a degree of control over their own situation that effectively disqualifies claimants from state support. Surveys of public attitudes have also revealed prevalent perceptions of asylum seekers as undeserving "economic migrants" who create a burden for Australian communities (Klocker 2004). While at the height of public hysteria about "boat people," letters published in national newspapers have reflected views of asylum seekers as "parasites," "leeches," and "the greatest peril imaginable" (Corlett 2000). In a clear articulation of how asylum seekers are thought to have failed tests of deservingness, the Federal Minister for Immigration and Border Protection stated, in May 2017, that asylum seekers who arrived without immigration documents were "fake refugees," "ripping off" the Australian taxpayer, and selfishly seeking to access "welfare, taxpayer benefits" (Maguire 2017).

Sentiments of kinship between current citizens and asylum seekers—another measure of deservingness—are rarely expressed in mainstream Australian discourse. Studies have shown that many Australian communities overlook asylum seekers' marginal existence as former detainees and holders of precarious visas (see, e.g. Haggis and Schech 2010). The use of pejorative terms in public discourse such as "illegals," "human cargo," "queue-jumpers" (or worse) not only dehumanise asylum seekers (Rowe and O'Brien 2014) but also render them ineligible for the criteria of belonging to the nation or docile compliance. Underlying concerns about injustice or the lack of fairness in global forced migration permeate public perceptions, leading to views of asylum seekers as not being "genuine" refugees, not taking their place in the "queue," and unnecessarily consuming public resources (McHugh-Dillon 2015).

Counter-narratives of asylum seekers as deserving and vulnerable migrants wanting to build a life as new Australians are typically reserved for advocates, service providers, and community-based organisations—often with little discernible influence over welfare policy directions. Economic rationalist positions that highlight asylum seekers' potential contributions, should they be extended employment opportunities and a stronger safety net (Fleay et al. 2016; Lueck et al. 2015), have also proven ineffective in shifting public opinion towards appreciating the potential for reciprocity.

The suspicion with which many Australians view people seeking asylum, and the failure of advocates to convince the public that asylum seekers meet crucial benchmarks for welfare deservingness, provide decision-makers with justifications to exclude them. The state is thus emboldened to exercise full control over territorial border crossings (despite the exorbitant impacts on public budgets), to maintain a high degree of selectivity in the composition of the immigration program, and to create substantial socioeconomic impediments for asylum seekers who do reside in Australia.

In-country deterrence

While policies designed to deter unwanted immigrants are often manifest at the territorial border—for example, policed checkpoints, fortified detention centres, or armed military operations—a growing body of literature has examined the social, discursive, and virtual spaces in which states practice forms of border control. "In-country deterrence" (Hynes 2011) takes many forms: the use of racialised "othering" in official government language (Rumford

2006), anti-immigrant public information and marketing campaigns (Watkins 2017), employing citizens and police as "virtual border guards" (Yuval-Davis et al. 2018; Weber 2011), and surveillance technologies and identity management techniques (Vaughan-Williams 2010). While successive Australian governments have utilised variations of all these strategies, here we focus on the use of restricted socio-legal rights and entitlements (De Genova 2013) as the main form of in-country deterrence for asylum seekers who reside in Australia.

Withholding state welfare from non-citizens is considered a deterrent if one accepts the notion that generous government support incentivises unauthorised migration (Vogl 2019). Restricting migrants' access to government support—such as cash payments, healthcare, housing, and other basic services—can create situations of poverty and social exclusion for migrant welfare claimants, notionally deterring future unwanted arrivals. Various EU, UK, and US governments have used welfare restrictions to create the threat of destitution and marginalisation for asylum seekers in attempts to keep entries and applications as low as possible (see, e.g. Lomba 2006; Mayblin 2014; Nessel 2015). In Australia, recent policy and legislative decisions targeting asylum seekers and other non-citizens are part of a growing lineage of in-country deterrence policies (see, e.g. Mansouri 2002; McNevin and Correa-Velez 2006; Schloenhardt 2002).

At the time of writing there were approximately 100,000 people seeking asylum living in Australia who could be considered targets of deterrence policies. This includes almost 13,000 people who arrived by boat and hold a Bridging 'E' visa subclass (BVE) (DHA 2020a). The *Migration Act 1958 (Cth)* refers to these individuals as irregular or "illegal maritime arrivals" (IMAs), with the BVE allowing the individual to remain lawfully in Australia on a short-term basis while awaiting an immigration decision or preparing to leave the country. BVE holders are arguably the most vulnerable asylum seekers in Australia; their visas are subject to review or cancellation at any time, they are easily detained or deported if they breach the stipulated "code of behaviour," and they typically experience high levels of unemployment and homelessness (Fleay and Hartley 2016; Smith et al. 2020; Vogl 2019).[2]

Asylum seekers on BVEs may be eligible for Status Resolution Support Services (SRSS), which provide a basic safety net of a fortnightly income support payment, access to a caseworker, torture and trauma counselling, and subsidised medication (Okhovat 2018). In 2018, however, the Federal Government moved to restrict eligibility criteria for SRSS. People seeking asylum who had work permissions and did not meet a high threshold of vulnerability—defined by significant physical and mental health barriers, family issues, or emergencies—were to be exited from the program, even if they were unemployed and did not have any other source of income (ACOSS 2018). Those who stayed on the program no longer had access to the full suite of support. During parliamentary hearings, in May 2018, representatives from the Department of Home Affairs explained that the changes were designed to enable a "focus on people's capacity for self-agency and status resolution through granting of a visa or departure from Australia" (The Senate, Legal and Constitutional Affairs Committee 2018). Further, "individuals on a bridging visa with work rights, and who have the capacity to work, are expected to support themselves while their immigration status is being resolved. People have been referred to *Jobactive* [Australia's public employment services] if they need assistance finding work" (Hekmat 2018).

According to the Federal Government, the SRSS is not a "social welfare program," but rather a form of temporary support during immigration status resolution (Hekmat 2018). Since the SRSS is not enacted in welfare legislation, changes do not need the Prime Minister's Cabinet approval or to be passed by the legislature; the recent tightening of eligibility criteria were made via additions to the SRSS Operational Procedures Manual (RCOA 2019). In response, advocates and community sector organisations warned that most asylum seekers would be pushed into situations of poverty, homelessness, and destitution (Doherty 2018; St Vincent de Paul Society 2018; van Kooy and Ward 2018).

The second sub-category of asylum seekers targeted by the government's in-country deterrence framework are the approximately 17,000 boat arrivals that have been granted either a temporary protection visa (TPV) or safe haven enterprise visa (SHEV) (DHA 2020b). TPVs and SHEVs are 3–5-year visas granted to asylum applicants who are recognised as refugees or who otherwise satisfy Australia's humanitarian protection obligations. However, in keeping with the deterrence logic of the regime, the Australian Government has promised that as illegal boat arrivals they will never be permanently resettled in Australia (Reilly 2016). In 2018–19, the average duration from lodgement to primary decision for SHEV grants was 617 days (The Senate, Legal and Constitutional Affairs Committee 2019), meaning that asylum seekers on bridging visas may be waiting for periods exceeding two years only to be granted another temporary and conditional visa. This is in addition to the several years that people have been waiting before being allowed to apply for a visa.

TPV and SHEV holders do not have access to the SRSS program, nor are they eligible for the suite of settlement services available to permanent refugees. Under certain conditions they may access a modest income support payment, but unlike permanent refugees they are not eligible for government-subsidised education, housing, disability and mental health services, or public transport concessions (AHRC 2019).

After their visa expires, TPV and SHEV holders may reapply for another TPV or SHEV, but they may not apply for permanent refugee protection. In addition, SHEV holders, should they meet the stipulated condition of living, working, and/or studying in a designated regional area for at least three-and-a-half out of five years, are technically eligible to apply for a subsequent family or skilled visa. However, the visa fees, English language requirements, and skills tests associated with these visas make the bar "very high to clear" for any refugee group (Reilly 2018), as acknowledged by the then Minister for Immigration and now Prime Minister Scott Morrison in 2014:

> [W]hat we are doing here is not providing a pathway to welfare, and generational welfare at that. There is an opportunity here but I think it is a very limited opportunity . . . at the end of the day, no-one is getting a permanent protection visa.
>
> (Morrison 2014)

Temporary protection arrangements have been used in the EU to manage cross-country asylum flows (Beirens et al. 2016) and in the United States to allow migrants to remain during extraordinary circumstances in their home countries (USCIS 2020). UNHCR (2014) guidelines on temporary protection explicitly state that such arrangements should enable states to respond quickly to complex humanitarian crises but are not to be used to discourage people from seeking asylum under international law. In Australia, however, enforcement of a temporary and conditional visa system for people, who otherwise engage the state's refugee protection obligations, creates long-term uncertainty for its subjects and, therefore, adds another dimension to Australia's in-country deterrence regime.

Methodology

We conducted an inductive, thematic analysis of 49 de-identified transcripts from consultations facilitated by the Refugee Council of Australia (RCOA) in 2017–18. The RCOA is a national, membership-based peak body representing service providers and community-based and ethno-specific organisations that support refugees and people seeking asylum. RCOA regularly assesses the perspectives and experiences of its members through consultation forums across the country. Participants are asked a series of questions about asylum and refugee policy in Australia, invited to share lived experiences, and given the opportunity to raise concerns about service provision and support needs for migrant communities. Our sample was representative of community-level perspectives from each state and territory in Australia, a variety of stated migrant situations, residence status and duration of time in Australia, as well as a range of government-funded and charitable, not-for-profit organisations.[3] Consultations adhered to the RCOA's Ethical Guidelines for Research.

We imported an initial sample of 63 transcripts into the Nvivo software package and conducted a text keyword search to sort and rank priority transcripts for analysis. The search terms we used were based on the major themes of this book and our review of relevant literature, and included the following:

> "asylum" OR "seeker" OR "income support" OR "SRSS" OR "status resolution" OR "deterrence" OR "bridging visa" OR "BVE" OR "legacy caseload" OR "TPV" OR "SHEV" OR "temporary protection" OR "safe haven enterprise visa" OR "welfare" OR "deport" OR "fast track"

This query returned 49 transcripts with 697 individual references to the aforementioned terms. Following Thomas (2006), we then applied an inductive analytical approach, involving multiple readings of the transcripts and iteration of a coding structure. The lead author, who developed a two-level coding frame using Nvivo, read all transcripts after which transcripts were re-read and select passages coded by the co-author. We developed 13 top-level codes with a further eight second-order codes. The most densely coded themes in the sample were then grouped to arrive at broad themes for discussion.

Waiting and dependence while seeking asylum

Both asylum seekers and community sector respondents repeatedly raised the significance of long waiting periods during visa processing, with attendant impacts on individual and family mental health as well as financial and material well-being. The precarious situations in which asylum seekers found themselves while waiting for status resolution led to widespread dependence on state welfare, but more so on community and charitable sources of support and emergency relief.

Immigration processes and visa applications

The refugee status determination process for people seeking asylum in Australia has been shown to be extremely difficult to navigate for individuals who are not proficient in English and who lack adequate legal support (AHRC 2019; Ghezelbash 2020). People who arrive in Australia without a valid visa are not eligible for funded legal assistance (Kaldor Centre 2019). Both community sector organisations and migrants in our sample described a complex, opaque system characterised by uncertain application procedures, frequently changing rules or conditions, and inconsistent messages from the Department of Home Affairs. Some respondents described the problem in terms of bureaucratic inefficiencies: one representative of a Brisbane-based service provider referred to a "chaotic, hopeless system" with a "lack of transparency and consistency around the visa process," particularly for BVE holders. Decisions on asylum applications were largely considered arbitrary or unpredictable. Several asylum seekers corroborated this view: one male asylum seeker in regional New South Wales said, "I don't know in what order they process the applications. It's just by chance." Other asylum seeker respondents compared their situations with those of people who had been awarded permanent protection visas, unable to explain the justifications for different visa outcomes.

Organisations providing support to asylum seekers were more likely to see malevolent intent in the design of the asylum system. For example, a Sydney-based service provider described the government as waging "nothing short of war against the humanitarian visa space," with "unbelievable decisions and discretion being exercised in some very distressing situations." Referring to the stipulated requirements for accessing income support payments, another service provider in the Northern Territory made the direct link to the government's deterrence strategy, commenting, "I think they're hoping that they'll starve [asylum seekers] out . . . and they'll just go home." These responses reflect service sector perceptions of a system designed to be harsh and unjust.

Asylum seeker respondents often mentioned long periods of time waiting for decisions or information from immigration officials, leaving them with significant uncertainty about their long-term future. Waiting in anticipation of an outcome was commonly referred to as "limbo"—for example, one female asylum seeker in a Melbourne consultation said:

> Now it's been more than four years, [many asylum seekers] are just waiting in this limbo situation. No one is going to answer our questions. We don't know if we are going to stay here or not and how long it will take for us to get a clear answer.

The experience of waiting for an outcome that could come at any time, with the outcome itself characterised by perceived "chaos" or randomness, creates high levels of stress for those affected. A dialogue between two male asylum seekers in one Sydney consultation also reflected how waiting for an immigration decision could cause interrelated experiences of fear, anxiety, and social isolation:

> Respondent 1: "It has become quite a sensitive time for me. I am living with fear now. Every time the phone rings, I get nervous that I am going to receive a bad call. It is a constant fear and a sensitive time. It has become quite unbearable for us. Both for my wife, and for myself . . ."
>
> Respondent 2: "I can relate to that. Because you are waiting and you don't know what the decision is, every day when the postman comes around, you start getting panic attacks. Because you don't know if the letter is there . . . Social isolation as well, because you do not want to meet up with people. Because you cannot afford to go and catch up for a coffee. You don't want people to see you are still in the same position. [For] years, everyone is advancing in their lives, getting married, getting new jobs, buying a house but then you are stuck in the same situation and not getting anywhere. So you end up cutting yourself off from everybody else."

This exchange is emblematic of the deterrence logic underpinning Australia's onshore asylum system: waiting under threat of a negative decision creates "fear" and "panic" that makes life "unbearable" for subjects; it prevents the development of social ties and networks between migrants and leaves subjects "stuck" in social and economic stasis, unable to progress and build a better life for themselves. Similarly, some asylum seeker respondents described how long waiting periods for immigration decisions negatively impacted on the quality of their relationships with family members overseas.

Mental health impacts

Scholars have continued to document the pervasive mental health effects of being an asylum seeker with unresolved immigration status (see, in particular, Campbell and Steel 2015; Procter et al. 2018). According to respondents in our sample, fear, stress, and anxiety induced by waiting in the asylum system led to significant mental health issues or aggravation of pre-existing traumas. Many families, including children, were described as isolated, traumatised, and under severe mental strain. One male asylum seeker in a Sydney consultation expressed his frustration on behalf of his family, and his feelings of being trapped in this limbo situation:

> I lost everything . . . My wife, she has panic attacks. She is sick and has anxiety. We can't do anything . . . I do not know what is going on inside the government. I am confused. I am so crazy. . . . When I came to this country I was 24 years old. [Now] I am 31 years old; I can't do anything. I had a lot of plans; I had a lot of dreams. I wanted to make a future, but now, I lost everything. You can't get back to 24 years old. I am 31; I lost seven years. I lost everything. All my kids are sick, depressed. They can't talk to anyone. We aren't allowed to go out. We can't do anything.

Another male asylum seeker in a Sydney consultation described himself as "a bomb ready to explode," that he was "crushed and soulless," along with his deep concern that his child would be severely affected by these experiences and "never be able to contribute to this country." These responses highlight the deleterious effects of long-term limbo, with declining mental health a central concern for both adults and children. That a family of asylum seekers could wait seven years for a resolution of their claims for protection reflects both significant system inefficiencies, as noted by some respondents, and an intentional strategy to deter onshore asylum seekers through attrition.

The consultation data also points to a potential negative by-product of in-country deterrence: that in creating precarious conditions for asylum seekers, Federal Government policies place aggrieved individuals, with fragile mental health and frustrations with public institutions and administration, directly into communities. In this vein, one respondent asked rhetorically, "Violence and fights and even car accidents asylum seekers are involved in, why do they happen? All are caused because of anxiety, because of constant worries and uncertainty."

The mental health impacts of waiting in the asylum system, for minors, was a particularly concerning theme to emerge from the RCOA consultations. Several migrant and community sector respondents described situations such as single mothers being isolated without access to childcare services and unable to attend to their children's mental health needs, teachers struggling to engage students who had significant unacknowledged trauma, and non-disclosure of mental health issues among young people from asylum seeking backgrounds. One representative of a Melbourne-based service provider described a situation emblematic of these problems:

> I'm working with one young person who's just like given up, she's like [quoting asylum seeker], "What's the point in trying at school because I feel like I'm going to be sent back to [her home country]? I have no future here." School doesn't know how to deal with her, she won't engage with mental health services, the parents are concerned about how they will be found by the community. So there's also a lot of shame when talking about mental health issues, they're concealing a lot of information as well, and not disclosing, and it's six months down the track and they're only starting to tell you the significant trauma . . . before they get to that really tertiary level of talking about suicide.

This response highlights how young people from asylum-seeking backgrounds in Australia may not be engaging with critical mental health supports, either by choice or because of obstacles built-in to the service system.

Financial and material hardship

The financial and material difficulties associated with being an asylum seeker in Australia are well documented (see, e.g. Hartley and Fleay 2014; Okhovat 2018; van Kooy and Bowman 2018). Our data corroborate these accounts, with additional emphasis on asylum seekers' dependence on forms of community support—both formal and informal. A central theme in many respondents' comments was asylum seekers' capacity to meet their costs of living, constrained by poor employment prospects and lack of access to government support or subsidies. This stands in contrast to the welfare entitlements of recognised, permanent refugees, and is thought to lead to dependency on community organisations, volunteers, emergency relief and homelessness services, as well as informal support from families and wider migrant communities. For example, a male asylum seeker during a Perth consultation described his relative destitution: "I am in the situation I have not got any job yet. For me personally, I do not know where I am going to sleep tonight. I have not got any place to sleep and to eat."

Given the restricted access to welfare, it is perhaps unsurprising that people in this situation would be quickly rendered homeless or without money to afford food. As noted earlier, people seeking asylum on BVEs are now only eligible for SRSS income support if they meet high thresholds of physical or mental vulnerability; it is incapacity to work, not unemployment, that renders them eligible to access SRSS payments. SHEV and TPV holders may access an income support payment (special benefit), reserved for people with severe financial hardship—but this comes with job-seeking requirements as part of Australia's system of labour market activation policies.

One Brisbane-based service provider representative noted the high levels of unemployment amongst asylum seekers in their region, with an assessment that the "generosity of volunteers" was making up the gap in publicly funded services. The respondent also verified the widespread poverty of asylum seekers:

> There are people becoming homeless and destitute, family issues, child safety issues . . . They've got no money for food, no money for rent. They're living in this hell with nowhere to go or no supports. There is no plan for them.

During a Sydney consultation, another service provider representative described a "huge gap" in the sector's visibility of asylum seekers who are not receiving any formal services, suggesting that some may be working illegally, and others are "just relying on family and friends." The lack of accurate information about this situation makes estimation of its true scale difficult to ascertain; however, there is clearly a significant proportion of people amongst the 30,000 who are the target of Australia's in-country deterrence policies who rely on informal support to survive. There were numerous personal accounts in our sample that corroborated these claims of dependence, including those who noted that people exited SRSS "into nothing." This resulted in service providers seeing significant increases in demand for emergency relief (e.g. food banks) and homelessness services.

Discussion and conclusions

This chapter illuminates how welfare policy in Australia is used as a tool of migration control, to coerce current asylum seekers and deter future arrivals from seeking asylum. It aimed to develop a critical understanding of the nature, impacts, and outcomes of recent changes to Australia's (already minimal) welfare safety net for people seeking asylum on bridging and temporary visas, and how restrictions on their access to welfare force them into situations of limbo, waiting, and dependence on community support. We focused on two significant themes from our analysis of consultation data provided by the RCOA—waiting and dependence—which characterise how many people seeking asylum experience life in Australia. Following other scholars in the field (Fleay and Hartley 2016; Schloenhardt 2002; Vogl 2019; Weber and Pickering 2014), we argue that these experiences are part of an intentional deterrence strategy targeting current and future unauthorised immigration.

The first component of in-country deterrence is the creation of universally negative experiences of the status resolution system, with severe impacts on people's mental health. Both migrant and service provider respondents in our sample described complex and obfuscatory processes characterised by long periods of uncertainty and ultimately unjust outcomes. While a lack of English language skills and financial and legal resources may contribute to negative outcomes for many applicants, it is the lack of transparency and efficiency in government decision-making that is the primary driver of ongoing hardship for this group. Our analysis shows that prolonged periods of waiting and not knowing about official decisions create high levels of stress and anxiety for asylum seekers—and in more extreme cases, depression and suicidal ideation. Individuals, families, children, and young people are equally at risk. In addition, the forging of strong social connections between migrants and non-migrants is obstructed by asylum seekers' pervasive fear, anxiety, and mistrust.

The second component of in-country deterrence is the material precarity of people seeking asylum, manufactured by minimal state welfare provisions and over-exposure to market conditions. Asylum seekers on bridging and temporary visas face a range of difficulties gaining paid employment, in addition to those faced by other migrant workers, such as restricted access to employment services, subsidised vocational education and training, and transport concessions (van Kooy and Randrianarisoa 2017). High levels of unemployment, underemployment, and exploitative work amongst people seeking asylum (see, e.g. Fleay et al. 2016) intersects with fragile mental health and social isolation to create untenable living conditions. Our analysis shows that this leads to asylum seekers' widespread dependence on local sources of support provided by volunteers, charity organisations, family, and friends. However, these are simply coping strategies that exist in lieu of adequate welfare provision, unlikely to improve asylum seekers' quality of life while awaiting resolution of their immigration status.

Maintaining control over the state's resources and preserving the mainstream way of life are central to the logic and functioning of welfare states. Conditional systems, such as Australia's, draw a hard line at unauthorised immigration—the *sans papiers* who, without an invitation, are clearly differentiated as undeserving or "never deserving" claimants for state support. The disqualification of people seeking asylum from welfare deservingness enables the Australian Government to enact the twin strategies of in-country deterrence: slow, confusing, and often unjust immigration processes, combined with restricted access to forms of support that would enable a better standard of living. The aim may well be attrition—forcing onshore asylum applicants to choose between a destitute existence in Australia, with the promise that they will "never be permanently resettled," or returning to their countries of origin. Ultimately, the outcome has been the creation of a virtual underclass of people in the community who face a tortured existence while seeking asylum in Australia.

Notes

1 See further, Chapter 1 in this volume.
2 See further, Chapter 5 in this volume.
3 It should be noted, however, that we did not have access to comprehensive data concerning individual participant characteristics and their specific backgrounds to inform our analysis.

References

Australian Council of Social Services. (2018) 'We implore the government to stop the cuts to people seeking asylum', *Media release*. 18 June 2018. ACOSS.

Australian Human Rights Commission. (2019) *Lives on Hold: Refugees and Asylum Seekers in the "Legacy Caseload"*. AHRC.

Beirens, H., Maas, S., Petronella, S. and van der Velden, M. (2016) *Study on the Temporary Protection Directive: Final Report*. European Commission.

Cameron, M. (2013) 'From "Queue Jumpers" to "Absolute Scum of the Earth": Refugee and organised criminal deviance in Australian asylum policy', *Australian Journal of Politics & History*, 2: 241.

Campbell, E. J. and Steel, E. J. (2015) 'Mental distress and human rights of asylum seekers', *Journal of Public Mental Health*, 14: 43.

Corlett, D. (2000) 'Politics, symbolism and the asylum seeker issue', *University of New South Wales Law Journal*, 23: 13.

De Genova, N. (2013) 'Spectacles of migrant 'illegality': The scene of exclusion, the obscene of inclusion', *Ethnic and Racial Studies*, 36: 1180.

Department of Home Affairs. (2020a) *Illegal Maritime Arrivals on Bridging E visa*. DHA, Australian Government.

Department of Home Affairs. (2020b) *IMA Legacy Caseload: Report on Processing Status and Outcomes*. DHA, Australian Government.

Derrida, J. (2002) *Acts of Religion*. Routledge.

Doherty, B. (2018) '"New dose of cruelty": Up to 7,000 asylum seekers to lose income support' *The Guardian*, 30 March.

Fleay, C. and Hartley, L. (2016) 'I Feel Like a Beggar': Asylum seekers living in the australian community without the right to work', *International Migration & Integration*, 17: 1031.

Fleay, C., Lumbus, A. and Hartley, L. (2016) 'People seeking asylum in Australia and their access to employment: Just what do we know?', *Cosmopolitan Civil Societies: An Interdisciplinary Journal*, 8: 63.

Ghezelbash, D. (2020) 'How refugees succeed in visa reviews: New research reveals the factors that matter', *The Conversation*, 9 March.

Goot, M. and Watson, I. (2011) *Population, Immigration and Asylum Seekers: Patterns in Australian Public Opinion*. Parliamentary Library of Australia, Canberra.

Haggis, J. and Schech, S. (2010) 'Refugees, settlement processes and citizenship making: An Australian case study', *National Identities*, 12: 365.

Hartley, L. and Fleay, C. (2014) 'Policy as punishment: Asylum seekers in the community without the right to work', *Centre for Human Rights Education, Curtin University*, February.

Hekmat, A. (2018) 'Asylum seekers' benefits cut by Home Affairs', *The Saturday Paper*, 14–20 April.

Hirsch, A. L. (2017) 'The Borders beyond the border: Australia's extraterritorial migration controls', *Refugee Survey Quarterly*, 36: 48.
Hynes, P. (2011) *The Dispersal and Social Exclusion of Asylum Seekers: Between Liminality and Belonging*. Bristol University Press, Policy Press.
Kaldor Centre. (2019) *Do People Seeking Asylum Receive Legal Assistance?* Andrew & Renata Kaldor Centre for International Refugee Law, UNSW.
Klocker, N. (2004) 'Community Antagonism Towards Asylum Seekers in Port Augusta South Australia', *Australian Geographical Studies*, 42: 1.
Larsen, C. A. (2008) 'The Institutional Logic of Welfare Attitudes: How Welfare Regimes Influence Public Support', *Comparative Political Studies*, 41: 145.
Lomba, S. D. (2006) 'The Threat of Destitution as a Deterrent against Asylum Seeking in the European Union', *Refuge: Canada's Journal on Refugees*, 81.
Lueck, K., Due, C. and Augoustinos, M. (2015) 'Neoliberalism and nationalism: Representations of asylum seekers in the Australian mainstream news media', *Discourse & Society*, 26: 608.
Maguire, A. (2017) '"Fake refugees": Dutton adopts an alternative fact to justify our latest human rights violation', *The Conversation*, 22 May.
Mansouri, F. (2002) 'The legacy of Australia's treatment of onshore asylum seekers', *Mots Pluriels*, 21: 1.
Mayblin, L. (2014) 'Asylum, welfare and work: Reflections on research in asylum and refugee studies', *International Journal of Sociology and Social Policy*, 34: 375.
McHugh-Dillon, H. (2015) '"If they are genuine refugees, why?" Public attitudes to unauthorised arrivals in Australia', Victorian Foundation for Survivors of Torture.
McNevin, A. and Correa-Velez, I. (2006) 'Asylum seekers living in the community on bridging visa E: Community sector's response to detrimental policies', *Australian Journal of Social Issues*, 41: 125.
Morrison, S. (2014) 'Reintroducing TPVs to resolve Labor's asylum legacy caseload; Cambodia', Transcript of press conference: Parliament House, Canberra: 25 September 2014.
Nessel, L. A. (2015) 'Deliberate destitution as deterrent: Withholding the right to work and undermining asylum protection', *San Diego Law Review*, 52: 313.
Okhovat, S. (2018) *With Empty Hands: How the Australian Government Is Forcing People Seeking Asylum into Destitution*. Refugee Council of Australia.
Pickering, S. (2001) 'Common sense and original deviancy: News discourses and asylum seekers in Australia', *Journal of Refugee Studies*, 14: 169.
Procter, N. G., Kenny, M. A., Eaton, H. and Grech, C. (2018) 'Lethal hopelessness: Understanding and responding to asylum seeker distress and mental deterioration', *International Journal of Mental Health Nursing*, 27: 448.
Refugee Council of Australia. (2019) *Starving Them Out: How the Australian Government Is Forcing People Seeking Asylum into Destitution*, 2 February 2019. RCOA.
Reilly, A. (2016) 'Same old rhetoric cannot justify banning refugees from Australia', *The Conversation*, 30 October.
Reilly, A. (2018) 'The vulnerability of safe haven enterprise visa holders: Balancing work, protection and future prospects', *University of New South Wales Law Journal*, 41(3): 30.
Rowe, E. and O'Brien, E. (2014) '"Genuine" refugees or illegitimate "boat people": Political constructions of asylum seekers and refugees in the Malaysia Deal debate', *Australian Journal of Social Issues*, 49: 171.
Rumford, C. (2006) 'Theorizing Borders', *European Journal of Social Theory* 9: 155.

Sandelind, C. (2019) 'Can the welfare state justify restrictive asylum policies? A critical approach', *Ethical Theory & Moral Practice*, 22: 331.

Schloenhardt, A. (2002) 'Deterrence, detention and denial: Asylum seekers in Australia', *University of Queensland Law Journal*, 22: 54.

Smith, D., McKay, F. H. and Lippi, K. (2020) 'Experiences of homelessness by people seeking asylum in Australia: A review of published and "grey" literature', *Social Policy & Administration*, 54: 441.

St Vincent de Paul Society. (2018) *The Destitution of Asylum Seekers in Australia: Cuts to Status Resolution Support Service Payments*. St Vincent de Paul Society National Council.

The Senate, Legal and Constitutional Affairs Committee. (2018) 'Question on notice no. 99, 2017–18', Additional Estimates.

The Senate, Legal and Constitutional Affairs Committee. (2019) 'Question on notice no. 180, 2019–20', Supplementary Budget Estimates.

Thomas, D. R. (2006) 'A general inductive approach for analyzing qualitative evaluation data', *American Journal of Evaluation*, 27: 237.

United Nations High Commissioner for Refugees. (2014) *Guidelines on Temporary Protection or Stay Arrangements*. UNHCR.

US Citizenship and Immigration Services. (2020) *Temporary Protected Status*. www.uscis.gov/humanitarian/temporary-protected-status (accessed 30 May 2020).

van Kooy, J. and Bowman, D. (2018) 'Surrounded with so much uncertainty': Asylum seekers and manufactured precarity in Australia', *Journal of Ethnic and Migration Studies*, 45(5): 693.

van Kooy, J. and Randrianarisoa, A. (2017) *Giving Asylum Seekers a Chance: Insights from a Pilot Employment Program*. Brotherhood of St Laurence, Fitzroy.

van Kooy, J. and Ward, T. (2018) *An Unnecessary Penalty: Economic Impacts of Changes to the Status Resolution Support Services (SRSS)*. RCOA.

van Oorschot, W. (2000) 'Who should get what, and why', *Policy and Politics*, 28: 33.

Vaughan-Williams, N. (2010) 'The UK border security continuum: Virtual biopolitics and the simulation of the sovereign ban', *Environment and Planning D*, 28: 1071.

Vogl, A. (2019) 'Crimmigration and refugees: Bridging visas, criminal cancellations and "Living in the Community" as punishment and deterrence', in Billings, P. (ed.) *Crimmigration in Australia: Law, Politics, and Society*. Springer, p. 149.

Watkins, J. (2017) 'Australia's irregular migration information campaigns: Border externalization, spatial imaginaries, and extraterritorial subjugation', *Territory, Politics, Governance*, 5: 282.

Weber, L. (2011) 'It sounds like they shouldn't be here': Immigration checks on the streets of Sydney', *Policing and Society* 21: 456.

Weber, L. and Pickering, S. (2014) 'Constructing voluntarism: Technologies of 'intent management' in Australian Border Controls', in Schwenken, H. and Ruß-Sattar, S. (eds) *New Border and Citizenship Politics, Migration, Diasporas and Citizenship Series*. Palgrave Macmillan, p. 17.

Yuval-Davis, N., Wemyss, G. and Cassidy, K. (2018) 'Everyday bordering, belonging and the reorientation of british immigration legislation', *Sociology*, 52: 228.

Chapter 5

The growing challenge of precarious housing and homelessness for refugees and asylum seekers in Australia

Emma Fell

Introduction

Access to safe, stable housing is established as a fundamental human right in numerous international treaties to which Australia is a party.[1] However, asylum seekers and refugees granted temporary protection living in the Australian community face significant, and often insurmountable, barriers to accessing secure accommodation (Fozdar and Hartley 2013: 50; Yeung 2014: 26). These housing needs have been largely ignored in homelessness policy debate (Liddy et al. 2010). Since 2013 the Australian Government has targeted a group of refugees and asylum seekers, described as the "Legacy Caseload," with punitive policies, including increasingly restricted access to income support and the denial of work rights to some members of this cohort (van Kooy and Ward 2018: 3; AHRC 2019: 50). This policy framework has pushed many people into destitution, rendering stable accommodation impossible to attain (Okhovat 2018: 11; Olliff 2014: 8).

It has largely fallen to non-governmental organisations (NGOs), community groups, faith-based networks, and some state governments to fill the resulting housing gap. A range of innovative community-based responses has been adopted around Australia, often with minimal government support or recognition (Smith et al. 2020: 447). However, despite the value of such efforts, this piecemeal, *ad hoc*, approach is insufficient to meet the current level of need (JSS 2015: 2). While increased state government support for such schemes may go some way to addressing this growing challenge, ultimately, a long-term solution requires substantial policy change at both the federal and state government levels. Given that the punitive nature of the current federal policy regime is designed to both control asylum seekers and refugees already in Australia and deter potential future irregular migrants, realising a tenable solution to this issue is highly challenging in the present political context.

This chapter explores the connection between the processes of seeking asylum in Australia for certain "boat arrivals" and homelessness or housing precarity. It is argued that the denial of stable housing to members of the Legacy Caseload is one element of policies designed to punish members of this cohort,

DOI: 10.4324/9781003298595-10

encourage them to return to their countries of origin, and deter future irregular migration (Tazreiter 2017: 243). By contrast, the treatment of people arriving lawfully (i.e. with prior authorisation) by plane who subsequently seek asylum appears far less punitive and usefully can be compared with the Legacy Caseload.

The "Legacy Caseload"

The so-called Legacy Caseload is a cohort of approximately 30,000 refugees and asylum seekers who arrived in Australia by boat between 13 August 2012 and 1 January 2014 who were not subject to offshore processing on Nauru or Manus Island (Kaldor Centre for International Refugee Law 2019c: 1). This cohort is subject to different rules and processes from other asylum seekers and refugees due to a range of substantial changes to Australia's immigration laws implemented by the conservative Federal Government since 2013 (Kaldor Centre for International Refugee Law 2019c: 1; Karlsen and Phillips 2017: 34). Many view the approach adopted towards the Legacy Caseload as punitive, especially in contrast to the approach to other aspects of the refugee-humanitarian program (van Kooy and Bowman 2019: 694; Hugo 2014: 869; AHRC 2017: 41). Government rhetoric tends to dehumanise asylum seekers and refugees, particularly those who arrived by boat, and significantly influences community perceptions (Everuss 2020: 6; McKay et al. 2011: 117; McAdam 2013: 435). Due to this restrictive policy regime, members of the Legacy Caseload are particularly vulnerable to experiences of precarity and "physical, psychological and emotional trauma" (van Kooy and Bowman 2019: 697).

Members of the Legacy Caseload are barred by law from applying for permanent protection visas (PPV) and are instead restricted to temporary protection visas (TPVs) and safe haven enterprise visas (SHEVs). These visas last for three and five years respectively before a subsequent application must be lodged (AHRC 2019: 65; DHA 2020a). This group is also subject to a "fast track" application process, which provides for only a limited form of merits review, conducted on the papers without an oral hearing and generally without new information being permissible (AHRC 2019: 28; Karlsen and Phillips 2017: 30; McDonald and O'Sullivan 2018: 1005). There are serious concerns about the procedural fairness and rigour of this process (McDonald and O'Sullivan 2018: 1006; Kenny and Procter 2016: 64). Furthermore, government-funded legal assistance for this cohort has been withdrawn, increasing the challenge of navigating this process (Kaldor Centre for International Refugee Law 2019a: 4; AHRC 2019: 26). Despite the process being described as "fast track," there have been lengthy delays in the processing of these applications (AHRC 2019: 26).

Many members of the Legacy Caseload were barred from applying for protection for up to four years after their arrival by boat, placing them in a prolonged state of limbo (Kaldor Centre for International Refugee Law 2019c: 1; Okhovat 2018: 7). The Federal Government then imposed an arbitrary deadline of 31 October 2017 for all applications to be lodged, which almost all members of the cohort met (AHRC 2019: 28). At 31 March 2020, 5,958 members of the Legacy Caseload were still awaiting either a primary or limited merits review decision (DHA 2020c: 2). Of those awaiting a decision, 3,173 were living in Victoria, 2,211 were living in New South Wales, and 240 were living in Queensland (DHA 2020c: 4). 17,317 had received a positive protection status determination and been granted either a TPV or a SHEV (DHA 2020c: 2). A further 7,761 had received a negative outcome (DHA 2020c: 5). An unknown number of those who received a negative outcome on the merits of their claim may be pursuing judicial review of the adverse decision.

Visa categories

TPVs and SHEVs

Members of the Legacy Caseload who are recognised as refugees are granted either a TPV or a SHEV. At 31 March 2020, 8,431 TPVs and 16,647 SHEVs had been granted (DHA 2020c). There are restricted pathways to permanent residency for SHEV holders and the requirements are extremely difficult to satisfy (Reilly 2018: 876; Taylor 2018: 211; AHRC 2017: 43). No such pathway exists for TPV holders (AHRC 2019: 68). The temporary nature of these visas is widely criticised, as the need to regularly reapply exacerbates stress and can significantly worsen mental health problems (AHRC 2017: 42, 2019: 66; Hafeez-Baig 2016: 128). TPV and SHEV holders have no right of family reunification and must apply for permission to travel overseas (Hafeez-Baig 2016: 124, 125; Taylor 2018: 212). TPV and SHEV holders have access to Medicare, have work rights, and are entitled to minimal social security payments through Centrelink (Hartley et al. 2019: 5). However, there are limits on SHEV holders' ability to access these payments and also satisfy the SHEV pathway requirements (Hartley et al. 2019: 5).

Bridging visas

Most members of the Legacy Caseload who are still awaiting an initial visa decision, or who are engaged in some form of review, hold a Bridging Visa E (BVE) (AHRC 2019: 49). BVEs are subject to regular renewal, causing ongoing uncertainty for asylum seekers. At 31 March 2020, 12,742 members of the Legacy Caseload held BVEs in Australia, with 5,860 of those in Victoria, 4,764 in New South Wales and 867 in Queensland (DHA 2020b: 4).

Most, but not all, people seeking asylum on BVEs have work rights, but they may struggle to secure employment (Okhovat 2018: 12). BVE holders are not eligible for social security through Centrelink, resulting in many asylum seekers on BVEs living in the community without adequate income and unable to support themselves and their families (AHRC 2019: 50). Some BVE holders may be eligible for support through the Status Resolution Support Scheme (SRSS). However, the support available through SRSS is often insufficient to meet basic needs, and access to this service has been severely restricted over recent years (AHRC 2019: 51; Olliff 2014: 17; ASRC 2019: 6). This has resulted in many BVE holders being exited from the program, leaving them without the necessary welfare supports (Okhovat 2018: 18), and others have had the support they receive significantly reduced (van Kooy and Ward 2018: 5). Most BVE holders have access to Medicare, although it can be difficult to consistently access medical treatment due to the short nature of BVEs (Okhovat 2018: 13).

Asylum seekers who receive a negative refugee status determination at the primary decision-making stage and upon review are referred to as "finally determined." Notwithstanding that they still have legal avenues open to them, including judicial review and ministerial intervention, which can ultimately lead to the grant of a substantive visa (AHRC 2019: 54). These processes can be lengthy and yet asylum seekers are generally ineligible for SRSS, which may leave them without income for an extended period while the legal challenges are pursued (AHRC 2019: 54).

Rejected asylum seekers without a valid visa

There are also some members of the Legacy Caseload who are now living in the community without any visa. These are asylum seekers whose applications have been "finally determined," and who either have no appeal options left or have disengaged from legal processes (Smith et al. 2020: 442). These unsuccessful visa claimants have no entitlement to any income support, no work or study rights, and no access to Medicare (Smith et al. 2020: 442). Additionally, as immigration detention is mandatory for unlawful non-citizens, they are at real risk of being detained and, in principle, removed to their country of origin at any time, despite Australia's *non-refoulement* obligations (AHRC 2019: 95). Irrespective of the determination that they are not entitled to refugee status, these asylum seekers may maintain their claims for protection and therefore be unwilling to voluntarily return home. This creates a situation of extreme vulnerability. Worryingly, as more asylum seekers receive negative refugee status determinations and exhaust their legal (review or ministerial intervention) options, there are likely to be increasing numbers of people in this precarious situation.

Some members of the Legacy Caseload are deprived of their liberty in immigration detention, pending verification of their identity or national security checks, for example. These people may be released into "community detention," in which case they are provided with housing and services to meet their basic needs but are not permitted to work (AHRC 2019: 101). At 31 March 2020, there were 512 asylum seekers, who arrived by boat, held in immigration detention (DHA 2020d: 4).

Impact of this policy context on members of the Legacy Caseload

All members of the Legacy Caseload experience significant levels of disadvantage, but asylum seekers, particularly those without any government support, are viewed as the most vulnerable segment of this cohort (Weber 2019: 232). Most members of the Legacy Caseload, excluding some BVE holders and those without a visa, are entitled to work, and asylum seekers and refugees generally report that they do want to work to support themselves (JSS 2015: 4). However, while the Federal Government has frequently stated that those with work rights are expected to support themselves, asylum seekers and refugees face significant barriers to accessing stable work (van Kooy and Ward 2018: 5; van Kooy and Bowman 2019: 698; Curry et al. 2018: 436). The continuing impacts of trauma, a lack of English skills, and difficulty having overseas qualifications and experience recognised in Australia can all make it difficult to secure stable employment (Reilly 2018: 884; JSS 2015: 4). This cohort also lacks proper access to English language tuition and employment support services (Kaldor Centre for International Refugee Law 2019b: 4; Olliff 2014: 24). Employers may not properly understand the work rights attached to temporary visas (JSS 2015: 4; Smith et al. 2020: 443). Additionally, the temporary nature of BVEs severely limits employment opportunities, as it can be very challenging to find an employer willing to accept these unstable conditions (JSS 2015: 4; van Kooy and Bowman 2019: 699).

These structural barriers may leave asylum seekers and refugees vulnerable to exploitation in the workplace, but given their vulnerable situation many are reluctant to report unscrupulous employers (Reilly 2016: 11). Where work is secured it is likely to be low-paid and short-term with highly variable hours, and asylum seekers and refugees are likely to have a high turnover of jobs (Curry et al. 2018: 436; van Kooy and Bowman 2019: 700–701). These conditions often contribute to a sense of precarity, even though the person may have an income (van Kooy and Bowman 2019: 701). In this context, work rights can be of limited value, particularly for asylum seekers (van Kooy and Bowman 2019: 704). Without work most asylum seekers have no income, and this financial hardship often leads to destitution and deterioration in physical and mental health (AHRC 2019: 54).

Asylum seekers and refugees often experience severe physical and mental health issues due to their experiences in their home countries, during their journeys to Australia, and throughout the visa application process (Hedrick et al. 2019: 2; Procter et al. 2018: 451; Okhovat 2018: 20). The temporary visa status of Legacy Caseload members leaves them vulnerable to precarity, and asylum seekers in particular are subject to ongoing insecurity due to their unresolved immigration status (Rutherford 2015: 96; Smith et al. 2020: 443). Many members report that living in the community without adequate support compromises their "sense of humanity through undermining [their] autonomy and independence" (Hartley and Fleay 2017: 57; Fleay et al. 2013: 483). Because of the protracted nature of the asylum process for this cohort, many have now lived in a state of limbo for many years enduring poverty and chronic uncertainty (Hartley and Fleay 2017: 57). Such experiences of enforced poverty are known to negatively impact mental health (Hartley and Fleay 2017: 56; Hartley et al. 2017: 1194). In these circumstances, members of the Legacy Caseload may be severely limited in their ability to exercise agency over their lives and safeguard their sense of humanity (Hartley and Fleay 2017: 59).

In this context of vulnerability and financial hardship, members of the Legacy Caseload, particularly asylum seekers, are often forced to turn to community organisations for support, although such resources are generally scarce (AHRC 2019: 52). There is also significant pressure on established refugee communities to voluntarily support vulnerable members of the Legacy Caseload (AHRC 2019: 53). Asylum seekers and refugees in this cohort are placed in an extremely vulnerable position due to the denial of services on many fronts, and the challenges faced in securing stable accommodation must be understood in this context.

Comparison to air arrivals

By contrast, asylum seekers who arrive in Australia by plane, with a valid visa, and then apply for a protection visa, are treated significantly differently. First, asylum seekers arriving by air are eligible for permanent protection visas (Smith et al. 2020: 443). This is a very important distinction, as permanent status fosters a sense of stability and security and leads to better employment and housing outcomes. PPV applicants have access to a fairer refugee status determination process including an independent, *de novo*, review at the Administrative Appeals Tribunal (AHRC 2019: 29). PPV holders can access a wider range of social security, settlement support services, and employment services; have the same access to education as any other permanent resident; and may access free English language education (Kaldor Centre for International Refugee Law 2019b: 4; AHRC 2017: 44). They may also sponsor immediate family members to come to Australia and need not request permission to travel (Kaldor Centre for International Refugee Law 2019b: 4).

All asylum seekers and refugees are vulnerable due to their experiences of trauma, and those who arrive in Australia by air and then apply for protection do face significant challenges, including many of those experienced by members of the Legacy Caseload (McDonald and O'Sullivan 2018: 1007; van Kooy and Ward 2018: 4). However, the increased vulnerability created by the punitive policy framework relating to boat arrivals significantly exacerbates these issues and increases people's likelihood of experiencing homelessness (Olliff 2014: 3).

Experiences of housing precarity and homelessness

In Australia, homelessness is understood through a three-tier definition from Chamberlain and MacKenzie (2003: 1–2):

> *Primary homelessness*, which aligns with the prevailing perception that homelessness is "rooflessness". This includes anyone without conventional accommodation, such as; "people living on the streets, sleeping in parks, squatting in derelict buildings, or using cars or railway carriages for temporary shelter".
>
> *Secondary homelessness*, which includes those who move frequently between various forms of temporary shelter, such as; people staying in transitional or emergency accommodation, people staying temporarily with others, and "people staying in boarding houses on a short-term basis" for 12 weeks or less.
>
> *Tertiary homelessness*, which includes people living in boarding houses for 13 weeks or longer. The accommodation is not self-contained, meaning residents do not have their own bedroom, living room, kitchen or bathroom facilities. These people also do not have the security provided by a lease.

People who are homeless or at risk of homelessness are among the most marginalised and vulnerable members of society (Liddy et al. 2010: 12; Steen 2018: 167). Homelessness destroys stability and connection and has long-lasting impacts (Olliff 2014: 7; Steen 2018: 167). While asylum seekers and refugees face the same challenges experienced by many people living in poverty in the Australian community, these experiences are compounded by their histories of trauma (Fozdar and Hartley 2013: 28). As these people have been forced to flee their homes, stable housing is also central to creating a new home and sense of belonging (Fozdar and Hartley 2014: 168). For members of the Legacy Caseload, accessing appropriate, affordable, and sustainable accommodation is a significant challenge due to a range of barriers (RCOA 2016: 1; Olliff 2014: 3). While all members of the Legacy Caseload are vulnerable to experiences of homelessness and housing precarity, asylum seekers with exceptionally low incomes are particularly vulnerable.

Factors affecting homelessness

Financial hardship

Many challenges faced by asylum seekers and refugees, including access to housing, are "mediated by poverty" (Fozdar and Hartley 2013: 28). Commonly, asylum seekers and refugees arrive in Australia with extremely limited resources

(Olliff 2014: 11). Further, as outlined earlier, members of the Legacy Caseload have limited income opportunities (Smith et al. 2020: 53; Olliff 2014: 11; Baric 2014: 9). Many cannot access social security and the most vulnerable members of this cohort may not have work rights (Yeung 2014: 26). For those who do have work rights numerous barriers to securing stable employment exist (Flatau et al. 2015: 75; Forrest et al. 2012: 192). Many asylum seekers and refugees also have family members overseas to whom they must send money (Olliff 2014: 6; Reilly 2016: 10). Therefore, in this context, the private rental market is usually inaccessible for those without stable employment (Olliff 2014: 6). This can become cyclical, whereby financial hardship creates an unstable housing situation which then reinforces the barriers to securing an income (van Kooy and Ward 2018: 9; Fozdar and Hartley 2014: 163).

Shortage of accommodation

There is a lack of affordable housing in the private rental market in Australia (Anglicare Australia 2020: 7; RCOA 2016: 2; Fozdar and Hartley 2014: 151). This issue is particularly severe in urban centres, such as Sydney and Melbourne, where many refugees and asylum seekers are concentrated (JSS 2015: 5; Spinney and Nethery 2013: 179), and this situation has been worsening due to increasing competitiveness in the market (Olliff 2014: 3). A lack of affordable properties renders private rental accommodation unattainable for many in the Legacy Caseload. Even where a property is secured the tenants may not be able to keep up with rising rents (Flanagan 2007: 65; Olliff 2014: 10). This can mean that the property is lost or that an exceedingly high proportion of income is spent on rent making it impossible to meet other basic needs (Olliff 2014: 10).

Difficulty navigating the housing market

Many members of the Legacy Caseload do not have strong English skills and may struggle to navigate the housing market independently. Some may have difficulty searching for available properties or determining how to arrange and travel to inspections (Flanagan 2007: 64; Olliff 2014: 13). Completing tenancy application forms and organising the necessary documentation can also be challenging or impossible alone (Olliff 2014: 13). Additionally, the mental health issues many asylum seekers and refugees experience, as a result of past trauma in their country of origin, experiences of immigration detention, the protection application process, and the stress of living in the community without adequate support, can further compromise their ability to effectively navigate the housing market (Baric 2014: 9; Olliff 2014: 14).

Many refugees and asylum seekers have limited knowledge of tenancy rights and obligations in the Australian rental market, which may prevent them from exercising their rights and ensuring they fulfil their responsibilities as tenants (Olliff 2014: 13; Fozdar and Hartley 2013: 37). This lack of knowledge also exposes refugees and asylum seekers to exploitation by unscrupulous landlords and heightens the risk of unfair or illegal leasing arrangements (Hartley and Fleay 2017: 56; Olliff 2014: 7). Equally, those who do not understand tenant's legal responsibilities are more likely to lose their bond, be charged for expensive repairs, or face eviction for unwitting breaches (Olliff 2014: 15).

Employment and rental history

Members of the Legacy Caseload often lack documentation, including evidence of rental history, references, and identification (Olliff 2014: 13; Yeung 2014: 26; Forrest et al. 2012: 197). Failure to produce a positive rental history can result in failure to secure a property in competitive housing markets. This issue is particularly relevant to new arrivals but may still impact those who have been living in the community for an extended period (as many in the Legacy Caseload have been) if they have spent significant periods couch-surfing or unofficially subletting. The high rate of unemployment and the insecure nature of any employment secured also means that asylum seekers and refugees are unlikely to be able to provide documentation to demonstrate they have the income necessary to sustain a lease (Flatau et al. 2015: 24).

Discrimination in the housing market

Asylum seekers and refugees commonly experience prejudice and discrimination in the housing market. The lack of stability and security for members of this cohort may make them less appealing as prospective tenants, and where there is high demand for properties landlords have more scope to discriminate between tenants (Flatau et al. 2015: 24, 28). Furthermore, real estate agents or landlords may not understand a refugee or asylum seeker's visa entitlements or status in Australia (Flatau et al. 2015: 24) or may be unwilling to invest additional effort to overcome any communication or knowledge barriers (Olliff 2014: 7; Smith et al. 2020: 455). Some real estate agents and landlords may also hold biased misconceptions about asylum seekers and refugees as difficult tenants, influenced by the acrimonious nature of the political debate about asylum seekers in Australia (Olliff 2014: 16; Everuss 2020: 6; Greenhalgh et al. 2015: 483). Such discrimination may further complicate the experience of finding housing and drive people to accept unfit accommodation (RCOA 2016: 3).

Experiences resulting from these factors

For many members of the Legacy Caseload, these factors lead to experiences of homelessness and housing precarity, as they are unable to secure access to the private rental market (Smith et al. 2020: 456). Some are confronted with primary homelessness and experiences such as rough sleeping. These people report that they felt unsafe during these experiences, and that this is not what they expected from their life in Australia (Flatau et al. 2015: 67).

Many are faced with a shortage of appropriate accommodation options and experience secondary or tertiary homelessness. Large families often struggle to find a single property that is large enough to meet their needs; especially as such properties are likely to be prohibitively expensive (Flatau et al. 2015: 27). This can result in overcrowding, which may lead to family conflict and breakdown, or a single family being split between multiple properties resulting in familial fragmentation and impeding recovery from trauma (Flanagan 2007: 67).

Another common challenge is that accessible housing is often of unacceptably poor quality or even unsafe (Fozdar and Hartley 2014: 165; Flanagan 2007: 65). Where appropriate accommodation cannot be sourced asylum seekers and refugees may feel forced to accept unsuitable housing, such as "boarding houses, carports, garages, sheds and caravan parks, as well as . . . severely overcrowded conditions" (Olliff 2014: 12). Moreover, inappropriate placements in shared properties may make the tenants feel uncomfortable or unsafe. For example, in one case a woman and her husband were placed in a house with ten single men (Hartley and Fleay 2017: 57) and in another case, a single, elderly woman felt she had no choice but to share a house with single men experiencing drug addiction issues (Olliff 2014: 12).

Others experience secondary homelessness through couch-surfing with family or friends, moving between boarding houses or emergency accommodation, or living in overcrowded conditions (Flatau et al. 2015: 66; Olliff 2014: 7). Strong community links can significantly reduce or even prevent experiences of primary homelessness by providing the option of couch-surfing (Flatau et al. 2015: 76). However, the pressure on these communities to provide accommodation can lead to overcrowding (Fozdar and Hartley 2013: 38), which may result in conflict, heightened stress, and a lack of privacy (Olliff 2014: 16). These circumstances can result in relationship breakdowns and domestic and family violence that can further expose people to homelessness (Flatau et al. 2015: 27; Beckwith et al. 2018: 13; Baric 2014: 9). Informal sharing arrangements can also present risks, such as eviction, for the primary tenants (Olliff 2014: 16). In these unstable circumstances asylum seekers and refugees must often move frequently within the community, which can negatively impact their rental history and hinder applications for future properties (Olliff 2014: 15; ARC 2013: 16; Smith et al. 2020: 450).

Nonetheless, asylum seekers and refugees may not consider these experiences of homelessness, although they do satisfy the Australian definition (Flatau et al. 2015: 22; Couch 2017: 2). In fact, some people feel that experiences such as couch-surfing, living in overcrowded accommodation, or regularly moving are part of their natural transition into Australian society and, therefore, reject characterisation of these experiences as homelessness (Flatau et al. 2015: 28). Due to such attitudes, and the hidden nature of secondary homelessness, it is likely that many experiences are not accounted for (Olliff 2014: 8).

For many others, these constraints on sustainable housing cause them to be pushed out of urban areas to more affordable regions. This decentralisation can leave people more socially isolated and vulnerable (Olliff 2014: 11). Important welfare support services are less likely to be available outside urban centres. Furthermore, outer regions often lack affordable and accessible transport options and the resultant cost of transport can become unsustainable, meaning people are unable to access necessary support services or social functions that maintain their connection to cultural communities (Fozdar and Hartley 2014: 164). Asylum seekers and refugees often face isolation, particularly due to their separation from their cultural communities and families, making proximity to community and support services critically important (ARC 2013: 16; Hartley et al. 2017: 1191).

In this context, experiences of housing precarity and homelessness can become chronic, particularly for asylum seekers who cannot plan for their future and who may have been without income for extended periods. Even TPV and SHEV holders face ongoing insecurity due to the temporary nature of their protection visas (Hafeez-Baig 2016: 128). Additionally, those who are unaware of the available support may go without any assistance for extended periods and so prolong these experiences (Couch 2017: 5). Experiences of homelessness and of long-term destitution are stressful for asylum seekers and compromise their health and well-being (Ziersch et al. 2017: 1; Couch 2017: 1; Smith et al. 2020: 444).[2] This can also compromise their ability to satisfy the requirements of, and participate in, the refugee status determination process and, thus, may contribute to a negative visa outcome (Yeung 2014: 27). It may also influence people's ability to accept the outcome of the status determination process where there is a negative decision (Olliff 2014: 8; Liddy et al. 2010: 12).

Comparison to air arrivals

Asylum seekers who arrive by plane and apply for a PPV are also vulnerable to experiences of homelessness and housing precarity while waiting for an outcome on their application. Many PPV applicants experience financial hardship, and certain members may have additional particular vulnerabilities. However, compared with the Legacy Caseload they are eligible for more support services and benefit from a quicker, more robust refugee status determination process. This means they are less likely to face the prolonged destitution experienced by many members of the Legacy Caseload (Kaldor Centre for International Refugee Law 2019b: 4). Further, once granted a PPV, these refugees become permanent residents, with access to far more support services and stability than TPV and SHEV holders (Kaldor Centre for International Refugee Law 2019b: 4). These differences make members of this cohort less likely to have prolonged experiences of homelessness and housing precarity. Those with permanent refugee status have been found to more frequently enter the private rental market and to be far less likely to experience homelessness compared with those with only temporary protection (Flatau et al. 2015: 64; Smith et al. 2020: 444).

State government response

The Australian Government's policy settings, outlined earlier, have created a situation of extreme precarity for asylum seekers and refugees from the Legacy Caseload. The progressive restriction of social security and support services has pushed increasing numbers of people into destitution. These decisions have also shifted the responsibility of supporting these people away from the Federal Government and onto other sectors. Indeed, some states have made efforts to fill the welfare support vacuum and provide supports to the Legacy Caseload; however, significant gaps remain. For instance, in Queensland, TPV and SHEV holders are eligible for social housing if they satisfy the assets test and meet the relevant income threshold (Queensland Government 2020b; Blythe et al. 2018: 21). Unfortunately, asylum seekers are ineligible, although those who have applied for a PPV, as well as PPV holders, may apply (Queensland Government 2020b). However, despite their eligibility, it is highly unlikely that TPV and SHEV holders will gain timely access to public housing given the complex nature of the system, the order of priority imposed, and the lengthy waiting list (Olliff 2014: 12; Blythe et al. 2018: 18; Smith et al. 2020: 444). However, in New South Wales and Victoria, no members of the Legacy Caseload are eligible to apply for social housing (NSW Government 2019; State Government of Victoria 2020; Blythe et al. 2018: 21). In both states, PPV holders are eligible as permanent residents but asylum seekers are not (NSW Government 2019; State Government of Victoria 2020).

State governments may also provide support for other housing solutions for members of the Legacy Caseload, such as limited rental assistance schemes (Blythe et al. 2018: 25). Additionally, in Queensland, the State Government has provided $3.6 million for a two-year program to provide a range of supports to members of the Legacy Caseload, including emergency relief and housing support (Queensland Government 2020a). This program cannot meet all of an individual's needs, or support every member of the Legacy Caseload, but it does go some way to alleviating the extreme financial hardship members of this cohort experience (Asylum Circle 2019).

Community support

Current strategies

Due to the significant challenges impacting access to housing for members of the Legacy Caseload, and the lack of robust government support, many people are forced to rely primarily on community support and the not-for-profit sector to meet their housing needs (Flatau et al. 2015: 28). For many years, and with little to no resourcing from government, non-profit welfare agencies, community services, church networks and other informal groups have channelled vast amounts of time, energy, and resources into alleviating the housing crisis for people seeking asylum through personal offers of accommodation (Olliff 2014: 24; Okhovat 2018: 21). This work is largely decentralised and informal and, as such, can be invisible and difficult to quantify.

Individuals, religious groups, and other informal associations provide a significant amount of support. A commonly adopted approach is to utilise donated properties or spare rooms from members of the community and church or faith groups for temporary housing. For example, Refugees Welcome Australia links members of the community willing to provide rent-free accommodation with refugees and asylum seekers in need of housing (Refugees Welcome Australia 2020). Since 2017, this group has facilitated more than 100 placements in Brisbane, Sydney, and Melbourne (Refugees Welcome Australia 2020). Another approach that relies on community support is pooling donations to assist refugees and asylum seekers with rent (BRASS Network 2018). Established refugee communities are also critical in providing these forms of informal support through family, social, and community connections (Olliff 2014: 52). Such voluntary community efforts are often crucial in supporting vulnerable asylum seekers and refugees.

NGOs have also adopted a range of innovative strategies in response to the welfare challenges facing asylum seekers and refugees. Some organisations may provide money to pay rent, bills, and utilities or to cover associated expenses such as bond and moving costs (ASRC n.d.; Olliff 2014: 31). Many NGOs coordinate or manage donated properties to provide housing and casework support or even take on the head lease or purchase property in order to provide free or low-cost housing (Olliff 2014: 40; Baptcare 2020). For example, Asylum Circle in Queensland coordinates a block of units released by the Queensland Government to provide free transitional accommodation to asylum seekers experiencing financial hardship (Asylum Circle 2020). The organisation self-funds administrative costs and casework support associated with this project (Asylum Circle 2020). Another successful example is the Lentara Project in Melbourne, which coordinates 18 donated properties to house at-risk asylum seekers and refugees (Lentara Uniting Care 2020). Families are generally provided with an entire property, while single men and women may be placed in share houses with other people of the same gender. Alongside rent-free housing, tenants are provided with casework support, a basic living allowance, and assistance with other bills (Lentara Uniting Care 2020). Similarly, Providence House in Sydney is a property donated and maintained by the Sisters of Charity Foundation and managed by the Asylum Seekers Centre to provide emergency and transitional housing support to asylum seekers. Tenants can also access casework support, financial assistance for living expenses, and educational and recreational activities (Sisters of Charity Foundation n.d.; Asylum Seekers Centre n.d.).

For those who do have an income and are able to pay rent some NGOs provide support to identify appropriate and affordable properties, assist in completing application forms, and provide reference letters (Migrant Information Centre n.d.; AMES Australia 2018; Olliff 2014: 27). This type of assistance is valuable in overcoming many of the non-financial challenges facing refugees and asylum seekers, such as difficulty navigating the housing market and a lack of rental history and documentation to compete in the private rental market. Some organisations have also found that building up relationships with real estate agents and housing providers can be effective in assisting potential tenants to secure properties (Olliff 2014: 34). However, in the context of the Legacy Caseload, these forms of assistance will likely be beneficial only for some TPV and SHEV holders, or BVE holders who have managed to secure a stable income. Asylum seekers with very low or no income will not have the resources to take advantage of this form of assistance.

While all of these approaches can be extremely valuable, they also come with risks. First, informal, decentralised, and *ad hoc* assistance can make it extremely hard to prevent some members of the cohort, potentially those who are most isolated and in need of support, from falling through the cracks. Furthermore, some of these arrangements, particularly those relying on community donations, do not provide ongoing security for asylum seekers or refugees; they could become highly vulnerable at any time if this support is unexpectedly withdrawn. Additionally, the strategies adopted by NGOs are resource-intensive and often cannot be maintained without external funding (Olliff 2014: 27). Additionally, the current approach is necessarily *ad hoc* and piecemeal and so not the most efficient use of resources.

The need for reform

Without adequate government support, NGOs working with the Legacy Caseload must self-fund services and rely on community donations to provide assistance to this vulnerable group (Yeung 2014: 27). These organisations are increasingly overwhelmed by the level of need (JSS 2015: 2) and cannot possibly provide comprehensive support to all members of this cohort. Many organisations are therefore in the difficult position of witnessing the "physical and psychological deterioration" of refugees and asylum seekers, without being able to offer the necessary assistance (JSS 2015: 2). Concerningly, with increasingly restricted access to social security, and as more members of the Legacy Caseload receive negative visa status determinations, the demand on this sector is increasing (Okhovat 2018: 21; ASRC 2019: 3).

The present situation places too great a burden on NGOs, established refugee communities, and the broader community, who should not bear primary responsibility for supporting the asylum legacy cohort. Without significant government investment, the innovative models developed by the community cannot provide the requisite level of support (Okhovat 2018: 21). Many of the strategies developed and implemented by NGOs provide effective and extremely valuable support to members of the Legacy Caseload, and further investment in these strategies could increase capacity to provide such support (Olliff 2014: 4). However, this cohort of refugees and asylum seekers has lived for many years with protracted uncertainty and desperately needs the underlying causes of their precarity rectified, as well as investment in these support schemes.

Asylum seekers and refugees need a holistic framework to support access to stable housing. The current level of government support is wholly inadequate and fundamental change is required. The most significant and urgent needs are eligibility of all members of the Legacy Caseload for social security payments, expanded and realistic pathways to a secure future in Australia, and an increase in affordable housing stock. These changes would provide the stability and income necessary to allow many more asylum seekers and refugees to access the private rental market (Olliff 2014: 8). Further, access to public housing should be improved through an increase in housing stock and broadened eligibility criteria, ideally for all members of the Legacy Caseload, but at minimum for TPV and SHEV holders in all states (Blythe et al. 2018: 22). For asylum seekers who remain vulnerable to housing precarity government-funded, medium-term, housing for those who are awaiting the outcome of the visa application has long been advocated (Liddy et al. 2010: 31). Implementation of these changes would, appropriately, shift the burden of providing basic living necessities back towards government and away from the wider community. These measures would also likely provide long-term housing solutions for this cohort, rather than the transitional support that is the current focus. Members of the Legacy Caseload should also be provided with increased access to English language tuition and employment support to further promote their autonomy and independence. In this context, further investment in NGO initiatives such as tenancy education and casework would be particularly meaningful (Olliff 2014: 24). With increased financial stability for much of the cohort, the strategies NGOs have adopted to provide emergency housing could then be reserved for the most vulnerable who continue to face barriers to secure accommodation.

Conclusion

Asylum seekers and refugees in the Legacy Caseload have been subjected to a suite of harsh and punitive policies due to their "irregular" method of arrival. The Australian Government has an obligation to provide safety and fair treatment to these people, and access to appropriate, affordable and sustainable housing is a related essential element of this obligation (Liddy et al. 2010: 58). Access to housing is known to underpin a range of other well-being factors, such as health and educational and economic participation in society, and is widely viewed as a cornerstone of successful integration for asylum seekers and refugees (Flatau et al. 2015: 75; JSS 2015: 9). Many members of the Legacy

Caseload, particularly asylum seekers, experience severe financial hardship and are constantly struggling against destitution. Housing stress is only one strand in a complex web of challenges facing this cohort. The challenge of securing housing must be viewed in this broader context. Not only is access to housing affected by a range of other factors but also insecure housing can compromise other things, such as physical and mental health, the ability to secure an income, and the capacity to engage in the refugee status determination process (Ziersch et al. 2017: 1; Smith et al. 2020: 444). Most members of the Legacy Caseload require not only housing assistance but also support to meet all their fundamental needs. While innovative strategies are being implemented and advocated for by the community sector, the resources available cannot meet the level of need. However, the federal policy landscape gives little cause for optimism about substantial reform in the near future (van Kooy and Ward 2018: 12).

The hardship experienced by members of the Legacy Caseload is not accidental. Rather, it is the intended result of the punitive policy approach adopted towards the welfare of this cohort. The policies affecting the Legacy Caseload are not designed to provide stability or security to refugees and asylum seekers. Instead, these policies serve the conservative Federal Government's political objectives of punishing refugees and asylum seekers who are already in Australia, encouraging them to return to their countries of origin (potentially to acute danger), and deterring others from trying to reach Australia in future. By constructing a context in which members of the Legacy Caseload are denied access to secure accommodation, alongside other basic welfare needs, the government increases the marginalisation and vulnerability of this cohort and inhibits their effective integration into the community and development of a sense of belonging. Thus, these asylum seekers and refugees are incentivised to return to their countries of origin, as they are unable to fully establish their lives in Australia. Given the contentious nature of the political discourse surrounding boat arrivals, and the effectiveness of the current policy regime in serving the government's objectives, it is difficult to foresee substantial law and policy reform in the short term.

There is some indication that certain state governments may be more willing to extend support to the Legacy Caseload (Blythe et al. 2018: 21). However, there is already a significant demand on public housing stock and state resources, and it is unreasonable to shift too much of this burden to the states, where this support has traditionally been the responsibility of the Australian Federal Government (van Kooy and Ward 2018: 12). It seems highly unlikely that the states will be willing, or able, to provide the level of support necessary to prevent this cohort from living in poverty. Accordingly, it is highly difficult to envision a viable solution to the issue of housing precarity and homelessness for members of the Legacy Caseload. Without a fundamental shift in the Federal Government's approach in relation to the management of this cohort (and refugees and asylum seekers more broadly), members of the Legacy Caseload who have lived in the community for years now will likely remain in a protracted state of destitution, without access to stable accommodation.

Notes

1 For example, the *International Covenant on Economic, Social and Cultural Rights*, opened for signature 16 December 1966, 999 UNTS 171 (entered into force 23 March 1976) art 11(1); *Convention on the Rights of the Child*, opened for signature 20 November 1989, 1577 UNTS 3 (entered into force 2 September 1990) art 27(3); *Convention on the Elimination of All Forms of Discrimination against Women*, opened for signature 18 December 1979, 1249 UNTS 13 (entered into force 3 September 1981) art 14(2)(h); *International Convention on the Elimination of All Forms of Racial Discrimination*, opened for signature 21 December 1965, 660 UNTS 195 (entered into force 4 January 1969) art 5(e)(iii); *Convention Relating to the Status of Refugees*, opened for signature 28 July 1951, 189 UNTS 137 (entered into forced 22 April 1954) art 21.
2 See further, Chapter 6 by Due et al.

References

AMES Australia. (2018) *Accommodation Services*. AMES Australia. www.ames.net.au/settle-in-aus/accommodation-services

Anglicare Australia. (2020) *Rental Affordability Snapshot*.

Asylum Circle. (2019) *Asylum Seeker and Refugee Assistance (ASRA) Program*. Asylum Circle. www.asylumcircle.com.au/asylum-seeker-and-refugee-assistance-asra-program/

Asylum Circle. (2020) *Transitional Housing Project*. Asylum Circle. www.refugeeswelcome.org.au/who-we-are/

Asylum Seeker Resource Centre. (2019) *Cutting the Safety New: The Impact of Cuts to Status Resolution Support Services*. ASRC.

Asylum Seeker Resource Centre. (n.d.) *Rental Support*. ASRC. www.asrc.org.au/home/our-services/how-we-help/justice/casework/

Asylum Seekers Centre. (n.d.) *Accommodation, Legal & Financial Support*. ASC. https://asylumseekerscentre.org.au/support/.

Australian Human Rights Commission. (2017) *Asylum Seekers, Refugees and Human Rights: Snapshot Report*. AHRC.

Australian Human Rights Commission. (2019) *Lives on Hold: Refugees and Asylum Seekers in the 'Legacy Caseload'*. AHRC.

Australian Red Cross. (2013) *Inaugural Vulnerability Report: Inside the Process of Seeking Asylum in Australia*. ARC.

Baptcare. (2020) *Accommodation for People Seeking Asylum*. Baptcare. www.baptcare.org.au/services/housing/accommodation-for-people-seeking-asylum

Baric, I. (2014) 'Asylum seekers and homelessness', *Parity*, 27(10): 8.

Beckwith, S., Gottardo, C., Brown, M. and Rego, N. (2018) *Free from Violence Against Women and Girls*. Jesuit Refugee Service.

Blythe, R., Clarke, J., Connell, T., Wallace, J. and Woods, C. (2018) *States of Refuge: Access to Health, Housing and Education for People Seeking Asylum and Refugees in Australia*. Rights Advocacy Project, Victoria.

BRASS Network. (2018) *Urgent Need for Housing*. Brisbane Refugee and Asylum Seeker Support Network. www.brassnetwork.org/urgent-need-for-housing-for-people-seeking-asylum/

Chamberlain, C. and MacKenzie, D. (2003) *Counting the Homeless 2001*. Australian Bureau of Statistics cat no. 2050.0.

Couch, J. (2017) '"Neither here nor there": Refugee young people and homelessness in Australia', *Children and Youth Services Review*, 74: 1.

Curry, O., Smedley, C. and Lenette, C. (2018) 'What is "successful" resettlement? Refugee narratives from New South Wales in Australia', *Journal of Immigrant & Refugee Studies*, 16(4): 430.

Department of Home Affairs. (2020a) *Applying for a Subsequent TPV or SHEV*. https://immi.homeaffairs.gov.au/what-we-do/refugee-and-humanitarian-program/onshore-protection/applying-for-a-subsequent-tpv-or-shev/information-for-tpv-and-shev-holders

Department of Home Affairs. (2020b) *Illegal Maritime Arrivals on Bridging E Visa*. Australian Government, Canberra.

Department of Home Affairs. (2020c) *IMA Legacy Caseload: Report on Processing Status and Outcomes*. Australian Government, Canberra.

Department of Home Affairs. (2020d) *Immigration Detention and Community Statistics Summary*. Australian Government, Canberra.

Everuss, L. (2020) 'Mobile sovereignty: The case of "boat people" in Australia', *Political Geography*, 79: 1.

Flanagan, J. (2007) *Dropped from the Moon: The Settlement Experiences of Refugee Communities in Tasmania*. Anglicare Tasmania.

Flatau, P., Smith, J., Carson, G., Miller, J., Burvill, A. and Brand, R. (2015) *The Housing and Homelessness Journeys of Refugees in Australia*. Australian Housing and Urban Research Institute Report no. 256.

Fleay, C., Hartley, L. and Kenny, M.A. (2013) 'Refugees and asylum seekers living in the Australian community: The importance of work rights and employment support', *Australian Journal of Social Issues*, 48(4): 473.

Forrest, J., Hermes, K., Johnston, R. and Poulsen, M. (2012) 'The housing resettlement experience of refugee immigrants to Australia', *Journal of Refugee Studies*, 26(2): 187.

Fozdar, F. and Hartley, L. (2013) 'Refugee resettlement in Australia: What we know and need to know', *Refugee Survey Quarterly*, 32(3): 23.

Fozdar, F. and Hartley, L. (2014) 'Housing and the creation of home for refugees in Western Australia', *Housing, Theory and Society*, 31(2): 148.

Greenhalgh, E., Watt, S. and Schutte, N. (2015) 'Mechanisms of moral disengagement in the endorsement of asylum seekers policies in Australia', *Ethics & Behaviour*, 25(6): 482.

Hafeez-Baig, M. J. (2016) 'Putting the "protection" in "Temporary Protection Visa"', *Bond Law Review*, 28(2): 115.

Hartley, L., Baker, S., Fleay, C. and Burke, R. (2019) '"My study is the purpose of continuing my life": The experience of accessing university for people seeking asylum in Australia', *Australian Universities' Review*, 61(2): 4.

Hartley, L. and Fleay, C. (2017) '"We are like animals": Negotiating dehumanising experiences of asylum-seeker policies in the Australian community', *Refugee Survey Quarterly*, 36: 45.

Hartley, L., Fleay, C. and Tye, E. (2017) 'Exploring physical activity engagement and barriers for asylum seekers in Australia coping with prolonged uncertainty and no right to work', *Health and Social Care in the Community*, 25(3): 1190.

Hedrick, K., Armstrong, G., Coffey, G. and Borschmann, R. (2019) 'Self-harm in the Australian asylum seeker population: A national records-based study', *SSM—Population Health*, 8: 1.

Hugo, G. (2014) 'Change and continuity in Australian international migration policy', *International Migration Review*, 48(3): 868.

Jesuit Social Services. (2015) *The Living Conditions of People Seeking Asylum in Australia*. JSS.

Kaldor Centre for International Refugee Law. (2019a) *'Fast track' Refugee Status Determination*. University of New South Wales.

Kaldor Centre for International Refugee Law. (2019b) *Temporary Protection Visas (TPVs) and Safe Haven Enterprise Visas (SHEVs)*. University of New South Wales.

Kaldor Centre for International Refugee Law. (2019c) *The 'legacy caseload'*. University of New South Wales.

Karlsen, E. and Phillips, J. (2017) *Developments in Australian Refugee Law and Policy: The Abbott and Turnbull Coalition Governments (2013–2016)*. Parliamentary Library, Canberra.

Kenny, M.A. and Procter, N. (2016) 'The fast track refugee assessment process and the mental health of vulnerable asylum seekers', *Psychiatry, Psychology and Law*, 23(1): 62.

Lentara Uniting Care. (2020) *Asylum Seeker Project*. www.unitinglentara.org.au/page/58/asylum-seeker-project

Liddy, N., Sanders, S. and Coleman, C. (2010) *Australia's Hidden Homeless: Community-based Approaches to Asylum Seeker Homelessness*. Hotham Mission Asylum Seeker Project.

McAdam, J. (2013) 'Australia and asylum seekers', *International Journal of Refugee Law*, 25(3): 435.

McDonald, E. and O'Sullivan, M. (2018) 'Protecting vulnerable refugees: Procedural fairness in the Australian fast track regime', *University of New South Wales Law Journal*, 41(3): 1003.

McKay, F., Thomas, S. and Kneebone, S. (2011) '"It would be okay if they came through the proper channels": Community perceptions and attitudes toward asylum seekers in Australia', *Journal of Refugee Studies*, 25(1): 113.

Migrant Information Centre. (n.d.) *Housing*. Migrant Information Centre Eastern Melbourne. http://miceastmelb.com.au/our-services/housing/?doing_wp_cron=1590861834.2058610916137695312500

New South Wales Government. (2019) *Eligibility for Social Housing*. www.facs.nsw.gov.au/housing/help/eligibility/social-housing

Okhovat, S. (2018) *With Empty Hands: How the Australian Government Is Forcing People Seeking Asylum to Destitution*. Refugee Council of Australia.

Olliff, L. (2014) *The Home Stretch: Challenges and Alternatives in Sustainable Housing for Refugees and Asylum Seekers*. Refugee Council of Australia.

Procter, N., Kenny, M.A., Eaton, H. and Grech, C. (2018) 'Lethal hopelessness: Understanding and responding to asylum seeker distress and mental deterioration', *International Journal of Mental Health Nursing*, 27: 448.

Queensland Government. (2020a) *Asylum Seeker and Refugee Assistance Program*. Queensland Government Department of Local Government, Racing and Multicultural Affairs. www.dlgrma.qld.gov.au/multicultural-affairs/programs-and-initiatives/asylum-seeker-refugee-assistance-program.html

Queensland Government. (2020b) *Check Your Eligibility*. Queensland Government. www.qld.gov.au/housing/public-community-housing/eligibility-applying-for-housing/eligibility-for-housing/check-your-eligibility

Refugee Council of Australia. (2016) *Submission to the Affordable Housing Working Group—Innovative Financing Models*. RCOA.

Refugees Welcome Australia. (2020) *The Who, What and How*. www.refugeeswelcome.org.au/who-we-are/

Reilly, A. (2016) 'Asylum seekers in the community: The importance of work for a decent life', *Australian Journal of Human Rights*, 22(1): 1.

Reilly, A. (2018) 'The vulnerability of Safe Haven Enterprise Visa holders: Balancing work, protection and future prospects', *University of New South Wales Law Journal*, 41(3): 871.

Rutherford, E. (2015) 'Removing protection from Australia's asylum laws: A study of Temporary Protection Visas', in Cadwallader, R. (ed.) *We Are Better Than This: Essays Addressing Policies on Asylum Seekers*. ATF Press, p. 91.

Sisters of Charity Foundation. (n.d.) *Asylum Seekers Housing Program*. Sisters of Charity. https://sistersofcharityfoundation.com.au/donations/asylum-seekers-housing-program/

Smith, D., McKay, F. and Lippi, K. (2020) 'Experiences of homelessness by people seeking asylum in Australia: A review of published and "grey" literature', *Social Policy & Administration*, 54: 441.

Spinney, A. and Nethery, A. (2013) '"Taking our houses": Perceptions of the impact of asylum seekers, refugees and new migrants on housing assistance in Melbourne', *Social Policy & Society*, 12(2): 179.

State Government of Victoria. (2020) *Social Housing Eligibility*. Housing Victoria. www.housing.vic.gov.au/social-housing-eligibility

Steen, A. (2018) 'The many costs of homelessness', *The Medical Journal of Australia*, 208(4): 167.

Taylor, S. (2018) 'Refugee family reunion: What might have been', *Alternative Law Journal*, 43(3): 209.

Tazreiter, C. (2017) 'The unlucky in the "lucky country": Asylum seekers, irregular migrants and refugees and Australia's politics of disappearance', *Australian Journal of Human Rights*, 23(2): 242.

van Kooy, J. and Bowman D. (2019) '"Surrounded with so much uncertainty": Asylum seekers and manufactured precarity in Australia', *Journal of Ethnic and Migration Studies*, 45(5): 693.

van Kooy, J. and Ward, T. (2018) *An Unnecessary Penalty: Economic Impacts of Changes to the Status Resolution Support Services (SRSS)*. RCOA.

Weber, L. (2019) 'From state-centric to transversal borders: Resisting the "structurally embedded border" in Australia', *Theoretical Criminology*, 23(2): 228.

Yeung, P. (2014) 'Whose problem is it anyway? Moving towards a shared responsibility approach to reducing asylum seeker homelessness', *Parity*, 27(10): 27.

Ziersch, A., Walsh, M., Due, C. and Duivesteyn, E. (2017) 'Exploring the relationship between housing and health for refugees and asylum seekers in South Australia: A qualitative study', *International Journal of Environmental Research and Public Health*, 14: 1.

Chapter 6

Financial precarity and health for temporary refugee and asylum-seeking visa holders in Australia

Moira Walsh, Clemence Due and Anna Ziersch***

Introduction

Pre- and post-migration stressors mean that people from refugee and asylum-seeking backgrounds are at higher risk of poor mental and physical health, relative to both the general population and other migrant groups (Hollifield et al. 2002; Fazel and Stein 2003; Fazel et al. 2005, 2012). In a post-migration setting, there is a range of factors that contribute to this health inequity, including immigration and welfare policies in resettlement countries which frequently function to place refugees and asylum seekers at greater risk of financial and visa precarity. For those on temporary visas, in particular, these policies often lead to extended periods of uncertainty, with associated negative health impacts (Fleischman et al. 2015; Hynie 2018). While the health impacts for refugees and asylum seekers associated with temporary visa status and financial insecurity are well known (Silove et al. 2000; Steel and Silove 2001; Porter and Haslam 2005; Johnston et al. 2009; Bogic et al. 2015; Chen et al. 2017; Hynie 2018), less is known about how these elements interact in the particular immigration and welfare context of Australia. Through in-depth interviews with fourteen people from refugee and asylum-seeking backgrounds residing on temporary visas and receiving emergency relief through a charitable organisation and six service providers working with this group of people, this chapter explores the health impacts of financial precarity for temporary refugee visa holders in Australia.

A note on terminology: For the purposes of this chapter, refugees are people who have been successful in their claims for refugee status under the 1951 *Convention relating to the Status of Refugees* ("Refugees Convention") or in their application for a protection visa in Australia under s 36(2)(a) or s 36(2)(aa) of the *Migration Act 1958* (Cth). Asylum seekers are people awaiting their claims for refugee status or complementary protection to be determined in Australia or overseas. In this chapter, for concision we use the terms "refugee" and "asylum seeker" but recognise the complex identities these terms contain. We take the World Health Organization (WHO) definition of health as "a state of complete physical, mental and social well-being and not merely the absence of disease or infirmity" (WHO 1946). This definition views physical and mental

DOI: 10.4324/9781003298595-11

health as intertwined insofar as mental health impacts are likely to have physical health impacts and vice versa (Savic et al. 2016).

Background

Immigration and welfare policy in Australia

Over the last several decades, immigration and welfare policies of successive Australian governments have generated much controversy; namely changes to refugee status determination, the reintroduction of temporary protection, mandatory detention of undocumented asylum seekers while their refugee claims are processed, and the reintroduction of regional processing (AHRC 2019).

In 2014 temporary protection visas (TPVs) were reintroduced as well as a new temporary visa class known as safe haven enterprise visas (SHEVs), for "declared" refugees who arrive in Australia without valid visas. The TPV provides protection for three years and the SHEV provides protection for five years (Migration Regulations 1994, Schedule 2). The main feature of the SHEV is that visa holders must intend to work or study in a part of "regional Australia" (Department of Home Affairs 2020a). Holders of TPVs and SHEVs are ineligible for family reunion and can travel only with permission from the Department of Home Affairs (DHA). They are eligible for most welfare services, such as Medicare, though there are some restrictions (discussed in more detail ahead). Asylum seekers awaiting determination of their claim are most often granted a bridging visa (BV) which is a general visa given to people while other substantive visa applications are processed, though they can be held in detention if they arrive without a visa or re-detained if they breach the visa criteria (including the behavioural "code of conduct"). BVs vary in length (generally between three and 12 months) depending on visa determination and provide varied access to work rights and other entitlements and also have travel restrictions (Reilly 2016). These restrictive immigration policies create labour market precarity for asylum seekers and refugees through short-term, conditional visas which can make them unappealing to employers, over-represented in insecure work, and at risk of exploitation/discrimination (Ziersch et al. 2021; van Kooy and Bowman 2019).

From June to August 2020, of those asylum seekers among the so-called Legacy Caseload permitted to remain in Australia in order to lodge applications for substantive visas,[1] 12,450 people remain on BVs or are awaiting BV extensions, of which 10,245 are living in the community (Department of Home Affairs 2020b). Another 5,594 people have been granted TPVs and 12,084 people have been granted SHEVs—valid for three and five years respectively, after which time the visa holder must have their refugee claims reassessed (Department of Home Affairs 2020c). There were also 8,413 applicants who had their applications for SHEVs and TPVs refused, some of whom have been removed (deported), and many of whom continue to live in the community pending review of these refusal decisions or pending their deportation (Department of Home Affairs 2020c).

In order to assess the backlog of refugee claims from approximately 30,000 asylum seekers who had arrived in Australia by boat prior to January 1 2014 (the "Legacy Caseload"), changes were made to the refugee status determination process through the introduction of a "fast track process" which limited decision review opportunities (Kenny and Procter 2016; McDonald and O'Sullivan 2018). After this date all asylum seekers attempting to reach Australia by boat were turned back or transferred to Pacific Island nations for offshore regional processing. By contrast asylum seekers arriving by plane, usually entering the country legally on visa and then submitting to immigration authorities, are not treated as punitively as maritime arrivals. From the 2014–15 to 2018–19 financial years, 92,071 asylum seekers arrived by plane (Davidson 2019).

In mid-2018, cuts were made to the Status Resolution Support Services (SRSS) comprising a "special benefit" payment that is equivalent to 89% of NewStart allowance (this amounts to approximately $500 per fortnight for a single person, approximately $450 for a partnered person, and approximately $575 per fortnight for a single person with dependent children or for a single person, 60 years or older after nine continuous months on payment), casework support, and counselling for people awaiting status determination (Services Australia 2020). Asylum seekers who do not meet a high threshold of vulnerability, as assessed by the DHA and SRSS providers, were made ineligible for the special benefit and consequently receive no income support. The vulnerability assessment includes the following criteria: ongoing physical health barriers, permanent disability, or cognitive impairment; mental health barriers where there is a current diagnosis and treatment plan in place from a medical clinician; sole parents with preschool-age children, women who are pregnant, or a primary caregiver of a highly vulnerable person; those ages 70 and over; and, individuals dealing with a major crisis (family/domestic violence) (Department of Home Affairs 2020d).

Those asylum seekers of adult workforce age receiving the SRSS benefit payment are required to meet "mutual obligations requirements" (actively searching for work) and are given no additional support to find employment other than the most basic support under Jobactive (access to a computer and internet to search for jobs). It is noteworthy that these assessments of "job-readiness" do not reflect an understanding of pre- and post-migration challenges, which can compound to negatively impact resettlement outcomes including employment (Siriwardhana et al. 2014; Bogic et al. 2015; Li et al. 2016). Importantly, asylum seekers are ineligible for English language tuition, through the Adult Migrant English Program, whereas those on TPVs or SHEVs can access 510 hours of free tuition. Asylum seekers are eligible for the Skills for Education and Employment Program to support further English, computer, and other skills for employment. However, there is limited uptake of this program due to inadequate referral processes from Jobactive employment providers (Refugee

Council of Australia 2019). Of those who have been granted a TPV or a SHEV, income support can be interrupted for several weeks while Centrelink adjusts to their new status and can be cancelled all together if the recipient commences a program of study (without eligibility for Austudy).

According to the Refugee Council of Australia (RCOA 2017), the asylum seekers impacted most acutely by the cuts to SRSS have the lowest skills and qualifications, meaning that many are unable to find basic employment and cannot access social security or mental health support services. This cohort of people is relying on not-for-profit organisations for assistance with living costs, accommodation, and legal support.

Social determinants of refugee and asylum seeker health

People from refugee and asylum-seeking backgrounds constitute a marginalised and often vulnerable section of the global community for whom pre-migration experiences of violence, trauma, and dislocation lead to increased risk of poor mental and physical health, including higher rates of PTSD, communicable diseases (e.g. respiratory, gastrointestinal, and dermatologic infections) and chronic pain due to experiences of torture and trauma (e.g. see Fazel et al. 2005; Silove et al. 2007; Steel et al. 2009; Alemi et al. 2014; Pavli and Maltezou 2017). Importantly, refugees and asylum seekers' physical and mental health are also influenced by post-migration factors. For example, experiences of racism and discrimination, ongoing uncertainty associated with visa status for those on temporary visas, and acculturative stress resulting from living in a new social and cultural context (Hynie 2018; Ziersch et al. 2020; Savic et al. 2016) with cumulative and compounding impacts for those experiencing multiple stressors for mental and physical health (Siriwardhana et al. 2014; Bogic et al. 2015; Li et al. 2016). Importantly, studies have repeatedly demonstrated the adverse effect of family separation on the mental health of refugees. Alongside pre-migration trauma exposure, family separation has been associated with elevated depression, post-traumatic stress and anxiety symptoms, increased disability and reduced quality of life (Nickerson et al. 2010; Savic et al. 2013; Miller et al. 2018).

In general, post-migration impacts on physical and mental health for refugees and asylum seekers can be viewed through a social determinant of health (SDH) lens. Social determinants of health are defined by the WHO as "the conditions in which people are born, grow, live, work and age" and include material factors (access to safe environments, adequate food and housing, high-quality healthcare, and appropriate employment) and interpersonal factors (social exclusion, discrimination, and low social status), which are mostly responsible for health inequities (World Health Organisation 2008). Social determinants influence health through psychological states, such as stress, anxiety, depression, and perceptions of control as well as through biological pathways via neuroimmune, neuroendocrine, and epigenetic responses (Miller et al. 2009; Bambra et al.

2010; Braveman and Gottlieb 2014). Of particular relevance for this chapter, income is a key SDH, and financial difficulties are known to pose a risk to health and well-being. For example, where a lack of sufficient income can mean an inability to pay for medications and health services, adequate food and other resources for health, as well as stress responses to the circumstances (Marmot 2002; Lund et al. 2010; Funk et al. 2012, Lund 2012).

As with the general population, people from refugee and asylum-seeking backgrounds are influenced by SDH. However, pre-settlement experiences as well as post-settlement stressors that are framed by the immigration and social welfare policies of receiving countries present particular risks for health post-migration (Hynie 2018). Research has highlighted that low socio-economic status for refugees (often associated with barriers to economic opportunity such as rights to work, barriers to employment, and limited welfare) contributes to psychological trauma, distress, and depression (Porter and Haslam 2005; Bogic et al. 2015; Chen et al. 2017; Hynie 2018). The impacts of insufficient income (at or below the poverty line) together with other SDH such as unsuitable housing and unemployment on the physical health of refugees and asylum seekers have also been documented in the literature, particularly in relation to barriers accessing healthcare (Taylor and Haintz 2018). This includes consultation fees, cost of transportation to appointments, and paying for medication (Hadgkiss and Renzaho 2014).

In addition to financial precarity, both temporary visas and the process of seeking asylum are also SDH (Hynie 2018). In relation to asylum-seeking processes, research has highlighted the adverse psychological impacts of negative detention experiences (e.g. exposure to violence and other stressful events as well as prolonged detention) and TPVs that cause uncertainty, fear, and insecurity (Silove et al. 2000; Steel and Silove 2001; Marston 2003). The uncertainty associated with TPVs has been found to exacerbate and reproduce the existing high levels of psychological distress experienced by many people with refugee backgrounds (Marston 2003), manifesting as ongoing worries and intrusive thoughts relating to fears about deportation (Procter 2004; Coffey et al. 2010). Moreover, research has indicated that temporary visa holders report greater negative psychological outcomes than those with secure visa status even when experiences of detention are accounted for. These include anger, sense of injustice and of feeling dehumanisation, perceived lack of control and reported PTSD symptoms, depression symptoms, anxiety symptoms and suicidality (Steel et al. 2011; Newnham et al. 2019; Nickerson et al. 2019; Marston 2003; Johnston et al. 2009; Hartley and Fleay 2017).

Temporary visas can also lead to negative impacts on physical health as a result of ongoing stress and difficulty accessing healthcare service providers and cycles of poverty and disadvantage (Omeri et al. 2006; Silove et al. 2007). Previous Australian research has also indicated that asylum seekers in the "Legacy Caseload" undergoing the complex "fast track" administrative process have significant difficulties understanding and participating in the process, often because of existing stress and psychological trauma (Kenny and Procter 2016). The reduction in government funding for legal assistance exacerbate these difficulties and combine to compound existing stress and psychological trauma (Kenny et al. 2016).

In this chapter, building on the body of research outlined earlier, we aim to explore the health impacts of financial precarity for temporary refugee visa holders in the context of current immigration and welfare policies in Australia. We draw on in-depth interviews with individuals from refugee and asylum-seeking backgrounds in financial difficulty who were seeking emergency relief, and the service providers who support them.

Methods

Participants

The research participants were fourteen people from refugee and asylum-seeking backgrounds and six service providers working with refugee and asylum-seeking clients. All fourteen participants from refugee and asylum-seeking backgrounds were recipients of the St Vincent de Paul (SVDP) Migrant and Refugee Centre emergency relief program: the asylum seeker assistance fund (ASAF). The ASAF provides welfare assistance (short-term living allowance, rent assistance, contribution towards utility bills, food vouchers, and SVDP assistance cards, which can be used in SVDP second-hand shops) to people from asylum-seeking and refugee backgrounds whose income support has been interrupted or cancelled.

All of these participants were asylum seekers who had experienced or were experiencing cuts to their SRSS payments and were experiencing extreme financial hardship in Australia. They comprised six women and eight men ranging from 23 to 72 years of age, with an average age of 36 years. The majority came from the Middle East (Iran and Afghanistan = 10). Others were from Asia (Myanmar, Sri Lanka, Vietnam = 5). Participants had been in Australia for an average of 5.5 years (range: 4–7 years). Interviews/focus groups were also conducted with six service providers (all female) from organisations working with asylum seekers and providing emergency relief. Taken together, these twenty participants provided nuanced accounts of lived experience, as well as service provider perspectives representing several key non-government organisations.

Procedure

Ethics approval was obtained from the researchers' institutional ethics committee and close consideration was given to potential issues of coercion and informed consent, confidentiality, and anonymity, as well as the presence of power imbalances between researchers and participants (Ziersch et al. 2019). Potential participants were told that taking part was entirely voluntary and that they could withdraw at any time. Several of the refugee and asylum seeker participants presented with recognisable physical and mental health issues. Three participants were unable to sit in a chair for a long period of time, and two revealed various scars and injuries to their backs, arms, and legs (sustained in their country of origin) that had not healed properly. Others displayed signs of fatigue, confusion, sadness, and despair during the interviews. In line with an ethical approach to research with vulnerable populations (Ziersch et al. 2019) the researcher was guided by these factors during the interview process in terms of how she phrased questions and probed for details. Additionally, participants were offered several opportunities throughout the interview to discontinue if they wished to. Information about support and counselling service were made available to all participants. One participant was referred to a refugee health organisation for counselling, and the researcher conducting the interviews followed up on the well-being of this participant on two occasions. Informed consent was gained from all participants prior to participation and interpreters were available. Data collection involved semi-structured in-depth interviews, which took place between September and December 2018 at mutually agreed-upon locations including public libraries, offices at universities, cafes, community organisations, and the participants' home.

A female researcher from a non-migrant, Caucasian background, with extensive experience interviewing people from refugee backgrounds, conducted the interviews and time was taken prior to the interview commencing for building rapport. Six participants elected to use an interpreter. The interviews covered people's overall resettlement experiences, financial circumstances, visa status and conditions, and their health and well-being. Interview questions were developed based on existing literature and input from service providers and built iteratively over the interviews as new issues emerged. While the overall time spent with participants was longer (e.g. to develop rapport and trust), the average duration of the interviews with refugees and asylum seekers was 32 minutes, and for the service providers it was 52 minutes.

Data analysis

The interview data were thematically analysed using the five stage framework approach (Ritchie and Spencer 1994): familiarisation with the data (reading and re-reading transcripts); the development of a thematic framework (done inductively and iteratively from the data); indexing (coding with NVivo Version 12 [QSR International 2019], with a subset double coded by members of the research team); charting (thematic matrices charting each participant against emergent themes); and, mapping and interpretation (where experiences relating to visa uncertainty and health impacts are outlined). In this chapter, we use pseudonyms and include visa status (bridging visa [BV] and safe haven enterprise visa [SHEV]), country of origin and gender (where this is not clear from the context), for direct quotes.

Findings

Analysis of the interview data revealed significant financial precarity for participants. This precarity was located in the context of the participants' temporary visa status and the associated immigration and welfare policies, which affected their overall financial security, their inability to secure work, and ongoing visa (and residency) uncertainty. Participants reported that, together, these factors were having a significant impact on their health and well-being, particularly mental health. Importantly, participants also reported that health itself had an impact on employment prospects and associated financial status (with poor health leading to difficulties in securing employment), highlighting the intertwined nature of the relationships between financial and visa precarity and health. These findings are discussed in more detail ahead.

Financial precarity in the context of temporary visas

All but two of the participants of this study were on temporary visas—the other two had had their bridging visas cancelled. They were all experiencing financial precarity because of cuts and/or interruptions to their income support, difficulties finding work or being unable to work, and no access to a range of social supports such as childcare subsidies, Medicare, and the National Disability Insurance Scheme (NDIS). In terms of work rights and income support, eight participants were on short-term bridging visas with work rights and no income support. Three of these participants were awaiting a decision regarding SHEV applications and were deemed job ready. The SHEV applications of the other five had been refused, initially by immigration officials and then upon appeal by the Administrative Appeals Tribunal (AAT). Consequently, their SRSS payments had been immediately ceased. Four participants were on SHEV visas, with two unemployed receiving the meagre special benefit (income support) and two full-time tertiary students (with fee-paying scholarships) who were ineligible for a special benefits payment because they had undertaken a period of study in excess of the 12-month limit to receive a special benefit. Last, two participants had no visa, with no income support and no work rights, due to their lack of lawful immigration status.

Eleven of the fourteen participants were relying exclusively on charitable organisations for survival. Three of the fourteen were employed—all on a casual basis—as an interpreter and in the manufacturing sector, which they reported did not provide them with enough income to live on. The community service that participants were recruited from provided a $60 supermarket card and a $120 per month living allowance for a period of six months, as well as some food and clothing. All participants also indicated that the service assisted them with one-off payments of their rent, and occasionally assisted them with bills and other expenses.

In the interviews, service providers specifically noted the financial precarity of their clients, many of whom had been subject to cuts and interruptions to their income support, with one participant saying, "There's no safety net for these people." Another service provider gave the example of clients who have had their claims for asylum accepted but who were left with no income for long periods of time due to the difficulties many had navigating welfare bureaucracy and protracted wait time for income support to be reinstated:

> So they were on a bridging visa and then they got their SHEV. So instantaneously, Centrelink's cut off straight away. So we had these clients who all of a sudden, had no income. Then you've just got to reapply, and it takes forever. I mean, it's a nightmare [and] the landlords are not always sympathetic.
>
> (Service Provider)

Refugee and asylum seeker participants also reported instances of cuts and interruptions to their income support. Esteri, an asylum seeker and single mother from Iran, applied for a SHEV twelve months prior to the interview and was still awaiting a decision. Esteri was ineligible for income support and, while she had causal work as an interpreter, the work was often intermittent and she struggled financially:

> Right now I do not receive any money from Centrelink because they cut it off . . . So yeah, so the $120 [per month] that I get from [charitable organisation] is one week worth of groceries for me [my finances] are really not anywhere near good at all.

Similarly, Hashem, a 47-year-old Iranian asylum seeker, had had his claim for a visa refused and was awaiting a judicial review of that adverse determination by the Federal Circuit Court of Australia. At the time, Hashem was receiving the same $120 as the other participants from a charitable organisation to assist with living costs. Of his situation he said:

> Financially I'm actually at zero. I'm only living by the aid of the church. I don't have anything . . . Since May they [DHA] have put us into this extreme hardship . . . I have to live with $100 for about one month and it's very hard to do that.

Another participant, Sara, a SHEV holder and full-time university student, was ineligible for income support because she was undertaking a course longer than twelve months duration. She described the consequences of having her income support cut: "it was so difficult because I spent my whole savings and I had a car, I sold my car and spent the money as well. Then so I end up had nothing [sic]."

In addition to seeking support from community organisations, participants noted that borrowing money from friends or family was a key means to surviving when experiencing financial vulnerability. As such, finding work often meant repaying debts rather than working towards financial security. For instance, Abdul, an Afghani asylum seeker, described finding work after a difficult period of searching. He and his wife's claims for asylum were rejected and so their income support was cut. This was particularly challenging given the recent birth of their first child. For Abdul, however, returning the money that he had borrowed was at the forefront of his mind:

> I can't say that I'm economically strong . . . I've started work for the last three or four weeks and it's been well. So, I have some money that needs to be returned back to people that I've got a loan from other people.

Participants were also often required to sell possessions to survive. For example, Marduk, an asylum seeker from Iran, described how he sold most of his possessions after his claim for refugee status was refused, leading him to borrow several thousands of dollars from friends to pay for a migration lawyer, and this resulted in homelessness.

Navigating immigration and welfare bureaucracy

Finding and engaging in employment as a pathway to financial security was reported as a significant issue for all participants, with their temporary visa status and associated conditions highlighted as a key barrier to work. Although, notionally, a majority of the participants had work rights allied to their visas, only four were employed in any way at the time of the interview, and all were casual employees. Casual employment and difficulties finding employment more generally meant that financial precarity remained a reality for all of the participants. There were a range of barriers to employment, associated with their visa, for the participants that contributed to their financial precarity, including work rights status, length of visa, and access to English language programs. Marduk, who arrived in Australia in 2013 and was not allowed to work, applied for a SHEV in 2015. However, his visa claim was rejected, and he was placed on a six-month BV pending an appeal. He was ineligible for income support because, like several other participants, he did not meet the stringent "financial hardship" criteria and was of a working age. While Marduk's work rights were reinstated at the time of the interview, he was unable to find a job because of his temporary visa:

> I have visa, six-month visa. One or two months you're searching for job, and then when someone interview someone, "Marduk, what's your visa?", 'This is my visa." "Oh, just three months left? [Get] out, out!"

Similarly, Esteri, from Iran, also noted that her temporary visa was a direct barrier to securing work. Esteri was working as an interpreter but seeking extra work in hospitality during the evening when her ex-partner could care for their child. She had been unsuccessful because "when they find out about your visa, they're not very keen on it." Esteri also noted that having no access to childcare benefits, due to her bridging visa status, was an additional barrier to finding work: "I'm not eligible for day care benefits or anything, although I am working and paying tax. So I can't work full time because I'm going to have to pay everything I earned for day care." Relatedly, other participants described a lack of education and English language skills as a major obstacle to finding work despite being deemed "work-ready "by the DHA, with limited access to English language education services. Through an interpreter, Denpa, an asylum seeker from Myanmar, detailed his despair at being unable to find work to support his family because of a lack of education and English language skills: "The money matter and job matter. My payment was cut and I'm illiterate, I'm not educated, it's not good for me to find a job for me. With not a job, no income and life become not meaningful."

Much like Marduk, Denpa was not granted work rights for two years after arriving in Australia, nor did he have access to English language classes that likely impacted his capacity to find a job once he had the right to work. Other participants also faced English language difficulties including Marduk, who, while studying at a local high school for a week, received notification from Australian immigration that he was no longer eligible to attend school because of a change in policy. While he reported that he was able to learn English independently he shared his dismay that many other asylum seekers would be left undesirable to employers without the right to attend school and develop appropriate English language skills:

> It was government's notice. When they change, they ask to—now in my visa I can't study. They write, yeah, you can't study. Why I can't study? [If] our English good, you can work. Start to work. But they didn't even let us to learn English. Why? [sic].

As a result of these various barriers to employment for refugees and asylum seekers on temporary visas, service providers noted that many people spent significant amounts of time seeking financial support. In this way, navigating financial precarity in the context of precarious employment or no employment could be a full-time job in itself:

> [People] spend a lot of their time running around trying to get support . . . it would be great to think that on top of this [people] could be engaged in some sort of training or something to upskill but they don't have the time because it's spent trying to survive . . . their day is spent going to here there or other places trying to get money.
>
> (Service Provider)

Overall, participant accounts highlighted the complex ways that financial and visa precarity intersected for people on temporary visas. Combined, this insecurity was exacerbated by difficulties navigating the complex terrain of immigration and welfare bureaucracy without financial support. For example, Marduk offered a clear account of the relationship between visa precarity and financial precarity: "I sold my everything to lawyers . . . I lost my everything [sic]." Unsurprisingly then, when asked what kinds of support would be most helpful, several participants said legal representation: "I need a lawyer now, a helpful lawyer" (Abdul Jaleel, Afghan male, bridging visa) and "If they could help with getting the visa granted—apply for the visa" (Minh, Vietnamese male, bridging visa).

Health impacts of financial and visa precarity

A range of health impacts related to financial and visa precarity were reported by participants, particularly emotional responses to the stress of financial precarity and visa temporariness, such as despair and hopelessness, anger and frustration, fear of deportation, and shame in having to rely on others for financial resources. Reportedly, people's health was also affected by not having money to access services as well as direct health costs. In turn, health also affected financial security through creating barriers to finding and keeping work, and subsequent financial security, creating a mutually reinforcing cycle of difficulty. Participants saw these health effects as compounded by other aspects of visa conditions, such as the barriers to family reunion.

Emotional responses

The processing of visa applications for people from the Legacy Caseload has often meant long and protracted visa determinations and, as a consequence, ongoing financial precarity. Refugees, asylum seekers, and service providers reported this as taking a toll on mental health in particular, through despair and hopelessness. Service providers described the poor mental health of those clients who are without income support after having their claims for asylum refused:

> The people who come here who have nothing, they're very depressed. They present as depressed. They look sad. They have—they really have no hope. They don't know where they're going. They're just living from day to day. They're vulnerable and desperate.
>
> Despair. I think despair . . . it's just despair . . . they get a tiny little bit of hope and then something else just throws them back. A little thing you know. I mean, well to us, a little thing, but it's magnified to them.

All participants, regardless of visa status or work rights, reported emotional difficulties associated with financial precarity and visa insecurity. Denpa, for example, said, "With not a job, no income and life become not meaningful." While others described their frustration and despair as a result of their precarious immigration status and financial situation making them "sick" and "broken":

> I told [Immigration] "why are you giving me hard time? Do you need a sick person to live in the community or a healthy person?" . . . they have put me under so much pressure that I have changed, and I've become another person. I was not like this back home in Iran.
>
> (Hashem, Iranian male, bridging visa)

> I never touch someone in my life as a fighting. Now, looking from last year, two years ago, I'm really different. I punch more than 20 times to glasses. My car glass—I broke two or three times, four times . . . when you start to problem here [points to head], finish! When here [points to head] is broke, it's too hard to back [recover] [sic].
>
> (Marduk, Iranian male, bridging visa)

Ongoing uncertainty associated with visa precarity also resulted in fear and worry in relation to being sent back to their country of origin or placed in detention. One service provider described the trauma experienced by asylum seeker clients denied refugee status, who feared deportation:

> [The government] say, well you can go back [to a part of the country] most of them have never been to and their families are in another part of the country, or in another country. It's—we're dealing with that trauma.
>
> (Service Provider)

Another service provider gave an account of accompanying an asylum seeker client to a meeting with the DHA:

> Just going to a bloody meeting with someone—any kind of meeting or any kind of bureaucratic meeting is—I mean one of our clients had to go to the immigration department the other day and they were terrified they were going to be taken to detention. They thought they were going to be taken to detention and they were absolutely terrified.
>
> (Service Provider)

Another participant, Khanh, an asylum seeker from Vietnam, had no visa and was awaiting a merits review before the AAT. She described her fear as a result of her visa precarity and, like Hashem, spoke of the impact of high levels of pressure on her mental health:

> I am very concerned, also—we don't have a valid visa. So, you know, we're living here unlawfully. So, in that case, they can just detain us anytime, and take us to the detention centre . . . and I have nightmares about the fact that

> they would send us back to Vietnam. So, the pressure is very, very high, for my mental [health].

In addition to uncertainty associated with temporary visa status, refugees and asylum seekers holding such visas do not have the opportunity to apply for family reunion in Australia. Ongoing uncertainty in relation to seeing family again and worry about their well-being was also reported as having a significant bearing on the mental health and well-being of a number of participants. For example, one service provider said, "They've all got bad mental health because they're all separate from their families."

Tabish, a bridging visa holder, also believed that his poor mental health was a direct result of being separated from his wife and five children, ranging in age from ten to nineteen years, for more than six years, especially in relation to his fear for their safety:

> I'm very worried about their safety as you're aware that in Afghanistan there is a lot of risk . . . so I very worried about them and that's one of the causes of my mental condition . . . my mental condition is getting worse [sic].

Another source of emotional discomfort related to reliance on support from community organisations. Refugee and asylum seeker participants frequently indicated that seeking support was not a preferred option. However, as highlighted earlier, many refugees and asylum seekers on temporary visas were forced to search for support from various organisations, often leading to feelings of shame:

> Anybody who told me that there is a place that they could possibly help you, I have gone there and I have tried to seek help. I have to and I don't have a choice and I don't have anybody here that could help me. (Hashem, male, Iran, bridging visa)
>
> It is not very good relying on or asking—I don't feel like asking for help from the service like this, all the time. (Minh, Vietnam, bridging visa)
>
> I don't like this job [seeking financial support] but sometimes my life very pressure me, I have to come here . . . Actually I be shy every time I came here [sic]. (Amir, Iran, SHEV)

Moreover, service providers referenced feelings of shame experienced by clients in the context of prolonged financial precarity:

> I think probably underlying that is probably a sense of shame and . . . I think they're—all these people are adults so, I'm sure there is a lack of—or they've lost a lot of pride in this process.
>
> (Service Provider)

For some participants, this range of emotional difficulties culminated in significant mental health issues and in some cases suicidality. For example, in addition to Marduk's account of his deteriorating mental state as a consequence of his visa and financial precarity (described earlier), he detailed his feelings of distress and suicidal thoughts in relation to the sustained period of uncertainty or "bad luck" that he has experienced:

> Not knowing what's happening . . . Every night, every night I'm thinking about this . . . There was a storm in 2016 when I start my bad luck. And I thinking about it every night when I sleep. I feel really really bad. I almost kill myself two or three times, and then I only I think about my mums and my family [sic].
>
> (male, Iran, bridging visa)

In another example, Sara, a SHEV holder who arrived with her sisters (without their) parents in 2013, was hospitalised for depression after a long period of uncertainty on a bridging visa without work rights and following the death of one of her sisters.

Inability to afford health and other services

In addition to emotional responses to financial and visa precarity, participants and service providers also reported difficulties paying for medical care as a consequence of cuts to income support: "people with health conditions, if they don't have a healthcare card the cost is very high. That's prohibitive in some cases and some of them have—it's life—they have life threatening sicknesses. So, they need their medication" (Service Provider). Similarly, Hashem reported delaying seeing his doctor about his debilitating back pain because of the financial precarity he was experiencing due to cuts to his income support: "last night I was awake because of my back pain until 5:00 a.m. Because it's been three months that I haven't gone to the doctor, because my Centrelink has actually stopped. And I don't have any money to purchase medication" (Iranian male, bridging visa). Service providers said their clients often reported forgoing medication or medical treatment because of financial precarity. Those with dependents were described as particularly vulnerable to poor health outcomes:

> The consequences for their health are quite serious. One lady has a number of health issues and she's now having to come off medication because she can't afford it, which then puts her in a position where her health is going to deteriorate and then what capacity is she going to have to care for her children as a single mother? . . . These are the impacts we see of people not having money or access to money.
>
> (Service Provider)

Moreover, both refugee and asylum seeker parents described difficulties affording medical treatment/care for their children. Kiana, a single mother with two young children with special needs was recently granted a SHEV and receives the special benefit payment. However, with limited English language skills, the prohibitive cost of childcare and no local experience in the labour market, Kiana has been unable to find suitable work. Furthermore, support from the government to facilitate therapies and treatment for her children's condition is not available to SHEV holders. Kiana noted:

> I'm always each month—each month I am going to—I go to hospital, Women's and Children's Hospital about my son . . . But NDIS doesn't support because my visa is different and difficult for support and my son eligible for NDIS, but they can't support me.
>
> (Iranian female, SHEV)

Another parent to two young children, Minh from Vietnam, was on a bridging visa with no income support or work rights. Minh was upset during the interview when describing his worries about not having the means to pay for potential medical expenses, particularly for his children:

> Before, when I was working—so, I had the money. When the children are sick, you can call the ambulance, and I'm able to pay for the fees—the doctor's fees, and all that. But now, I'm not working. So, when they are sick again, I'm not sure if I can afford to call the ambulance for the children. That's what is making it so difficult.

Poor health as a barrier to employment/income

Participants also reported their health issues as impacting their access to employment and subsequent financial security, highlighting the intertwined nature of these factors. For example, some described physical injuries, sustained in their countries of origin, as a barrier to employment. Tabish, for example, had been in Australia for six years after fleeing Afghanistan. Tabish had endured mental and physical torture, described living with physical pain, and was taking medication for his depression. He was awaiting a judicial review after having his claims for refugee status denied twice, which meant he was immediately ineligible for income support. Tabish was unable to find suitable work that accommodated his physical injuries although he had made numerous attempts: "the injury my head and my lower back . . . doesn't let me to work, the condition of the pain get worse."

Amir, an Iranian refugee, was also unable to find work because of a serious back injury: "my position body, all my document doctor say me 'Don't sit two hours more driving, your medicine is sleepy and you cannot working" [sic]. Likewise, Hashem said that a back injury prevented him from even looking for work: "if I put strain on my back a little bit then my legs get locked and then I will fall. Most of the time I have to spend sitting or lying down."

Service providers also described the financial vulnerability of older clients and those with compounding health issues, particularly from Afghanistan, who, though deemed "work ready," were not in fact able to work:

> So they have no money and they can't work because they're elderly [in their] seventies it's really the older people, or the people with chronic health problems who can't work. They're the ones who're disadvantaged. (Service Provider)
>
> I don't think there's enough investigation into that, into people's health to just—to see whether they are work ready. You can't just say someone is work ready.
>
> (Service Provider)

Service providers also noted the emotional and mental vulnerability of many individuals in this group, and though they may have work this did not necessarily translate to being able to fulfil the requirements of one's job: "[someone] can be fine [able to work and with a job] and the next day [they're] not."

In the context of compounding stressors, such as having no income, searching for work, seeking support from various services, and ongoing uncertainty about the future vis-à-vis their temporary visas, one service provider noted "a lot of confusion and a lot of forgetfulness" amongst their clients in navigating the complex immigration and welfare systems. Another service provided shared a similar account:

> They can't hold onto that information. They don't remember to bring things that you've told them can you bring that piece of paper in, and they can't deal with it [then there's] despair and shame when they realise they have forgotten vital paper work.
>
> (Service Provider)

Tabish articulated this dilemma:

> Because of my tension or depression I [hope to] receive some help regarding my visa application, that will be very grateful . . . my mental condition is getting worse because I also have, I suffer from the short of memory [sic] (Afghan male, bridging visa).

Discussion

This chapter has highlighted the financial and visa precarity of refugees and asylum seekers associated with immigration and welfare policies and their impacts on health and well-being. Financial precarity was a central feature of the accounts of participants in the context of their temporary visas. This transient state affected their ability to secure work, as well as their capacity to seek greater visa security more generally and enjoy other human rights such as family reunion. Impacts on health and well-being, particularly mental health, were evidenced through the reporting of a range of difficult emotional responses as well as barriers accessing essential health and other services. Findings also indicated that poor health status had reciprocal effect on employment prospects and associated financial status, highlighting the interwoven nature of the relationships between financial and visa precarity and health. This relationship was also noted where participants struggled to navigate immigration and welfare bureaucracy in the context of poor mental health, financial precarity, and limited financial support with legal appeals. This chapter concludes with some recommendations in light of these findings.

Cuts to income support for temporary visa holders were found to be a key contributing factor to financial precarity. This was particularly the case for asylum seekers who had had their claims for refugee status denied (and were seeking judicial review) or who were still undergoing visa determination but did not meet the "financial hardship" criteria and were of a working age. The transition period between asylum seeker bridging visas and substantive refugee visas (SHEV or TPV) was also a time during which income support was interrupted or cut, resulting in periods of extreme financial vulnerability. Three quarters of the participants were relying exclusively on community organisations for financial support and only three were employed, all on a casual basis with wages that they reported were not enough to live on. These findings reflect many of the concerns voiced by advocacy organisations, such as the RCOA, about temporary visas.

Barriers to employment as a pathway to financial security was reported as a significant issue for all refugee and asylum seeker participants as well as service providers, with their temporary visa and associated conditions highlighted as limiting employment options, reflecting findings of previous research (van Kooy and Bowman 2019; Ziersch et al. 2021). Many participants had been on temporary bridging visas without work rights for extended periods of time after arriving in Australia. Even when work rights were granted, participants had experienced long periods without involvement in the workforce and the associated financial and other benefits of employment (e.g. opportunities to develop English language skills, social connections, confidence and a sense of purpose) (Warfa et al. 2012). These missed opportunities, as well as the short length of some bridging visas and limited access to English language programs, contributed to ongoing difficulties many people faced in finding work. A lack of access to other benefits, such as childcare subsidies, was also found to be an obstacle to finding secure employment. The particular mandate around job-readiness that arose after changes to welfare policy for people seeking asylum was also found to be problematic given the lack of understanding of refugee resettlement challenges that can impede employment prospects (Ziersch et al.

2020). As van Kooy and Bowman (2019) argue, these challenges constitute a "manufactured precarity" that are a consequence of immigration policies that compound to undermine the efforts of asylum seekers to build new lives in Australia.

This study indicated that financial precarity and visa insecurity (as well as drawn out visa determination processes and restrictive visa conditions, such as no family reunification) were important factors that impacted the social determinants of health for refugee and asylum seeker participants. In particular, emotional responses to the stress of financial precarity and visa temporariness were evident including despair and hopelessness, anger and frustration, and fear of deportation/being returned to detention and for the safety of family in countries of origin. These findings build on previous research highlighting the negative health impacts of temporary visas through stress, uncertainty, and insecurity (Silove et al. 2000; Steel and Silove 2001; Marston 2003; Nickerson et al. 2019) and emphasise the negative impacts of family separation on well-being (Nickerson et al. 2010; Savic et al. 2013; Miller et al. 2018). The study also revealed self-reported feelings of shame in having to rely on others for financial resources, rather than being self-sufficient, reflecting findings from earlier research noting the importance of having a sense of control over one's life (Marston 2003; Johnston et al. 2009).

Our findings, discussed in this chapter, also add to emerging evidence that temporary visas impact health through poverty and disadvantage (Omeri et al. 2006; Silove et al. 2007; Sengoelge et al. 2020) and cause difficulties in accessing healthcare (Hadgkiss and Renzaho 2014; Bambra et al. 2010; Taylor and Haintz 2018). While difficulties affording healthcare (medication, consultation fees, transportation fees to appointments) are universal experiences for those living in poverty, refugees and asylum seekers are at higher risk of health issues and temporary visas are an additional barrier to accessing healthcare services (Omeri et al. 2006). We also identified a reciprocal relationship between health and financial security, whereby health issues also affected financial security through creating barriers to finding and keeping work, such that they were mutually reinforcing difficulties. For a number of participants these compounding stressors were associated with significant mental health difficulties.

This study examined the lived experiences of a group of refugees and asylum seekers living on the margins and gained insights into the impact of financial precarity on their lives. However, there were a number of limitations. For instance, given that all refugee and asylum seeker participants were financially precarious it was not possible to unpack how different levels of financial precarity might affect health, and the small sample size prohibited a systematic examination of the impact of different factors, such as country of origin, time in Australia, and family circumstances. However, the study was able to provide a detailed and nuanced picture of the lived experiences of a hard-to-reach group of financially precarious individuals on temporary visas, as a way of identifying the compounding factors impacting health and well-being. Service provider accounts supplemented refugees' and asylum seekers' testimony by giving their experiences of working with a broad range of clients.

Recommendations

It was clear from the findings that current immigration and welfare policy in relation to temporary refugee and asylum seeker visas contributed significantly to financial precarity and poor health for the participants. Ongoing visa uncertainty and lack of family reunion, limited access to services, and inappropriate determinations of work readiness worked in concert to damage health. Key policy implications that can be drawn from the findings highlight the need for urgent immigration law reform through the abolishment of the "fast track" process. Additional resources are required to increase the capacity of the Home Affairs Office to process claims for asylum in an appropriate time frame and legal funding is required to assist asylum seekers with their claims. Ultimately, SHEVs and TPVs should be abolished: if people are successful in their claim for refugee status then they should be provided with a permanent protection visa with related rights, including the opportunity to apply for prompt family reunion. We acknowledge the need for bridging visas while claims to asylum are being processed but argue that these should come with the same welfare and work rights as other temporary visas.

Targeted support is critical to assist many people seeing asylum to develop the skills (including English language) and confidence they need to find secure employment. The present mainstream employment support service, Jobactive, has been found to be ineffective for the broader population (permanent residents and citizens) not least people from asylum seeking backgrounds (RCOA 2017; Parliament of Australia 2019). Funding is critical for culturally appropriate services that are trauma informed to improve the chances of people on temporary visas achieving financial security through employment.

Last, the research highlighted the impact of a lack of access to social security benefits. The COVID-19 pandemic and the lack of access of some temporary visa holders to social security response measures further demonstrated the extreme precarity of temporary visa holders and their dependence on changing policies introduced by governments without consideration to health and well-being (Kenny 2020; Farhart 2020; van Kooy 2020). Those on temporary visas should have access to the full suite of relevant social security benefits to ensure an equitable safety net for those who are unable to search for or undertake employment.

Conclusion

In summary, current immigration and welfare policies associated with asylum seeker processes and temporary visa conditions compound the risk factors for ill-health for refugees and asylum seekers by placing people at financial risk and exposing them to long periods of uncertainty. The adverse health impacts of this can be significant and long lasting and, therefore, law and policy settings warrant urgent reform.

Note

1 See Chapter 1 for an explanation of the Legacy Caseload and temporary protection measures.

References

Alemi, Q., James, S., Cruz, R., Zepeda, V. and Racadio, M. (2014) 'Psychological distress in Afghan refugees: A mixed-method systematic review', *Journal of Immigration Minority Health*, 16(6): 1247.

Australian Human Rights Commission. (2019) *Lives on hold: Refugees and asylum seekers in the 'Legacy Caseload'*. AHRC.

Bambra, C., Gibson, M., Sowden, A., Wright, K., Whitehead, M. and Petticrew M. (2010) 'Tackling the wider social determinants of health and health inequalities: Evidence from systematic reviews', *Journal of Epidemiology & Community Health*, 64(4): 284.

Blythe, R., Clarke J., Connell, T., Wallace, J. and Woods, C. (2018) *States of Refuge: Access to Health, Housing and Education for People Seeking Asylum and Refugees in Australia.* Liberty Victoria.

Bogic, M., Njoku, A. and Priebe, S. (2015) 'Long-term mental health of war-refugees: A systematic literature review', *BMC International Health Hum Rights*, 15(1): 29.

Braveman, P. and Gottlieb, L. (2014) 'The social determinants of health: It's time to consider the causes of the causes', *Public Health Reports*, 129(1_suppl2): 19.

Chen, W., Hall, B., Ling., L. and Renzaho, A. (2017) 'Pre-migration and post-migration factors associated with mental health in humanitarian migrants in Australia and the moderation effect of post-migration stressors: Findings from the first wave data of the BNLA cohort study', *Lancet Psychiatry*, 4(3): 218.

Coffey, G., Kaplan, I., Sampson, R. and Tucci, M. (2010) 'The meaning and mental health consequences of long-term immigration detention for people seeking asylum', *Social Science & Medicine*, 70(12): 2070.

Davidson, H. (2019) 'Australia on track for record number of asylum seekers arriving by plane, Labor says', *The Guardian*, 8 October.

Department of Home Affairs (DHA). (2020a) 'Safe haven enterprise visa'. https://immi.homeaffairs.gov.au/visas/getting-a-visa/visa-listing/safe-haven-enterprise-790

DHA. (2020b) 'Visa statistics- statistical information on visit, study, work, migration and humanitarian visas'. www.homeaffairs.gov.au/research-and-statistics/statistics/visa-statistics/live/humanitarian-program

DHA. (2020c) 'Illegal maritime arrivals on bridging E visa'. www.homeaffairs.gov.au/research-and-stats/files/illegal-maritime-arrivals-bve-june-2020.pdf

DHA. (2020d) 'Status resolution service'. https://immi.homeaffairs.gov.au/what-we-do/status-resolution-service/status-resolution-support-services

Farhart, C. (2020) 'Scott Morrison urged to extend coronavirus assistance to one million "vulnerable" temporary visa holders', *SBS News*, 4 May.

Fazel, M., Reed, R., Panter-Brick, C. and Stein, A. (2012) 'Mental health of displaced and refugee children resettled in high-income countries: Risk and protective factors', *The Lancet*, 379(9812): 266.

Fazel, M. and Stein, A. (2003) 'Mental health of refugee children: Comparative study', *British Medical Journal*, 327(7407): 134.

Fazel, M., Wheeler, J. and Danesh, J. (2005) 'Prevalence of serious mental disorder in 7000 refugees resettled in western countries: A systematic review', *The Lancet*, 365(9467): 1309.

Fleischman, Y., Willen, S., Davidovitch, N. and Mor, Z. (2015) 'Migration as a social determinant of health for irregular migrants: Israel as case study', *Social Science & Medicine*, 147: 89.

Funk, M., Drew, N. and Knapp, M. (2012) 'Mental health, poverty and development', *Journal of Public Mental Health*, 11(4): 166.

Hadgkiss, E. J. and Renzaho, A. M. (2014) 'The physical health status, service utilisation and barriers to accessing care for asylum seekers residing in the community: A systematic review of the literature', *Australian Health Review*, 38(2): 142.

Hartley, L. and Fleay, C. (2017) '"We are like animals": Negotiating dehumanising experiences of asylum-seeker policies in the Australian community', *Refugee Survey Quarterly*, 36(4): 45.

Hollifield, M., Warner, T., Lian, N., Krakow, B., Jenkins, J., Kesler, J., Stevenson, J. and Westermeyer, J. (2002) 'Measuring trauma and health status in refugees: A critical review', *Jama: The Journal of the American Medical Association*, 288(5): 611.

Hynie, M. (2018) 'The social determinants of refugee mental health in the post-migration context: A critical review', *Canadian Journal of Psychiatry*, 63(5): 297.

Johnston, V., Allotey, P., Mulholland, K. and Markovic, M. (2009) 'Measuring the health impact of human rights violations related to Australian asylum policies and practices: A mixed methods study', *BMC International Health & Human Rights*, 9(1): 1.

Kenny, M. A. (2020) *Temporary Visa Holders Left Behind in Australia*. Public Policy Institute, The University of Western Australia.

Kenny, M. A. and Procter, N. (2016) 'The fast track refugee assessment process and the mental health of vulnerable asylum seekers', *Psychiatry Psychology and Law*, 23(1): 62.

Kenny, M. A., Procter, N. and Grech, C. (2016) 'Mental health and legal representation for asylum seekers in the "legacy caseload"', *Cosmopolitan Civil Societies—An Interdisciplinary Journal*, 8(2): 84.

Li, S. S., Liddell, B. J. and Nickerson, A. (2016) 'The relationship between post-migration stress and psychological disorders in refugees and asylum seekers', *Current Psychiatry Reports*, 18(9): 82.

Lund, C. (2012) 'Poverty and mental health: A review of practice and policies', *Neuropsychiatry*, 2(3): 213.

Lund, C., Breen. A., Fisher, A., Kakuma, R., Corrigall, J., Joska, J., Swartz, L. and Patel, V. (2010) 'Poverty and common mental disorders in low and middle income countries: A systematic review', *Social Science & Medicine*, 71(3): 517.

Marmot, M. (2002) 'The influence of income on health: Views of an epidemiologist', *Health Affairs*, 21(2): 31.

Marston, G. (2003) *Temporary Protection, Permanent Uncertainty: The Experience of Refugees Living on Temporary Protection Visas*. Centre for Applied Social Research, RMIT University.

McDonald, E. and O'Sullivan, M. (2018) 'Protecting vulnerable refugees: Procedural fairness in the Australian Fast Track regime', *University of New South Wales Law Journal*, 41: 1003.

Miller, G., Chen, E. and Cole, S. W. (2009) 'Health psychology: Developing biologically plausible models linking the social world and physical health', *Annual Review of Psychology*, 60: 501.

Miller, A., Hess, J., Bybee, D. and Goodkind, J. (2018) 'Understanding the mental health consequences of family separation for refugees: Implications for policy and practice', *American Journal of Orthopsychiatry*, 88(1): 26.

Newnham, E. A., Pearman, A., Olinga-Shannnon, S. and Nickerson, A. (2019) 'The mental health effects of visa insecurity for refugees and people seeking asylum: A latent class analysis', *International Journal of Public Health*, 64(5): 763.

Nickerson, A., Bryant, R., Steel, Z., Silove, D. and Brooks, R. (2010) 'The impact of fear for family on mental health in a resettled Iraqi refugee community', *Journal of Psychiatric Research*, 44(4): 229.

Nickerson, A., Byrow, Y., O'Donnell, M., Mau, V., McMahon, T., Pajak, R., Li, S., Hamilton, A., Minihan, S., Liu, C., Bryant, R., Berle, D. and Liddell, B. (2019) 'The association between visa insecurity and mental health, disability and social engagement in refugees living in Australia', *European Journal of Psychotraumatology*, 10(1): 1688129.

Omeri, A., Lennings, C. and Raymond, L. (2006) 'Beyond asylum: Implications for nursing and health care delivery for Afghan refugees in Australia', *Journal of Transcultural Nursing*, 17(1): 30–39.

Parliament of Australia. (2019) 'Jobactive: Failing those it is intended to serve'. https://parlinfo.aph.gov.au/parlInfo/download/committees/reportsen/024217/toc_pdf/Jobactivefailingthoseitisintendedtoserve.pdf;fileType= application%2Fpdf

Pavli, A. and Maltezou, H. (2017) 'Health problems of newly arrived migrants and refugees in Europe', *Journal of Travel Medicine*, 24(4).

Porter, M. and Haslam, N. (2005) 'Predisplacement and postdisplacement factors associated with mental health of refugees and internally displaced persons: A meta-analysis', *JAMA: Journal of the American Medical Association*, 294(5): 602.

Procter, N. G. (2004) 'Re-traumatisation, fear and suicidal thinking: A case study of 'boatpeople' from Australia', *Migration Letters*, 1(1): 42–49.

Refugee Council of Australia. (2017) *Not working: Experiences of refugees and migrants with jobactive*. RCOA.

Refugee Council of Australia. (2019) *Barriers to education for people seeking asylum and refugees on temporary visas*. RCOA.

Reilly, A. (2016) 'Asylum seekers in the community: The importance of work for a decent life', *Australian Journal of Human Rights*, 22(1): 1.

Ritchie, J. and Spencer, L. (1994) 'Qualitative data analysis for applied policy research', in Bryman, A. and Burgess, B. (eds) *Analyzing Qualitative Data*. Routledge, 173.

Savic, M., Chur-Hansen, A., Mahmood, M. and Moore, V. (2013) 'Separation from family and its impact on the mental health of Sudanese refugees in Australia: A qualitative study', *Australian and New Zealand Journal of Public Health*, 37(4): 383.

Savic, M., Chur-Hansen, A., Mahmood, M. and Moore, V. (2016) '"We don't have to go and see a special person to solve this problem": Trauma, mental health beliefs and processes for addressing "mental health issues" among Sudanese refugees in Australia', *International Journal of Social Psychiatry*, 62(1): 76.

Sengoelge, M., Solberg, Ø., Nissen, A. and Saboonchi, F. (2020) 'Exploring social and financial hardship, mental health problems and the role of social support in asylum seekers using structural equation modelling', *International Journal of Environmental Research and Public Health*, 17(19): 6948

Services Australia (SA). (2020) 'How much you can get', www.servicesaustralia.gov.au/individuals/services/centrelink/jobseeker-payment/how-much-you-can-get

Silove, D., Steel, Z., Susljik, I., Frommer, N., Loneragan, C., Chey, T., Brooks, R., le Touze, D., Ceollo, M., Smith, M., Harris, E. and Bryant, R. (2007) 'The impact of the refugee decision on the trajectory of PTSD, anxiety, and depressive symptoms among asylum seekers: A longitudinal study', *American Journal of Disaster Medicine*, 2(6): 321.

Silove, D., Steel, Z. and Watters, C. (2000) 'Policies of deterrence and the mental health of asylum seekers', *JAMA: Journal of American Medical Association*, 284(5): 604–611.

Siriwardhana, C., Ali, S., Roberts, B. and Stewart, R. (2014) 'A systematic review of resilience and mental health outcomes of conflict-driven adult forced migrants', *Conflict Health*, 8(1): 13.

Steel, Z., Chey, T., Silove, D., Marnane, C., Bryant, R. and van Ommeren, M. (2009) 'Association of torture and other potentially traumatic events with mental health outcomes among populations exposed to mass conflict and displacement: A systematic review and meta-analysis', *JAMA: Journal of American Medical Association*, 302(5): 537–549.

Steel, Z., Momartin, S., Silove, D., Coello, M., Aroche, J. and Tay, K. (2011) 'Two year psychosocial and mental health outcomes for refugees subjected to restrictive or supportive immigration policies', *Social Science Medicine*, 72(7): 1149.

Steel, Z. and Silove, D. M. (2001) 'The mental health implications of detaining asylum seekers', *The Medical Journal of Australia* 175(11–12): 596.

Taylor, J. and Haintz, G. L. (2018) 'Influence of the social determinants of health on access to healthcare services among refugees in Australia', *Australian Journal of Primary Health*, 24(1): 14.

van Kooy, J. (2020) *The Impacts of COVID-19 on People Seeking Asylum and Refugees on Temporary Visas*. Refugee Council of Australia.

van Kooy, J. and Bowman, D. (2019) '"Surrounded with so much uncertainty": Asylum seekers and manufactured precarity in Australia', *Journal of Ethnic and Migration Studies*, 45(5): 693.

Warfa, N., Curtis, S., Watters, C., Carswell, K., Ingleby, D. and Bhui, K. (2012) 'Migration experiences, employment status and psychological distress among Somali immigrants: A mixed-method international study', *BMC Public Health*, 12(1): 749.

World Health Organisation. (1946) *Preamble to the Constitution of the World Health Organization*, as Adopted by the International Health Conference.

World Health Organisation. (2008) (Commission on Social Determinants of Health), *Closing the gap in a generation: Health equity through action on the social determinants of health – Final report of the commission on social determinants of health*. World Health Organisation.

Ziersch, A., Due, C. and Walsh, M. (2020) 'Discrimination: A health hazard for people from refugee and asylum-seeking backgrounds resettled in Australia', *BMC Public Health*, 20(1): 108.

Ziersch, A., Due, C., Arthurson, K. and Loehr, N. (2019) 'Conducting ethical research with people from asylum seeker and refugee backgrounds', in Liamputtong, P. (ed.), *Handbook of Research Methods in Health Social Sciences*. Springer, 1871.

Ziersch, A., Walsh, M., Due, C. and Reilly, A. (2021) 'Temporary refugee and migration visas in Australia—An occupational health and safety hazard', *International Journal of Health Services* 51(4): 531.

Chapter 7

Navigating the threat of *refoulement* arising from the trifecta of welfare conditionality, behavioural codes, and short-term visas

Hanne Worsoe and Greg Marston***

Introduction

This chapter examines situations for those protection seekers who fail Australia's refugee status determination scheme (known as "fast-track") for designated maritime arrivals. Introduced in December 2014, under the *Migration and Maritime Powers (Resolving the Asylum Legacy Caseload) Act 2014 (Cth)* (*Asylum Legacy Caseload Act*, hereafter), "fast-track" is a truncated administrative scheme of "due process" applying to over 30,000 "unauthorised maritime arrivals" arriving in Australia after 12 August 2012. It also includes some "unauthorised maritime arrivals" from before this time, whose claims were not finalised by the government by 8 September 2013 (RCOA 2020). Based on official statistics from the Department of Home Affairs (DHA), at the time of writing, there are 10,467 people in the community on temporary visas having failed to secure a substantive protection visa via "fast-track" processes, with 2,275 awaiting the reissuing of a further, short-term, bridging visa (BVE). (Department of Home Affairs 2020).

Asylum seekers whose visa claims fail under the "fast-track" are impacted in diverse ways by several intersecting policies that push them to consider returning to a place of potential persecution and serious harm; a process known in international law as constructive *refoulement* (Mathew 2019). This chapter provides a de-identified case study to show how people navigate the threat of *refoulement*, sometimes with help from allies from within the Australian community. Truncated refugee status determination processes, minimal welfare supports, temporary (short-term) visas, and behavioural monitoring of asylum seekers are key features of the regulation of asylum seekers subject to the "fast-track" scheme.

The first part of this chapter outlines the policy background to the "fast-track" regime. The second part outlines a conceptual framework and methodology that helps illuminate this regime. The third part presents a detailed, de-identified case study demonstrating how asylum seekers attempt to navigate their way through legal procedures, welfare restrictions, behavioural monitoring,

DOI: 10.4324/9781003298595-12

and short-term visas to defy/contest constructive *refoulement* or simply, coerced return to a place of persecution.

Policy background

Gill and Good (2019: 3) have referred to a "schizophrenia" of states' competing models on how to approach refugee issues: a tussle between the need to recognise individual asylum seeker cases on their merits and an instrumentalised security model focusing on control of refugees and minimising their "perceived risks" to the host country. In Australia, this has morphed into competitive strong-arming tactics, as successive governments of both political persuasions attempt to outdo each other in their quests to "keep borders secure" from people seeking asylum. The last two decades have seen increasingly punitive policies introduced to deter and deflect unauthorised arrivals by sea (Billings 2013; Briskman et al. 2008; Marr and Wilkinson 2004; Phillips 2014). In 2012, as "unauthorised sea-arrivals"[1] climbed to their highest numbers since the Indo-Chinese refugee crisis of the 1970s (Higgins 2017; Phillips and Sprinks 2013) the Labor Government's "No Advantage" policy included a freeze on the processing of asylum claims for those within Australia ("onshore"). Denied English language classes, work rights, and family reunion, these asylum seekers instead had to live off a financial allowance that was 89% of the Australian unemployment benefit, placing them below poverty line.[2]

The "No Advantage" policy has been described as "policy as punishment" (Hartley and Fleay 2014), with people unable to afford food or medical treatment and experiencing mental ill-heath from their unresolved status and separation from family in home countries (see, e.g. Fleay and Briskman 2013; Fleay and Hoffman 2014; Hartley and Fleay 2014; Fleay et al. 2015). Once work rights were granted in 2015, asylum seekers struggled to find secure work; few employers wanted workers on short-term visas who could not speak English (Fleay and Hartley 2016; Fleay et al. 2016; Hartley and Fleay 2017).

Moreover, from December 2013, all asylum seekers who arrived unauthorised by sea issued with bridging visas had to sign a behaviour contract (Methven and Vogl 2014, 2019), threatening detention-deportation if they breached any law, however minor, and which forbade them from engaging in anti-social or disruptive behaviours. These requirements and expectations have rightly been described as legal overreach, conspiring to induce a state of fear in asylum-seeking people (Vogl and Methven 2015).

The *Asylum Legacy Caseload Act 2014* introduced both "fast-track" procedures and, for successful claimants, heralded temporary protected status: via a three-year temporary protection visa (TPV) or a five-year safe haven enterprise visa (SHEV).[3] Those rejected on the merits of their claim under "fast-track" remained on the shorter "Bridging E" visas (BVEs), periodically renewable every one to six months pending completion of all available legal avenues for redress (including judicial review).

The *Asylum Legacy Caseload Act 2014* implied that asylum-seeking people were a "caseload" and a "problem" that needed "resolving" rather than people needing fair and robust assessment for refugee recognition. After "fast-track" came into force, social and medical research indicated that "fast-track" processing, on top of previous punitive policies, and the act of seeking refuge, induced a state of "lethal hopelessness" (Proctor et al. 2018) among asylum-seeking people subject to its processes. People struggled to complete application forms in English without publicly funded legal assistance, faced official suspicion about the veracity of their refugee claim, and experienced ongoing job marginalisation and difficulties accessing social welfare supports.

The abridged "fast-track" refugee processing regime, limits on welfare support, temporary visas, and behavioural monitoring have become technologies of punitive control within a structurally violent administrative regime, leaving people in "manufactured precarity" (van Kooy and Bowman 2019).

From biopolitics to necropolitics

For this chapter, we draw on conceptual frameworks that include a range of complementary ideas about the exercise of power, including biopolitics (Foucault 1978, 1979, 2008), structural and cultural violence (Galtung 1990), and necropolitics (Mbembe 2019), in order to examine the subjectification of people rejected under "fast-track" refugee processing. This conceptual bridge is in keeping with the move, over the past decade, in Australian asylum seeker policy to outright punitive policy. In keeping with a tendency in countries of the Global North—particularly the United States (Miller 2005), but also the United Kingdom (Mayblin 2020) and Europe (van der Woude et al. 2017)—these policies essentially criminalise the actions of many people seeking refugee protection; an aspect of what Stumpf has characterised as "crimmigration" (Stumpf 2014). The racialised suspicion of many seeking refugee status, particularly after the terrorist attacks in New York on 11 September 2001, equates people of Middle Eastern and Muslim origins with terrorism, even if they are themselves fleeing from such terror (Miller 2005). In appreciating asylum seeker policy in terms of "crimmigration," we can recognise the expansion of state power that collapses migration, security, and ethnicity with crime (Stumpf in Billings 2019, 6). Such "crimmigration" is inherently biopolitical, governing bodies as they attempt to seek safety by restricting their capacity to gain full membership in the destination country.

Biopolitics refers to technologies and rationalities used to regulate and govern a given population at the juncture between the body and population (Foucault 1978). Foucault was concerned with how scientific knowledge and measurement produced governable subjects for the state to pursue certain ends: minimising disease, reducing crime rates, or protecting sovereign borders from "risky arrivals." The *telos* of government "makes things better" for society, by deploying scientific and juridical expertise to gain knowledge about the population (in this case, the population of those who arrived by boat without a visa). It then folds this knowledge back into the body politic to promote self-governing subjects consistent with various forms of liberalism. Biopolitics, therefore, seeks to examine *all* mechanisms of power, not just those regarded as oppressive. However, there is a close relationship between security and freedom that fuses productive and oppressive mechanisms of power. In the case of refugee policy, technologies of security come to legitimise detention and a protracted and invasive assessment process for asylum-seeking people arriving in Australia uninvited. Harsh policies directed at unauthorised arrivals are publicly justified in the interests of respecting the "rule of law," emphasising state sovereignty through the "strengthening" of border controls and protecting the security of citizens. These policies are backed through political discourse labelling sea-arriving people as "illegal" (Abbott 2013, 2012; Karlsen 2017), impatient "queue jumpers" (Houston 2012), and "unruly" individuals who have disregarded the Australian visa system despite the fact that they could not readily access it (Zagor 2015). This policy framing glosses over of lack of access to efficient and timely refugee processing in transit countries where many people are left waiting decades for resolution of refugee status (Glendinning 2015).

This chapter recognises "fast-track" refugee processing and associated policies directed at the Legacy Caseload as "structurally violent." Galtung first coined "structural violence" to conceptualise violence committed without a direct perpetrator (Galtung 1969), his later work conceptualising violence as constituted by three mutually supporting sides of a "triangle of violence" (Galtung 1990). "Direct violence" referred to acts of violence directly inflicted on another person by a direct perpetrator. "Structural violence" conceptualised bureaucracy as violent, with differential damaging effects according to race, gender, ethnicity or, in this instance, mode of (maritime) arrival in the destination country as an asylum seeker. "Cultural violence" referred to the ideological underpinnings of structural violence and direct violence, the beliefs and normative assumptions justifying policy (structural violence) and behaviour (direct violence) (Galtung 1990).

Writing a decade ago, criminologists Weber and Pickering noted that border controls in many international contexts where people seek safety involve violence in the form of death or some form of harm to the individual (Weber and Pickering 2011). Yet violence seeps over the border and into the community where "necropolitical" acts of bordering continue in asylum-seeking and refugee people's lives, more hidden than the overt "bordering" practices that may occur globally, such as in the United States for example (Riva 2017), including state neglect of those on the "migrant trail" into the southern United States (De Leon 2015). Two brief examples in the European context illustrate how subtler forms of state neglect can occur.

In Sweden, Barker (2018) analysed the Swedish welfare system, which defines people according to their degree of "Swedish-ness" rather than birth or visa status granting people the right to live in Sweden. Those who are refugees and migrants, and those who are children of refugees and migrants, are indirectly excluded in Swedish society through what she characterises as "penal nationalism." Such practices are not unique to Sweden. Similar tactics have long been employed in Great Britain with meagre levels of welfare support for asylum seekers (Mayblin et al. 2020).

Galtung's triangle of violence can be said to characterise much of the aforementioned state policies and practices. Australian asylum seeker policy particularly affects those seeking refuge who are not part of a "humanitarian intake." Those from countries in the Global South, where it is difficult to obtain a visa to fly into Australia to seek asylum, must cross into Australian waters by taking dangerous sea journeys on boats managed by people smugglers. Violence is apparent in the "cultural violence" where maritime arrivals seeking protection are verbalised as "illegal" by political leaders, in policy, and on government websites. Violence is apparent in the "direct violence" of immigration detention, random re-detention, and threatened *refoulement* for petty public order misdemeanours. Finally, violence is apparent in the "structural violence" of legislation such as the "fast track" refugee status determination regime (which elevates speedy determinations over procedural justice) and associated welfare policies for the Legacy Caseload.

Law and policy levers become technologies of control within a structurally violent system enabling a refugee-processing regime that is "necropolitical" in its effects, keeping people in marginalised states of being for prolonged periods. This is not simply the destitution of asylum seekers described by Mayblin (Mayblin 2020; Mayblin et al. 2020) or the dangerous boat crossings described by Weber and Pickering (2011) and others (Papailias 2019; Stümer 2018). This also entails the temporary visas and attendant insecurity that creates long-term harm to people (Momartin et al. 2006; Steel et al. 2011). Also, it involves bureaucratic inertia, by design: the slow or non-processing of people's visa claims that leaves them frustrated and in uncertain states of limbo (Davies and Isakjee 2019; Davies et al. 2017; Fleay and Hoffman 2014; Hartley and Fleay 2014, 2017; van Kooy and Bowman 2019).

Governmentality uses certain asylum seekers as corporeal examples of the consequences of punitive policy, with ripple effects of fear felt by others undergoing refugee status determination or facing rejection and expulsion. The re-detention of a Sri Lankan Tamil family from the remote Queensland town of Biloela is a case in point (Kenny and Procter 2019). Promised new bridging visas by DHA, this family's home was raided at dawn in March 2018, and the couple and their young children were forcibly put back into immigration detention for several years; first in Melbourne and then, in August 2019, on Christmas Island (Billings and Lelliott 2019; Davidson 2019a, 2019b, 2019c) where they remained isolated and in limbo until May 2021, when they were released into "community detention" (legally still detained but able to reside at a specified address and engage with the local community and access welfare supports). This type of immigration enforcement action crystallised implied threats of violence for asylum seekers in any interaction with government or official representatives. It could happen to them too.

Building on Foucault's concept of biopolitics, acknowledging that power can be both productive *and* repressive (Foucault 1978), Mbembe saw Foucault's notions of biopower and biopolitics working together with other technologies of power that operated more directly on subjectivity in an oppressive, disciplinary fashion. Mbembe (2019) developed the term "necropolitics" as the "other side" of the biopolitics coin, describing forms of oppressive governing with populations kept in "conditions that confer upon them the status of the *living dead*" or "deathworlds" (Mbembe 2019: 92). Necropolitics has already been used to conceptualise punitive refugee policy and refugee neglect in some European contexts: the lack of assistance for those making the Mediterranean crossing leading to drownings (Papailias 2019; Stümer 2018); the Calais refugee camps in France: first neglected, then bulldozed, then rebuilt, only to be bulldozed again (Davies et al. 2017); and, the UK government's hostile approach of keeping asylum-seeking people in states of poverty in the United Kingdom with minimal welfare payments and no work rights (Mayblin and James 2019; Mayblin 2020; Mayblin et al. 2020).

Consistent with these European "deathworlds" (Mbembe 2019: 62) of danger, neglect, poverty, and "bare-life" (Agamben 1998), Australia's asylum-seeker policies formulated, in part, to stop drownings at sea and "save lives" (Abbott 2012, 2013; Houston 2012), have created insecurity, destitution, and even death for asylum seekers, refugees, and those rejected as refugees under the "fast-track" administrative decision-making regime. As several contributors to this edited collection have shown,[4] an absence of assorted welfare supports and durable protection for refugees deliberately and progressively produce dire or "necropolitical" conditions for people. There is a "funnel" through which people seeking asylum are thrust by government policies, legislation, and administration, so that their behaviour and actions comply with the desired state outcome (Johansen 2013), even as they may resist that punitive law/policy pressure with the aid of advocates and other supporters. Their entrapment through this "funnelling"—whether via policy denying them welfare payments or law/policy labelling them as bad characters—leaves asylum seekers in "precarious and often immiserated lives" (Vecchio and Gerard 2018: 9).

Methodology

Based on ethnographic research undertaken over two years, from 2017 to 2019, at a voluntary asylum seeker support hub in a church in an Australian city, this chapter's first author, Hanne Worsoe, undertook fieldwork following the trajectory of "fast-track" refugee processing: from application for refugee status through to acceptance or rejection. However, this was not simply an observation of the administration of legal processes; its anthropological approach means this project "speaks back to policy" (Marston and McDonald 2006: 277), examining the social effects of law and policy (Nader 2016: 191), to discern the distinctive contexts of the operation of law (Gill and Good 2019: 310) and policy. Corroborating participant-observation fieldwork was supplemented with twenty semi-structured interviews: three interviews with advocates, and seventeen with those working professionally with asylum seekers: counsellors, psychologists, lawyers, migration agents, medical staff, social workers, and advocates. These interviews triangulated fieldwork observation.

Those recognised as refugees have a limited chance of resettlement, granted only three-year "temporary protection visas," or five-year "safe haven enterprise visas," rather than permanent resettlement with a clear path to citizenship. Those failing "fast-track" are subject to shorter, month-by-month "bridging E visas" (BVEs), making it difficult to sustain employment. As soon as the limited "fast-track" appeals process is finalised, all access to social benefits ceases for those whose claims are rejected. In focusing this chapter on the situations of those who have failed to obtain a positive outcome via "fast-track," we de-identified one situation encountered in the fieldwork, adding in elements from similar cases to protect peoples' identities. Exact dates have been altered; however, the trajectory was similar for all people appealing their visa rejection through the Federal Circuit Court on legal-procedural grounds. Therefore, the balance of this chapter focuses on one Afghan Hazara man, "Reza," whose protection visa claim was rejected under the "fast track" process.

Reza and "fast-track" rejection

In 2012 "Reza" fled Afghanistan, leaving behind his wife and 5-year-old daughter after being targeted by Taliban insurgents. Given the cost of a people smuggler he and his wife decided it was safer and cheaper for him to go first, and then bring the family to Australia once he was resettled. Reza arrived late in 2012 by sea, on a boat facilitated by people smugglers. However, the "No Advantage" policy had just been introduced by the then Labor Government, so people arriving irregularly by sea who were not sent offshore to Nauru or Manus Island, for regional processing purposes, had their claims for asylum frozen in Australia. Reza could not formally apply for refugee recognition after arrival. In limbo, Reza lived off 89% of an income support welfare benefit, because he was refused work rights under the "No Advantage" policy. He sent home what money he could to his wife who was unable to work in their Taliban-dominated province in Afghanistan. The necropolitical character of the "No Advantage" policy affected Reza immediately upon arrival in Australia.

In 2013 a change of federal government meant a change in policy. Reza now had to sign a behaviour contract (Vogl and Methven 2015), warning him he would be re-detained in an immigration detention centre if he contravened Australian laws. He did not see the point of signing such a document as he had always been law abiding, and the document mentioned him committing potential acts of terrorism and sexual abuse, which he found offensive. He had come to Australia to escape terrorism, not to commit it. However, upon being told he would be returned to Afghanistan if he did not sign, he felt he had no choice, and he signed the behaviour contract.

In December 2014, two years after Reza's arrival, Australia passed laws enacting an expedited, "fast-track" refugee status determination regime. Six months later Reza was finally given work rights. He found a job, using *Gumtree*, relying on Google Translate to help navigate the site, as he had been refused access to English lessons under the "No Advantage" policy. He was proud of the fact that he quickly found a job as a tiler after showing his employer photographs on his phone of his completed jobs in Afghanistan. It had been hard to explain to his family back home why he could not work for three years, yet still send them the money they needed to live. He had lived off two small meals daily, sharing quarters with three other Hazara men he'd met while in immigration detention. Reza was relieved to work. Not only could he send more money home but also he could now afford to have his refugee protection claim prepared. Under "fast-track" processing, most asylum seekers received no publicly funded legal assistance and representation, and access to pro bono legal support is limited.

In 2016, four years after waiting, Reza received a letter from the Immigration Minister "inviting" him to apply for a visa via the bespoke "fast-track" processing scheme for maritime arrivals in the Legacy Caseload. This letter signalled that the Minister had chosen to lift the statutory bar that had prohibited a valid protection visa lodgement, allowing refugee processing to formally progress. He engaged a migration agent, a middle-aged, middle-class, Iranian man. In speaking to the man Reza felt as if his Hazara Afghan dialect was not of equal value to the Mashhad-accented Farsi spoken by the migration agent, but he told himself it did not matter if the man was preparing his case. Reza attended several interviews to fill out the 41-page visa application form, listing all his places of residence, all his schooling, and all his places of employment throughout his life. It was hard to remember such details and he did not have all relevant documents. His wife had to send them from their remote province, a difficult task given her remoteness and the precarity of her Hazara status with the Taliban now occupying their province.[5] However, she managed to scan and transmit the documents. It took Reza several weeks to complete the application. Once submitted it was another year before the interview with Australian immigration officials. Reza then waited six months more for the visa decision. Plainly, there was nothing fast about "fast-track."

In mid-2018, six years after arriving in Australia, Reza received a letter notifying him that he had not been officially recognised as a refugee. The migration agent he had employed told him that he should be fine going through "fast-track" because Hazara Afghans were usually approved, therefore Reza was shocked by the rejection. Surely there had been a mistake? His case was automatically referred to the Immigration Assessment Authority (IAA), which was his one chance of appealing against the merits of the immigration department's adverse determination. He asked the migration agent if they could prepare additional information, only to discover this was prohibited by statute unless the IAA asked for it. The IAA would only re-examine the decision made by the Department based "on the paperwork." The laws were arguably designed to uphold the initial "fast-track" decision in the IAA appeal, and while the legislation does allow for the IAA to request further information, this discretion is rarely exercised in practice (RCOA 2019).

Reza could not afford any more legal fees. He feared his case had not been adequately prepared. This was a common refrain at the Asylum Seeker Hub, where this research was undertaken, and anecdotally verified in interviews with migration agents, lawyers, and paralegal volunteers, who said that without the usual government screening and funding of migration agents for maritime arrivals, migration agent "sharks" had surfaced as a significant problem in poorly prepared "fast-track" cases. Reza decided to try to obtain help from the Asylum Seeker Hub, waiting all afternoon in a church hall full of similar anxious faces. He was comforted by the fact that church elders told him and others they could do their afternoon prayers upstairs in the church. It re-centred him, and he felt he belonged somewhere.

The lawyer on duty at the Asylum Seeker Hub explained that he could now challenge the case only on limited legal-procedural grounds through the Federal Circuit Court. The merits of his refugee case could not be contested after the negative IAA decision. If he failed this appeal (a "judicial review") too, she warned him that he would be liable for both his court costs *and* those of the DHA. Reza had now been in Australia for six years without seeing his family. All the family's savings were spent getting him to Australia with good reason. He needed to try everything he could. His chances were limited, but how could he not be recognised as a refugee? He went ahead with the judicial review.

He started volunteering at the church's Asylum Seeker Hub on weekends. This was the time when he missed family most. Each Saturday afternoon he set up the Asylum Seeker Hub for all those who poured into the clinic after receiving their "fast-track" rejections. He oversaw the food pantry. Then at the end of the afternoon he dismantled tables, stacked chairs. This is how Hanne came to know him. In broken English, he said he had tried to get into English at TAFE (Technical and Further Education) but was rejected because of the conditions attached to his BVE. Necropolitical visa restrictions meant that Reza was excluded from the government's Adult Migrant English Program for resettled refugees, making it more difficult for him to successfully operate in Australian society. The first author offered to help him with his English. Another volunteer, a former English as a Second Language teacher, provided old, photocopied sheets of word exercises. In fieldwork notes, Hanne recalls,

> We Google-translated, chatting about family, writing random vocabulary encountered in conversations and the worksheets. He helped me with my

Farsi, laughing at my fumbling attempts to write the script. Unwittingly, I had stumbled upon a "decolonising" method of participant observation. It felt good to provide comic relief.

Short-term visas, work rights, and welfare

After the judicial review was unsuccessful, DHA reissued Reza's BVE for two months. One volunteer refers to these BVEs as a "lottery" because one never knows how long one will get—a month, two months, or more. Reza had to keep reapplying for such temporary visas every couple of months, which meant filling out more forms at the Asylum Seeker Hub. His employer had already written a letter to the DHA, speaking highly of Reza's work ethic, requesting Reza remain in Australia to work for him. This letter formed part of an appeal, for a discretionary and non-reviewable "ministerial intervention" after the Federal Circuit Court appeal failed. But Reza's letter went unanswered. Reza's two-month visas then dwindled to monthly visas.

The employer let him go, incorrectly fearing government trouble for hiring someone on such a short-term visa. Now Reza had no income, and because he had failed "fast-track" he was ineligible for income support via Status Resolution Support Services. Reza lived off savings while still sending remittances to family. He tried finding work, but as soon as potential employers saw his month-long BVE, they would not employ him even though he had work rights. He lacked the English to be able to contract his own work, despite volunteers advertising his services in closed online refugee support groups. He could not set up his own tiling business as he could not afford the insurance. Necropolitical policy closed in around Reza. Ultimately, Reza moved to Melbourne, where a large Afghan migrant population meant he could work for Afghan Australian contractors with whom he could communicate easily. The structural violence of the "fast-track" regime diminished Reza's chances of refugee recognition, and any chance of being able to function effectively in mainstream Australian society. "Fast-track" rejection and associated welfare policies left Reza to negotiate the marginalisation and destitution of his visa rejection.

Debt, the behaviour contract, and character grounds

After failing before the Federal Circuit Court, Reza had to pay all court costs both for himself and the DHA: a $7000 debt to the Australian Government. While he had waited so long for his "fast-track" processing, now the Debt Collection Service (DHA) rang Reza soon after the Federal Court failure; there was no pause to repay the court costs incurred. In Foucauldian terms, the state exercised the logic of governmentality upon one it deemed an outsider, yet rationalised that Reza still had a financial obligation to a society from which he had been effectively purged through necropolitical refugee status processes, theoretical work rights and minimal welfare supports. In broken English, Reza related to author one that he did not understand why he had to repay so much each month. He had tried to object.

The immigration department asked Reza for $250 a month to repay court costs over two years, based on their access to asylum seekers' bank accounts. The department had used that information to calculate the money that Reza should repay. However, they had not considered the fact that Reza was no longer employed and, also, did not receive income support as a refused refugee claimant. Those who owe money to the department have their bank accounts monitored to ensure they pay their debt, otherwise their short-term visas are not renewed.[6] Surveillance in this case does not make Reza a self-governing subject (Foucault 1979) but a failed subject, punished for that failure of refugee recognition. Biopolitics seamlessly morphs into necropolitics. Reza had tried to negotiate to pay less than $250 per month, using broken English to explain that he had no work and, thus, no income coming into his bank account. In late May 2019 he requested assistance at the Asylum Seeker Hub to ring the department, asking Hanne to intercede on his behalf.

She relays in her field notes, "The number on the letter put me straight through to an officer who turned out to be the woman who had spoken with Reza and who had also signed the letter of demand. On speaker phone, we verified I was speaking on Reza's behalf. I asked if we could reduce the amount of debt Reza was repaying each month. The woman said this was not possible, Reza had 'agreed to a plan.' I asked her, 'Did she understand that Reza spoke little English?' She affirmed this fact, but reaffirmed that Reza had agreed to the plan, and had to pay the debt. She then said he risked being refused another BVE 'on character grounds' if he did not pay the court costs." At the time, I (mistakenly) assumed this referred to the Behaviour Contract, resurfacing as a tool of financial coercion. However, the Behaviour Contract can only be used to *cancel* a temporary visa, not prohibit its granting. The Home Affairs Debt Collector had actually made an oblique reference to section 501 of the *Migration Act 1958 (Cth)*, which deals with the "character" of a non-citizen. Reza, it appeared, would be refused a new BVE because he owed a debt to the Commonwealth. Seemingly, as a "debtor" he infringed the "character grounds" in section 501 of the *Migration Act*.

Hanne again relates from field notes, "I explained to the woman on the phone how Reza was sacked from his job because of the short-term visa granted to him by the DHA. How could he pay the debt when he earned nothing?" Reza watched intently. The woman paused, then snapped, 'Well, if he can't pay the money, he needs to tell us in writing, because he agreed to repay that amount. We will consider his request, but nothing is guaranteed.' Thanking the officer, I immediately drafted an email, which the volunteer Farsi translator on duty read to Reza, who nodded as he comprehended each sentence. The letter was then emailed to Reza who immediately forwarded it to Home Affairs Debt Collection Service."

This incident highlights how, from the Immigration Minister down to frontline bureaucrats, the DHA acts with impunity. This was Butler's "petty sovereign" in action (Butler 2003). Structurally violent policy parses unwanted bodies from the state: the state demands money over the phone in a language Reza can barely speak, having denied him access to learning that language. The state monitors his bank account and then creates a repayment plan through surveillance of his bank account and engages in what seemed to be repeated bullying over the phone, labelling Reza a debtor if he could not repay. Reza struggled to repay his Federal Circuit Court debt because he had lost his job owing to a short-term visa issued by that same department. The repayment schedule was then used to threaten him with denial of a new visa if he did not meet certain repayment amounts. Short-term visas and debt collection coalesced pushing Reza towards repatriation (arguably, "constructive *refoulement*"). This is necropolitical power that is directly, structurally, and culturally violent, keeping Reza in a state of heightened anxiety, financial precarity, and ongoing uncertainty.

Reza was successful in his request to have the repayment instalments reduced, so far managing them with repeated trips to Melbourne for work, several months at a time. He continues to send money to his wife. But he struggles. He messaged Hanne some months after this event, "I not sleep. I sick, I sore back and head." She suggested he go to Foundation House, the Melbourne counselling service for those with refugee trauma backgrounds. She recalled in her notebook, "It felt an inadequate response, over a thousand kilometres away. I hoped his old friend Google Translate would help him understand." Later, I noticed on Messenger that he had removed that part of our conversation. Had he felt too vulnerable? Was he concerned about state surveillance of his phone, too?[7] I still don't know. He messaged again, a few months later, to tell me he could not sleep, as he missed his daughter, whom he had not seen now for over seven years. He told me she cried each time he spoke to her via WhatsApp. 'When will I hear from the ministerial intervention?' he asked me via a translating friend over speaker phone, when I later rang him on his mobile. 'I want to speak to a lawyer' he said. I told him that I would help him find a lawyer and through networks in Melbourne, a Dari-speaking advocate found Reza legal assistance. In trying to resist the state's capacity to render Reza abject, this "intervention" felt minimal, but the lawyer helpfully informed Reza that he should not worry about not hearing back from the DHA on his ministerial intervention. It was 'actually a good sign' that his letter had been unanswered because only ministerial intervention refusals received an immediate answer. Through the state's neglect of his ministerial appeal, Reza was learning that an unanswered letter is a 'good letter': Reza could continue working, send home remittances, repay a $7000 Federal Circuit Court debt to the department, and renew his BVE every month or so. The state's apparent inactivity, having created painfully long waiting through "fast-track" refugee processing, paradoxically now helps Reza by keeping him in Australia. The state's rush to *refoule* Reza has not yet been successful. Now the state ignores him, as long as he keeps renewing his BVE, pays off his Federal Circuit Court debt, and "behaves." Reza tries to develop some small peace of mind while desperately missing his wife and child, dealing with the pressure of earning enough to send them money, and repay his debt. This is how Reza lives: in a state of ongoing limbo.

Article 31 of the 1951 *Convention relating to the Status of Refugees* ("Refugees Convention") outlines that Reza should not be punished for his "irregular" mode of arrival in Australia as a refugee protection seeker; however, for the Legacy Caseload, many of Australia's human rights obligations were not respected. Had Reza been able to obtain a visa and arrive in Australia lawfully by plane, he would have been treated very differently and may have had a positive outcome. Instead, Reza went through a procedurally deficient refugee recognition process in an alien language, faced opaque and costly court processes, was denied government-funded legal assistance impeding effective access to the courts (contrary to Article 16, Refugees Convention), struggled to find employment because of his short-term visa (conflicting with Articles 17–19, Refugees Convention), was denied welfare support when he couldn't find work (arguably, contradicting Article 23, Refugees Convention) and hasn't seen his family, whom he worries about constantly, for eight years.

Life after failing the "fast-track" process becomes a cat-and-mouse game of evading *refoulement* whilst negotiating limited forms of appeal and intervention, applying for bridging visa renewals within the prescribed time frame, finding sustainable employment, and "behaving" in accordance with the Code. The disciplinary gaze of the sovereign state and the necropolitical threat of *refoulement* limits Reza's capacity to have any sense of ontological or material security. Through the capillaries of oppressive state practices, the prospect of self-*refoulement* (notionally "voluntary return") is never far away, but so too is a subtle resistance.

This chapter shows that the *telos* of the Australian Government is more than to "discourage" asylum seekers, refugees, and those who have failed "fast-track" processing from continuing to live in Australia. Having purportedly created a timely and cost-efficient system through the "fast-track" process, law and policy settings serve to erode any hope or possibility of humanity, except through where people collaborate with civil society. Technologies of surveillance and technologies of security are the final pieces of sovereign power wielded over the Legacy Caseload. "Failed" asylum seeker subjects owing money from their Federal Circuit Court appeal are branded debtors, risking detention and expulsion if they cannot repay. Government surveillance of asylum seekers' bank accounts, to gain knowledge about their financial situations, is knowledge then folded back into the management process through the debt recovery arm of DHA. Productive and oppressive mechanisms of power fuse to ensure that the DHA recoups its court costs and continues to coerce asylum seekers to consider repatriation (constructive *refoulement*).

Conclusion

The past two decades of asylum-seeker policy in Australia is a history of increasingly punitive deterrence (Marr and Wilkinson 2004; Phillips 2014). Bureaucrats charged with dispensing public powers are, as Robert Manne (2017) says, unable to see what it is they are doing in the Arendtian sense—to "think what [they] are doing" (Arendt 1998: 5). Those immigration officers no longer *think* about what they *do*, because the nation has become accustomed to thinking of what they are doing as perfectly normal (Manne 2017).

"Cultural violence," the thinking that Manne refers to as "absolutism," a political determination that no asylum seeker on a boat should ever reach Australia and be resettled, justifies and enables the "structural violence" of necropolitical asylum policy: to punish people who attempt to arrive, or who have arrived, in Australia "unauthorised" by sea. This is the operation of power in society at its most pervasive; however, the dominance of social norms and modes of juridical and scientific thought that constitute "problems" and "problem populations" is never complete. Contestation is a constant; there are always cracks and fissures enabling moments of reframing and progressive change. Mbembe's concept of necropolitics implies a passive state of "near death," but when armed with knowledge and community allies Reza's case illustrates that asylum seekers can navigate their way through structurally violent "deathworlds" (Mbembe 2019) to maintain some semblance of "living" in Australia, however insecure and imperfect.

Accordingly, this chapter has shown that there is always pushback, as people live on in the face of indifferent, or antagonistic, bureaucratic systems, to survive the governance of neglect. However, Reza's case also demonstrates that material precarity and ontological uncertainty are constant states of being for "failed" asylum-seeking people in Australia.

Notes

1 Termed "illegal maritime arrivals" by the Department of Home Affairs since a change of government in September 2013.
2 The Australian unemployment benefit is $40 a day or $280 weekly and has not increased in real terms since 1994, over 26 years ago (Australian Council Of Social Services (ACOSS) 2018; Hewson 2019). The Status Resolution Support Services (SRSS) payment is thus $35 a day, or $243 weekly for a single person, with some extra funding for children, rental costs, and basic mental and physical health access (van Kooy and Ward 2018, 5). The Australian Council of Social Service (ACOSS), the peak body for social services in Australia, estimates that the cost for "basic essentials"—housing, groceries, transport, and clothing—is $433 per week for a single person (ACOSS 2018), so both the unemployment benefit and SRSS do not meet a basic living allowance.
3 See further, Chapter 1 by Peter Billings and Chapter 4 by John van Kooy and Asher Hirsch.
4 See, for example Chapter 2 by Leanne Weber.

5 Hazaras are one of the persecuted minorities in Afghanistan by the Taliban who ruled the province between 1996 and December 2001 (Ibrahimi and Maley 2018; Maley 2020) and who later re-claimed power in August 2021 following the withdrawal of U.S. and allied forces from Kabul.
6 The Department of Home Affairs links the receipt of government payments to visa status, so when asylum-seeking people cannot find work, and are on the Status Resolution Support Services (SRSS) payment (the 89% of an unemployment stipend), if they have unexplained amounts in their account, or evidence of a money transfer overseas, their SRSS payment is reduced. Likewise, for those who owe money to the Department of Home Affairs after the Federal Circuit Court appeal, there is the same regime of supervision of bank accounts by the state.
7 Fieldwork observation has demonstrated on several occasions how state surveillance of asylum-seeking people's Facebook accounts has been used as part of evidence to discredit refugee claims.

References

Abbott, T. (2012) *The Coalition's plan for more secure borders: Address to the Institute of Public Affairs, Melbourne* [Online]. Institute of Public Affairs. https://parlinfo.aph.gov.au/parlInfo/download/media/pressrel/1603644/upload_binary/1603644.pdf;fileType=application%2Fpdf#search=%22media/pressrel/1603644%22

Abbott, T. (2013) *Operation sovereign borders policy launch* [Online]. NSW Liberal Party website. https://members.nsw.liberal.org.au/tony-abbott-transcript-joint-press-conference-brisbane

Australian Council of Social Services. (2018) *Analysis of the impact of raising benefit rates Australian Council of Social Service September 2018 report by Deloitte access economics*, commissioned by ACOSS.

Australian Council of Social Services. (2020) *Briefing note: Raise the rate of newstart and other allowances*. ACOSS. www.acoss.org.au/wp-content/uploads/2020/01/200229-Newstart-Increase-Briefing-Note.pdf

Agamben, G. (1998) *Homo Sacer: Sovereign power and bare life*. Stanford University Press.

Arendt, H. (1998 [1958]). *The Human Condition*. University of Chicago Press.

Barker, V. (2018) *Nordic nationalism and penal order: Walling the welfare state*. Routledge.

Billings, P. (2013) 'Irregular maritime migration and the pacific solution mark II: Back to the future for refugee law and policy in Australia?', *International Journal on Minority and Group Rights*, 20: 279.

Billings, P. (2019) *Crimmigration in Australia: Law, Politics, and Society*. Springer.

Billings, P. and Lelliott, J. (2019) 'Minister's 'god-like' powers can be put to better use in Biloela Tamil family's case', *The Guardian*. www.theguardian.com/commentisfree/2019/sep/06/ministers-god-like-powers-can-be-put-to-better-use-in-biloela-tamil-familys-case

Briskman, L., Goddard, C. and Latham, S. (2008) *Human Rights Overboard: Seeking Asylum in Australia*. Scribe Publishing.

Butler, J. (2003) *Precarious Life: The Powers of Mourning and Violence*. Verso.

Davidson, H. (2019a) '"The cruelty is the point": What's behind the treatment of the Biloela Tamil family', *The Guardian*. www.theguardian.com/australia-news/2019/sep/04/no-explaining-why-the-treatment-of-the-biloela-tamil-family-distresses-so-many

Davidson, H. (2019b) 'The hypocrisy, double standards and micro-cruelties at heart of Biloela case', *The Guardian*. www.theguardian.com/australia-news/2019/sep/18/the-biloela-tamil-case-has-prompted-a-festival-of-double-standards

Davidson, H. (2019c) 'Legal experts question fast-track process that refused Biloela Tamil family's claim', *The Guardian*. www.theguardian.com/australia-news/2019/sep/06/legal-experts-question-fast-track-process-that-refused-biloela-tamil-familys-claim

Davies, T. and Isakjee, A. (2019) 'Ruins of empire: Refugees, race and the postcolonial geographies of European migrant camps', *Geoforum*, 102: 214.

Davies, T., Isakjee, A. and Dhesi, S. (2017) 'Violent inaction: The necropolitical experience of refugees in Europe', *Antipode*, 49: 1263.

De Leon, J. (2015) *The land of open graves: Living and dying on the migrant trail*. University of California Press.

Department of Home Affairs, Australian Government. (2020) *Onshore Processing Statistics (DHA)*. www.homeaffairs.gov.au/research-and-statistics/statistics/visa-statistics/live/onshore-processing

Fleay, C., Ali Rezai, N. and Hartley, L. (2015) 'Hidden: Living behind bricks and wire', *Griffith Review*, 299.

Fleay, C. and Briskman, L. (2013) 'Hidden men: Bearing witness to mandatory detention in Australia', *Refugee Survey Quarterly*, 32: 112.

Fleay, C. and Hartley, L. (2016) 'I feel like a beggar': Asylum seekers living in the Australian community without the right to work', *Journal of International Migration and Integration*, 17: 1031.

Fleay, C. and Hoffman, S. (2014) 'Despair as a governing strategy: Australia and the offshore processing of asylum-seekers on Nauru', *Refugee Survey Quarterly*, 33: 1.

Fleay, C., Lumbus, A. and Hartley, L. (2016) 'People seeking asylum in Australia and their access to employment: Just what do we know?', *Cosmopolitan Civil Societies: An Interdisciplinary Journal*, 8(2): 63.

Foucault, M. (1978) *The History of Sexuality, Vol. 1: An Introduction*. Pantheon Books.

Foucault, M. (1979) *Discipline and Punish: The Birth of the Prison*. Penguin.

Foucault, M. (2008) *The Birth of Biopolitics Lectures at the Collège de France, 1978–1979*. Palgrave Macmillan.

Galtung, J. (1969) 'Violence, peace, and peace research', *Journal of Peace Research*, 6: 167.

Galtung, J. (1990) 'Cultural violence', *Journal of Peace Research*, 27: 291.

Gill, N. and Good, A. (2019) *Asylum Determination in Europe*. Springer.

Glendinning, P. (2015) 'Asylum seekers, refugees and human dignity', *Social Alternatives*, 34: 27.

Hartley, L. and Fleay, C. (2014) *Policy as Punishment: Asylum Seekers in the Community Without the Right to Work*. Centre for Human Rights Education, Curtin University.

Hartley, L. and Fleay, C. (2017) '"We are like animals": Negotiating dehumanising experiences of asylum-seeker policies in the Australian community', *Refugee Survey Quarterly*, 36: 45.

Hewson, J. (2019) *Increase in Newstart Allowance Long Overdue*. Crawford School of Public Policy, ANU College of Asia and the Pacific. www.austaxpolicy.com/increase-newstart-allowance-long-overdue/

Higgins, C. (2017) *Asylum by Boat: Origins of Australia's Refugee Policy*. New South Publishing.

Houston, A., Aristotle, P. and L'Estrange, M. (2012) *Report of the Expert Panel on Asylum Seekers. Expert Panel on Asylum Seekers*. Australian Government.

Ibrahimi, N. and Maley, W. (2018) *Afghanistan: The Hazaras Are Not Safe*. Lowy Institute. www.lowyinstitute.org/the-interpreter/hazaras-not-safe

Johansen, N. B. (2013) 'Governing the funnel of expulsion: Agamben, the dynamics of force, and minimalist biopolitics', in Aas, K. F. and Bosworth, M. (eds) *The Borders of Punishment: Migration, Citizenship, and Social Exclusion*. Oxford University Press.
Karlsen, E. and Phillips, J. (2017) 'Developments in Australian refugee law and policy: The Abbott and Turnbull coalition governments (2013–2016)', *Research Paper Series 2017–18*. Parliamentary Library.
Kenny, M. A. and Procter, N. (2019) 'How the Biloela Tamil family deportation case highlights the failures of our refugee system', *The Conversation*.
Maley, W. (2020) *Why Hazaras Are in Danger in Afghanistan: Expert Opinion*. Refugee Council of Australia (RCOA). www.refugeecouncil.org.au/hazaras-opinion/
Manne, R. (2017) *Australia's Uniquely Harsh Asylum Seeker Policy: How Did It Comes to This?* Australian Broadcasting Commission. www.abc.net.au/religion/australias-uniquely-harsh-asylum-seeker-policy—how-did-it-come/10095226
Marr, D. and Wilkinson, M. (2004) *Dark Victory*, 2nd edition. Allen & Unwin.
Marston, G. and McDonald, C. (2006) *Analysing Social Policy: A Governmental Approach*. Edward Elgar.
Mathew, P. (2019) 'Constructive refoulement' in Juss, S. (ed) *Research Handbook on International Refugee Law*. Edward Elgar Publishing.
Mayblin, L. (2020) *Impoverishment and Asylum: Social Policy as Slow Violence*. Routledge.
Mayblin, L. and James, P. (2019) 'Asylum and refugee support in the UK: Civil society filling the gaps?', *Journal of Ethnic and Migration Studies*, 45: 375.
Mayblin, L., Wake, M. and Kazemi, M. (2020) 'Necropolitics and the slow violence of the everyday: Asylum seeker welfare in the postcolonial present', *Sociology*, 54(1): 107–123.
Mbembe, A. (2019) *Necropolitics*. Duke University Press.
Methven, E. and Vogl, A. (2014) 'Asylum-seeker code is a rhetorical tool—With severe consequences', *The Conversation*. https://theconversation.com/asylum-seeker-code-is-a-rhetorical-tool-with-severe-consequences-35083
Methven, E. and Vogl, A. (2019) 'Australia's asylum seeker code of behaviour', *Asylum Insight*.
Miller, T. A. (2005) 'Blurring the boundaries between immigration and crime control after September 11th', *Boston College Third World Law Journal*, 25(1): 81.
Momartin, S., Steel, Z., Coello, M., Aroche, J., Silove, D. and Brooks, R. (2006) 'A comparison of the mental health of refugees with temporary versus permanent visas', *The Medical Journal of Australia*, 185: 367.
Nader, L. (2016) 'The impact of militarism on anthropology', *HAU: Journal of Ethnographic Theory*, 6: 463.
Papailias, P. (2019) '(Un)seeing dead refugee bodies: Mourning memes, spectropolitics, and the haunting of Europe', *Media, Culture & Society*, 41: 1048.
Phillips, J. (2014) *A Comparison of Coalition and Labor Government Asylum Policies in Australia since 2001*. Parliamentary Library. https://parlinfo.aph.gov.au/parlInfo/download/library/prspub/3024333/upload_binary/3024333.pdf
Phillips, J. and Sprinks, H. (2013) *Boat Arrivals in Australia since 1976*. Parliamentary Library. https://parlinfo.aph.gov.au/parlInfo/download/library/prspub/5P1X6/upload_binary/5P1X6.pdf
Proctor, N., Kenny, M. A., Eaton, H. and Grech, C. (2018) 'Lethal hopelessness: Understanding and responding to asylum seeker distress and mental deterioration', *International Journal of Mental Health Nursing*, 27: 448.

Refugee Council of Australia. (2019) *Fast Tracking Statistics. What Are They Deciding?*. RCOA. www.refugeecouncil.org.au/fast-tracking-statistics/6/

Refugee Council of Australia. (2020) *Fast Tracking Statistics*. RCOA. www.refugeecouncil.org.au/fast-tracking-statistics/

Riva, S. (2017) 'Across the border and into the cold: Hieleras and the punishment of asylum-seeking Central American women in the United States', *Citizenship Studies*, 21(3): 309.

Steel, Z., Momartin, S., Silove, D., Coeelo, M., Aroche, J. and Tay, K. (2011) 'Two year psychosocial and mental health outcomes for refugees subjected to restrictive or supportive immigration policies', *Social Science & Medicine*, 72: 1149.

Stümer, J. (2018) 'The dead are coming border politics and necropower in Europe', *Cultural Politics*, 14(1): 20.

Stumpf, J. P. (2014) 'Crimmigration. Encountering the leviathan', in Pickering, S. and Ham, J. (eds) *The Routledge Handbook on Crime and International Migration*. Routledge.

Van Der Woude, M., Barker, V. and Van Der Leun, J. (2017) 'Crimmigration in Europe', *European Journal of Criminology*, 14(1): 3.

van Kooy, J. and Bowman, D. (2019) '"Surrounded with so much uncertainty": Asylum seekers and manufactured precarity in Australia', *Journal of Ethnic and Migration Studies*, 45: 693.

Vecchio, F. and Gerard, A. (2018) *Entrapping Asylum Seekers*. Palgrave Macmillan.

Vogl, A. and Methven, E. (2015) 'We will decide who comes to this country, and how they behave: A critical reading of the asylum seeker code of behaviour', *Alternative Law Journal*, 40: 175.

Weber, L. and Pickering, S. (2011) *Globalization and Borders: Death at the Global Frontier*. Palgrave Macmillan.

Zagor, M. (2015) 'The struggle of autonomy and authenticity: Framing the savage refugee', *Social Identities*, 21(4): 373.

Chapter 8

Asylum seekers, healthcare, and the right to have rights

The political struggle over Australia's "medevac" law

David Neil and Michelle Peterie***

Introduction

Since its inception, Australia's policy of processing asylum seekers "offshore" has attracted international condemnation. As part of this policy, people travelling to Australia by boat in search of asylum are intercepted at sea and subject to prolonged and indefinite detention (or containment) in Papua New Guinea (PNG) and Nauru. Medical professionals and human rights organisations have highlighted the serious physical and psychological harms suffered by detainees at these "regional processing" facilities, as well as the inadequate healthcare provided. Yet the Australian Government has actively fought against attempts to bring even critically ill detainees to Australia for medical treatment.

Healthcare is often considered the most basic welfare right because health is a precondition for the enjoyment of most other benefits, and because access to medical treatment can be the difference between life and death. Although the right to health is recognised as a fundamental human right (United Nations, Office of the High Commissioner for Human Rights 2008), access to healthcare largely depends on states recognising this obligation to displaced persons within their territory. Hannah Arendt (1951: 279) saw the most poignant paradox of contemporary politics in the discrepancy between the idealistic insistence on the "inalienability" of human rights and the utterly alienated circumstances of the rightless themselves. The struggle in Australian domestic politics to hold the Federal Government accountable for its human rights violations and to afford asylum seekers some semblance of a right to health is an important object lesson in why human rights must be codified in national laws.

Drawing on Arendt's insights, this chapter examines the political struggle over access to emergency medical treatment for asylum seekers and refugees in Australia's offshore processing facilities on PNG and Nauru respectively. It begins with a brief exegesis of Arendt's (1951) writing on "the right to have rights." Next, it provides an overview of Australia's historical treatment of people seeking asylum, before expounding the key elements of the humanitarian emergency that developed in Australia's offshore processing facilities between 2012 and 2018. The chapter then considers a short-lived "medevac" law to

DOI: 10.4324/9781003298595-13

grant critically ill detainees easier access to emergency healthcare in Australia and the political furor that ensued. The chapter concludes with a discussion of what this situation reveals about the purpose of Australia's offshore processing regime in light of Arendt's work. In keeping asylum seekers outside the boundary within which an effective rights claim can be raised, we argue offshore processing is an elaborate strategy for refusing desperate people the right to have rights. Australia's denial of suitable healthcare to refugees and asylum seekers in PNG and Nauru is therefore a function of a more fundamental denial.

The right to have rights

The French Revolution's *Declaration of the Rights of Man* (1789) is the foundation stone and template for the development of the modern conception of human rights. It declares Man to be the source of law, rather than God, custom, or history. The Rights of Man belong to people purely in virtue of their being human and—since rights must be independent of and immune to the whims of all governments—these rights are *inalienable*. The Declaration posits an abstract human being as the wellspring of rights. If rights belong in full measure and equally to all humans everywhere, they can only attach to a universal human essence possessed by every human being.

There is a direct line of descent from the *Declaration of the Rights of Man* to the 1948 *Universal Declaration of Human Rights* (UDHR),[1] whose preamble asserts that the "inherent dignity and . . . equal and inalienable rights of all members of the human family is the foundation of freedom, justice and peace in the world." In human rights theory, there is no consensus on what dimension or attributes of the "human" serve to ground the authority of human rights. Arguments have been made for agency and autonomy, equality and freedom, fairness, dignity, basic needs, fundamental interests, human well-being, moral capacity, practical reason, and various other human qualities as the basis of this authority (Nickel 2019). Intrinsic to the orthodox conception of human rights, however, is the claim that human rights do not depend on jurisdictional authority for their existence. Rather, human rights are supposed to function as a constraint on sovereign legislative authority. In international law, states are the primary duty bearers of human rights obligations, comprising both an "obligation to respect" (non-interference with the enjoyment of rights) and an "obligation to protect" individuals and groups from rights violations (United Nations, Office of the High Commissioner for Human Rights 2008).

In *The Origins of Totalitarianism*, Arendt argues that rights conferred on the basis of mere species membership turn out to be worthless coin for those excluded from any political community capable of enforcing those rights. The declaration in the UDHR's preamble, that member states must respect the universal and inalienable rights of all humans, contradicts the legal and territorial autonomy that is the basis of the sovereign state. Human rights have been conferred on an abstract human being, without history or place, extracted from all social and political relations. Yet meaningful rights must be claimable. For Arendt, the plight of refugees throughout the 20th century shows that people who are not accepted as members by any state are unable to make effective rights claims. In practice, the loss of national rights entails the loss of human rights (Arendt 1951: 299).

If states are the only juridical authorities capable of ensuring human rights, then the contradiction between national sovereignty and the universality of human rights can be resolved only through the recognition of a "right to have rights," which Arendt defines as a "right to belong to some kind of organised community" (1951: 298). For Arendt, substantive rights are civic rights, meaning that they depend on membership of a political community to be realised. The recognition of one's standing and personhood within a community is the politico-legal precondition for enjoyment of other rights. Rights that can protect basic human needs must be underwritten by a state that is able to institute and enforce those rights, and so make them real for all its members.

In Arendt's conception, refugees are effectively stateless persons. Arendt herself was stateless for 18 years—between fleeing Germany in 1933 and being granted US citizenship in 1951—and in *The Origins of Totalitarianism* she examines the plight of the millions of displaced and homeless people in the interwar period who were without effective rights. A person, Arendt argues, may be *de jure* stateless where there is no state that legally recognises them as a citizen, but they may also *de facto* stateless when the state itself is their persecutor, or where the state they live in cannot or will not protect them against persecution. Under this definition, even resident non-citizens, such as migrant workers, can be *de facto* stateless when they find themselves without legal entitlements or protections in the host country. What matters, for practical purposes, is the condition of acute vulnerability that results when a person does not have effective membership of a state that guarantees them basic rights. Statelessness and rightlessness are essentially the same thing, and to ensure any of the rights enumerated on canonical lists of human rights, people must first be rescued from statelessness. As Arendt explained:

> The calamity of the rightless is not that they are deprived of life, liberty, and the pursuit of happiness, or of equality before the law and freedom of opinion—formulas which were designed to solve problems within given communities—but that they no longer belong to any community whatsoever. Their plight is not that they are not equal before the law, but that no law exists for them; not that they are oppressed but that nobody wants even to oppress them.
>
> (Arendt 1951: 295)

In the formula of a "right to have rights," Arendt asserts that human rights must be grasped, in the first instance, as anchored in a right to belong to a body politic, rather than as a list of particular rights that can be exercised only by people who already belong to such a community.

Arendt identifies a deep tension between "nation" and "state" in the hybrid notion of the nation-state. Historically, the nation and the state have been separate entities: the state is the sovereign power that makes and enforces laws in its territory, while the nation is a genealogical entity, a historical people whose membership is determined by birth. The primary function of the state is the protection of the inhabitants of its territory, regardless of nationality, and to act as a supreme legal institution. With the emergence of the modern nation-state, political sovereignty and nationality are fused into a single entity. What Arendt (1951: 230) calls the "secret conflict between state and nation" arose after the French Revolution. The Republic was declared to be subject to laws that flow from the Rights of Man, but at the same time held to be sovereign, "bound by no universal law and acknowledging nothing superior to itself" (Arendt 1951: 230). Under the nation-state model, the nation became the *raison d'être* of the state. Nationalism became a glue to bind the populace into a unified political entity and reciprocally popular will transformed the function of the state into protection of the nation. For Arendt (1951: 231), nationalism is in essence, "the expression of this perversion of the state into an instrument of the nation and the identification of the citizen with the member of the nation."

It is, in large part, the emergence of a national conception of citizenship that has rendered modern states vulnerable to dangerous ideologies premised on nationalist myths. Arendt's work offers a useful framework for interpreting the actions of countries, such as Australia, that have consistently failed to fully recognise the rights of refugees and asylum seekers despite their in-principle commitment to universal human rights. The tension between human rights and national sovereignty sheds some light on Australia's consistently fearful and pitiless response to people seeking refuge by boat.

Australia: a proud history as a state of asylum?

Australia represents itself domestically and on the international stage as a country with a strong commitment to human rights. Australia was a founding member of the United Nations and, at Eleanor Roosevelt's invitation, was one of the eight nations involved in drafting the UDHR. Dr Herbert Vere Evatt, an Australian judge and politician who had been a justice of the High Court and Attorney General, served as president of the United Nations General Assembly in 1948–49, when the UDHR was adopted and ratified (Edge and Arnold 2017). Evatt was instrumental in achieving the inclusion of social and economic rights in the UDHR, alongside civil and political rights. Australia was one of the original 26 participating states at the 1950 United Nations conference in Geneva, held in December 1950, to complete the drafting of, and to sign the *Convention relating to the Status of Refugees*. Additionally, Australia is a party to core human rights treaties, including the (1966) *International Covenant on Civil and Political Rights*,[2] the (1966) *International Covenant on Economic, Social and Cultural Rights*,[3] and the (1989) *Convention on the Rights of the Child*.[4] The right to health is enshrined in several human conventions, including the *International Covenant on Economic, Social and Cultural Rights*, which identifies a right to "the highest attainable standard of physical and mental health" and, by extension, to the "facilities, goods, services and conditions" (United Nations Committee on Economic, Social and Cultural Rights 2000) necessary for this standard to be realised.

The United Nations has a Universal Periodic Review process that provides an analysis of participating nations' compliance with their international human right obligations. In the 2015 review process, Australia used its opening statement to underline this history of human rights involvement and to assert an ongoing commitment to its international obligations:

> Australia has a long tradition of robust commitment to human rights and supporting and promoting human rights internationally. This includes a long history of positive and constructive engagement with the UN human rights system. We believe that the protection and promotion of human rights is an essential component of a rules-based global order upon which lasting peace, security, freedom and dignity for all depend.
>
> (Australian Mission to the United Nations 2015: 2)

Yet Australia's record on human rights falls far short of such rhetoric. This is starkly evident in Australia's long history of colonial violence and racial exclusion, as enshrined in the "white Australia policy," which did not officially end until 1973 (see McMaster 2001). It is also apparent in Australia's responses to certain asylum seekers.

Compare Australia's affirmation to the United Nations (cited earlier) with a recent address by Professor Gillian Triggs, former President of the Australian Human Rights Commission (AHRC) (2012–17) and Assistant Secretary-General of the United Nations from 2019. Triggs (2019) lamented that Australia had "let down the Evatt vision and his courage" and suggested Evatt would have been astonished to learn that 70 years after the UDHR was established, Australia was yet to implement it in domestic law. Triggs warned that Australia had become "isolated and exceptional in its failure to protect the human rights of some of the most vulnerable in our community." She also suggested that the courts had been either complicit or negligent in facilitating the Australian Government's nonconformity with human rights, particularly with respect to asylum seekers.

Australia's treatment of maritime asylum seekers, in particular, has declined considerably since the first asylum seeker boat, carrying five Indochinese refugees, arrived in Australia in 1976 (Peterie 2016). The vessel marked the beginning of Australia's first "wave" of boat arrivals (McMaster 2001). The then Federal Government, led by centre-right Liberal Prime Minister Malcolm Fraser, responded by asking neighbouring countries to prevent these boats embarking for Australia. Fraser also increased Australia's refugee intake from these countries, providing a safe resettlement path for those who might otherwise come by sea. Between 1977 and 1982, Australia resettled over 54,000 Vietnamese refugees from these regional camps, as well as the over 2,000 asylum seekers who had come by boat (Stevens 2012). In the years that followed Australia's response to asylum seekers would become increasingly hostile. Indeed, even the Fraser Government hardened in its response as the years progressed and doubts were raised as to whether, years after the end of the Vietnam War, Indochinese asylum seekers were still in genuine need of protection (Stevens 2012).

In 1992 the Australian Government, led by Labor Prime Minister Paul Keating, responded to a new "wave" of asylum seeker boats by introducing mandatory detention (Gleeson 2016). Prior to 1992 immigration detention was used in Australia only on a discretionary basis, but the policy of mandatory detention for "unlawful non-citizens" has become an entrenched feature of Australian immigration/asylum policy for several decades (Phillips and Spinks 2013a, 2013b). In its initial iteration, mandatory detention was framed as a short-term emergency measure. The policy—which required those entering Australia without a valid visa to be detained while their asylum claims were assessed—permitted detention for a period of up to 273 days. However, the policy was subsequently amended to exclude the temporal limitation, making Australia the only country in the world allowing *indefinite* mandatory detention for unlawful non-citizens including maritime arrivals (Phillips and Spinks 2013a).

Latent anxieties about border security had been building in the Australian community for years (McMaster 2001; Papastergiadis 2004), but the tipping point came in 2001 when the Norwegian merchant ship *MV Tampa (Tampa)*, rescued 433 asylum seekers and sought permission to bring them to Christmas Island. The *Tampa* had been alerted to the small fishing boat's distress by the Australian Maritime Safety Authority and—after rescuing the passengers—was instructed to take them to Indonesia. Learning of their proposed destination, however, asylum seekers petitioned the captain, Arne Rinnan to take them to Australia. Rinnan consulted Australia's search and rescue authorities who advised him to do as he saw fit. He headed for Christmas Island, where he was told local police would meet the ship (Mares 2002). In the hours that followed, the Australian Government warned Rinnan that, if he proceeded, he could be charged with people smuggling. Senior Government officials would later admit that the government's aim, in seeking to keep the *Tampa* outside Australian waters, was to ensure "that none of the fundamental rights accorded to non-citizens under the Migration Act 1958 (Cth) accrue to the asylum seekers" (Lynch and O'Brien 2001: 215). Rinnan stopped the ship just outside Australian territorial waters but did not turn back (Mares 2002).

The standoff that ensued marked the beginning of a new chapter in Australia's response to maritime asylum seekers (Nethery 2019; Mares 2002; Hatton and Lim 2005). The Prime Minister, John Howard, declared that the *Tampa* would not be permitted to enter Australia. Howard's bellicose declaration made headlines around the world and was met with widespread approval in Australia where the government and media "constructed the arrival of 'unauthorized' asylum seekers to Australia on board the *Tampa* as a 'crisis' that threatened Australia's 'border security' and 'sovereignty'" (O'Doherty and Augoustinos 2008: 577). Aboard the *Tampa*, Rinnan requested urgent medical help because some of the passengers were seriously ill, and there were reports that asylum seekers had begun a hunger strike (O'Doherty and Augoustinos 2008). After multiple requests for assistance met with no positive response, Rinnan proceeded towards Christmas Island. The military response was swift. Forty-five armed Special Air Services troops boarded the ship and took control (Lynch and O'Brien 2001).

Australia proceeded to negotiate with neighbouring countries to find an alternative destination for the asylum seekers interdicted on the *Tampa*. Two Pacific nations—both in desperate financial need (Nethery 2019)—ultimately agreed to take the interdictees, in exchange for significant remuneration. As Banks and McGregor (2011: 233) explain:

> The former Australian colonial territory of Papua New Guinea, which allowed Manus Island to be used as a "human processing zone", and the tiny island state of Nauru (whose once bountiful supplies of phosphate had long since been diminished by Australian mining companies and used to enhance the New Zealand and Australian agricultural economies) became sites to "outsource" and "offshore" humanitarian responsibilities.

In September 2001 laws were introduced excising almost 5,000 small islands, including Christmas Island, from Australia's migration zone, and allowing all maritime asylum seekers who arrived in these "excised" places to be transferred to Nauru or PNG for refugee status determination (McAdam and Chong 2014; Hatton and Lim 2005). This new policy of deterring boats and sending asylum seekers offshore for processing was dubbed the "Pacific Solution." It is hard to credit the historical tone-deafness of naming a network of internment camps with the word "solution," yet the policy met with resounding approval in Australia.

The *Tampa* episode was still fresh in the public consciousness when the events of 2001 September 11 rocked the western world. In Australia, Howard—now actively campaigning for re-election—affirmed Australia's long-standing "friendship" with the United States and committed to fight a "War on Terrorism" (Brangwin and Rann 2010). Ignoring the reality that many of the asylum seekers arriving on Australia's doorstep were fleeing the same regimes opposed by the United States and Australia (Martin 2015), Howard vilified asylum seekers—maligning them as fraudulent "queue jumpers" and as potential terrorists (Marr and Wilkinson 2003; Poynting et al. 2004; Peterie 2017). The events of September 2001 allowed Howard to "fight a law and order election and pitch it in terms of national survival" (Marr and Wilkinson 2003: 93). Australia's international human rights obligations were subordinated to the sovereignty and integrity of the state.

Howard won a decisive electoral victory and, in the years that followed, boat arrivals to Australia all but ceased (Hatton and Lim 2005). The issue of "the boats," however, would remain at the forefront of Australian politics. By 2008 Australia appeared to have lost some of its appetite for hardline asylum policies and the newly elected Labor Government closed Australia's offshore processing centres (Phillips and Spinks 2013a). Most of the refugees who had previously been detained offshore had, by this time, been resettled in Australia or elsewhere (Phillips 2012). Yet, as Nethery and Holman (2016: 1020) note, the closure seemed "largely symbolic" as "[c]onstruction continued on the high-security Christmas Island Immigration Detention and Reception Facility, which ... continued to fulfil many of the criteria of keeping detention centres out of sight."

The Labor Government's purported desire for a more humane policy was to be short lived. A steep rise in the number of maritime asylum seekers arriving in Australia precipitated political panic (Lacertosa 2014). The Labor Government searched for a strategy to stem the flow. After a number of false starts (Lacertosa 2014; Nethery 2019), an Expert Panel was created to advise the government on the best way forward:

> Most significant, the panel advocated reviving the Pacific Solution by re-opening refugee processing centers in Nauru and Papua New Guinea. The panel also recommended "irregular maritime" arrivals not be permitted to apply for asylum anywhere in Australian territory, regardless of whether they reached the shores of the Australian mainland. This made all boat arrivals eligible for transfer to third party countries.
>
> (Lacertosa 2014: 335)

The government accepted the recommendations, and *The Migration Legislation Amendment (Regional Processing and Other Measures) Act 2012* took effect in August 2012.

In 2013, the newly elected Liberal Government established a "zero tolerance'" militarised border protection program called "Operation Sovereign Borders." A key feature of Operation Sovereign Borders was maritime interdiction coupled with offshore processing, and these policies and practices worked in tandem with a complete bar upon refugee resettlement in Australia for anyone arriving without a visa (a policy introduced under the former Labor Government immediately prior to the federal election). The cost of Australia's preoccupation with sovereignty and territorial integrity would be counted in human lives.

A "humanitarian emergency"

By 2015 there was mounting evidence of serious health and safety problems in Australia's offshore processing centres on Nauru and Manus Island (PNG). In recommending the resumption of offshore processing, in 2012 the Expert

Panel had included a number of caveats, stressing the importance of "no arbitrary detention, appropriate accommodation, adequate health services, access to education and training, legal assistance with protection applications, appropriate appeal mechanisms, and independent monitoring" (McAdam and Chong 2014: 119). However, these safeguards had not been put in place. Rather, evidence was growing that Australia's offshore processing system was "characterised by poor facilities; neglect of the medical, welfare and educational needs of detainees; dehumanising treatment by staff; widespread mental illness and rates of self-harm; and pervasive physical and sexual abuse of detainees, including children" (Nethery and Holman 2016: 1032). Detention offshore was *causing* physical and psychological injury (Isaacs 2016).

The harm that children were experiencing within these offshore centres was a particular concern and attracted considerable attention among activists and human rights organisations. A AHRC inquiry into children in detention found "that the prolonged, mandatory detention of asylum seeker children causes them significant mental and physical illness and developmental delays" (AHRC 2014). In 2015 a government inquiry was conducted into allegations of rapes and other assaults on detainees at the Nauru processing centre. *The Moss Review* substantiated several specific allegations and found that sexual abuse at Nauru was underreported (Moss 2015). The following year a cache of 2,116 incident reports from Nauru was leaked to the public. The "Nauru Files," as the documents became known, included seven reports of sexual assaults involving children, 59 reports of assault involving children and 30 reports of self-harm involving children (Farrell et al. 2016).

Offshore detainees were not only experiencing physical and psychological illness as a result of their detention (AHRC 2017) but also being denied essential medical care, as (non-medically trained) senior executive officials or government bureaucrats overrode clinical advice regarding the medical transfer of detainees to Australia. In 2014 an Iranian asylum seeker, Hamid Khazaei, presented to the clinic at the Manus Island facility with a small lesion on his leg, caused by a common tropical skin infection. The clinic did not have the required antibiotic to treat the infection and his condition deteriorated rapidly. Doctors' request for an emergency transfer to Australia was rejected by the Department of Immigration. Mr Khazaei's condition worsened and after more urgent pleading a transfer was approved, but to a hospital in Port Moresby. There Mr Khazaei was misdiagnosed, incorrectly treated, and left unattended as he became critically ill. He suffered a series of cardiac arrests and severe brain damage and was finally transferred to a Brisbane hospital where he died (Doherty 2018). In another incident in 2016 an Iranian refugee at Nauru, Omid Masoumali, set himself alight. A transfer to the mainland was delayed for 30 hours because he had refugee status and the medical contractor was authorised to treat only asylum seekers. Mr Masoumali died slowly over two days, although an inquiry found that he would have had a high chance of survival had he been treated at a major hospital in a "timely fashion" (Vujkovic 2019).

The process of securing a medical evacuation to the Australian mainland was prohibitively complex. If health service providers in either PNG or Nauru determined that they were unable to treat a detainee, a non-statutory process called an overseas medical referral (OMR) process could be commenced. Under this process, medical staff could recommend a patient's transfer, but relocation decisions were at the minister's discretion. Medical professionals working with this system cautioned that the process was prioritising political considerations over detainees' well-being (AHRC 2019). As a senior medical officer for International Health and Medical Services (IHMS) on Nauru disclosed:

> While on Nauru, evacuation deadlines which either my staff or I recommended were frequently not met and at times appeared to be ignored by the Australian government and patients were often in constant pain as their conditions worsened. Follow-up requests by myself or my staff would also not be met with substantive responses. Clinical decisions and recommendations which were made by IHMS medical staff were referred to and often questioned by non-medical staff.
>
> (AHRC 2019)

In some instances, detainees were granted medical transfers but were relocated to medical facilities in other countries where appropriate treatment options were not available. In 2016, for example, a young woman who fell pregnant after being raped on Nauru was transferred to Port Moresby without her consent. This occurred against the advice of healthcare providers on Nauru and despite abortion being illegal in PNG. She was brought to Australia only after the Federal Court ruled, in the case of *Plaintiff S99/2016*, that she would be of heightened risk of very serious physical and/or psychological harm if she terminated her pregnancy in PNG.[5] The Australian Government endeavoured to formalise this practice of third-country medical treatment in 2017, when it signed a deal with Taiwan. This was a troubling development, not least because Taiwan is not a signatory to the *Refugees Convention* (RCOA 2019b).

Despite significant healthcare needs, Manus Island detainees, in particular, were rarely permitted treatment in Australia. In the 18-month period from January 2017 to July 2018, only nine Manus Island detainees were granted medical transfers (RCOA 2019b). Australian officials, who were under no legal obligation to follow the medical advice, often rejected applications for medical transfers. As discussed in Chapter 1 of this volume, lawyers had to litigate in court to bring their sick clients to Australia for emergency treatment. As the Refugee Council of Australia (2019b) stated, the medical transfers process was "slow, non-transparent and involved overuse of judicial resources."

In November 2017 the United Nations Human Rights Committee released its *Concluding Observations on the Sixth Periodic Report of Australia*. The report was scathing. With respect to asylum seekers, the Committee expressed concern about:

> The conditions in the offshore immigration processing facilities in Papua New Guinea (Manus Island) and Nauru, which also hold children, including inadequate mental health services, the serious safety issues and instances of assault, sexual abuse, self-harm and suspicious deaths, and the fact that the harsh conditions have reportedly compelled some asylum seekers to return to their country of origin, despite the risks that they face there.

Yet, despite this public denunciation, access to medical treatment in Australia's offshore processing facilities further deteriorated. In October 2018 Médecins Sans Frontières (MSF) doctors working at the Nauru centre had their visas abruptly cancelled (Burton-Bradley and Raines 2018). The Nauruan Government issued a statement claiming that MSF had failed to provide promised health services to its nationals, and accusing MSF of a "ruse":

> It has become very clear that they were never here to help Nauruans as was their initial representation to Government to gain entry into Nauru. They were here as political activists and it was self-evident from the statement made by MSF representatives referring to our sovereign nation, which is our beloved home, as an "open air prison."
>
> (Davidson 2018)

In response an MSF spokeswoman said the organisation's only goal was "to provide the best medical and mental healthcare to Nauruan asylum seekers and refugees on the island and alleviate their suffering" (Davidson 2018). In December 2018 MSF released a report, *Indefinite Despair*, documenting the extreme mental health situation on the island:

> Close to one-third of MSF's refugee and asylum seeker patients attempted suicide, while 12 patients were diagnosed with the rare psychiatric condition of "resignation syndrome". . . . The data shows that the mental health suffering on Nauru is among the worst MSF has ever seen, including in projects providing care for victims of torture.
>
> (MSF 2018: 4)

Also, the Australian Medical Association delivered a letter, signed by 6,000 doctors, to the Prime Minister, describing the situation on Nauru as a humanitarian emergency and demanding that children and their families be transferred to Australia for treatment (AMA 2018).

As public pressure mounted and the Australian Government faced dissent within its own ranks, it became clear that subjecting children to the trauma of offshore processing was no longer politically tenable. The government acted swiftly to remove all children from Nauru. Some were brought to Australia while others were transferred to the United States as part of a refugee resettlement agreement brokered in 2016 under the Obama administration (Department of Home Affairs 2019). However, for hundreds of adult refugees and asylum seekers offshore containment persisted.

"Medevac" laws and subsequent repeal

In late 2018 the balance of power shifted in the Australian Parliament following a by-election that resulted in the Liberal/National Coalition Government losing its slender majority. The Opposition (Labor Party) joined with independents to introduce legislation to improve access to adequate healthcare for offshore detainees. The *Home Affairs Legislation Amendment (Miscellaneous Measures) Act 2019*, commonly known as the "medevac" law, came into force in March 2019 against the wishes of the ruling Coalition Government. Under the medevac provisions, qualified medical professionals oversaw decisions regarding medical transfers to Australia as part of a statutorily defined process. A medical transfer to Australia needed to be recommended by two doctors. The Minister for Immigration then had 72 hours to approve or refuse this recommendation. A refusal could be made on security, adverse character, or medical grounds. If it was made on medical grounds, however, an eight-person medical panel reviewed the decision. If a decision was not forthcoming within required 72 hours, the transfer was considered approved (Legal and Constitutional Affairs Legislation Committee 2019).

The law was short lived. Following a Federal election in May 2019, the Coalition Government, arguing that the law was a "border protection" risk and a "loophole" that asylum seekers could exploit, managed to construct a deal with an independent senator to repeal the medevac legislation in December 2019 (Martin 2019). But in its short life medevac had a considerable—if contradictory—impact on the lives of the 192 people who were transferred to Australia under its provisions (RCOA 2020). One the positive side of the ledger, transferred detainees were able to access medical and psychiatric assessments and treatments that were not available at their offshore processing locations (Legal and Constitutional Affairs Legislative Committee 2019). Conversely, transferees found that conditions in Australia were far from hospitable. After years of preventing refugees and asylum seekers from reaching Australian territory and accessing its legal protections, the government seemed intent on containing and swiftly expelling those who had made it to Australia for medical care.

With their transfer to Australia, detainees—already subject to years of offshore detention—hoped that this traumatic chapter had come to an end. Instead, many found themselves interned in Australia's onshore immigration detention system: a network of prison-like detention centres and "alternative places of detention," including commercial hotels. Detainees in these facilities were not permitted to leave their places of detention and often spent months waiting for the medical treatment they had been brought to Australia to receive (ASRC 2019; Taylor 2019). In theory, the medevac legislation allowed transferees to be returned to PNG or Nauru after their treatment (Legal and Constitutional Affairs Legislation Committee 2019). As lawyers fought these forced returns in the courts, however, the government reasserted its commitment to mandatory detention and insisted that, regardless of their refugee status, these individuals would never be settled permanently in Australia. Thus, many detainees faced the prospect of indefinite mandatory detention within the onshore system. While Australia's onshore immigration detention network is less overtly violent than its offshore counterpart, the logic of "deterrence" infuses all aspects of institutional life, pressuring detainees to abandon their visa claims and return to their countries of origin (Peterie 2018a, 2018b).

The parliamentary committee reviewing the *Migration Amendment (Repairing Medical Transfers) Bill 2019* received over 100 submissions, all of which argued strongly in support of medevac. The medevac legislation merely asserted a fundamental principle of medical practice: that doctors are responsible for treatment decisions and that doctors' first obligation is to the health of their patients. The restoration of the pre-medevac arrangements was carried out over strenuous objections from the medical profession. The repeal of the medevac law brought a fresh round of international and domestic condemnation that the Australian Government appeared determined to abandon its international obligations under the *Refugees Convention*, the *International Covenant on Civil and Political Rights*, and the *Convention on the Rights of the Child* (Cousins 2019).

The government's strenuous effort to repeal the medevac law seems markedly disproportionate given the relatively small group of people the law applied to. When the medevac provisions were repealed there were fewer than 600 people left offshore (RCOA 2019a). It is striking that the financial costs associated with Australia's hardline approach are far higher than would be incurred by a more humane system. Research conducted by Equity Economics found that the "true cost to Australian taxpayers of offshore processing and onshore mandatory detention between 2016 and 2020 was in fact $9 billion" and that "on the available public information, offshore processing is costing the Australian Government in excess of $573,000 per offshore person, per year" (Asylum Seeker Resource Centre, Save the Children and Get Up 2019: 8). That compares with around $10,221 per person per year for those living in the community, in Australia, on bridging visas (Asylum Seeker Resource Centre, Save the Children and Get Up 2019). Nonetheless, the Australian Government has been prepared to incur heavy moral, reputational, and financial losses—and inflict immense harm on people—for the perceived symbolic significance of "border security."

Claims about the security threat posed by the few relatively helpless individuals transferred under the medevac legislation were exaggerated. The question that Arendt directs us to ask, therefore, is why the ostensibly unrelated matter of providing medical treatment to some seriously ill asylum seekers and refugees was framed, in official discourse, as an existential threat to the nation? The answer lies in the conflation of national sovereignty with a requirement that the state must maintain an unqualified prerogative to deny the rights claims of non-citizens. In other words, the struggle against medevac was largely motivated by a nationalist fear that extending welfare rights to outsiders constitutes an erosion of the rights of Australians over *their* resources.

A global story

Much has changed since Arendt wrote *The Origins of Totalitarianism* and there are many critics of Arendt's skepticism about human rights instruments like the UDHR. Jeremy Waldron (2006), for instance, argues that Arendt fundamentally misunderstood how legal norms develop. She could not foresee that, in the half century after the publication of *The Origins of Totalitarianism*, the "soft law" of declarations, treaties, and conventions would become a "dense thicket of human rights law whose influence is felt in every corner of the legal world" (Waldron 2006: 96). Arendt might well reply, however, that 70 years after the *Refugees Convention*, the scale of statelessness is an order of magnitude larger than the human catastrophe described in *The Origins of Totalitarianism*. The United Nations High Commissioner for Refugees (2020) reports 79.5 million people forcibly displaced worldwide at the end of 2019. As Larking (2012: 69) explains, these individuals—"a mix of political refugees, members of persecuted minorities, and individuals trying to escape poverty, generalised war, or otherwise unsustainable living conditions"—share much in common with the stateless individuals of Arendt's time.

Australia's punitive treatment of these "stateless" individuals is not unique. Rather, it reflects a global trend. One hundred and forty-five states are now parties to the 1951 *Convention relating to the Status of Refugees* and 146 are signatory to the 1967 *Protocol*. Certainly, there are many reasons why the *Refugees Convention*, primarily designed as a response to those displaced by the war that engulfed Europe, is not well suited to the circumstances of forced migration in the 21st century. The point to emphasise here, however, is that in the last two decades most of the wealthy countries in the world have adopted harsh deterrence measures in response to asylum seekers (Nethery and Silverman 2015; Peterie 2018a).

Although Australia's immigration detention policy is among the harshest in the world, the detention of asylum seekers and other undesired immigrants is now the norm in the United States and most of Europe (The Migration Observatory 2020). In the United Kingdom between 2009 and 2019, the number of people held in immigration detention varied between 24,000 and 32,000 per year (The Migration Observatory 2020). Before the 1990s the United Kingdom had no permanent detention centres; by 2015 it had 11 "immigration removal centres" and several short-term holding facilities (Griffiths 2015). France has

22 "administrative detention centres," which held 46,800 people during 2017, including 2,797 minors (Global Detention Project 2018). In 2016 the United States detained 44,270 asylum seekers, as a subset of over 300,000 immigration detainees. A total of 446,223 persons were expelled in that year, and daily population of immigration detainees in the United States hovers around 30,000 (Global Detention Project 2016).

Many countries have also moved beyond immigration detention policies to externalise their borders, preventing asylum seekers and other undocumented non-citizens from entering their territories and, by extension, accessing rights. As Hirsch and Bell (2017: 417) explain:

> While refugees are protected from refoulement once they make it to the jurisdiction or territory of a state, they face an ever-increasing array of non-entrée policies designed to stymie access to state territory. Without being able to enter a state capable of securing their claims to safety and dignity, refugees cannot achieve the rights which ought to be afforded to them under international law.

In the United States and Europe, boats carrying asylum seekers are regularly intercepted by navy and custom vessels and turned back to their country of origin. Agreements have also been reached with the governments of transit countries to ensure that potential asylum seekers do not embark for these destination countries (Hirsch and Bell 2017). "Remote control" strategies of this kind prevent "stateless" individuals from accessing territories in which they could access their rights (Fitzgerald 2019). Australia's offshore processing regime is a graphic illustration of this phenomenon. Despite the fact that the offshore detention facilities were funded, built, staffed, and administered by Australia, the Australian Government has consistently argued that they are not Australia's legal responsibility because the asylum seekers are located in another sovereign state (Department of Home Affairs 2019).

Conclusion

Contemporary responses to people seeking asylum offer a vivid illustration of Arendt's argument regarding the inherent tension that exists between principles of sovereignty and an abstract commitment to universal human rights. More specifically, perhaps, they demonstrate that the political prioritisation of the former can impose profound human costs. This chapter's discussion of the political struggle surrounding the provision of emergency healthcare to refugees and asylum seekers detained in Australia's offshore processing system offers a case in point. From an Arendtian perspective, the mechanisms developed under offshore processing since 2012 have functioned as mechanisms for denying asylum seekers the standing to make an effective claim upon Australia. Political efforts to deny individuals in PNG and Nauru access to timely and adequate healthcare were, thus, a function of a more fundamental denial: a denial of the right to have rights at all.

Notes

1 UN General Assembly Resolution 217A (adopted 10 December 1948).
2 Opened for signature 16 December 1966, 999 UNTS 171 (entered into force 23 March 1976).
3 Opened for signature 16 December 1966, 993 UNTS 3 (entered into force 3 January 1976).
4 Opened for signature 20 November 1989, 577 UNTS 3 (entered into force 2 September 1990).
5 See the discussion of *Plaintiff S99/2016 v Minister for Immigration and Border Protection* (2016) 243 FCR 17, in Chapter 1.

References

Arendt, H. (1951) *The Origins of Totalitarianism*. Harcourt, Brace and Company.

Asylum Seeker Resource Centre. (2019) *Sick People Transferred from PNG and Nauru Detained without Medical Oversight* (Media Release), 19 December.

Asylum Seeker Resource Centre, Save the Children and Get Up. (2019) *At What Cost? The Human and Economic Cost of Australia's Offshore Detention Policies 2019*.

Australian Human Rights Commission. (2019) *Migration Amendment (Repairing Medical Transfers) Bill 2019 [Provisions] Submission 54*. https://humanrights.gov.au/our-work/legal/submission/migration-amendment-repairing-medical-transfers-bill-2019

Australian Human Rights Commission. (2017) *Asylum Seekers, Refugees and Human Rights: Snapshot Report*, 2nd edition, 30 March. AHRC.

Australian Human Rights Commission. (2014) *The Forgotten Children: National Inquiry into Children in Immigration Detention*, November 2014. AHRC.

Australian Medical Association. (2018) 'Unconscionable to leave children on Nauru', *Australian Medicine*, 31 October. https://ama.com.au/ausmed/unconscionable-leave-children-nauru

Australian Mission to the United Nations. (2015) Opening Statement by Australia. *Universal Periodic Review Working Group: 23rd Session Universal Periodic Review of Australia*. www.ag.gov.au/rights-and-protections/human-rights-and-anti-discrimination/united-nations-human-rights-reporting/australias-universal-periodic-review

Banks, G. and McGregor, A. (2011) 'Pacific 'solutions' and imaginaries: Reshaping pacific relations or re-Colonising the "sea of islands"', *Asia Pacific Viewpoint*, 52(3): 233.

Brangwin, N. and Rann, A. (2010) *Australia's Military Involvement in Afghanistan since 2001: A Chronology* (Parliamentary Library, Parliament of Australia), 16 July. Commonwealth of Australia.

Burton-Bradley, R. and Raines, S. (2018) 'MSF Mental Health Team Confirms It Has Been Ordered to Get Off Nauru by Government', *ABC News*, 10 October.

Cousins, S. (2019) 'Australia Repeals Medical Evacuation Law', *The Lancet*. DOI: 10.1016/S0140-6736(19)33067-3

Davidson, H. (2018) '"They conspired against us": Nauru government accuses MSF of activism', *The Guardian*, 12 October.

Department of Home Affairs. (2019) *Submission to the Inquiry into the Migration Amendment (Repairing Medical Transfers) Bill 2019 [Provisions]*, Senate, Legal and Constitutional Affairs Legislation Committee.

Doherty, B. (2018) 'Hamid Kehazaei: Australia responsible for 'preventable' death of asylum seeker', *The Guardian*, 30 July.

Edge, A. and Arnold, S. (2017) 'Rights and freedoms: The United Nations and the universal declaration of human rights as global education', *Agora*, 52(4): 47.

Farrell, P., Evershed, N. and Davidson, H. (2016) 'The Nauru Files: Cache of 2,000 Leaked Reports Reveal Scale of Abuse on Children in Australian Offshore Detention', *The Guardian*, 9 August.

Fitzgerald, D. S. (2019) *Refuge Beyond Reach: How Rich Democracies Repel Asylum Seekers*. Oxford University Press.

Gleeson, M. (2016) 'Offshore processing: Failing those we should protect', *Law Society of NSW Journal*, 23: 24.

Global Detention Project. (2016) 'United States immigration detention'. www.globaldetentionproject.org/countries/americas/united-states

Global Detention Project. (2018) 'France immigration detention'. www.globaldetentionproject.org/countries/europe/france

Griffiths, M. (2015) 'A proud tradition'? Immigration detention in the United Kingdom', in Nethery A. and Silverman, S. J. (eds) *Immigration Detention: The Migration of a Policy and Its Human Impact*. Routledge.

Hatton, T. and Lim, A. (2005) 'Australian asylum policy: The Tampa effect', *Agenda*, 12(2): 115.

Hirsch, A. L. and Bell, N. (2017) 'The Right to Have Rights as a Right to Enter: Addressing a Lacuna in the International Refugee Protection Regime', *Human Rights Review*, 18: 417.

Isaacs, D. (2016) 'Are Healthcare Professionals Working in Australia's Immigration Detnetion Centres Condoning Torture?', *Journal of Medical Ethics*, 42: 413.

Lacertosa, J. L. (2014) 'Unfriendly Shores: An Examination of Australia's Pacific Solution under International Law', *Brooklyn Journal of International Law*, 40(1): 321.

Larking, E. (2012) 'Human Rights, the Right to Have Rights, and Life Beyond the Pale of the Law', *Australian Journal of Human Rights*, 18(1): 57.

Legal and Constitutional Affairs Legislation Committee. (2019) *Migration Amendment (Repairing Medical Transfers) Bill 2019 [Provisions]: Report*, 25 September. Commonwealth of Australia.

Lynch, P. and O'Brien, P. (2001) 'From Dehumanisation to demonisation: The MV Tampa and the denial of humanity', *Alternative Law Journal*, 26(5): 215.

Mares, P. (2002) *Borderline: Australia's Response to Refugees and Asylum Seekers in the Wake of the Tampa*. University of New South Wales Press.

Marr, D. and Wilkinson, M. (2003) *Dark Victory: How A Government Lied Its Way to Political Triumph*. Allen and Unwin.

Martin, S. (2019) 'Medevac repeal bill passes after Jacqui Lambie makes 'secret deal' with coalition', *The Guardian*, 4 December.

Martin, G. (2015) 'Stop the boats! Moral panic in Australia over asylum seekers', *Continuum* 29(3): 304.

McAdam, J. and Chong, F. (2014) *Refugees: Why Seeking Asylum Is Legal and Australia's Policies Are Not*. NewSouth Publishing.

McMaster, D. (2001) *Asylum Seekers: Australia's Response to Refugees*. Melbourne University Press.

Médecins Sans Frontières (MSF). (2018) *Undefinite Despair: The Tragic Mental Health Consequences of Offshore Processing on Nauru*, December. Médecins Sans Frontières.

Moss, P. (2015) *Review into Recent Allegations Relating to Conditions and Circumstances at the Regional Processing Centre in Nauru: Final Report*, 6 February. Commonwealth of Australia.

Nethery, A. (2019) 'Australia's refugee detention regime: Offshore and unaccountable', *Current History*, September, p. 221.

Nethery, A. and Holman, R. (2016) 'Secrecy and human rights abuse in Australia's offshore immigration detention centres', *The International Journal of Human Rights*, 20(7): 1018.

Nethery, A. and Silverman, S. J. (2015) *Immigration Detention: The Migration of a Policy and Its Human Impacts*. Routledge.

Nickel, J. (2019) 'Human Rights', in Zalta, E. N. (ed) *The Stanford Encyclopedia of Philosophy*. Stanford University Press.

O'Doherty, K. and Augoustinos, M. (2008) 'Protecting the nation: Nationalist rhetoric on asylum seekers and the Tampa', *Journal of Community and Applied Social Psychology*, 18: 576.

Papastergiadis, N. (2004) 'The invasion complex in Australian political culture', *Thesis Eleven*, 78(8): 8.

Peterie, M. (2016) '"These few small boats": Representations of asylum seekers in Australia's 1977 and 2001 elections', *Journal of Australian Studies*, 40(4): 433.

Peterie, M. (2017) 'Docility and desert: Government discourses of compassion in Australia's asylum seeker debate', *Journal of Sociology*, 53(2): 351.

Peterie, M. (2018a) 'Deprivation, Frustration and Trauma: Immigration Detention Centres as Prisons', *Refugee Survey Quarterly*, 37(3): 279.

Peterie, M. (2018b) 'Technologies of control: Asylum seeker and volunteer experiences in Australian immigration detention facilities', *Journal of Sociology*, 55(2): 181.

Phillips, J. and Spinks, H. (2013a) *Immigration Detention in Australia*, Parliamentary Library, Parliament of Australia, 20 March.

Phillips, J. and Spinks, H. (2013b) *Boat Arrivals in Australia Since 1976*, Parliamentary Library, Parliament of Australia, 23 July.

Phillips, J. (2012) *The 'Pacific Solution' Revisited: A Statistical Guide to the Asylum Seeker Caseloads on Nauru and Manus Island*, Parliamentary Library, Parliament of Australia, 4 September.

Poynting, S., Noble, G., Tabar, P. and Collins, J. (2004) *Bin Laden in the Suburbs: Criminalising the Arab Other*. Sydney Institute of Criminology Series.

Refugee Council of Australia. (2019a) *Offshore Processing Statistics*. www.refugeecouncil.org.au/operation-sovereign-borders-offshore-detention-statistics/

Refugee Council of Australia. (2019b) *Migration Amendment (Repairing Medical Transfers) Bill 2019 [Provisions] Submission 43*. www.aph.gov.au/Parliamentary_Business/Committees/Senate/Legal_and_Constitutional_Affairs/RepairMedicaltransfers/Submissions

Refugee Council of Australia. (2020) *Australia's Offshore Processing Regime: The Facts*. www.refugeecouncil.org.au/offshore-processing-facts/8/

Stevens, R. (2012) 'Political debates on asylum seekers during the Fraser government, 1977–1982', *Australian Journal of Politics and History*, 58(4): 526.

Taylor, J. (2019) 'Asylum seekers transferred to Australia under Medevac laws held in Melbourne hotel', *The Guardian*, 19 December.

The Migration Obervatory. (20 May 2020) *Immigration Detention in the UK*. https://migrationobservatory.ox.ac.uk/resources/briefings/immigration-detention-in-the-uk/

Triggs, G. (2019) 'From good international citizen to pariah? The decline of human rights protection in Australia', *Evatt Journal*, 18(2).

United Nations Committee on Economic, Social and Cultural Rights. (2000) *General Comment No 14: The Right to the Highest Attainable Standard of Health*, 22nd sess, UN Doc E/C.12/2000/4 (11 August 2000) 3.

United Nations Human Rights Committee. (2017) *Concluding Observations on the Sixth Periodic Report of Australia* CCCPR/C/Aus/CO/6, 1 December 2017.

United Nations, Office of the High Commissioner for Human Rights (2008) *Fact Sheet No. 31, The Right to Health.* https://www.ohchr.org/sites/default/files/Documents/Publications/Factsheet31.pdf

Vujkovic, M. (2019) 'His burns were 'very survivable' but Omid Masoumali died slowly over two days', *ABC News*, 1 March.

Waldron, J. (2006) 'Cosmopolitan norms', in Post, R. (ed.) *Another Cosmopolitantism, by Seyla Benhabib*. Oxford University Press.

Part 3

Protecting and promoting respect for refugees' human rights

Part 3: commentary

Countering the toxic policy exchange: Reflections on UK and Australian approaches to 'immigration control' and academic-activist partnerships of resistance

Margaret Greenfields

Introduction

As a British academic-activist and policy practitioner who is watching the United Kingdom move seemingly inexorably towards an increasingly "hostile (immigration) environment," driven by the political rhetoric of "taking back our borders" in the wake of the Brexit vote to leave the EU (UK Government/Home Office 2021); writing this commentary has been a deeply sobering experience.

Despite the horrors occasioned by the COVID-19 pandemic in the United Kingdom in which Black and ethnic minority community members, particularly those living in poor-quality accommodation and experiencing poverty, are disproportionately likely to contract or die of the virus (UCL Centre for Health Informatics 2020; Boyle 2020); where abundant evidence exists (tested and proven in courts of law) of the deeply negative physical and mental health impacts on recently arrived vulnerable asylum seekers of being confined to poor-quality, non-COVID–secure former army barracks (Bulman 2021a); existing under a 23-hour-a-day curfew in hotel accommodation (Taylor 2021) or experiencing destitution on refusal of asylum claims (Sisters Not Strangers Coalition 2020), the current British political regime is ideologically committed to a model of immigration control and associated asylum "support" which owes a considerable debt to the influence of right-wing politicians and pundits (Sumption 2019; Pegg and Lewis 2020) advocating policy transfer of the Australian model to nation-states which share commonalities of approach to deterring irregular migration (Weisbrot 2018; Bar-Tuvia 2018; Mainwaring and Cook 2019).

Indeed, the recently announced "New Plan for Immigration" (UK Government/Home Office 2021) for the first time adopts the explicitly differentiated approach to treatment of asylum seekers utilised in Australia, with those persons

DOI: 10.4324/9781003298595-15

accepted through international resettlement schemes being entitled to access support packages and being awarded indefinite leave to remain status, whilst individuals who have entered via "safe third countries" will, at best, should an asylum appeal succeed, be entitled only to temporary protection status and "*will be regularly reassessed for removal from the UK . . . have limited family reunion rights and . . . no recourse to public funds*" (UK Government/Home Office 2021: foreword). Further, emphasising once again the preoccupation with irregular migration by boat which is a common strand found also in Australian immigration policy and discourse (see, e.g., Briskman, Chapter 9), the new British policy will create harsh new criminal penalties for those found to be aiding and abetting asylum seekers and migrants to enter the country illegally, punishable by up to life imprisonment (Dathan 2021). Similarly, we will see an increased used of immigration detention for those deemed to have arrived in an irregular manner, with the announcement in early 2021 (The Home Office [UK] and Rt. Hon. Caroline Noakes, MP. 2018; Women for Refugee Women 2021) of the opening of the first newly constructed detention centre since 2014, intended to house 80 women (Gates-Lincoln 2021; Cobain 2018) contrary to Government commitments to reduce the number of asylum seekers in detention.

Although it has been unlawful to hold children in immigration detention in the United Kingdom since 2010, it is unclear what will happen to the children of such detainees if their mothers are accommodated in such centres and there is no other family carer in the country. The UK civil society agency, Bail for Immigration Detainees, in their policy briefing on proposed asylum changes (BiD 2019) provides evidence of significant numbers of children of detained asylum seekers (and those facing immigration removal after failure of their claims) being placed in state care, highlighting the potential for social workers to become unwittingly complicit in supporting a damaging immigration system, as explicated by Linda Briskman (Chapter 9) in the Australian context, in her discussion on the tensions between "care and control."

Thus, activist practitioners, civil society, and academics, who are engaged in humanitarian and legal practices to support asylum seekers and refugees in the United Kingdom, are facing broadly similar ethical and practical challenges to those described by Briskman and Caroline Fleay et al. in their chapters in this volume (albeit without *yet* having to contend with the horrors of "offshoring" of irregular migrants who arrive by boat: Grierson and Walker 2021; Doherty 2021). In the remainder of this commentary, I explore the themes and issues raised by the authors in Part 3 of this edited collection, drawing comparisons with the UK and European situations, where appropriate.

The paradox of provision of social welfare

Briskman's thoughtful chapter on the conflictual relationship and moral responsibilities of health and social welfare professionals attempting to deliver high-quality services and support (categorised as "second generation" human rights) to asylum seekers and refugees denied civil and political ("first generation") human rights, opens up an important line of enquiry into the moral philosophy and dilemmas underpinning humanitarian engagement with those individuals who are victimised by harsh asylum systems. Whilst agreeing fully with the argument propounded by Briskman that the mode of arrival of refugees and asylum seekers in Australia (and now the United Kingdom) plays into the binary of the "good refugee" who is compliant, judged worthy of support and, hence, entitled to humane treatment and access to material resources, versus those irregular migrants who are framed as dangerous, unlawful, and in need of control, it seems to me that the "futility argument" is in danger of undermining the value of incremental gains and the inherent power of collaborative solidarity movements focused on practical change, explored by Fleay et al. (Chapter 10).

Briskman's eloquent claim-making for the necessity of the profession of social work being rooted in radical approaches that challenge structural oppressions enacted by a governmental state which engages in "slow violence" (Coddington 2019) on those subject to immigration control, and the indignities of lacking permanent refugee protection, is highly persuasive when faced with the lived experience of those subject to such a "state of injury" (Mbembe 2019). The cool fury in her reflections on the Kafkaesque bureaucratic nightmare experienced by those on temporary visas seeking employment or basic levels of welfare payments, or subject to the horrors of detention (and the way in which she links the dispossession of Aboriginal peoples to the underpinning racist project woven through the political history of Australia) neatly underpin Briskman's argument for the indivisibility of first- and second-generation human rights. And, hence, the imperative for social workers, and other professions, to recognise their moral responsibility in acting as neo-liberal agents of the state whilst providing a cloak of humanitarian respectability.

However, whilst in agreement with her theoretical interpretation of the necessity of alertness to the interdependence of first- and second-generation human rights when considering the plight of refugees and asylum seekers under current regimes (remorselessly reduced to Agamben's [2017] "bare life" by the carceral state which forcibly situates them in a "state of exception"), I am unable to concur with Briskman's despairing claim that the provision of welfare services and social work to those labouring under diminished human rights is both "ineffective and futile."

It is largely self-evident that welfare professionals are overwhelmingly focused on seeking to mitigate the harm caused by economic and social abuses of the asylum seeking and refugee population, rather than attempting to engage with the first-generation rights of the client group. However, to imply (as Briskman appears to) that, by definition, social workers will fail to fulfil human rights and social justice responsibilities when working in detention settings, risks setting up an argument which proposes either the withdrawal of all but minimal levels of welfare services (which may then be delivered by those who are untrained as social workers and are simply employed wholly by detention authorities, reducing important external contact with those out-with the "system") or undermines the values, motivations, and opportunities for supporting individuals working in such settings.

Indeed, Briskman's case study commentary on the typology of responses of health professionals to working in detention settings (Briskman and Zion 2014), whilst both illuminating and deeply concerning, through focusing on individual response rather than systemic consequences of mode of action, does not seek to engage with the argument of what does, or may, occur in practice when staff "retreat from employment." Or worse still, if calls for a boycott on working in such sites should succeed, thus leaving internees in even greater danger than at present. It would also have been interesting to learn more about the characteristics and motivations of staff who "stay the course" in such punitive and challenging asylum detention regimes (as well as how those working in community settings consider their role and opportunities to engage in "street level bureaucracy" [Lipsky 2010] to subvert harsh asylum control regimes).

This interface between the theoretical, philosophical, and service-based approach to working within a system where human rights abuses or negation of dignities are widespread, and the scope for resistance and challenge may be infrequent and small scale, are to some extent teased out in the section of Briskman's chapter dealing with the inherent contradictions of the social worker's role, and the clarion call for adoption of the Global Agenda for Social Work's commitment to promoting social and economic in the context of recognition of human dignity and worth of the individual. However, the challenge remains—explored in greater detail in Chapter 10 (Fleay et al.), for which Briskman creates a gateway to reflection—on how the individual social worker or welfare practitioner can move beyond the values-based theoretical formulation of support for indivisible human right, to bringing about practical change and supporting the agency of those trapped in the asylum system. Briskman ends her chapter with a reflection on the opportunities which are paradoxically inherent in the context of the COVID-19 pandemic, as greater public awareness emerges about the risks faced by individuals and families constrained in detention camps or living in community settings who are precluded from the social welfare supports available to other Australian residents.

The increased attention paid to the many refugees on temporary protection visas, who are now at risk of destitution with high levels of job loss, and highly vulnerable to COVID-19 and other preventable health conditions due to barriers to accessing to healthcare has, Briskman notes, created a catalyst for policy change. Academics, professionals in diverse roles, and the OPCAT Network have all called for a fundamental reconsideration of the conditions under which asylum seekers and refugees are subjected to in Australia.

COVID-19 as an opportunity to reframe the asylum regime debate?

This opportunity to rethink and challenge repressive carceral regimes impacting refugees and asylum seekers (and undocumented migrants) is gaining traction globally, even in contexts which are not as punitive as Australia. Through the work of activists working in partnership with those with lived experience (as explored by Fleay et al.), backed by evidence of the potentially devastating impacts of COVID-19 on vulnerable migrants (Reidy 2021), there are growing calls internationally (UN 2020; WHO 2020) for a change of approach which takes account of the impacts of brutal "bordering" regimes (Yuval-Davis et al. 2019) and ensures that "nobody is left behind" (Kluge et al. 2020).

Conversely, across the United Kingdom and Europe, as we see growing alertness to opportunities for transnational bodies, such as the WHO and UNHCR, and national anti-racist and "open borders" activist networks, to challenge the default binary representations of "deserving" versus "unwelcome/fraudulent" asylum claimants, in some countries there has been a stark and opportunistic reduction in support for refugees and those seeking asylum, coupled with enhanced levels of hostile media reporting who have doubled down on narratives of disease-ridden "illegal" migrants (and similarly stigmatised Roma communities) risking the health of national citizens (Hargreaves and Logie 2020; Sevencan 2020; Follis et al. 2020; Andreou 2020). Thus, there is a paradoxical risk/opportunity nexus at play which follows the interplay of electoral politics in diverse nation-states that may themselves have been hard hit by the pandemic, leading to the election of more conservative or right-wing regimes that are hostile to migrants and asylum seekers, as is common in times of economic downturn (Pearce 2014).

Indeed, a UK House of Commons Library briefing note on the "Effect of the Covid-19 pandemic on Refugee communities" stated that in some refugee-hosting countries:

> Fears of refugees in the general public may be compounded by Covid-19 fears, increasing discrimination against these groups. The social stigma associated with Covid-19 may encourage illness concealment, delay early detection and treatment, increase distrust in health authorities, lower the likelihood of compliance and prolong recovery.
>
> (House of Commons Library 2020: 4)

This concern supports earlier findings from a major Equalities and Human Rights Commission report (2018) which reported that refugees, asylum seekers, and undocumented migrants in the United Kingdom were afraid of seeking healthcare over fears that medics would share their data, or adverse implications for their asylum claim of accessing treatment. As well as concerns over structural barriers, such as financial constraints, impacting their ability to travel for medical appointments. These challenges to appropriate healthcare seeking are exacerbated further by deep levels of confusion amongst both asylum seekers and healthcare professionals in relation to entitlements for refugees, asylum seekers and other migrants' ability to access otherwise "universal, free at the point of delivery" healthcare in Britain (Tomkow et al. 2020). Despite reassurances from the British Government that undocumented migrants are encouraged to access free medical treatment if unwell, and that everyone is entitled to COVID-19 vaccinations without risk of deportation, reports exist of unnecessary deaths from COVID-19 of undocumented migrants or failed asylum seekers living in liminal circumstances who have not sought medical help, as a result of fear of State incarceration or deportation (Bulman 2020).

Accordingly, despite growing calls in the United Kingdom, in parts of Europe, and Australia for reconsideration of how refugees and asylum seekers are treated in the wake of the pandemic, and increased awareness of the failure of human rights protection for the most vulnerable members of society, it cannot be assumed that we will see a shift towards greater acceptance of indivisible human rights for these groups amongst the larger populace. On the contrary, it can be seen that some states have exploited the disruption occasioned by the pandemic to further reduce humanitarian support and protection available to asylum seekers (Crawley 2021). Therefore, although in a number of European countries there has been a reduction in numbers of asylum seekers in detention centres since the pandemic struck in 2020, there is also an apparent and growing divide at nation-state level, with Italy having imposed the compulsory detention of asylum seekers in unhygienic and overcrowded boats held offshore, in the name of public health, leading to multiple self-harm incidents. Similarly, Greece imposed lockdowns on refugee camps which even precluded emergency transfers to hospital for children with serious non-COVID-related medical conditions (Andreou 2020; D'Ignoti 2021; Fallon and Grillmeie 2020).

Concerningly, not only is the United Kingdom expressing an interest in "offshoring"/externalisation of asylum seekers until their applications can be determined, but even in mainland Europe this concept is gaining traction. In June 2021 Denmark passed legislation enabling refugees to be removed from Danish soil to asylum centres in a non-European partner country for case reviews and possibly the provision of humanitarian protection in that third country, paid for by Denmark (Reuters 2021). Similarly, in April 2021 Sweden announced changes to their asylum regimes which would initially only grant temporary leave to remain for a three-year period, and should an applicant subsequently apply for permanent residency they would need to fulfil much tougher eligibility requirements (including knowledge of the Swedish language and culture) and, should they wish to apply for family reunification, be required to provide proof of sufficient income to support themselves and family members who wished to join them (Esteves 2021).

Faced with such concerning and rapidly changing approaches to immigration and asylum law and policy in multiple countries, there is increasing evidence of collective rallying against such restrictive regimes, led by coalitions and networks of faith groups and professionals. The practices of resistance emerging from these increasingly popular, grassroots-led migrant solidarity movements that exist in several diverse countries typically composed of religious believers, civil society agencies, academics, students, and other young people (English et al. 2019). And are fully aligned to the theory of the indivisibility of first- and second-generation human rights discussed by Briskman. They are exemplified in Fleay et al.'s discussion of the Western Australia (WA) advocacy network, to which attention now turns in the following section.

Advocacy practice to influence existing political systems

In Chapter 10, Fleay et al. analyse the co-production processes utilised by the WA Refugee and People Seeking Asylum Network. They explore the range of processes and techniques used to influence politicians and policy makers so as to improve the situation of individuals impacted by the harsh Federal Government requirements placed on safe haven enterprise visa (SHEV) holders.

The mode of multi-level political engagement and advocacy presented within Chapter 10, which brings together those individuals negatively impacted by legislation, academics, civil society agencies, and a range of other stakeholders, is a method of resistance with which I'm personally familiar and engage with regularly in my own professional practice. In a chapter on the role and dilemmas of the "ethical academic" seeking to influence policy formation with marginalised populations (Greenfields 2018: 250), I expound on the argument that "three legs" of the tripod that support the design and delivery of meaningful policy interventions are first, empowerment ("voice") of those directly affected by legislation; second, high-quality research and data to support moral and practical arguments for change; and third, engagement with and knowledge of appropriate policy design gained through close working with policy professionals and those who can influence change, including politicians. Such changes in policy and practice, which progressively accrue value for the individuals directly impacted, are typically incremental, calibrated to particular circumstances or geographical locations (WA, in the case of Chapter 10), and gain traction and wider adoption over time (policy transfer at micro, meso, and macro level), facilitating a slow build-up of influence and impact as the benefits of a particular approach can be appreciated.

Accordingly, such pragmatic but effective methods of ally-building and selection of deliverable "asks," based on an understanding of political opportunity structures and refined through working collaboratively with politicians and policy professionals on a more localised level, offer an effective method of leveraging change through advocacy. One key element of effective "quiet, localised, relational" work to bring about change lies, I would suggest, in the fact that policy professionals, civil servants, and politicians who are typically holding multiple portfolios, are time poor and may have a relatively weak prior knowledge of the impacts of Federal (National) state policies. By engaging in relational work with advocacy networks they are, thus, supported in their functional role by the provision of clear, accessible data and relatable human narrative to underpin their activities and discussions with influential colleagues, in order to generate change.

The discussion in Chapter 10 on the processes utilised to collect evidence, engages with particular SHEV holders who were empowered to present their narratives to political and policy actors, and the success of their advocacy in bringing about a series of positive changes at the local, State, level. This does not (as the authors acknowledge) address the failures of Federal immigration policies. Nor does it address the underpinning racist structures that permit the design and popularity of an immigration model predicated on closed borders and an inherent suspicion of, and hostility to, those fleeing persecution though irregular routes. Rather, the value of the authors' approach is in creating a more positive and welcoming environment for refugee and asylum-seeking residents of WA. Regardless of whether the Federal Government eventually responds positively to the call to designate Perth, and other areas of WA, as "regional areas" for the purposes of establishing a pathway to permanent residency, through the work of advocacy network and the agreement of the WA Government to request such recognition, steps have been taken to restore dignity and humanity to those caught in the toils of the asylum system.

The delicately phrased discussion on the hostility articulated towards political and policy actors by some activists, and the negative effects of media representations of protests and other forms of direct action portrayed as disruptive or subversive to the well-functioning state, articulates clearly the tensions in differing approaches to migrant solidarity, which are often associated in public discourse with youth-oriented, left-wing or anarchist practices, and by proponents of political solidarity movements as radical contestation of the power of the State (English et al. 2019).

For the typical pragmatic (and well-meaning) policy actor, protests or acts of relatively unorganised solidarity, such as taking vanloads of food and sanitary supplies to large-scale informal encampments of migrants (e.g. 'The Jungle" in Calais), or high-profile direct actions undertaken by loosely affiliated members of solidarity movements working outside of the parameters of established civil society agencies, are anathema to the design and implementation of effective policy solutions. Indeed, whilst potentially effective in bringing about short-term or reactive change, such as halting a deportation flight or alleviating destitution for those without recourse to public funds and services, arguably such modes of action are more effective in raising awareness or creating an environment in which more traditional policy processes can come into play than they are in bringing about long-term change. Cairney, in a discussion on the political processes underpinning policy development proposes that academics (and by extension one may add many solidarity activists) "should identify how the policy process works and seek to influence it on that basis—not according to how they would like it to be" (Cairney 2015: 9).

It is in bridging this gap between the demand for radical change in the overall immigration system (articulated by Briskman, in her call for welfare practitioners to foreground human rights discourse and recognise the futility of alleviation of individual economic or social exclusion in the face of an unjust regime), and a micro-level focus on individual cases, such as form the workload of lawyers and social workers, that I would argue that Fleay et al. are undertaking their most effective practice. Thus, not only are the Network members engaged at the level of influencing policy and practice in WA, with the potential to grain traction in reshaping the pathways to obtaining permanent residency for temporary visa holders (should Perth be redesignated and recognised as a designated "regional area") but also their mode of engagement has clearly delivered personal benefits to individual SHEV holders beyond the immediate gains associated with transport concessions and enhanced educational opportunities.

These "secondary benefits" occur through facilitating recognition of refugees' and asylum seekers' agency and power, supporting their "speaking their truth to power," and enhancing their relationship with structures of the state, as well as in building personal confidence through activism. As is evidenced in the reflections on politicians' responses to meeting SHEV holders. Collaborative methodologies have also shifted the narrative and parameters of understanding for politicians, as political stakeholders who may have not have knowingly met an asylum seeker previously and who would have been solely reliant on policy briefings or media representations to inform their stance.

Conclusion

Fleay et al.'s pragmatic approach to operationalising political opportunity through networks of influence offers a contrasting approach to Briskman's call (no less valid, if perhaps more idealistic) for high-level action that demands recognition of the indivisible relationship between categories of human rights to facilitate dignified positive outcomes for refugees and asylum seekers. Briskman provides examples of activism which led to the withdrawal of planned engagement between Royal Melbourne Institute of Technology and an immigration detention facility, underpinned by the belief that provision of education in such settings represented a clash of first-generation (liberty) and second-generation (educational) human rights. Without knowing the full details of the situation, the troubling question remains, however, for this commentator, of whether the principle of not engaging with the immigration system should outweigh the importance of delivery of high-quality education to those in detention: given the importance of such opportunities in supporting detainees to build skills and knowledge which could support their release from incarceration, alleviate the crippling boredom and depression which is a common experience for those incarcerated, and aid asylum seekers in obtaining employment once released into the community. Precisely the same question, of whether a greater harm is committed by collaborating with state agencies with which one disagrees, or by failing to deliver needed services, is raised by the call by some medics for a boycott on delivery of medical services in detention settings, as detailed by Briskman in Chapter 9. Perhaps more prosaically, one could ask if an individual medic or university refusing to deliver support services to those in detention simply harms the individual asylum seeker by a delay in their accessing second-generation rights, or merely if another provider will take on the role instead, leading to limited impact on the system of state control?

The moral philosophy argument that any form of collusion with cruel immigration regimes (of asylum detention or highly restricted rights for asylum seekers in community settings) is akin to condoning such state practices is clearly a contested issue. In response I find that my mind returns repeatedly to considering the ethical limits and reasonable expectations on community workers engaged with populations at greatest risk in the context of war or other disasters, even when there is a necessity of having contact with those whose views are diametrically opposed to one's own (e.g. medics and humanitarian workers passing through check points in war zones). My own stance is that there is a moral imperative for professionals not to refrain from action to alleviate suffering in the face of great unjustness or evil. Instead, there is an ethical duty incumbent on those empowered or privileged enough to launch challenges to the status quo (through engaging in dialogue, legal proceedings, or other administrative processes) and, thus, to support activities which may (albeit incrementally) bring about positive change.

Mayblin (2019: 7) refers to the "policy imaginary" through which legislators and policy makers create a conceptual image of asylum seekers, which can exist and allow harm to occur only "where moral distance is already physically and emotionally established between asylum seekers and policy decision makers [such that] imaginaries are protected and enclosed for policy actors through the everyday workings of the state."

By breaking down this imaginary and presenting those responsible for developing and implementing policies negatively affecting asylum seekers and refugees with contact with people most directly affected by the consequences of their decisions (via face-to-face meetings in which lived experience is presented, or more adversarially through legal proceedings) it can be argued that the greater good is served more effectively than by withdrawing from the fray.

In conclusion, to return to the UK context with which I am most familiar. In 2021 ahead of the implementation of the most chilling proposals for immigration reform to occur in decades (UK Government/Home Office 2021), there have been several successful civil society and community organisation–led campaigns and legal battles which are piecemeal but proving effective in challenging the worst excesses of a hostile environment on vulnerable migrants. We have seen examples of popular community resistance to detention and deportation of local residents (Brooks 2021) and also members of the Prison Inspectorate and the judiciary, supported by evidence from social workers and medics, who have upheld human rights and the rule of law (*R (MD) v Secretary of State for the Home Department* [2021] EWHC 1370 (Admin)), condemning conditions under which asylum seekers are held and requiring the government to mitigate the horrors and risks of severe physical and mental illness on incarcerated migrants. Therefore, it can be argued that through working in collaboration with, rather than ideological opposition to, political and policy allies, and by utilising the levers of establishment resources and power, our best chance exists for creating processes and reception conditions for asylum seekers and refugees that treat those in need of protection with dignity, compassion, and justice.

Bibliography

Agamben, G. (2017) *The Omnibus: Homo Sacer*. Stanford University Press.

Andreou, A. (2020) 'Europe's Far-Right Exploits COVID-19 for Anti-Refugee Propaganda', *Balkan Insight Online News Item*, 4 June. https://balkaninsight.com/2020/06/04/europes-far-right-exploits-covid-19-for-anti-refugee-propaganda/

Bar-Tuvia, S. (2018) 'Australian and Israeli agreements for the permanent transfer of refugees: Stretching further the (Il)legality and (Im)morality of western externalization policies', *International Journal of Refugee Law*, 30(3): 474.

BiD. Bail for Immigration Detainees. (2019) *Policy Briefing: Families Separated by Immigration Detention and Deportation*, February. London: BiD.

Boyle, C. (2020) 'Missing voices: Why asylum seekers are uniquely vulnerable in the coronavirus crisis', *Left Foot Forward*, 1 April. https://leftfootforward.org/2020/04/missing-voices-why-asylum-seekers-are-uniquely-vulnerable-in-the-coronavirus-crisis/

Briskman, L. and Zion, D. (2014) 'Dual loyalties and impossible dilemmas: Health care in immigration detention', *Public Health Ethics*, 7(3): 277.

Brooks, L. (2021) 'Glasgow protesters rejoice as men freed after immigration van stand-off', *The Guardian Newspaper*, 13 May. www.theguardian.com/uk-news/2021/may/13/glasgow-residents-surround-and-block-immigration-van-from-leaving-street

Bulman, M. (2020) 'Undocumented migrants dying of coronavirus because they're too afraid to seek help, MPs and charities warn', *The Independent Newspaper*, 18 April. www.independent.co.uk/news/uk/home-news/coronavirus-undocumented-migrants-deaths-cases-nhs-matt-hancock-a9470581.html

Bulman, M. (2021a) 'Vulnerable asylum seeker kept at Napier Barracks for weeks after attempting to take his life', *The Independent Newspaper*, 15 April. www.independent.co.uk/news/uk/home-news/asylum-seeker-napier-baracks-suicide-b1832157.html

Bulman, M. (2021b) 'Dozens of vulnerable asylum seekers wrongly placed in Napier Barracks despite watchdog warnings', *The Independent Newspaper*, 22 May. www.independent.co.uk/news/uk/home-news/dozens-of-vulnerable-asylum-seekers-wrongly-placed-in-napier-barracks-despite-mental-health-warnings-b1850679.html

Cairney, P. (2015) *The Politics of Evidence-Based Policymaking*. Palgrave MacMillan.

Cobain, I. (2018) 'UK immigration authorities separating children from parents', *The Guardian Newspaper*, 3 July. www.theguardian.com/uk-news/2018/jul/03/uk-immigration-authorities-separating-children-from-parents

Coddington, K. (2019) 'The slow violence of life without cash: Borders, state restrictions, and exclusion in the U.K. and Australia', *Geographical Review*, 109(4): 527.

Crawley, H. (2021) 'How COVID-19 became a cover to reduce refugee rights', *The Conversation*, 21 March. https://theconversation.com/how-covid-19-became-a-cover-to-reduce-refugee-rights-156247

Dathan, M. (2021) 'People smugglers will be jailed for life, vows Priti Patel', *The Sunday Times*, 21 March. www.thetimes.co.uk/article/people-smugglers-will-be-jailed-for-life-vows-priti-patel-brhb8g892

D'Ignoti, S. (2021) 'Pressure grows on Italy to abolish migrant quarantine ships', *Politico EU*, 7 January. www.politico.eu/article/italy-migrants-offshore-quarantine-incidents-deaths/

Doherty, B. (2021) 'As UK considers offshore asylum plan, why Australia's system was a dangerous failure', *Guardian*, 22 March. www.theguardian.com/australia-news/2021/mar/22/as-uk-considers-offshore-asylum-plan-why-australias-system-was-a-dangerous-failure

English, C., Grazioli, M. and Martignoni, M. (2019) 'Migrant solidarity in post-colonial Europe: Challenging borders, creating mobile commons', in Kinna, R. and Gordon, U. (eds) *The Routledge Handbook of Radical Politics*. Routledge.

Equalities and Human Rights Commission. (2018) *Research report 122. People seeking asylum: Access to healthcare lived experience*. Manchester: EHRC. www.equalityhumanrights.com/sites/default/files/research-report-122-people-seeking-asylum-access-to-healthcare-lived-experiences.pdf

Esteves, J. (2021) 'Sweden's aid groups rally ahead of restrictive migration proposals', *Catholic News Service Online*, 21 April. https://cruxnow.com/church-in-europe/2021/04/swedens-aid-groups-rally-ahead-of-restrictive-migration-proposals/

Fallon, K. and Grillmeieir, F. (2020) 'Greece's refugees face healthcare crisis as Lesbos Covid-19 centre closes', *The Guardian Newspaper*, 31 July. www.theguardian.com/global-development/2020/jul/31/greece-refugee-healthcare-crisis-island-camps-lesbos-moria-coronavirus

Finlay, R., Benwell, M. C. and Hopkins, P. (2020) 'Covid-19: Responding to the needs of asylum seekers in challenging and dangerous times', *Discover Society*. https://eprints.ncl.ac.uk/file_store/production/266736/A5D1755B-885D-4D59-A277-CEC6C5B2B060.pdf

Follis, A., Neagu, B., Nikolov, K. and Makszimov, V. (2020) 'Less blame, little action for Europe's Roma during second COVID wave', *EuActiv*, 8 December. www.euractiv.com/section/non-discrimination/news/less-blame-little-action-for-europes-roma-during-second-covid-wave/

Gates-Lincoln, A. (2021) 'Plans for new women's detention centre in Durham are challenged', *Electronic Immigration Network*, 24 May. www.ein.org.uk/blog/plans-new-womens-detention-centre-durham-are-challenged

Greenfields, M. (2018) 'Policy input on the front line. Dilemmas of the ethical academic', in Beck, S. and Ivasiuc, A. (eds) *Roma Activism Reimagining Power and Knowledge*. Berghahn Books.

Grierson, J. and Walker, P. (2021) 'UN official raises concerns over UK offshore asylum plan', *The Guardian*, 18 March. www.theguardian.com/uk-news/2021/mar/18/gibraltar-isle-of-man-rule-out-housing-asylum-seekers-uk

Hargreaves, J. R. and Logie, C. H. (2020) 'Lifting lockdown policies: A critical moment for COVID-19 stigma', *Global Public Health*, 15(12): 1917.

The Home Office [UK] and Rt. Hon. Caroline Noakes, MP. (2018) 'New pilot schemes to support migrants at risk of detention', 3 December. www.gov.uk/government/news/new-pilot-schemes-to-support-migrants-at-risk-of-detention

House of Commons Library. (2020) *Research Briefing: Effect of the Covid-19 Pandemic on Refugee Communities*. House of Commons. https://commonslibrary.parliament.uk/research-briefings/cdp-2020-0134/

Kluge, H. H. P., Jakab, Z., Bartovic, J., d'Anna, V. and Severoni, S. (2020) 'Refugee and migrant health in the COVID-19 response', *The Lancet*, 395(10232): 1237. www.thelancet.com/journals/lancet/article/PIIS0140-6736(20)30791-1/fulltext?rss=yes

Lipsky, M. (2010) *Street Level Bureaucracy: Dilemmas of the Individual in Public Services*, 30th Anniversary Edition. Russell Sage Foundation.

Mainwaring, C. and Cook, M. L. (2019) 'Immigration detention: An Anglo model', *Migration Studies*, 7(4): 455. https://doi.org/10.1093/migration/mny015

Mayblin, L. (2019) 'Imagining asylum, governing asylum seekers: Complexity reduction and policy making in the UK Home Office', *Migration Studies*, 7(1): 1.

Mbembe, A. (2019) *Necropolitics* (trans. Steve Corcoran). Duke University Press.

Pearce, J. (2014) 'Racism and Xenophobia in economic downturns', *Skeptic-Ink*. https://skepticink.com/tippling/2014/10/07/racism-and-xenophobia-in-economic-downturns/

Pegg, D. and Lewis, P. (2020) 'Australian-style offshore asylum plan driven by No 10', *The Guardian Newspaper*. www.theguardian.com/uk-news/2020/sep/30/australian-style-offshore-asylum-plan-driven-by-no-10

Reidy, E. (2021) 'One year on: How the pandemic has affected refugees, asylum seekers, and migration', *The New Humanitarian*. www.thenewhumanitarian.org/analysis/2021/3/10/one-year-how-pandemic-has-affected-refugees-asylum-migration

Reuters. (2021) 'Denmark passes law to relocate asylum seekers outside Europe', *The Guardian*, 3 June. www.theguardian.com/world/2021/jun/03/denmark-passes-law-to-let-it-relocate-asylum-seekers-outside-europe

Sevencan, S. (2020) 'Refugees, asylum seekers unfairly blamed for COVID-19', *Andalou Agency (Turkish News Agency)* 2 September. www.aa.com.tr/en/world/refugees-asylum-seekers-unfairly-blamed-for-covid-19/1960743

Sisters Not Strangers Coalition. (2020) *Hear us: The experiences of refugee and asylum-seeking women during the pandemic*. www.refugeewomen.co.uk/wp-content/uploads/2020/08/Hear-us-Sisters-Not-Strangers.pdf

Sumption, M. (2019) *The Australian points-based system: What is it and what would its impact be in the UK? Report*. The Migration Observatory, University of Oxford. https://migrationobservatory.ox.ac.uk/resources/reports/the-australian-points-based-system-what-is-it-and-what-would-its-impact-be-in-the-uk/

Taylor, D. (2021) 'Asylum seeker brings case against Covid 'curfew' at London hotel', *The Guardian Newspaper*, 19 February. www.theguardian.com/uk-news/2021/feb/19/asylum-seeker-brings-case-against-covid-curfew-at-london-hotel

Tomkow, L. J., Kang, C., Farrington, R., Wiggans, R., Wilson, R., Pushkar, P., Tickell-Painter, M., Lee, A., Whitehouse, E., Mahmood, N., Lawton K. and Lee, E. (2020) 'Healthcare access for asylum seekers and refugees in England: A mixed methods study exploring service users' and health care professionals' awareness,' *European Journal of Public Health*, 30(3): 527.

UCL (University College London) Centre for Health Informatics. (2020) *BAME groups two to three times more likely to die from Covid-19 than the general population*. www.ucl.ac.uk/health-informatics/bame

UK Government/Home Office. (2021) 'Home Secretary Priti Patel speech on immigration', 24 May. London: HMSO. www.gov.uk/government/speeches/home-secretary-priti-patel-speech-on-immigration

United Nations (UN). (2020) 'UN policy brief: COVID-19 and people on the move', June. www.un.org/sites/un2.un.org/files/sg_policy_brief_on_people_on_the_move.pdf

Weisbrot, E. (2018) 'Policy on the move: How policy advocates have framed the international transfer of Australia's asylum seeker policies', *Asia Pacific Journal of Public Administration*, 40(3): 147.

Women for Refugee Women. (2021) 'Stop the new detention centre for women at Hassockfield, county Durham', 26 February. www.refugeewomen.co.uk/stop-the-new-detention-centre/

World Health Organisation (WHO). (2020) 'Stories of hope as refugees help tackle the COVID-19 pandemic', 19 June. www.euro.who.int/en/countries/serbia/news/news/2020/6/stories-of-hope-as-refugees-help-tackle-the-covid-19-pandemic

Yuval-Davis, M., Wemyss, G. and Cassidy, K. (eds) (2019) *Bordering: Migration, Belonging and New Forms of Social Control*. Polity Press.

Chapter 9

Social welfare paradoxes for asylum seekers

Challenges for human rights

Linda Briskman

Introduction

Inadequate social welfare provision for asylum seekers and refugees is a topic of concern locally and globally. This chapter discusses this problematic from a human rights and social justice perspective by examining how competing rights have come to dominate the forced migration landscape in Australia. It does so by proposing that there exists a conflictual relationship between civil and political rights on the one hand, and economic and social rights on the other, advancing what I call the futility argument that posits that welfare provision as a "second-generation" human right cannot fulfil its aims unless violations of first-generation civil rights are eliminated. It draws on the discipline of social work, where critiques of social work reveal associated tensions between care and control that mirror the rights disjuncture. Social work is also beset with contradictions between different levels of social work from the clinical to the structural. Just as human rights remain contested the role and purpose of social work is divided between what Dominelli (1998) speaks of as therapeutic helping approaches, maintenance approaches, and emancipatory approaches. It is the emancipatory approach that places social justice and human rights to the forefront.

I am not claiming that social work has the sole prerogative regarding the question of welfare provision. I centre social work as welfare is its direct "business" and human rights and social justice are articulated within its mission. My focus is predominantly on asylum seeker boat arrivals, immigration detention (onshore and offshore) and aftermath, and detention alternatives. To set the context for what follows, I position myself as an activist academic as that shapes the lens through which I see the pursuit of justice for asylum seekers and refugees. For twenty years I have advocated, conducted research, and written for academic and media outlets about the depths of inhumanity into which Australia has plunged in its treatment of asylum seekers and refugees. I have visited detention centres throughout mainland Australia, Christmas Island, and abroad. I have directly witnessed the joy of people being released from detention under the official pretext of responding to their vulnerability, only to be demoralised

DOI: 10.4324/9781003298595-16

by temporary residency status with limited rights and limited sustenance. With the advent of community-based alternatives for asylum seekers I celebrated, with others, what seemed to be an end of the "mandatory"' aspect of immigration detention, only to see an ongoing diminishment of basic welfare provision for a life of dignity and worth, through indefinite waiting for refugee processing and through descent into poverty. Through these observations, and accumulated disappointment, I have concluded that until the punitive deterrence system of detention and its community alternatives are dismantled, welfare provision produces only short-term bolstering.

In line with this assertion, I argue that advocating for and implementing welfare provision for boat arrivals, either in detention or in the community, is ineffectual until their civil and political rights are recognised. Even though human rights are said to be indivisible, everyday understandings and official practice mitigate against this. The chapter first discusses what I call the "welfare problem." It then turns to outlining the disjuncture between first and second generations of human rights before presenting the futility argument. Following on, the chapter looks more overtly at social work and how this discipline and profession can undermine or advance the pursuit of human rights, illustrated by examples, and then a case study of health provision in immigration detention. Finally, I discuss prospects for a way forward, referring to the contemporary example of the COVID-19 pandemic, where there has been some unexpected convergence of rights in global advocacy and practice.

What is the welfare problem?

On a global scale, forced migration has increasingly become an exclusionary border security concern of nations rather than a person-centred approach of human security, protection, and safety. This constitutes what I have called a clash of paradigms (Briskman 2016) which aligns with the disjuncture presented in the futility argument. With unceasing migration flows, asylum seekers in destination countries encounter discrimination and challenges to their basic human rights (McCracken and Phillips 2017). Complicating the terrain within Australia is the binary between rights-holders and the rights-less. Those who have been formally invited to settle in Australia as refugees are immediately entitled to permanent residency and a range of settlement support services such as income, housing, education, and employment-seeking assistance. In such provision, Australia prides itself in accepting refugees through United Nations (UN) approval systems under its humanitarian program. Additionally, asylum seekers who arrive by plane are not routinely subjected to immigration detention, as they enter with a valid visa and are generally released into the community while awaiting claims processing. It is those asylum seekers who arrive "unauthorised" by boat, without a valid visa, frequently using Indonesia as a staging post, who have few substantive and diminished procedural rights, whether held offshore, or in immigration detention or community settings within Australia. This discriminates against asylum seekers based on their mode of arrival.

In detention, asylum seekers lack basic human rights including freedom of movement and freedom from inhumane treatment, although they receive such basic provision as shelter and food. Those in the community on bridging visas class E (BVEs)[1] are free to move and to be treated with some decency but are generally ineligible for social (income) security payments, federally subsidised tertiary education, or housing assistance, and they may lack entitlement to healthcare. The disjuncture of entitlements based on mode of arrival to Australia arguably contradicts the provisions and spirit of the 1951 *Convention relating to the Status of Refugees* ("Refugees Convention").

Australia's Refugee and Humanitarian program offers protection to "offshore" applicants who are usually refugees approved by the United Nations High Commissioner for Refugees and allocated for resettlement in Australia. It is this group who is offered immediate social welfare and other provision. This means they are provided with a "kick-start' as opposed to those asylum seekers who have entered "unauthorised," who may, at best, receive charitable handouts while their situation remains precarious. Entering formally through humanitarian programs sets up welcome through permanent protection for those situated as "good refugees" and not "queue jumpers" or bogus claimants as popular discourse would have it in respect of boat arrivals. Those people arriving directly by boat (excluding those arriving after July 2013, banished to Nauru or Papua New Guinea) have temporary and precarious residency status and rights-limitations. When refugees are demonised through border protection policies it becomes politically possible to deny them material resources. "Offshoring" in Nauru or Papua New Guinea (the practice examined in certain other chapters in this volume) exacerbates this trend with well-publicised and long-standing concerns about health and welfare provision, safety, and future uncertainty in those regional processing countries.

Looking broadly at popular constructions within increasingly conservative neoliberal states, there is an emphasis on welfare provision for "the deserving" and less emphasis on needs and rights. Social work ostensibly discarded the notion of deserving as it moved from individual charity-based approaches, largely attributed to the United Kingdom Charity Organisation Society, to a more critical and structural approach to understanding injustice and social disadvantage and constructing remedies that tackle systemic injustices and inequality. A critical turn for social work arose from the theorising of a pioneer in newly popularised structural social work from the late 1970s, Maurice Moreau. He postulated that the concern of social work is with groups who are marginalised by an ideology that supports, maintains, and legitimates the existing social order (Moureau 1979). The work of Moreau highlights the imperative for social work practice to account for the structural oppression of individuals, while also considering the individual, because of the interconnection between personal aspects of a problem and the institutional and political elements (Allan

2003). Combining individual and political dimensions in specific fields of practice has been a difficult undertaking experienced across disciplines in the asylum seeker and refugee realm and not just confined to social work.

A sustainable life is a core human right but a vexed one. The notion of social welfare gives rise to survival but not human dignity, and recourse to charity dispensed by community organisations and NGOs is both a necessity and a blight. Because of a lack of state provision, church and community groups specialising in assistance to asylum seekers are active sources of support for those who are otherwise unable to obtain income support, housing, and health services (Fentiman and O'Sullivan 2018). At the time of writing, however, these groups experience limits on what they can offer with volunteers routinely forced to stay at home, because of COVID-19 restrictions on free movement, and with the number of people requiring welfare support growing (Macken 2020a). The right to work creates more dignity and with some potential for increasing human connection, belonging, and routine which are foundational to human existence. Yet work for those experiencing temporariness, without permanent refugee protection, is another example of how government excludes, belittles, and creates barriers and destroys a trusting relationship between employer and employee, creating an underclass within the labour market. Work rights create a misconception of an altruistic government, albeit one where individualism prevails rather than an approach that works for the collective good of new arrivals and for the society as a whole. Asylum seekers are rendered powerless and, with a few exceptions, find it nigh impossible to exercise agency to advocate for their own inclusion, when enticements of permission (in reality expectation) to work (difficult to implement for people on temporary visas or whose qualifications go unrecognised) or basic payments (for the lucky few) imply expectation of gratitude on the part of the recipient.

Carens (2013) observes that irregular migrants are denied rights that would ordinarily be expected within the jurisdiction of the state. As posited by Davies et al. (2017: 1269), advanced states have "ample resources with which to ensure those within its borders are protected from hunger, provided with shelter and given the security required to live without constant fear. Welfare systems are relatively well funded." But like the slave discussed in Mbembe's (2003: 17) work, the asylum seeker and refugee are kept alive but in a "state of injury" where they experience calculated cruelty. For Lloyd et al. (2009–2010), criminalisation and exclusionary migration policies are forms of "civil death," where categories are created where people are not afforded the range of rights granted to most others in societies. Racism underlies the cruelty where, in Australian society, it has never been absent from politics and practice in a nation founded on race-based dispossession followed by race-based exclusion. Race for Mbembe (2003: 17) "has been the ever-present shadow in Western political thought and practice, especially when it comes to imagining the inhumanity of, or rule over, foreign peoples."

So great has the inhumanity been to asylum seekers and refugees that, according to Macken (2020b), Australia's treatment of refugees and asylum seekers constitutes a regime of cruelty and neglect amounting to torture. Trading human rights for borders breaches the UN *Convention against Torture*; Australia's mandatory detention system is cruel, inhuman, and degrading. Law, policy, and practice are punitive rather than offering protection as laid out in the *Refugees Convention*. As Robertson (2018: 36) explains in regards to offshore detention sites, although people held offshore are not experiencing waterboarding or electric shocks, "their lives are so miserable and devoid of hope and so psychologically crippling" as the Australian Government hopes they will return to their countries of origin. In 2017, the Supreme Court of Papua New Guinea ruled that Australia's detention of asylum seekers on Manus Island was illegal because it breached the right to personal liberty in the Papua New Guinea *Constitution*. Their eventual release from detention did not resolve the human rights concerns on Manus Island, claims Robertson, because there was a high possibility that resettlement in the Papua New Guinea community could result in violence.

In Australia, asylum seeker laws, policies, and practices are constantly changing and, for human rights advocates, in a downward sliding trajectory. Just when advocates believe that the situation cannot get worse more regulatory changes are introduced, including the pronouncement by the Labor Government, in July 2013, declaring that no asylum seeker who arrives by boat would ever be given the chance to settle in Australia. This combines with the resistance of successive Federal governments (from 2014 to date) to relocating people, entrapped for years in Nauru or Papua New Guinea, to Australia for much-needed physical and psychological health services that are caused or exacerbated by long-term detention. What does not change is the dominant belief that they are not entitled to human rights afforded to others in the society. In the official depiction of Australia as a country that welcomes refugees, stark contrasts emerge.

For life to be sustainable, people must be free from poverty and deprivation through access to welfare and health supports. This is a right and not a handout and it is best achieved by providing people with the means to attain these goals but with a safety net when this is not possible. Absence or withdrawal of welfare support has scant connection with the ability of a wealthy country like Australia to provide such support. For the federal government deems it necessary to maintain Australia's dominant interests to scapegoat one group of people, who have exercised their right to seek and enjoy asylum—effective protection from persecution and harm, in order to dissuade others from doing the same: a practice that uses cruel and inhuman punishment to advance the political goal of deterrence of irregular migration.

By sending a signal of the undeserving asylum seeker that is amplified by a narrative of fear, via the racialised construct of asylum seeker as potential terrorist (Perera 2002: 28), community protest is minimised and serves to preclude both freedom and welfare rights. It is here that legal and welfare provision collide with international law, with watered-down national law provision for welfare and the ideology of deterrence intersecting. Welfare support, which has long been a foundation of Australia's social policy regime even when weakened under conservative governments and neo-liberal ideologies that oppose the welfare state, is not considered the norm for asylum seekers. This is particularly problematic for asylum seekers on BVEs who have limited life provision and are in a state of limbo through slow administration of (temporary) visa claims and related appeals processes.

Economic arguments do not hold sway as deterrence and border protection motivations of governments and certain media outlets negate these viewpoints, even though it is well known that permanent refugee protection, work, and assistance with business development would benefit the national interest. The minimal costs of welfare provision for people in the community can be viewed alongside the exorbitant costs of offshore detention: it is estimated that Australia spends around $573,000 per year per asylum seeker (Munro and Joyce 2019). The right to receive public health provision (Medicare) for those without permanent visa status and who hold bridging visas is governed by legislation that is dependent on the conditions of the bridging visa held (Munro and Joyce 2019). For those without access to welfare services received by "worthy" refugees, the consequences can be dire, as the vast body of evidence about the poorer health and mental status of asylum seekers and refugees, compared with others in the population, attests. Munro and Joyce (2019) argue that if an applicant cannot receive medical services during the application process they will be in a worse physical and psychological state than when they first made an application and are less likely to engage with services if a visa is granted subsequently.

Generations of human rights

The generations typology of human rights, particularly what is known as the first and second generation, is useful in setting the scene for the human rights futility conundrum in the asylum seeker sphere and is a basis for critiquing the social work profession's mixed rights messages. First-generation human rights are civil and political rights, formally enshrined in the UN *International Covenant on Civil and Political Rights (ICCPR)*. These human rights are ones most commonly understood, and challenges to the treatment of asylum seekers is frequently framed within this domain, including protection from torture and freedom from discrimination. Bills of Rights, that are common in industrialised countries (but absent in Australia at the federal level), usually focus on first-generation rights and provide clarity and direction for human rights leaning practitioners (Ife 2012). In the "hierarchy" of human rights the term first-generation denotes that these are frequently viewed by rights bodies as being of most importance.

Second-generation human rights, enshrined in the UN *International Covenant on Economic, Social and Cultural Rights* (*ICESCR*), are most applicable to everyday social work practice and to forms of advocacy that strive for decent reception conditions for asylum seekers, either within or outside of immigration detention. According to Ife (2012: 45), these are the rights of people:

> to receive various forms of social provision or services in order to realise their full potential as human beings: the right to employment, the right to an adequate wage, the right to housing, the right to adequate food and clothing, right to education the right to adequate health care, the right to social security, the right to be treated with dignity in old age, the right to reasonable recreation and leisure time.

Discord for asylum seekers/refugees is revealed in selective attention to either first- or second- generation rights. This is where provision and advocacy unravel for asylum seekers because the denial of civil and political rights (such as freedom from arbitrary detention, freedom from torture, or non-discriminatory visa categories) sits alongside an absence of economic and social rights. This distinction is not confined to asylum seekers and refugees and also besets the professions. While a minority of social workers may be somewhat troubled by erosion of first-generation rights, most are attentive to helping people attain second-generation rights (Ife 2012: 59). But the precarity created by the lack of basic welfare provision cannot be addressed without holistic attention to human rights.

International dictates, including from the United Nations, declare human rights to be indivisible, interdependent, and interrelated. The indivisibility of human rights becomes disrupted in nations, such as Australia, where one set of rights is privileged over another. Unlike less resourced countries that may have to make rights-choices, the Australian problem has more to do with ideology and politics than human rights. As Chapman (2009) suggested, indivisibility implies that

> it is not possible to realize the obligations related to any one human right without also fulfilling the requirements of all other human rights. In addition, the affirmation of indivisibility suggests that the content of each human right is intrinsically related to, mutually supportive of, and perhaps even essential to the implementation of others.

In other words, civil and political rights cannot be achieved without the enjoyment of economic and social rights, and *vice versa*. Although this argument is contestable in practice, it leads to more detailed consideration of the futility argument, outlined in the following section.

You can't have one without the other

The question of indivisibility of human rights advances the notion of futility of welfarism that characterises social welfare provision as a component of second-generation human rights. This question is addressed by international aid scholarship, articulated by differentiating between humanitarianism and human rights. The paradox is akin to what can be observed in non-governmental aid presence in wartime, where humanitarian organisations endeavour to cure wounds but do not try to stop the wounding (Mills 2005). In this sense, dispensing welfarism creates a ruse of care and compassion to those rendered vulnerable through displacement. Humanitarian relief is dispensed without reference to the socio-political context in which it operates. In addition, the state has co-opted the notion of vulnerability while becoming increasingly punitive and through exerting what Aliverti (2020: 1117) calls, within the criminal justice system, "state-sanctioned pain."

The previous contentions can be illustrated through the situation of asylum-seeking children. In 2012 the International Detention Coalition (IDC) (n.d.) launched the Global Campaign to End Child Detention. This aligned with IDC proposals for alternatives to immigration detention that allow people to live freely in a community setting while waiting for their immigration status to be resolved. Despite expert evidence about the harms caused to children through prolonged detention, the practice has remained commonplace in many countries. It is beyond the scope and purpose of this chapter to detail the changes in scope and scale of the detention of children in Australia since mandatory immigration detention was legislated into being in 1992. However, in 2014 there were 584 children detained in immigration detention centres on mainland Australia, 305 children on Christmas Island, and a further 179 children were detained on Nauru (Australian Human Rights Commission 2014). Figures released by Australian Border Force in May 2020 reveal that although there are fewer than five children currently in immigration detention, there are 282 children living under what is known as a "Residence Determination" (Australian Border Force 2020) (frankly, "community detention") requiring families to live in provided designated accommodation with a small financial allowance and some services, but with minimal freedom of movement and choice. Another 1,949 children live within the community on BVEs with their parents and mostly without welfare support or care. Under COVID-19 restrictions, where people on BVEs have lost their jobs, many are facing significant levels of poverty which impacts badly on children. Resorting to dependence on charitable organisations for welfare provision diminishes people's self-esteem.

Not confining children to immigration detention provides them with access to some welfare services, including education without being transported by guards, creating an illusion of care. But the reality is that they are relegated to uncertainty and long-term visa-less existence along with their parents. In this formulation, children are blamed for directly and "irregularly" seeking asylum, rather than being recognised as vulnerable persons who have accompanied their parents who have fled from circumstances of war and oppression. Vulnerable children are subject to increased interventions and punishment, measures that are disproportionate to their perceived "crime" or wrongdoing. Two social work academics have been strident in their criticism of the detention of children, calling it organised and ritualised abuse (Goddard and Briskman 2004) and the transfer of children to Nauru as trafficking in children, consistent with the provisions of the UN *Convention against Trafficking* (Briskman and Goddard 2014). Despite two inquiries into the detention of children, the Human Rights and Equal Opportunity Commission (2004) and Australian Human Rights Commission (2014), detention of children has not been fully eliminated as it now appears in disguised forms ("community detention"), as noted earlier. The UN *Convention on the Rights of the Child* conveys an alternative and appropriate approach, with the "best interests of the child" to the forefront, including children seeking refugee status. Article 22(1) states:

> States Parties shall take appropriate measures to ensure that a child who is seeking refugee status or who is considered a refugee in accordance with applicable international or domestic law and procedures shall, whether unaccompanied or accompanied by his or her parents or by any other person, receive appropriate protection and humanitarian assistance in the enjoyment of applicable rights set forth in the present Convention and in other international human rights or humanitarian instruments to which the said States are Parties.

A second example, drawing from my direct experience, pertains to the academic realm. In 2002 a commercial-in-confidence proposal was leaked. The proposal, from the School of Education at the Royal Melbourne Institute of Technology (RMIT), was for RMIT to partner with a private detention operator to deliver education within immigration detention nationally. The ethics of such a partnership were questioned by two social work academics (Briskman and Fraser 2002) and others joined in a campaign that called for the University to prevent the bid from proceeding. What was at the heart of the objection was that freedom/liberty (first-generation right) was a key pillar of justice and that education provision (second-generation right) not only constituted collusion with the carceral state but also was a poor attempt to provide some rights to the rights-less for propaganda purposes. Contracting of services, as the RMIT example shows, is intended to suggest that humanitarianism is possible within a controlled punitive setting. But it is in these settings that health, welfare, and education personnel are stripped of their autonomy, professional ethics are negated, and an unsuspecting public is unaware that punitive practices are privileged over human rights considerations. The profit motive is hidden beneath ideological arguments by state and colluding non-state actors in an uncritical approach to service provision, illustrating in this instance the futility of providing the right to education without liberty and freedom from arbitrary detention.

Human rights and social work

Aspiration for human rights and human dignity is enshrined in social work values and documented in the Australian social work *Code of Ethics* (Australian Association of Social Workers 2020). This sits alongside the Global Definition of the Social Work Profession that states:

> Social work is a practice-based profession and an academic discipline that promotes social change and development, social cohesion, and the empowerment and liberation of people. Principles of social justice, human rights, collective responsibility and respect for diversities are central to social work. Underpinned by theories of social work, social sciences, humanities and indigenous knowledges, social work engages people and structures to address life challenges and enhance wellbeing.
>
> (International Federation of Social Workers and International Association of Schools of Social Work 2014)

The application of a human rights discourse to practice is under-developed in relation to asylum seeker boat arrivals in Australia. The civil/political and economic/social divide within social work extends to the wider advocacy sphere with rupture between those advocating for the end of mandatory immigration detention and those advocating for better conditions, either within detention or for those on temporary visas living in the community. Economic and social rights are the most directly relevant for social workers' practice, and this partly explains why the profession has been minimally focused on asylum seekers while delivering government-funded services for those refugees who entered Australia formally, through its orderly humanitarian visa programs.

Social work can be construed as a profession of conscience and is well positioned to promote social justice through working to eradicate multiple forms of oppression and to both help people in crisis and work for social change (van Wormer and Link 2018). Social workers who subscribe to progressive politically oriented constructs, particularly growing interest in critical social work, do not purport to be ideologically neutral. The dominant direct practice dimension of working with vulnerable groups creates a space for social workers to draw on experiential wisdom as practice ethnographers (Briskman 2009) that generates potential as change agents. Although codified ethics are imperfect mechanisms for reconciling differences, the 2010 Ethical Code of the Australian Association of Social Workers provides a benchmark through its human rights and social justice claims and its call to address unjust policies, which allow social workers to strive for social change and justice, often against political odds. For those who have been employed in offshore detention locations there has been some attention to the human rights dilemmas, similar to health workers situated in onshore immigration detention facilities. Both are discussed later in this chapter.

A divide exists between social work ideals and realities (Lymberry and Butler 2004), particularly in terms of access to justice. At the heart of this divide is the difficulty of overturning prevailing social values and vested interests, which determine what is considered to be a social problem requiring intervention (Martin 2015). Dominant interests, including politicians and media, have most sway and are pitted against social justice proponents who are rendered powerless and pejoratively labelled as "bleeding hearts." Social justice rhetoric that privileges emancipatory practices is depressingly weak when examined against forces seemingly antagonistic to social justice and human rights. As a profession, the law has more influence, even if it's marginal at times, including through judicial review cases that seek acknowledgement or restoration of people's rights and liberties. But lawyers too come in for criticism if they are seen to cross the barrier of objectivity enshrined within what is spoken of as the "rule of law," to take up legal and social justice advocacy. Other professions too subscribe to protect human rights, with the duty to do so outlined in various professional codes such as the Australian Medical Association, the Australian Psychological Society, and the Royal Australasian College of Physicians (Ryan 2020).

Critical theories in social work are largely derived from the radical tradition of the 1970s, influenced by Marxist, feminist, anti-racist, and postmodern theorising that cultivates a critical social work approach that shapes schools of social work thought (Ablett and Morley 2016). A critical social work perspective enables social workers to probe injustices, through attention to socio-political analysis and the nature of interventions that follow (Allan 2003). From a critical social work perspective, power is a key signifier in identifying how injustice and oppression operates and benefits dominant societal interests. Critical reflection is an important component of such practice. For example, social work student Candice Le developed critical consciousness during her tertiary education. She speaks of her former role as an Immigration Department employee. In so doing she goes to the heart of the problem by explaining how dominant discourses about asylum seekers had penetrated her worldview when facilitating deportation of failed asylum seekers (Le et al. 2019). She said she followed rules and regulations by which she was expected to abide and had little knowledge of the broader socio-political context within which those expectations were situated.

Despite human rights becoming a more common rhetorical device, social work practice is rarely framed in terms of human rights activity. Jim Ife (2016) points out dilemmas for social workers in modern constructions of human rights, which he sees as both progressive and conservative, with the latter limiting the transformational potential of social work. Nonetheless, as Ife advocates, if social workers saw themselves as human rights workers there would be more potential for progressive and transformative practice. Yet despite the important achievements of human rights law over half a century or more, this he suggests is limiting because of the liberalism inherent in modern western views of the law, noting that "the law is largely concerned with individuals" (Ife 2016: 5). A choice for social workers is to work within the system governed by law/ policy and bureaucratic decisions, challenge those rules/decisions, or subvert them. Although both law and social work strive for justice there are constraints for both, as each are dominated by legal, customary, and organisational expectations that beset practitioners. This dilemma confronted one social worker, "Jane Doe," in witnessing human rights violations in offshore detention, where asylum seekers were stripped of *(inter alia)* rights to autonomy and rights to adequate food and health provision (Briskman and Doe 2016), and care workers experienced nullification of professional expectations by working in a controlled punitive environment.

Social work is beset with contradictions, including the divide between "care" and "control." In a neoliberal climate, it is the control function that is privileged, although many social workers would be aghast to have this accusation levelled against them. Social work has become compliance-oriented in many fields, including child protection, where threats of state intervention face those who appear to be violating norms of child-rearing that are often racialised. In more recent times international social work organisations have emphasised the role of social workers in creating agency by arguing:

> A new world is only possible if social work and social development educators and practitioners unite in protecting people who are in vulnerable positions, but at the same time building their agency to engage in challenging and undoing oppression, discrimination, marginalization and exclusion.
> (International Association of Schools of Social Work et al. 2019: 5)

Neoliberal agendas that have crept into social work are reinforced by less direct public service provision and increased contracting to the non-government sector. To meet funding requirements, organisations and staff act at the behest of the state, with a consequent diminishment of discretion and public advocacy. For social workers in constrained organisations they are faced with ethical dilemmas regarding adhering to the social work value base while meeting organisational demands and policies which may frequently be misaligned with social work knowledge for practice that was imparted during their university education.

In 2010 the Global Agenda for Social Work was launched. Among its pillars was a commitment to promoting social and economic equalities and ensuring the dignity and worth of the person. In 2011 in Ghana, a determination was expressed by the three international social work organisations[2] that had crafted the Global Agenda to promote social work and social justice, while recognising that the full range of human rights were available to only a minority of the world's population (Truell and Jones n.d.). Alongside this the 2030 United

Nations agenda for sustainable development resulted in seventeen Sustainable Development Goals (SDGs), a number of which could be adopted for asylum seekers and refugees, including ending poverty, reducing inequalities, ensuring healthy lives, providing quality education and provision of clean water and sanitation. Although justifiably targeted towards the most disadvantaged groups in the Global South, they can be readily adapted to the economically developed Global North where inequalities exist for certain "unauthorised" persons.

Social work and social welfare services for people with diminished human rights have been shown to be ineffective and futile, including the insertion of social workers in offshore detention sites where welfare practices were antithetical to social work ethical practice paradigms. Evidence of this situation is revealed through the content of what have become known as the Nauru Files, released by *The Guardian* in 2016, with privations and abuse documented in casework notes. Earlier still, a group of Salvation Army workers that included social workers contacted to work in detention on Nauru issued a public statement after bearing witness to atrocities within detention (Salvation Army Workers 2013). As with health professionals (Ryan 2020), social workers are unlikely to fulfil human rights and social justice responsibilities while working in immigration detention settings. Social work practice with asylum seekers and temporary refugees in community settings has been less well documented. When the Australian Red Cross provided such services funded by the Federal government, and where social workers were among those employed, they were bound by their principle of Humanitarian Diplomacy which meant that there was no publicising of practices or problems, with concerns raised only by direct negotiation and attempts at persuasion with immigration authorities. They worked under Red Cross principles of neutrality and impartiality although witnessing human rights abuses of those under their care.

Case study of tensions

The following case study is an example of tensions that have arisen, revealing problems of the provision of health and welfare services in immigration detention and illustrating the futility argument when the right to health cannot be realised within an environment where people are stripped of civil rights and civil liberties.

From 2007 to 2009, I was an investigator (with Deborah Zion and Bebe Loff) on an Australian Research Council Discovery Project called "Caring for Asylum Seekers in Australia: Bioethics and Human Rights," which focused on detention within Australia. Although the right to health is enshrined in international law, the practice of implementing this human right created tensions. Health practitioners who we interviewed took on what they believed to be professional roles in service delivery. However, when people live without certain human rights protections, dual loyalty conflicts arise whereby obligations to patients clash with prescribed duties by employers and the state (Zion et al.

2012: 71). In the absence of liberty, combined with inadequate and controlled health provision, doctors, nurses, and mental health professionals were faced with ethical and moral dilemmas, resulting in differential responses (Briskman and Zion 2014).

Findings from interviews revealed four core reactions. One group delivered services in a manner required by their employers and, therefore, at the bidding of the state. A psychologist has explained this in a manner that illustrates first- and second-generation tensions in human rights. He described it as a situation whereby no matter how hard he worked, he could not change the causes of asylum seeker stress, saying it was like "having a patient coming into a hospital with a nail through their hand and you are giving them pethidine injections for pain but you don't remove the nail" (Human Rights and Equal Opportunity Commission (2004: 423). A second group delivered services and, where there was a dual loyalty conflict, were prepared to work in a mildly subversive manner on occasions, akin to what social work academic Bill Jordan (1990) refers to as isolated acts of banditry. This could entail nurses breaching rules by providing milk and fruit to children from their own supplies. Their actions invoked a politics of compassion and duty of care but did not necessarily align with concepts of justice and human rights. From a critical social work perspective, it can be described as covert action that can "right a particular wrong" but does not change the system and can serve to reinforce the status quo (Fine and Teram 2013: 1326). A third group retreated from their employment without public fanfare. And a fourth group were more activist in their protests, mostly after relinquishing employment within immigration detention. Some moved from acquiescence to subversion and then to advocacy, including whistleblowing that ignored confidentially clauses to which they had subscribed in order to champion the public interest.

Human rights and ethics are interrelated. Providing health services in immigration detention, even when trying to improve the way the system operates, does not redress the lack of civil and political rights. Some medical practitioners have been particularly outspoken, calling for boycotts against working in sites that violate human rights.

Conclusion: COVID-19 disrupting normative assumptions

I write this chapter during the COVID-19 pandemic. Worldwide restrictions on travel and other freedoms are mirrored in Australia with measures introduced to prevent community transmission and to offer support to those affected by enforced restrictions. Asylum seekers in detention and in the community on BVEs are not included. They either remain detained in conditions that cannot guarantee infection control, and those in the community with BVE status are provided with no Federal government support even when they have lost their only sources of income due to the retraction of employment opportunities. Advocacy that is occurring on a global scale may present some tentatively explored prospects for rights-convergence where the futility of one right without the other is brought into focus.

The rights dilemma is implicit in an article written by former Manus Island refugee Imran Mohammad, who relocated to the United States in 2018 under the "refugee swap deal" negotiated between Australia and the United States (see Billings 2022). He spoke of the pandemic interruption to his life and those of others who had been part of the transfer to the United States where there was disruption to education, work, and human connection. The situation, he explains, is reminiscent of Manus as fear and uncertainty prevail. Mohammad said (2020: 5) in what can be read as a dual rights–affirming statement, that his journey "actually began with my freedom . . . All we need as human beings is freedom education and a safe place to live."

The freedom/health nexus question further arises for offshored asylum seekers and refugees with health conditions who have been flown to Australia "temporarily" and relocated to hotels in Brisbane and Melbourne, where many have remained for an extended time period. The pandemic has been a source of deep concern to both advocates and those imprisoned within these hotel settings. Refugee Moz Azimi speaks of the experience from his guarded floor in the Mantra hotel, Melbourne, which he describes as his "luxury torture cell" as he reaches seven years of detention, in total, in different places. He refers to others who arrived by boat who now live in the Australian community, saying that his spirit is eroded through "the capriciousness of Australia's detention system—why some are allowed free while others are not." He believes that those in the Mantra are "sitting ducks" for COVID-19 (cited in Doherty 2020).

Unlike other countries, asylum seekers in detention or living in the Australian community have not been granted necessary health rights, even temporarily. For those in the community on bridging visas they have become dependent on over-stretched charities, as noted earlier. Oncologist and writer Ranjana Srivastava (2020) puts this into sharp relief in the volunteer work she has been doing with asylum seekers and refugees who are denied access to Australia's universal healthcare system and routinely denied care in public hospitals. As she bears witness in her activities, she speaks of injustices that are exacerbated at this time. She says of the pandemic that has

> left them in a particularly precarious position because they are ineligible for government subsidies. Many were gainfully employed but now there is no work. Others who had moved on from aid find themselves returning for assistance they were proud to have left behind.

John van Kooy (2020) has similarly emphasised that although the pandemic recession has resulted in increased unemployment, underemployment, and financial stress for very many people, asylum seekers are disproportionately affected because of their tendency to be employed in low-income and insecure jobs. van Kooy predicts that unemployment rates for refugees on temporary protection visas is set to double, resulting in homelessness and poor health.

The coming together of rights is apparent with those advocating for an end to detention, making a slightly different and perhaps strategic call for release from detention because of potential harms. The United Nations Network on Migration (2020), while advocating for the release of people from immigration detention centres worldwide as a result of the pandemic, uses it for wider leverage, by arguing for a human rights–based approach to use detention as a measure of last resort only. It also states that release from detention must not result in situations of homelessness or destitution and that provision is required to secure access to healthcare, housing, food, water, social security, and other welfare supports. As an interim measure, the suggestion is made that immigration detention centres introduce protective measures to prevent the spread of the coronavirus. On a global scale, Lancet Migration (2020) call for migrants and refugees to be included in responses to the pandemic with a focus on health. It notes that excluding migrants and refugees contradicts the commitment to leave no one behind in the ethics of justice that underpin public health, arguing that principles of solidarity, human rights, and equity must be central to the response (2020: 1482).

There have been examples throughout the world where immigration detention centres have significantly emptied as a result of COVID-19, including in Spain, the United Kingdom, Norway, and Zambia. Ireland has provided unemployment funds to all workers irrespective of legal status, with a guarantee not to report applicants to immigration authorities (United Nations Network on Migration 2020). In Australia, there has been considerable advocacy to release asylum seekers and refugees from detention during the pandemic, with health reasons prioritised. Given the long-term resistance of the Federal government to eliminate mandatory immigration detention, these campaigns have been tactical. For example, Academics for Refugees has argued for release on health grounds to avoid the virus spreading (Loughnan et al. 2020).

Members of the Optional Protocol to the Convention against Torture (OPCAT) Network in Australia presented a submission to Australian governments on places of detention and COVID-19. The working group stated that evidence from around the world shows that once COVID-19 enters a place of detention it "will spread like wildfire" (Lachsz and Hurley 2020), calling on the government to reduce numbers in detention and curb admissions, even on a temporary basis. But it went further than addressing temporary health concerns by suggesting that the pandemic presents an opportunity to rethink detention and to fully realise the vision of the OPCAT. The statement offers a challenge to government, communities of advocacy, and the professions. Securing freedom and attaining practical measures for well-being can overcome the rights disjuncture and the futility of having one without the other, including fulfilment of the *ICCPR* by ensuring that everyone has the right to liberty and security of person *and* the *ICESCR* to guarantee the right of everyone to an adequate standard of living. Beyond (or perhaps underpinning) international legal norms are norms of decency and dignity to be afforded to everyone in a society, citizen or non-citizen, with particular attention to the vulnerable.

Notes

1 For more information on this class of visa, see Chapter 1 by Peter Billings.
2 International Association of Schools of Social Work, International Council on Social Welfare, and International Federation of Social Workers.

Bibliography

Ablett, P. and Morley, C. (2016) 'Towards a history of critical traditions in Australian social work', *Social Alternatives*, 35(4): 7.

Aliverti, A. (2020) 'Benevolent policing? vulnerability and the moral pains of border controls', *The British Journal of Criminology*, 60(5): 1117.

Allan, J. (2003) 'Theorising critical social work', in Allan, J., Pease, B. and Briskman, L. (eds) *Critical social work: An introduction to theories and practices*. Allen and Unwin.

Australian Association of Social Workers. (2020) *Code of Ethics*. AASW.

Australian Border Force. (2020) *Immigration Detention and Community Statistics Summary*, 31 May. www.homeaffairs.gov.au/research-and-stats/files/immigration-detention-statistics-31-may-2020.pdf

Australian Human Rights Commission. (2014) *The Forgotten Children: National Inquiry into Children in Immigration Detention*. AHRC, Sydney. https://humanrights.gov.au/sites/default/files/document/publication/forgotten_children_2014.pdf

Billings, P. (2022) 'International crimes, refugee "prisoner swaps" and duplicity in Australia's refugee admissions', in Simeon, J. C. (ed) *Serious International Crimes, Human Rights and Forced Migration*. Routledge.

Briskman, L. (2016) 'A clash of paradigms for asylum seekers: border security and human security', in Goh, B. C., Offord, B. and Garbutt, R. (eds) *Activating Human Rights and Peace: Theories, Practice and Contexts*. Routledge.

Briskman, L. and Doe, J. (2016) 'Social work in dark places', *Social Alternatives*, 35(4), 73.

Briskman, L. and Zion, D. (2014) 'Dual loyalties and impossible dilemmas: health care in immigration detention', *Public Health Ethics*, 7(3): 277.

Briskman, L. (2009) 'Nation', in I. Shaw, Briar-Lawson, K. and Orme, J. (eds) *Sage handbook of social work research*. SAGE.

Briskman, L. and Fraser, L. (2002) 'Freedom first, then education', *The Age*, 7 August.

Briskman, L. and Goddard, C. (2014) 'Australia trafficks the asylum seeker children', *The Age*, 25 February. www.smh.com.au/opinion/australia-trafficks-and-abuses-asylum-seeker-children-20140224-33cxs.html

Carens, J. H. (2013) *The Ethics of Immigration*. Oxford University Press.

Chapman, A. R. (2009) 'The divisibility of indivisible human rights', *Economic Rights Working Paper Series*. The Human Rights Institute, University of Connecticut.

Court of Conscience Editorial Team. (2019) 'A brief primer on Australia's treatment of refugees and asylum seekers', *Court of Conscience*, 13: 7.

Davies, T., Isakjee, A. and Dhesi, S. (2017) 'Violent inaction: the necropolitical experiences of refugees in Europe', *Antipode*, 49(3): 1263.

Doherty, B. (2020) 'The Iranian refugee writing songs of love from his "luxury torture cell"', *The Guardian*, 28 May, www.theguardian.com/news/2020/may/28/the-iranian-refugee-writing-songs-of-love-from-his-luxury-torture-cell

Dominelli, L. (1998) 'Anti-oppressive practice in context', in Adams, R., Dominelli, L. and Payne, M. (eds), *Social Work: Themes, Issues and Critical Debates*. Macmillan.

Fentiman, K. and O'Sullivan, J. (2018) 'Social work with refugees and asylum seekers: An ever-changing partnership with the law', in Rice, S., Day, A. and Briskman, L. (eds) *Social Work in the Shadow of the Law*. The Federation Press.

Fine, M. and Teram, E. (2013) 'Overt and covert ways of responding to moral injustices in social work practice: Heroes and mild-mannered social work bipeds', *British Journal of Social Work*, 43(7): 1312.

Goddard, C. and Briskman, L. (2004) 'By any measure, it's official child abuse', *Herald Sun*, 18 February.

Human Rights and Equal Opportunity Commission (HREOC). (2004) *A Last Resort: National Inquiry Into Children in Immigration Detention*. Human Rights Unit, Sydney.

Ife, J. (2012) *Human Rights and Social Work: Towards a Rights-Based Practice*. Cambridge University Press.

Ife, J. (2016) 'Human rights and social work: beyond conservative law', *Journal of Human Rights and Social Work*, 1(1): 3.

International Detention Coalition (IDC). (n.d.) 'End immigration of children: there are alternatives', https://endchilddetention.org/solution/there-are-alternatives/

International Federation of Social Workers and International Association of Schools of Social Work. (2014) *Global Definition of Social Work, IFSW*. www.ifsw.org/global-definition-of-social-work/

Jordan, B. (1990) *Social Work in an Unjust Society*. Harvester Wheatsheaf.

Lachsz, A. and Hurley, M. (2020) 'OCPAT, Places of Detention and COVID-19', Joint submission to the Senate Select Committee on COVID-19, 28 May. Human Rights Law Centre.

Lancet Migration. (2020) 'Global call to action for inclusion of migrants and refugees in the COVID-19 response', *The Lancet*, 395(10235): 1482. www.thelancet.com/journals/lancet/article/PIIS0140-6736(20)30971-5/fulltext

Le, C., Morley, C. and Briskman, L. (2019) 'The role of critical social work education in improving ethical practice with refugees and asylum seekers', *Social Work Education*, 39(4): 403.

Lloyd, J., Burridge, A. and Mitchelson, M. (2009–2010), 'Thinking (and moving) beyond walls and cages: Bridging immigrant justice and anti-prison organizing in the United States', *Social Justice*, 36(2): 85.

Loughnan, C., Vogl, A., Fleay, C., Murray, P. and Dehm, S. (2020), 'Refugees need protection from coronavirus too, and must be released', *The Conversation*, 24 April. https://theconversation.com/refugees-need-protection-from-coronavirus-too-and-must-be-released-136961

Lymberry, M. and Butler, S. (2004) *Social Work Ideals and Practice Realities*. Palgrave Macmillan.

Macken, J. (2020a) 'Australian charities are struggling with demand: the coalition will rue turning its back on them', *Michael West Media*, 22 August. www.michaelwest.com.au/australian-charities-struggle/

Macken, J. (2020b) 'The melancholic torturer: How Australia became a nation that tortures refugees', *Journal of Sociology*, 56(1): 9.

Martin, S. (2015) 'Response to John Falzon's lecture on "we only have one enemy, it is called equality"', in C. Williams (ed) *Outrage: The Social Justice Papers*. RMIT University.

Martin, S. (2019) 'Offshore detention costs taxpayers up to $573,000 each person, report finds', *The Guardian*, 3 December. www.theguardian.com/australia-news/2019/dec/03/offshore-detention-costs-taxpayers-up-to-573000-each-person-report-finds

Mbembe, A. (2003) 'Necropolitics', *Public Culture*, 15(1): 11.

McCracken, K. and Phillips, D. R. (2017) *Global Health: An Introduction to Current and Future Trends*. Routledge.

Mills, K. (2005) 'Noble human rights defender or international band-aid? On contemporary humanitarianism', *Human Rights and Human Welfare*, 7: 25.

Mohammad, I. (2020) 'Setbacks and strengths', *The Saturday Paper*, 23–29 May.

Moureau, M. (1979) 'A structural approach to social work practice', *Canadian Journal of Social Work Practice*, 5(1): 78.

Munro, D. and Joyce, N. (2019), 'An asylum seeker's access to Medicare and associated health services while awaiting determination of a protection visa application in Australia', *Court of Conscience*, 13: 51.

New South Wales Council for Civil Liberties. (2007) 'Shadow Report prepared for the United Nations Committee Against Torture on the occasion of its review of Australia's Third Periodic Report under the Convention Against Torture and other Cruel, Inhuman or Degrading Treatment or Punishment', 27 July. NSWCCL.

Perera, S. (2002) 'A line in the sea', *Race and Class*, 44(2): 23.

Robertson, T. (2018) 'Australia's torture camps', *Arena*, 153: 36.

Ryan, E. (2020) *The Healthcare Community and Australian Immigration Detention: The Case for Non-violent Resistance*. Palgrave Macmillan.

Salvation Army Workers. (2013) 'Nauru staff condemn cruel conditions', *New Matilda*, 24 July. https://newmatilda.com/2013/07/24/nauru-staff-condemn-cruel-conditions/

Srivastava, R. (2020) 'Working with refugees has made me appreciate my good fortune', *The Guardian*, 13 May. www.theguardian.com/commentisfree/2020/may/13/working-with-refugees-as-a-volunteer-doctor-has-made-me-appreciate-my-good-fortune?CMP=Share_iOSApp_Other

Truell, R. and Jones, D. (n.d.) *The Global Agenda for Social Work and Social Development: Extending the Influence of Social Work*, IFSW. www.ifsw.org/wp-content/uploads/ifsw-cdn/assets/ifsw_24848-10.pdf

United Nations. (n.d.) *Sustainable Development Goals*. https://sustainabledevelopment.un.org/?menu=1300

United Nations Network on Migration. (2020) 'COVID-19 & Immigration Detention: What Can Governments and Other Stakeholders Do?', Working Group on Alternatives to Immigration Detention. https://migrationnetwork.un.org/sites/default/files/docs/un_network_on_migration_wg_atd_policy_brief_covid-19_and_immigration_detention_0.pdf

van Kooy, J. (2020) 'Covid-19 and humanitarian migrants contemporary visas: assessing the public costs', *Research briefing note 2*, July, Refugee Council of Australia. www.refugeecouncil.org.au/wp-content/uploads/2020/07/COVID-19-van-Kooy-.pdf

van Wormer, K. and Link, R. J. (2018) *Social Work and Social Welfare: A Human Rights Foundation*. Oxford University Press.

Zion, D., Briskman, L. and Loff, B. (2012) 'Psychiatric ethics and a politics of compassion: the case of detained asylum seekers in Australia', *Journal of Bioethical Inquiry*, 9: 67.

Chapter 10

"I spoke the truth about myself and that's when you connect with people"

Advocacy within the political system in response to living on a safe haven enterprise visa

Caroline Fleay, Mary Anne Kenny, Atefeh Andaveh, Salem Askari, Rohullah Hassani, Kate Leaney, and Teresa Lee*

Introduction

In this chapter we explore the negative and often-punitive policy impacts on people seeking asylum who arrived in Australia by boat between 2012 and 2013, and the advocacy of a group of community members in Western Australia (WA) that includes the authors. We highlight, in particular, the key welfare, employment, and well-being impacts experienced by people in WA who have been granted a safe haven enterprise visa (SHEV). Some of the negative impacts of the requirements of this visa have been evident since the visas were first issued, whereas other difficulties have emerged during the current COVID-19 pandemic.

We also explore here the advocacy network we have all been involved in for several years in WA and its efforts to bring about policy reform. The WA Refugee and People Seeking Asylum Network formed after the election of a new state (Labor) government in 2017, to advocate for improvements to policy at the state level that could make a difference to the welfare of people seeking asylum and refugees in WA. The network's advocacy in relation to the SHEV was a process of building allies through approaching WA Labor Members of Parliament (MPs) and requesting meetings with members. Most importantly, these meetings included people living on a SHEV who wanted to share their experiences with MPs. Over a period of 18 months, 25 network members visited more than 30 MPs in addition to a range of public servants.

Through their involvement in this network, Atefeh, Rohullah, and Salem have chosen to make visible their asylum-seeking backgrounds in their advocacy with government officials. They are all SHEV holders. Caroline, Mary Anne, Teresa, and Kate are network members who have no lived experience

DOI: 10.4324/9781003298595-17

of seeking asylum. Caroline and Mary Anne are academics who engage in collaborative research and advocacy projects with people seeking asylum in Australia. Teresa (Riverview Community Services) and Kate (Welcoming Australia) are both involved in community organisations that provide supports to people seeking asylum and refugees.

Advocacy is understood here to be a form of activism, entailing efforts that seek to bring about social and political change in response to social injustice (Burnett 2003: 141). In particular, we understand advocacy as "intentional actions aimed at changing policies and positions of decision-makers on specific issues of concern" (Lenette et al. 2020: 3). In relation to the context of the network with which we are involved, the aim of advocacy is to enable opportunities for people with lived experience of seeking asylum to participate in government policy decision-making processes.

Throughout the chapter we refer to refugees, people seeking asylum, and people from asylum-seeking backgrounds. People who go through a refugee status determination process and are found to be refugees or owed "complementary protection" in Australia are granted protection visas. The definition of a refugee in Australian legislation corresponds to the UN *Convention relating to the Status of Refugees* 1951 (as amended by the *Protocol relating to the Status of Refugees* 1967)—a person who is found to have a well-founded fear of persecution on the basis of their nationality, race, religion, membership of a particular social group or political opinion. We use the term "people seeking asylum" to refer to those who are still going through the legal process and are awaiting formal determination of their status. The term "people from asylum-seeking backgrounds" refers to those who came to Australia to seek asylum and have either been found to be a refugee or continue to wait for their claim to be finalised.

This chapter is informed by the conversations that Caroline and Mary Anne organised in January 2020 with the other co-authors. The intention of these conversations was to critically reflect on the advocacy processes we had engaged in together over the previous few years. Drawing on the methods adopted by Fleay et al. (2019) and Lenette et al. (2020) in their explorations of advocacy with people from a refugee background, Caroline and Mary Anne used a list of open-ended and semi-structured questions to guide each of their conversations with Atefeh, Salem, and Rohullah, and the group conversation they had with Kate and Teresa. To ensure that the experiences and views of all co-authors were privileged, however, all of the conversations deviated at times so that particular issues raised by each co-author could be further explored. Caroline and Mary Anne drew on the common themes evident in the transcriptions of these conversations to write the first draft of this chapter. This was followed by further discussion and editing by all co-authors. Our views are outlined in this chapter in two ways. We use "we" and "our" when discussions represent the experiences and views of all of us, and direct quotes from individual co-authors to highlight and respect each of our particular perspectives.

We outline here the processes through which the WA Refugee and People Seeking Asylum Network's advocacy priorities and strategies developed. As the quote from Salem in the title outlines, this involved enabling opportunities for people on a SHEV to speak directly to MPs. Through doing so, we highlight ways in which a quiet, localised, relational approach to advocacy, that includes people with lived experience of seeking asylum, can help build political allies who support policy reform. We also reflect on the prospects and limitations of further social and political change through this approach.

Policy context

Internationally the number of people displaced is at a historical high. The United Nations High Commissioner for Refugees (UNHCR) estimated that there were more than 79.5 million people displaced by conflict or persecution at the end of 2019 (UNHCR 2019). Australia is one of a relatively small number of countries that annually resettles refugees from overseas. In accordance with its international obligations under the UN *Convention relating to the Status of Refugees*, Australia also provides protection to people who arrive in Australia seeking asylum. However, historically Australia's policy response to people arriving unauthorised by boat has been punitive, with the direct intention to discourage others arriving by sea.

Between 2012 and 2013 more than 30,000 people seeking asylum arrived in Australia by boat. All were mandatorily detained in immigration detention centres upon arrival. Up until the 7 September 2013 election, the more progressive Labor Government was in office. However, in an effort to deter an increasing number of people seeking asylum arriving by boat, the government began to implement policies that included transferring some boat arrivals to sites of offshore processing in Papua New Guinea and Nauru. Those boat arrivals who were detained in Australia were denied the right to work for at least two years upon their release into the community and denied access to funded English language classes. Many were granted a succession of short-term bridging visas to enable them to live in the community as "lawful non-citizens" and forced to try to survive on 89% of social security payments (the Newstart allowance). Previous research highlights the distress and fear that was caused by the denial of work rights and ongoing uncertainty about their visa status (Hartley and Fleay 2014).

While most were given the right to work after several years, they were given no meaningful assistance to find employment; however, many found work despite the many barriers they faced, although there is certainly evidence of people working in exploitative situations (Asylum Seeker Resource Centre 2020). Those who were unable to find work due to illness or caring responsibilities were able to access the Status Resolution Support Services (SRSS),[1] which included a fortnightly minimal payment.

The election of the more conservative Liberal/National Coalition government in September 2013 meant the introduction of even tougher policies for people who had arrived by boat. Most were denied publicly funded legal assistance to help prepare their refugee claims, and they endured a worrying refugee claims process that minimises opportunities to have any rejection of their claims independently reviewed (the "fast track assessment process") (Kenny et al. 2016). All have had significant delays in the processing of their refugee claims, with some waiting more than seven years for their cases to be assessed. Government statistics from October 2019 showed that there were still around 6,500 waiting for their cases to be dealt with (Senate Legal and Constitutional Affairs References Committee 2019). As discussed in other chapters in this edited collection, increasing numbers of people who were accessing SRSS supports have been withdrawn from the program, whether or not they can in fact access employment.

Those processed and found to be refugees have only been given the option of a three-year temporary protection visa (TPV) or a five-year SHEV. While the SHEV visa holds some prospects for applying for a permanent visa, if certain conditions are satisfied, it is clear that most people on this visa, along with TPV holders, will be eligible to apply only for another temporary protection visa. As at April 2020 there were 16,882 people granted a SHEV (Department of Home Affairs 2020: 5). While there are no restrictions on where someone lives, works, or studies in order to be able to apply for a range of non-humanitarian visas at the end of this five-year visa, the SHEV holder must meet the "pathway requirements." These stipulate that for at least three and a half years (42 months) of the five-year visa they have been:

- Employed in a designated "regional area"[2] and not received prescribed social security benefits.
- Enrolled and physically attending full-time study in a designated "regional area."
- A combination of these.

Employment includes those who are self-employed or those who are employed by others on a permanent, temporary, or casual basis, and the visa holder must demonstrate they have worked for a period totalling 42 months or more.

However, many SHEV holders work or study in urban areas that are not included as SHEV regions—such as Perth, Brisbane, Sydney, and Melbourne. Many settled in these urban areas and found employment while waiting four or more years for their refugee claim to be considered. They have made ties with local communities and children attend schools. Some require specialised health services not available in most regional areas. For those who have found employment, they face great financial risks in moving to a SHEV regional area and trying to find employment all over again. To move also may break ties to community and disrupt the education of children.

If SHEV holders do not find employment in a regional area, they will not meet the SHEV pathway criteria and will be eligible to apply only for another temporary protection visa. However, assuming a SHEV holder does manage to meet this difficult pathway, their options are still limited. At the end of 42 months the only permanent visas they can apply for have difficult eligibility criteria regarding skills, age, and English language that will be challenging for most refugees to meet. All these factors mean SHEV holders are unlikely to be able to access any pathway to permanent residence. If they are re-determined to be refugees at the end of their visa they will be eligible only for another TPV or SHEV and continue to be barred from sponsoring family members to come to Australia.

Research by Kenny et al. (2016), based on interviews with migration agents and lawyers who work with this caseload, shows that the refugee status determination process causes mental distress due to the delays, uncertainty, and the complex nature of the legal process. In addition, the reduction in public funding for legal assistance, combined with the lack of access to a robust system of review, has led the Australian Human Rights Commission (2019) to conclude that some people may have been refused visas despite having good claims for refugee status.

Additionally, at the time of writing this chapter Australia is dealing with the impacts of the COVID-19 pandemic. Refugees on temporary visas are being impacted disproportionately, with many losing employment in sectors like construction. Their temporary visa status means they are ineligible for income support via the JobKeeper payment,[3] and many report reluctance to claim special benefits[4] through Centrelink[5] as they are concerned that it will impact upon their ability to meet the SHEV pathway (National Refugee-led Advisory and Advocacy Group [NRAAG] 2020).

In the next section, we further outline some of the difficulties endured by SHEV holders, with a particular emphasis on those who live in Perth.

Impacts of living on a SHEV in Western Australia

Atefeh, Rohullah, and Salem know well the difficulties of living on a SHEV in WA, especially given that Perth has not been designated a regional area for the purposes of this visa. As Salem explains:

> I came here in March 2013, so it's seven years now, and I have been living in Perth since then. Currently I am living on a SHEV, which is a five-year temporary visa. There are really difficult requirements to meet in order to apply for permanent residency, like moving to a regional postcode and working or studying for 3½ years. Especially at this point in time, if you can't get a job, you cannot get a Centrelink benefit either. If you do get a Centrelink benefit, that means that your stay in that regional postcode will not be counted for the pathway.

> There are also difficulties considering the fact that the majority of people on these visas have very little English or don't speak it at all, especially in my own community. I know many people who are highly skilled in trades like tiling, painting, plastering, etc. but they cannot communicate well enough to run that business alone by themselves. So therefore they need somebody else to partner up with to give them a helping hand with the communication and paper work. This technique has played a vital role in employment of those people with low English level and literacy in my community.
>
> It has a huge impact on people mentally as well, like I know a friend of mine who hasn't seen his family in 10 years, and now he is not really in a good situation mentally. If you speak to him regarding moving to a regional area, this is absolutely not an option for him. He is not really in a situation where he can consider moving to a regional area in order to get a permanent visa, because 10 years is not a short time. It's not 10 days or just a year or two. It's 10 years. It's a decade. So he is going through all these difficulties at this time. Now they are asking him to move to a regional area, when he's developed and established his life in Perth for this amount of time. I think it's really difficult.

After living and working in Perth for more than five years and developing strong community links, Rohullah felt he had to relocate to Canberra last year because of the SHEV pathway requirements:

> I had a job in Perth, I was doing ok with income. But the main thing I had stress with was not meeting the SHEV pathway, that's the main reason I moved to Canberra. I had gotten a forklift licence, truck driving licence, I did a course working in a confined space, all to get a job in regional WA. I applied for a lot of jobs but I couldn't get one so I moved to Canberra which is a SHEV region. Now I have got a job in Canberra and I am slowly settling down. But I'm worried about what will happen at the end of my visa, because of the pathway in this visa. It is not possible to get a permanent visa or something better than this visa because the pathway is impossible for most people.
>
> When I had a meeting with a department of immigration adviser, I showed him all my certificates. I told him I spent a lot of money to get these licences and certificates, I tried to get a job in regional WA, I applied for a lot of jobs. And then I moved here, but at the same time, I'm not getting any advantage. I can't sponsor my family, and I can't get a loan to have a business or invest for my future. He just shook his head.

Atefeh and her family have been living on a SHEV in Perth for seven years:

> Most refugees in our situation have not had access to proper English classes and so many cannot speak English well, including my parents who are

> over 60 and my mentally and physically disabled sister. The SHEV has also meant members of my family have not gotten access to the health services that are designed for permanent residents, which has put their mental and physical health in danger.
>
> The health system in Australia is very complicated and cannot be understood without help. I sacrifice a lot of my time and energy for my family to help them with all the difficulties they have been through since we escaped to Australia. I cannot imagine how refugees like my parents and my sister could go through all this without help. Every step has been so challenging and I try to make every single person we meet understand the situation of what a refugee has been through. Why can we not have the same rights as the other residents in this country? Seeing my family in this situation has affected me badly and raises a question in my mind about why I can't use my time, energy, and talent to do something that is worth my life, instead of fighting for the basic rights that every Australian has simply by being born in this country.

Other SHEV holders in Perth shared their experiences in workshops organised by the WA Refugee and People Seeking Asylum Network. Many spoke of having settled in the metropolitan area of Perth and found work through their communities and friends. Some spoke of the difficulties they faced in trying to get full-time work in regional areas, as seasonal work was the only work available. Their vulnerable position and lack of English skills meant they were offered positions that were low paid and without security, so if they were sick or injured, they lost their positions. Most who had tried to get work in a regional area ended up returning to Perth.

Many are working to support family members overseas. They face the dilemma of trying to meet the SHEV pathway by moving to work in a regional area, where work may only be seasonal, or remaining in a job in a metropolitan area where they have more secure work. As one SHEV holder said: 'If I go and move, and only work 3–4 months a year, how can I support my family?' (Kenny et al. 2019: 6). As Salem told the Joint Standing Committee on Migration in March 2020:

> We started from zero, and we've established our lives here. In my personal experience, I have learned a trade. Then we get a job. We work hard. Obviously, we have a family back home, so we try to support our families. We are paying our bills and paying our taxes. Honestly, we are always reminding ourselves to be responsible community members and to do our parts and contribute to the economy.
>
> (2020: 28)

Another barrier is that regional areas may not have particular services such as high-level medical services that some SHEV holders need, or specialist torture and trauma services. Recent research by the Australian Human Rights Commission (2019) reinforces the fact that there are worryingly high rates of mental health problems for people who continue to be forced to live on any of the temporary visas. For some the experience has become too overwhelming and in the past four years there has been at least 18 suspected or confirmed suicide deaths among those who have sought protection in Australia, and there are likely to be more who have self-harmed or made attempts to end their lives (Procter et al. 2018).

This punitive policy landscape places people in indefinite limbo even once recognised as a refugee, as they face having to re-apply for refugee status at regular intervals. It also means living with the terrible knowledge that they may never be able to get their family—their partner and children, their parents—to join them in Australia. The uncertainty surrounding their lives can never fully go away. Given the impacts of this punitive policy landscape on people granted a SHEV, we turn our attention to explore how the members of the WA-based civil society group, to which we all belong, have responded in an effort to bring about policy reform.

Refugee and People Seeking Asylum Network

The advocacy network was formed in 2017 in the aftermath of the election of the new WA Labor Government. While the WA Government is not responsible for broad immigration policy, it has legislative responsibility for public services such as transport, health, and education, which all affect the lives and well-being of people seeking asylum. A core group of individuals who had previously been involved in asylum seeker advocacy felt that the election of the WA Labor Government provided an opportunity to secure greater access to some services and supports for asylum seekers in WA.

Drawing on community-organising principles, this core group (including Caroline, Mary Anne, Kate, and Teresa) directed their efforts into working with a collective of individuals and agencies to develop strategic aims to bring about some desired change at the local level. This followed models from some of the other states and territories—the development of constructive relationships between advocates, agencies, and people seeking asylum and state/territory governments, which had resulted in the provision of greater supports to people seeking asylum. The group was also hopeful that the Labor Party would win the federal election in 2019, given their policy platform included replacing temporary protection visas with permanent ones.[6] So other than engaging with local Federal Labor MPs to ensure they were fully aware of the experiences of people seeking asylum in WA, most advocacy was focused at the state level where it was hoped there were greater prospects of changing the policy landscape.

Through initial meetings with refugee support agency representatives, academics, activists, church groups and others,[7] the network developed with a focus on understanding barriers that people seeking asylum and refugees face in accessing what they needed to settle in WA, and how this could be improved. This involved discussions with people with lived experience of seeking asylum, although the initial advocacy strategy was largely developed by a core group of academics, refugee support agencies, and those with links to the Labor Party. While members of this core group sought the views of people seeking asylum that they knew personally, during the early months of the network those without lived experience led the strategy development.

The network's key issues for change included the need for public transport concession cards for people seeking asylum, affordable access to Technical and Further Education (TAFE) colleges, and a request for postcodes in the Perth metropolitan area to be designated "regional" for the purposes of the SHEV pathway. It was this last area that became the focus of much of the network's efforts, however, driven by the increasing involvement in the network of people living on a SHEV visa.

As the network's meetings progressed, it became clear that it had to actively reach out to people seeking asylum in the community. Teresa, Kate, Caroline, and Mary Anne organised regular meetings over several months, which about 80 people seeking asylum from a range of backgrounds attended, including Atefeh, Rohullah, and Salem. We worked together in small and large groups to document the experiences and priorities of those who attended. A core group was keen to continue working with Teresa, Kate, Caroline, and Mary Anne to develop and carry out an advocacy strategy and they continue to meet regularly both as a group (composed mostly of Hazara men, including Salem and Rohullah) as well as individually with others (including Atefeh).

The network's efforts have thus become more focused on foregrounding the lived experience of people seeking asylum in strategy development and advocacy actions. It is also underpinned by the importance of building relationships. As with community organising, much of this work has involved "relational meetings" whereby we attend to each other and listen deeply to each other's experiences (Tattersall 2015: 383). Through these encounters over the past two years, we feel a level of trust has been built.

We discuss ahead specific examples of the network's direct advocacy through meetings between political decision makers and people seeking asylum. Other network activities have included the delivery of workshops/seminars for people seeking asylum and community stakeholders on legal and health issues identified by the group and public presentations by people seeking asylum to communicate their experiences to a broader community audience.

Based on our discussions with WA Government MPs who have become very supportive of the network over the past few years, we consider that the following outcomes have resulted directly from the network's advocacy:

- Securing access to transport concessions and affordable TAFE education and training in WA for people seeking asylum and refugees.
- The establishment of a cross-party group of MPs who act as advocates within the WA Parliament.

- Growing awareness within community stakeholders and people seeking asylum on a range of legal and health issues.
- The WA Government requesting that the Federal Government designate all Perth metropolitan postcodes as "regional areas" for the purpose of the SHEV pathway. Should the Federal Government enact this, it will enable all SHEV holders working and studying in Perth the opportunity to satisfy the first step of the restricted visa pathway to permanency.

In the following section we highlight how this network, composed of a coalition of different groups and individuals including people from asylum-seeking backgrounds, engaged in advocacy that led to these outcomes.

Building allies

Our focus on directing advocacy towards WA Government officials was underpinned by a belief that engaging in quiet advocacy through building allies within the political system was key to policy change at the state government level. We understand allies here as people who "belong to groups that have particular privileges, and work alongside people from groups that are subjected to power in relation to that privilege" (Reynolds 2013: 56). Our initial allies were those who understood the challenges facing people from asylum-seeking backgrounds and who were connected to the WA political system.

Seeking out allies is consistent with an understanding of political opportunity structure, "the degree of openness or closure of the formal political system," and the impact this has on how groups and individuals make claims for social change (Maddison and Martin 2010: 107). This structure includes a range of factors, such as the number of centres of decision-making power within the governing system, how decisions are made, how open the process is to other actors, the extent to which there are influential allies available, and when changes to this are made (Maddison and Martin 2010: 108; Tilly 2006: 44). An understanding of political opportunity structure helps explain why social movements or campaign groups who may have been without influence over policy decision-making, can become influential as social and/or political environments change (Maddison and Martin 2010: 108).

The decision to engage in advocacy through building allies within the political system is also consistent with an understanding of a government as being an entity that is not separate from society. This sees a government as being composed of individuals who may be approachable. This allows for the development of relationships with government officials to work together for positive outcomes (Gill 2010). Such an approach allows for connections to be made with a government through approaching particular MPs as opposed to seeing the government as hostile and not open to approach. This is in contrast to how the relationship between Federal Government officials and refugee advocates in Australia is often characterised—as an entrenched divisive space (Altman 2020: 2).

Divisiveness in Australia on asylum seeker policy is evident in a range of ways. There have long been negative portrayals of people seeking asylum who arrive in Australia by boat, often initiated by senior MPs (particularly in the Liberal Party) and perpetuated by some media outlets. These portrayals have contributed to asylum seeker policies becoming a divisive issue, particularly leading up to federal elections (Doherty 2015; Fleay et al. 2016). Suggestions that these portrayals and policies are having a negative impact on people seeking asylum are often met with hostile remarks from senior ministers. For example, in 2016 Department of Home Affairs Minister Peter Dutton responded to calls for people seeking asylum and refugees detained on Nauru and Manus Island to be brought to Australia by claiming that advocates encouraged people detained to self-harm (Doherty and Davidson 2016).

In addition, the actions of members of the refugee advocacy sector most visible in the public realm tend to be antagonistic forms of activism. For example, media coverage of a street protest in Brisbane in August 2020 calling for an end to the detention of people seeking asylum in Australia highlighted the arrest of six people for "public nuisance and disobeying police direction" (Siganto 2020). The visibility of these actions reinforces "a hostile 'status quo' relation with the state" (Altman 2020: 3). These actions are consistent with an understanding of a government from a statist perspective, where government and society are seen as separate entities, often in opposition. Such actions are likely to be public, oppositional forms of protest which can be very effective in raising public awareness of the treatment of people seeking asylum, but from the government's perspective may be seen as subversive. Expressing hostility towards a government through these actions is also often seen as a "morally accepted form of being a good activist" (Altman 2020: 11). However, the disadvantage in engaging in this form of activism is that activists do not appreciate potential allies within government (Gill 2010: 1057).

In the aftermath of the Labor Party winning the WA election in 2017, the network decided to adopt an advocacy approach that was based on building potential allies within this party. This was based on our knowledge that the party already had some members who understood the difficulties facing people seeking asylum in Australia and who we felt there was an opportunity to influence WA Government policies impacting on people from asylum seeking backgrounds through engaging with them. When we started to consult with those close to the Labor Party, we learned there were certain processes and key people who guided policy decision-making that needed to be understood. This early advice also included the need to reach out to other potential allies connected to the Labor Party. These initial discussions with allies helped guide the network's early decision making about how we could approach the government.

As Caroline recalls:

> We learned a lot in the early months from allies close to the government—that there were people within the WA Government who were open to at

> least learning about the experiences of people seeking asylum in WA, and the processes that might be best to follow. We also learned that you should not give up when our early attempts to get policies changed were met with negative responses.

Mary Anne also recalls the advice from those early allies who told us:

> You can expect to have your proposal rejected at first. It is really important that you build your allies, try to summarise and repackage your message. Make sure it is really clear and short, point to the positive aspects of your argument and the fact that the change is simple and will not cost government that much.

For Salem there was a sense of how important this process was, as well as learning about how best to engage with the Australian political system:

> Every MP we visited gave us a hint or some sort of way that "from here you can go to there," so there's an opportunity that if you go from this way you know alternatively to this way, that might help in the future. We learned a lot from the experience, and it was interesting for me. People that showed us the way, what we should do, that shouldn't be taken lightly. Because that is the foundation of what we have done today. What we are doing today is based on people's suggestions and the advice that we got at the start, and it worked, and we've improved so much from that starting point.

The advocacy we engaged in was often not visible outside of the officials we visited. We felt that this quiet advocacy was an important strategy to engage government on the problems SHEV holders were experiencing and to commit to relevant policy changes. As Kate puts it:

> I think that's how we've been able to be successful in contributing to getting the changes happening. If we were really outspoken and visibly critical of the state government in a public setting, we wouldn't have been able to make the progression that we have. It's slightly underground but things are happening.

In this WA political context, and at this time, approaching this government as a site of potential allies was useful.

Enabling the learning of MPs

A central strategy of the network's advocacy was to secure meetings with WA Government MPs in order to ultimately persuade the WA Government to request the Federal Government to designate the Perth metropolitan area as a SHEV region. These meetings became opportunities for SHEV holders to share their stories, enabling those MPs to learn about the lives of temporary protection visa holders in WA. These meetings were also central to building allies within the WA Government on this issue.

Salem considered that the learning experienced by MPs was due to the provision of detailed information about the SHEV and hearing directly from someone with lived experience:

> We're telling them the facts, that it is not possible for some of the SHEV holders to meet the visa requirements, it is just not possible. If it was possible, we could have done it. Even if it is not possible for a single person, then it is not fair. So that fairness that we all cherish as an Australian value, then it's vanished, it's gone away. So that's why when we talk facts to the MPs and to the politicians, most of them, even if they are not sympathetic from the beginning, when they listen and they find out the facts, the problems and the challenges we have, they come on board. The information and the facts have not been available to them.
>
> But the thing is I just spoke whatever I was going through, I spoke the truth about myself and that's when you can connect with the people.
>
> I was at that first meeting in Parliament House when we first talked about the SHEV. It was so nerve racking. I thought "you know, this is the moment that I have to at least let these people know what I'm going through."
>
> When people feel the story or the pain or the suffering, and when you are that powerful to pass that message of what you're going through to the people who are listening to it, that is the moment that you can connect with the people. If you fail to do that, then you can't get the people to be in favour of you. It is so important for everybody to go and speak their truth, to tell their stories to the people, because these people don't come from another planet. These are human beings, our fellow human beings who definitely understand the difficulties and the hardship of the others. It just needs to be told, their stories just need to be told.

Through years of advocating for her family, and the rights of other asylum seekers in Australia, Atefeh reflected:

> A lot of people don't understand what has happened to us. It doesn't make sense to them. And I understand it, obviously their life has been straight. They never think about it, and how much pressure and trauma one person can go through and still want to survive.
>
> When I went to see the Minister and explained to him what had happened in my life, it was something routine for me, it was talking about something that people in my community, everyone who is a refugee in

> Perth or in Australia, is experiencing. So I said something that is obvious for us.
>
> For them it is something that they had never heard. I was thinking that maybe because they are a Minister, they are a politician, they have a busy life, they don't think about these things. And they have to because we are part of this society. They have to know about what's happening. I thought maybe they are busy or they don't understand or they don't know about it. I didn't know their knowledge would be zero. So we have to go to explain it to them.
>
> The politicians we met said thank you for sharing your stories and letting us know about it. I found that both of them, they understood. And whenever I am trying to explain something, I try to say the truth that comes from my inside and with all my feeling. It's my life you know. If you experience it, you can explain it better.

After visits with MPs, Rohullah was aware of learning he gained as well as feeling understood:

> When we are approaching politicians, it is very good for us because we will learn how they are reacting when they hear about our background. We will learn their reaction to those who are coming as a refugee or who are coming by boat. I think there is a big gap. We feel bad because of the condition on our visa, but when we're talking about it they feel differently. I think it helps us when we are meeting politicians. We find out what's going on in that whole system. We find out how they are reacting about refugees, about people who are coming from a war zone. And we are requesting something from them, we can learn about what they are going to do, whether they are helpful or not.
>
> When we had a meeting with a local MP, I felt very comfortable because I thought the meeting was friendly. We talked in a very friendly way. She said she will refer the issue we raised to the Premier's office and discuss about these things, so she was helpful.
>
> But in general when we are talking, when we are sharing our daily life and our situation at the beginning of being in Australia, and then what we have achieved in terms of the scale and work and language, some of them get surprised how we have done this. They say "oh well done, you're doing very great," trying to encourage us and trying to treat us very well. This was with people from both major parties.

These encounters between MPs and people with lived experience as a SHEV holder activated a "relationship *between* the self and other" (Offord 2016: 2). Through these relationships, these connections between one another, it has become evident that most of the MPs we met have learned something about what it is like to live on a SHEV in Perth. Once they heard directly about the impacts of policies from those with lived experience, they appeared to understand the issues and be willing to take action within their party. This highlights that an important source of knowledge is that "generated from concrete, lived experiences" (Eschle and Maiguashca 2006: 129), and it can be informative and affective. Story telling in political advocacy is a legitimate form of messaging which can influence policy makers (Davidson 2017).

But there were challenges to enabling these learning encounters. The limited time some MPs were able to give, particularly if they had ministerial responsibilities, meant we had to be strategic about getting a clear message across quickly. Limited time also meant it was just not feasible in some meetings to allow access to people to explain their situation with an interpreter, and so it was people with better English skills who came to meetings with senior MPs. In addition, some politicians deflected and downgraded the lived experience of SHEV holders, giving preference to their own view that people would benefit by moving and working in a region outside of Perth. Thus, hearing directly from someone with lived experience is not necessarily experienced as a learning encounter and suggests perhaps it works best with officials already open to understanding and engaging with the lives of others. However, the vast majority of WA Government MPs who were visited on this issue did learn about the great challenges facing SHEV holders living in Perth and became allies of the network.

Positive outcomes of meetings

Most meetings resulted in MPs agreeing to raise the SHEV issue with senior ministers in the WA Government, as well as giving advice for us about which other MPs to approach and how. Ultimately, this process led to the WA Government agreeing to ask the Federal Government to include all of the Perth metropolitan area as a designated SHEV region in January 2019. Although the Federal Government is yet to agree to this request, we consider gaining the WA Government's support on this key issue (and the other issues outlined earlier) to be a significant outcome. These decisions, and each of those supportive meetings with MPs, were important sources of encouragement and hope that our actions have the potential to bring about some policy change.

For Salem:

> It's not often easy to get a politician to support a change or reform a policy, especially if it's a newly elected government, and we had these issues. But the positive and encouraging part was that once they heard our stories, they understood the hardship and challenges that we face in our lives, they became supportive, and some of them even kindly guided us to whom we should see next to be more effective. I have visited quite a number of MPs who eventually became sympathetic towards our proposal and every time

> after sharing my story with an MP, I felt accomplished and joyful and it gave me the motivation to go out and talk to another one till we got this done. And we did it.

Teresa, Kate, Mary Anne, and Caroline consider that if they did not work in this collaborative way to try to shift the policy landscape, the meaning they derived from being a researcher or social worker would be compromised. As Teresa expresses it:

> I feel like I would have no integrity about doing the work I do on an individual level if I didn't do this work. Every day I witness the unnecessary psychological torture experienced by people seeking asylum and refugees due to our current policies and legislation. My clients share stories of anguish about being forcibly separated from their families. Over the years I have watched my clients' mental health deteriorate with the increasing number of years they have been separated from their families. Each time I witness the trauma experienced by my clients as a direct result of current policy and legislation, it evokes a strong sense of responsibility both personally and professionally to respond not just on an individual level but also on a systemic level. I believe it is fundamental in response to this never-ending suffering to work alongside people seeking asylum and refugees to share these stories within the political context.

It also reflects the importance of the friendships they all have with people from asylum-seeking backgrounds. For Kate:

> I have relationships with people who are directly impacted by cruel policy. So with being present to people and hearing their pain, and knowing that because of the privilege and power that I hold I can attempt to effect change in things, I feel that I need to try. I don't feel that I can do the day to day work like helping people to apply for permission to travel without doing the work on the systemic issues as well. For example, my friend who I have known for eight years hasn't seen his mum for that whole time. Sitting with someone feeling that grief, and then walking away from it, I couldn't do that. That wouldn't be honouring that friendship and that relationship for me.

We recognise, however, that this process has been long, and will continue to be so as our efforts turn to the federal political system. As Salem reflects:

> I wanted to be committed to this, to get to the end of it. I didn't realise that it might take that long because at the beginning, I thought maybe after six or seven months we'll definitely get some answer because every MP we met was sympathetic and they have been so supportive.

For Rohullah:

> It's a very slow process, we can't expect more than that we have achieved.
>
> A lot of my friends said it's useless to attend the meetings because we're not going to change anything. My view was a bit different. Everyone can expect this reaction from the local government or the federal government when we are asking something which is opposite to their promise during the election. It is very hard to get the changes very quickly. I thought that by coming to the meetings, we will learn about the system and then we will know how to talk to the politicians, how to engage the community, and it's good for our language.
>
> Overall, through our meetings, we can say we are heading for a positive way. We have done a lot so far, we know it is very hard to get permanent visas or any other big change. We have achieved that the WA Premier agreed to send two letters to the federal government. It is a big achievement I think. It is little if you compare it with want we to achieve in the future, but it still is a good result.

As Atefeh expresses it, however, waiting for policy change over such a long period of time has huge mental health implications:

> The longer it takes to bring about policy change means the longer that all these problems will be around, and the longer that people like me will stay depressed. Being here for seven years, fighting for our simple rights almost every day, is enough to push someone to end their life. And every single life matters.

And as Rohullah also reflects, focusing on the SHEV regional area issue has meant little time for discussing other important issues:

> We spent a lot of time asking the WA government to request Perth as a SHEV region. Instead of some of that time, if we had meetings to talk about how to improve our daily life in the community, about human rights in our daily lives, about the environment, that would have been good. These areas need improving too.

While the gains we have made are still not what is ultimately needed for people on a SHEV to settle well in Australia, including getting their families here, we consider all of the encounters we had with MPs who were supportive are important outcomes. They provided encouragement and hope that we could affect at least some change at the political level, despite a hostile federal policy landscape. Focusing advocacy on engaging with individual members of the WA Government and finding that most became allies in our efforts has effectively humanised this government to us. We understand this in two ways: that the government is composed of humans with faces we can now picture, and as a government that has become more supportive of people from asylum-seeking backgrounds. Seeing a government in this way is to see it as potentially responsive to the concerns of the people within its borders, rather than impenetrable (Altman 2020: 14).

Limitations of advocacy at the state government level

The network's advocacy in relation to the SHEV was a process of building allies through meetings with more than 30 WA Labor MPs and other public servants that included people living on a SHEV who wanted to share their experiences with MPs. The vast majority of MPs agreed to raise the issue with senior ministers of the WA Government. This culminated in meetings with senior ministers and ultimately the WA Government's request that the Federal Government designate the Perth metropolitan area as a SHEV regional area.

However, at the time of writing, the Federal Government is yet to commit to making this change. The Federal Minister for Immigration is responsible for making the legislative instrument that stipulates what postcodes are designated as regional. Normally state governments, in consultation with the Federal Government, nominate those postcodes. Indeed, requests from other state governments to alter the SHEV regional areas within their jurisdictions have been agreed to by the Federal Government over the past few years. Following the Federal Government's inaction, the WA Government again requested that all of the Perth metropolitan area is designated a SHEV regional area in December 2019. As at September 2020, there continues to be no response from the Federal Government. As a consequence, network advocacy on this issue has become focused on engaging with WA-based Federal Government MPs in an attempt to gain their support on the issue.

In addition, even if Perth is designated a regional area, there remain significant challenges for SHEV holders to meet the eligibility requirements of the few visas available to them should they meet the pathway requirements. These difficulties are likely to be compounded by the impacts on employment wrought by the COVID-19 pandemic.

Focusing our efforts on engaging with the WA Government also does not address the federal policies that deny people seeking asylum the capacity to settle in Australia. It does not address the systemic social and cultural factors underlying Australia's treatment of people seeking asylum. Nor does it address the racist underpinnings of the settler colonialist state, or that the state "supports and maintains the processes of capitalist accumulation, profitability and growth" (Fisher and Shragge 2017: 464), processes that facilitate and exacerbate the forced migration of people across the globe. Addressing these systemic factors is vital. This is a long-term project that needs our attention.

Reflecting the political opportunities in WA we looked at what changes might be possible in the short term, changes that might emerge from within the localised system. Engaging with the WA Government seemed a way to move forward, and there have been positive outcomes from this.

Another challenge of this form of advocacy is that it relies on there being people within the state apparatus who are willing to collaborate. In relation to the WA Government, and the WA Parliament, this has been clearly evident. However, there is also a risk of being co-opted or socialised into state practices, and/or being exploited (Gill 2010: 1049–1050). We face the challenge of having predominantly engaged with Labor MPs, which places the gains made vulnerable if Labor does not win the next state election.

National efforts are needed to bring about social and political change at the federal level. To address this, our network has connected with the development of the broader national movement of refugee activists, agencies, and people seeking asylum. Since the re-election of the federal Coalition Government in May 2019, the WA network has participated in the development of a national advocacy strategy focused on the rights of people seeking asylum.

A year on, we see that this gives our work at the local level an expression at the national level and links into broader efforts to bring about change on a federal scale. This is a much more difficult project. We see that for social and political change to occur, there is a need for a range of strategies and activist practices, with some that engage directly with government officials and others that do not. Our contributions to national efforts (and others) may perhaps help "ground" the broader movement in "local work" which can enable greater representation, participation, and learning within that movement (Fisher and Shragge 2017: 455).

Conclusion

In this chapter we have highlighted how a quiet, localised, relational approach to advocacy, that includes people with lived experience of seeking asylum, has helped to build political allies in the WA Government. Through this approach in the wake of the opportunity that the election of the Labor Government provided, the WA Refugees and People Seeking Asylum Network has brought about tangible positive policy reforms at the state level. A key component in developing these allies were the meetings held between network members with lived experience of seeking asylum and MPs and other government officials. These meetings enabled connections to be established between participants, which led to MPs learning about what it is like to live on a temporary visa in WA, and network members learning about how to further engage with the WA political system.

Another key component was that so many WA Government MPs were willing to meet with people from an asylum-seeking background. The WA network (and others) continues to encounter difficulties in advocating within the federal political system where the primary responsibility for immigration policies lies.

Engaging with people within this system is needed in order to try to find and build allies at the federal level who may become pivotal in pushing for change from within the system. But we also recognise the challenges in doing so given the continued hard-line approach of the Coalition Government towards people seeking asylum who came to Australia by boat. There is a clearly a need for a diverse range of activist strategies and practices across the country to shift these policies. The voices and involvement of those with lived experiences need to be central to these strategies.

For SHEV holders and other temporary visa holders there is a great urgency for these punitive policies to be changed. As Atefeh, Rohullah, and Salem so powerfully remind us, the mental health implications of being forced to continue to live in such a precarious situation are profound. Their continued advocacy, as well as the actions of others with lived experience of seeking asylum, are striking acts of resistance to these policies.

Notes

1 SRSS is a payment made to a limited number of eligible people seeking asylum while they are waiting for their cases to be finalised. The payments are to help with basic living costs.
2 For the purpose of SHEV arrangements, "regional" includes all postcodes in the Australian Capital Territory, South Australia, Tasmania, and Northern Territory; this includes cities such as Adelaide, Hobart, Canberra, and Darwin. In other states it includes postcodes (mostly) other than those in the capital cities of Perth, Sydney, Melbourne, and Brisbane.
3 The JobKeeper payment is a wage subsidy payment funded by the Australian Government for employees of businesses who can demonstrate they have been significantly impacted by the COVID-19 pandemic.
4 Special benefits are fortnightly payments that provide financial assistance to people in severe financial need due to circumstances outside their control.
5 Centrelink is the name of the agency that delivers support to people with payments and services on behalf of the Australian Government Department of Human Services.
6 Leading up to the 2019 Australian federal election, it had been widely predicted that the Labor party would win government from the Liberal/National Coalition. However, the Coalition was re-elected, and the policy of temporary protection visas remains.
7 Members of the network now include people from asylum-seeking backgrounds, academics, activists, and representatives of community organisations and other stakeholders (including Curtin University's Centre for Human Rights Education, Centre for Asylum Seekers, Refugees and Detainees [CARAD], Riverview Community Services, Uniting Church in Australia, Southern Communities Advocacy Legal Education Service [SCALES], Refugee Rights Action Network [RRAN], and Unionists for Refugees).

Bibliography

Altman, T. (2020) 'Making the state blush: humanizing relations in an Australian NGO campaign for people seeking asylum', *Social Analysis*, 64(1): 1.

Asylum Seeker Resource Centre. (2020) *Submission to Select Committee on Temporary Migration Inquiry into and Report on the Impact Temporary Migration Has on the Australian Economy, Wages and Jobs, Social Cohesion and Workplace Rights and Conditions*. www.asrc.org.au/wp-content/

uploads/2013/04/ASRC-submission_Temporary-Migration_July-30-2020_formatted_final.pdf

Australian Human Rights Commission. (2019) *Lives on hold: refugees and asylum seekers in the "legacy caseload"*. www.humanrights.gov.au/our-work/asylum-seekers-and-refugees/publications/lives-hold-refugees-and-asylum-seekers-legacy

Burnett, C. (2003) 'Passion through the profession: both being activist and academic' *Social Justice*, 30(4): 135.

Davidson, B. (2017) 'Storytelling and evidence-based policy: lessons from the grey literature', *Palgrave Communications*, 3: 17093.

Department of Home Affairs. (2020) *IMA legacy caseload: report on processing status and outcomes April 2020*. www.homeaffairs.gov.au/research-and-stats/files/ima-legacy-caseload-april-2020.pdf

Doherty, B. (2015) *Call me illegal: the semantic struggle over seeking asylum in Australia*, University of Oxford. https://reutersinstitute.politics.ox.ac.uk/sites/default/files/2017-10/Call_me_illegal_The_semantic_struggle_over_seeking_asylum_in_Australia_0.pdf

Doherty, B. and Davidson, H. (2016) 'Peter Dutton accuses refugee advocates of encouraging suicide on Nauru', *The Guardian*, 3 May 2020. www.theguardian.com/australia-news/2016/may/03/peter-dutton-accuses-refugee-advocates-of-encouraging-suicide-on-nauru

Eschle, C. and Maiguashca, B. (2006) 'Bridging the academic/activist divide: feminist activism and the teaching of global politics', *Millennium: Journal of International Studies*, 35(1): 119.

Fisher, R. and Shragge, E. (2017) 'Resourcing community organising: examples from England and Quebec', *Community Development Journal*, 52(3): 454.

Fleay, C, Abbas, Ghulam, V., Vakili, M., Nasrullah, Hartley, L., Offord, B., Macfarlane, C. and Sayer, R. (2019) 'Enabling access to higher education for people seeking asylum: a collective approach', *Widening Participation & Lifelong Learning*, 21(2): 168.

Fleay, C., Lumbus, A. and Hartley, L. (2016) 'People seeking asylum in Australia and their access to employment: just what do we know?' *Cosmopolitan Civil Societies: An Interdisciplinary Journal*, 8(2): 63.

Gill, N. (2010) 'Tracing imaginations of the state: the spatial consequences of different state concepts among asylum activist organisations', *Antipode*, 42(5): 1048.

Hartley, L. and Fleay, C. (2014) *Policy as punishment: asylum seekers in the community without the right to work*. Curtin University Centre for Human Rights Education. https://apo.org.au/node/38122

Joint Standing Committee on Migration. (2020) *Inquiry into migration in regional Australia*, Committee Hansard, 19 March, Canberra.

Kenny, M., Procter, N. and Grech, C. (2016) 'Mental health and legal representation for asylum seekers in the "legacy caseload"', *Cosmopolitan Civil Societies Journal*, 8(2): 84.

Kenny, M. and Procter, N. (2019) 'Refugee status determination: mental distress and lethal hopelessness: challenges for legal professionals', Kaldor Centre Annual Conference 2019, good decisions: achieving fairness in refugee law, policy and practice, 26 November. www.kaldorcentre.unsw.edu.au/event/kaldor-centre-annual-conference-2019-good-decisions-achieving-fairness-refugee-law-policy-and

Kenny, M., Reilly, A. and Fleay, C. (2019) *Inquiry into regional migration in Australia submission 55*. www.aph.gov.au/DocumentStore.ashx?id=dd4a35c0-225c-46e7-b7a7-ca9f0cfdaaf4&subId=670327

Lenette, C, et al. (2020) '"We were not merely participating; we were leading the discussions": participation and self-representation of refugee young people in international advocacy', *Journal of Immigrant and Refugee Studies*, 18(4): 390.

Maddison, S. and Martin, G. (2010) 'Introduction to "surviving neoliberalism: the persistence of Australian social movements"', *Social Movement Studies*, 9(2): 101.

National Refugee-led Advisory and Advocacy Group (NRAAG). (2020) *Leaving nobody behind: COVID-19 national refugee community consultation: outcomes report*. https://drive.google.com/file/d/1RMbzM_m6Sc5zgbf7XYbNb3dsFIXSolpM/view

Offord, B. (2016) 'Ramping up cultural studies: pedagogy and the activation of knowledge,' in Hickey, A. (ed.) *The Pedagogies of Cultural Studies*. Routledge.

Procter, N, et al. (2018) 'Lethal hopelessness: understanding and responding to asylum seeker distress and mental deterioration', *International Journal of Mental Health Nursing*, 27(1): 448.

Reynolds, V. (2013) '"Leaning in" as imperfect allies in community work', *Narrative and Conflict: Explorations in Theory and Practice*, 1(1): 53.

Senate Legal and Constitutional Affairs References Committee. (2019) *2019–20 supplementary budget estimates*, Commonwealth of Australia. www.aph.gov.au/Parliamentary_Business/Senate_estimates/legcon/2019-20_Supplementary_Budget_Estimates

Siganto, T. (2020) 'Protesters march on Brisbane hotel where refugees and asylum seekers are being detained', *ABC News*, 15 August 2020. www.abc.net.au/news/2020-08-15/brisbane-protest-asylum-seeker-refugees-kangaroo-point/12562088

Tattersall, A. (2015) 'The global spread of community organizing: how "Alinsky-style" community organizing travelled to Australia and what we learnt?' *Community Development Journal*, 50(3): 380.

Tilly, C. (2006) *Regimes and Repertoires*. University of Chicago Press.

UNHCR. (2019) *Global Trends: Forced Displacement in 2019*. www.unhcr.org/globaltrends2019/#:~:text=By%20the%20end%20of%202019,record%20according%20to%20available%20data

Index

Page numbers followed by 'n' indicate a note.